D1766045

Ple
on

To
us

Yc

BLACK STRUGGLE
RED SCARE

Segregation and Anti-Communism

in the South, 1948–1968

JEFF WOODS

LOUISIANA STATE UNIVERSITY PRESS

BATON ROUGE

Published by Louisiana State University Press
Manufactured in the United States of America

Designer: Andrew Shurtz
Typeface: Trump Mediaeval
Typesetter: Coghill Composition Co., Inc.

Library of Congress Cataloging-in-Publication Data:
Woods, Jeff, 1970–
    Black struggle, red scare : segregation and anti-commu-
nism in the South, 1948–1968 / Jeff Woods.
        p. cm.
Includes bibliographical references (p.) and index.
    ISBN 978-0-8071-2926-5 (pbk. : alk. paper)
    1. African Americans—Segregation—Southern States—
History—20th century. 2. African Americans—Civil
rights—Southern States—History—20th century. 3. Anti-
communist movements—Southern States—History—20th
century. 4. Southern States—Race relations. 5. Southern
States—Politics and government—1951– I. Title.
    E185.61.W846 2004
    323.1196' 073075' 09045—dc22

                                        2003017756

to Andrea

CONTENTS

ACKNOWLEDGMENTS

I AM, OF COURSE, INDEBTED TO A NUMBER OF PEOPLE for their help with this study. Alonzo Hamby contributed more than anyone to its development. What I know of the craft of history is due largely to him. Randall Woods, who since I first began writing has reviewed and critiqued my work, has again offered the essential advice and encouragement that only a father and mentor can.

The original idea for this work came from Willard Gatewood, who helped me develop a section of it as a master's thesis. Without his help, the study in its entirety would not have been possible. My thanks also go to Neil McMillen, who far exceeded his professional duties in offering help to a young scholar who just showed up on his doorstep asking for instruction. In addition I am grateful to Anthony Badger, David Oshinsky, and Mike Parrish for reading rough drafts of chapters of this work. Thanks are due as well to John Gaddis, who opened my mind to history. And thanks to Chester Pach, Alan Booth, Joan Hoff, Steve Miner, Marc Selverstone, Ray Haberski, Jeff Coker, Steve Remy, Derek Catsum and all the professors and students at Ohio University and the Contemporary History Institute.

Thanks also go to Kara Dunfee, who made the daunting logistics of this undertaking manageable, and to my mother Rhoda Woods, whose copyediting greatly improved the manuscript.

The Lyndon Baines Johnson Presidential Library, the Contemporary History Institute, and the Ohio University History Department funded most of the research for this project. Thanks go as well to Arkansas Tech University and the student workers in the Social Sciences and Philosophy Department.

Finally, my deepest thanks to Annie and Cullen—you are the reason I write.

Naturally I take full responsibility for whatever mistakes are contained in this work.

ACKNOWLEDGMENTS

ABBREVIATIONS

ADA   Americans for Democratic Action

CDGM   Child Development Group of Mississippi

CICA   Committee to Investigate Communist Activities
(South Carolina)

COFO   Council of Federated Organizations

COINTELPRO   Counterintelligence Program (FBI)

CORE   Congress of Racial Equality

CP   Communist Party

CRC   Civil Rights Congress

ECLC   Emergency Civil Liberties Committee

FDP   Freedom Democratic Party

FOR   Fellowship of Reconciliation

GBI   Georgia Bureau of Investigation

GCE   Georgia Commission on Education

HUAC   House Committee on Un-American Activities

JLCS   Joint Legislative Committee on Segregation (Louisiana)

LCFO   Lowndes County Freedom Organization (Alabama)

LUAC   Joint Legislative Committee on Un-American
Activities (Louisiana)

OEO   Office of Economic Opportunity

PERM   Senate Permanent Subcommittee on Investigations

MFDP   Mississippi Freedom Democratic Party

NCC   National Council of Churches

NLG   National Lawyers Guild

RAM   Revolutionary Action Movement

SAI   Southern Association of Investigators

SCEF   Southern Conference Education Fund

SCHW   Southern Conference on Human Welfare

SCLC   Southern Christian Leadership Conference

SDS   Students for a Democratic Society

SISS   Senate Internal Security Subcommittee

SNCC   Student Nonviolent Coordinating Committee

SRC   Southern Regional Council

SSC   State Sovereignty Commission

STFU   Southern Tenant Farmers' Union

BLACK STRUGGLE, RED SCARE

"It is because a fellow is more afraid of the trouble he might have than he ever is of the trouble he's already got."

—WILLIAM FAULKNER,
Light in August

INTRODUCTION

IN THE WAKE OF THE 1957 LITTLE ROCK DESEGREGATION
crisis, columnist Holmes Alexander of the *Charleston News and Courier*
in South Carolina observed the return of "Southern nationalism." According to Alexander the "nationalism of the Old Confederacy now expresses
itself in the substitution of 'Dixie' for the national anthem at high school
football games and by the flaunting everywhere of the Stars and Bars."
After Little Rock, regional intransigence had hardened among southerners "offended by the appearance and aggressiveness of what could be
called a form of imperialism—Federal rule." This, according to Alexander,
while perhaps not Communism in name, was "Communism in nature."
Federally enforced desegregation, he implied, was the opening salvo in a
Marxist revolution that would end the southern and American way of life.
Southern nationalism had reemerged in response to the red and black
menace.[1]

In the five years after Little Rock, as both the struggle for black civil
rights and the cold war intensified, Alexander continued to sound the
alarm. In 1960 the columnist cautioned his readers about the "sinister similarities between Cuba and the Southern states." Where few had understood
that the "anti-Batista revolution in Cuba had communist colorations," he
wrote, fewer still realized that the black sit-ins then taking place all over
the South were similarly tainted. In 1964 Alexander suggested that, in preparing for the summer's black voter registration campaign, the country
brace "for a Negro insurrection which is nothing less than a communist invasion of American cities."[2]

Alexander's comments reflected the concerns of many white southern-

1. Holmes Alexander, "Ike Now Ally of World Communism's Forces," *Longview Daily
News*, undated, from Johnson Senate Papers, Box 395, Faubus Opposing Ike R–Z, Lyndon
Baines Johnson Library.

2. Holmes Alexander, "Cuba and Sitdowns and Red Strategy," *Charleston News and
Courier*, 10 May 1960, and "Attack from Within," *Charleston News and Courier*, 27 April
1964.

ers in the 1950s and 1960s that the forces of Communism and integration had signed a devil's pact to destroy the region's way of life. Rallying to defend Dixie against the perceived threat, southern segregationists and anti-Communists led a huge legal, political, and public-relations effort to expose and eliminate the Communist and integrationist enemy. These efforts amounted to a southern red scare.

This book offers a general overview of the southern red scare as it emerged in the eleven states of the Old Confederacy: Alabama, Arkansas, Georgia, Florida, Louisiana, Mississippi, North Carolina, South Carolina, Tennessee, Texas, and Virginia. The primary resources available on the subject in state and national archives are vast. The secondary literature is also extensive and growing. Given the breadth of the available material, tracing the entire course of the scare in all of its manifestations would constitute an enormous undertaking and serve as an overly ambitious introduction to the subject. Consequently this work concentrates on the phenomenon at its most intense, as it emerged in the South during the late 1940s, the 1950s, and the 1960s when segregation and anti-Communism acted as the mutually reinforcing components of an extreme southern nationalism.

Southern nationalism, as the term will be used here, had at its core a regional desire to protect the "southern way of life" from outside threats. An ideology outwardly expressed by symbolic gestures such as singing "Dixie" and waving the Confederate flag, southern nationalism embodied a set of shared values and traditions: a concern for personal and national honor, a suspicion of centralized power and a belief in states' rights, a fundamentalist faith in Protestant Christianity, and a view of history shaped by the region's experiences of slavery, the Civil War, and Reconstruction. But it was also a defensive regional ideology, defined as much by what its adherents opposed as what they favored. As historian Sheldon Hackney put it, southerners were most southern when they were "defending their region against attack from outside forces: abolitionists, the Union Army, carpetbaggers, Wall Street and Pittsburgh, civil rights agitators, the federal government, feminism, socialism, trade-unionism, Darwinism, Communism, atheism, daylight-saving time, and other by-products of modernity." The regional "siege mentality," Hackney rightly concluded, was "the heart of the southern national identity."[3]

3. Sheldon Hackney, "Southern Violence," *American Historical Review* 74 (February 1969), 924–25. See also Clifford Geertz, "Ideology As a Cultural System," in David E.

But while the defensive regional sense of self was the driving force behind southern nationalism, it also had less parochial and xenophobic applications. It should be remembered that even in the South's definitive act of [3 southern nationalism, secession, it adopted a governing document that incorporated most of the provisions of the United States Constitution. Truly, as historian Willard Gatewood wrote, "the Southerners' experience with separate nationhood endowed them with a double identity so that theirs is the only part of the country where a symbol of defiance against national authority, the Confederate flag, can be waved enthusiastically by one who considers himself a superpatriot of the 100% American variety."[4]

States rights catalyzed the southern nationalist mix of regional separatism and patriotic Americanism. Southern states, Dixie's nationalists argued, were the true keepers of the American flame. Democracy for these descendants of both Thomas Jefferson and John C. Calhoun was purest when federal power was minimized. National strength depended on local and regional majorities. Only cities, counties, and states could rightly determine the makeup of social and political institutions.

But the institution that was most sacred to southerners was also the least democratic and most regionally fixed—Jim Crow. White supremacy framed the South's concept of democracy and controlled its patriotic impulse. As historian Ulrich B. Phillips wrote, white people's resolve to keep

Apter, ed., *Ideology and Discontent* (London: Free Press of Glencoe, 1964), 48; Drew Gilpin Faust, *The Creation of Confederate Nationalism: Ideology and Identity in the Civil War South* (Baton Rouge: Louisiana State University Press, 1988), 3; David M. Potter, "The Historian's Use of Nationalism and Vice Versa," in *The South and the Sectional Conflict* (Baton Rouge: Louisiana State University Press, 1968); John McCardell, *The Idea of a Southern Nation: Southern Nationalists and Southern Nationalism, 1830–1860* (New York: W. W. Norton, 1979).

4. Willard Gatewood Jr., "The American Experience: The Southern Variable," in *The American Experience: Public Lectures in Honor of the Nation's Bicentennial* (Fayetteville: University of Arkansas Press, 1977), 35. See also Sheldon Hackney, "The South As a Counterculture," *American Scholar* 42 (Spring 1973): 286; John Shelton Reed, *The Enduring South: Subcultural Persistence in Mass Society* (Chapel Hill: University of North Carolina Press, 1972), 26–29; Dewey W. Grantham, "An American Politics for the South," in Charles Grier Sellers, Jr., ed., *The Southerner As American* (Chapel Hill: University of North Carolina Press, 1960); William C. Havard, ed., *The Changing Politics of the South* (Baton Rouge: Louisiana State University Press, 1972); Carl Degler, *Place over Time* (Baton Rouge: Louisiana State University Press, 1977); Ray Arsenault, "The Folklore of Southern Demagoguery," in *Is There a Southern Political Tradition?* (Jackson: University Press of Mississippi, 1996).

the South a white man's country was the "central theme of Southern history." The assumption that nonwhites and especially blacks "in the mass were incompetent for any good political purpose and by reason of their inexperience and racial unwisdom were likely to prove subversive" powered this determination. The good of the country and the region, white southerners incessantly argued, depended on a civil society controlled exclusively by whites. The preservation of regional and national strength thus meant the maintenance of what Phillips called "racial security."[5]

The preservation of racial security meant limiting black participation in civil society. Despite their claims to civic responsibility, southern nationalists were not what scholars Michael Ignatieff and Ernest Gellner have called "civic nationalists." Civic nationalists defined "membership in the nation in terms of shared adherence to civic values." They pursued goals "fully compatible with the necessary pluralism of civil society." Southern nationalists, on the other hand, were "ethnic nationalists." They defined belonging in terms of blood and ethnic origin. Ethnic nationalism, while compatible with civil society when it has ensured the rights of minorities, has proven destructive of civil society when political and social equality has been denied. Southern nationalists, in denying equal rights to blacks and civil rights activists through the southern red scare, practiced the kind of ethnic nationalism that undermined rather than reinforced American pluralist, democratic values.

While its defensive, regional, and ethnic brand of nationalism made the southern red scare unique, Dixie's scare shared a great deal with its national counterpart. As historian M. J. Heale argued, the South's segregationist, anti-Communist reaction developed out of a set of preconditions that were common to red scares nationally. The South had Communists, patriots, anti-Communist networks, political elites, and a federal example by the late 1940s and early 1950s. But the region lacked a final, crucial ingredient in those years—political and social turmoil. Its traditional one-party political apparatus had been free of significant ideological cleavages, keeping the region distanced from the national red scare. But once the status quo was challenged amid the racial struggles of the 1950s and 1960s, the South expe-

5. Ulrich B. Phillips, "The Central Theme of Southern History," *American Historical Review* 34 (October 1928): 35–42. See also W. J. Cash, *The Mind of the South* (New York: Knopf, 1941) and Bruce Clayton, *The Savage Ideal: Intolerance and Intellectual Leadership in the South, 1890–1914* (Baltimore: Johns Hopkins University Press, 1972).

4]

rienced the upheaval necessary to sustain its own brand of McCarthyism. It was also during this period that the southern red scare acquired its defining characteristic—race.[6]

The southern red scare was in many ways a byproduct of the region's massive resistance to integration. Its proponents' main goal was to discredit the civil rights movement by associating it with the nation's greatest enemy, Communism. The scare thus rose and fell largely in rhythm with southern efforts to counter the struggle for black equality. But the scare lingered beyond the most intense period of southern reaction. As historian William Billingsly suggested in his work on North Carolina's speaker ban, the more national criticism of the region's racial institutions grew, the more southern segregationists looked to anti-Communism to protect the traditional social order.[7]

An interlocking network of local, state, and federal institutions directed the southern red scare. Among the most effective components of the network were national congressional committees. Mississippi senator James Eastland, who chaired the Senate Internal Security Subcommittee (SISS), Louisiana representative Edwin Willis, who headed the House Committee on Un-American Activities (HUAC), and Arkansas senator John McClellan, who would take over Joe McCarthy's Permanent Subcommittee on Investigations (PERM), used their positions to hold public hearings on Communist influence in civil rights protests. Closely allied to the committees was the Federal Bureau of Investigation (FBI). Under its director, J. Edgar Hoover, the Bureau made the investigation of Communists in the civil rights movement one of its preeminent goals. Others willing to advance the southern nationalist agenda could even be found in the Central Intelligence Agency, Army Intelligence, and elsewhere in the federal security apparatus.

The national investigating committees and agencies served as models for similar state and local bodies in the South. They, far more than their federal counterparts, were dedicated to massive resistance through the exposure of Communists in the civil rights movement. State sovereignty commissions led the way with investigations and propaganda campaigns in Mississippi and Alabama. The Georgia Commission on Education, the

6. M. J. Heale, *McCarthy's Americans* (Athens: University of Georgia Press, 1998), 217, 294–96.

7. William Billingsly, *Communists on Campus: Race, Politics, and the Public University in Sixties North Carolina* (Athens: University of Georgia Press, 1999), xvi, 237–43.

6]

Johns Committee in Florida, Louisiana's Joint Legislative Committee on Un-American Activities, and similar organizations held hearings and advanced legislation to protect the South from the putative red and black threat. State bureaus of investigation and local law-enforcement officials also contributed manpower and research to the cause. The work of these agencies was buttressed by a regional propaganda machine led by the Citizens' Councils, their offshoots, the conservative press, and local and state politicos such as Leander Perez and Roy Harris. Professional anti-Communists also played a role. FBI informant Manning Johnson, former HUAC and PERM researcher J. B. Matthews, and Methodist minister Myers Lowman made a living providing southern segregationists with information about Communists in the civil rights movement. Together these and other federal, state, and local friends of the southern-nationalist cause devoted huge amounts of time, money, and human resources to exposing the alleged black and red conspiracy.

In many ways the network of agencies and individuals at the heart of the southern red scare took advantage of a domestic-security state left by the anti-Communists of the 1940s and early 1950s. Indeed, when the regional issue of race came to the fore in the late 1950s and the 1960s, southerners already had the tools of anti-Communism at hand. Loyalty oaths, public hearings, covert investigations, and Communist-control laws were easily converted into instruments capable of harassing civil rights organizations and activists. Although most of the state internal-security laws and oaths had been ruled unconstitutional by the Supreme Court by the early 1960s, the investigations and hearings continued to draw attention for another decade.

Not surprisingly, a conservative white-power elite led the southern red scare. Threatened by political and social changes that would undermine their power, white political and economic leaders looked to the scare to preserve the status quo. Still, the scare could not have existed without popular support. White working-class southerners needed little convincing from elites that Communism and integration were part of a unified threat to the region and the nation. They overwhelmingly supported both segregation and anti-Communism. Combining the two was an easy, culturally conditioned step. But the southern red scare also had a valuable, if less popular, appeal outside of the South. According to historian Dan Carter, it gave southern elites such as Alabama governor George Wallace "a rhetorical bridge to a national audience." Wallace understood that while most nonsoutherners living in the 1960s "were still ambiguous in their attitudes toward the rising civil rights movement; they were not ambiguous in their hatred for the Red Menace." The scare grew in strength in no small part because it was an exportable commodity.[8]

Wallace was the most prominent of many southern nationalists who attempted to use the southern red scare to gain electoral support. His ideological commitment to segregation and anti-Communism was real, but Wallace was a politician first. As John Kohn, one of Wallace's advisers in the 1960s, argued, if the Alabama governor "had parachuted into the Albanian countryside in the spring of 1962, he would have been head of a collective farm by harvesttime, a member of the Communist Party by midwinter, on his way to the district party meeting as a delegate by the following year, and a member of the Comintern in two or three years." Wallace, said Kohn, "could believe whatever he needed to believe." Arkansas governor Orval Faubus could similarly mold his beliefs to fit his political needs. As Faubus biographer Roy Reed has demonstrated, the governor's participation in the campaign against reds and blacks in the wake of the Little Rock crisis marked a sharp turn to the right designed to appease his segregationist critics.[9]

But the political benefits to be derived from publicly attacking Communists in the civil rights movement were not sufficient to explain the motivations of all southern red and black investigators. Some were more ideologues than opportunists. As his biographer Glen Jeansonne has suggested, Louisiana judge Leander Perez's frequent rants about Communists in the civil rights movement were more a matter of conviction than of political posture. J. Edgar Hoover was also a true believer, according to his biographer Kenneth O'Reilly. His red and black investigations were clearly influenced by his "dream of what America should be"—segregated and free of Communists.[10]

For most of the leaders of the southern red scare, the balance between political opportunism and true belief shifted frequently. Indeed, the quint-

8. Dan Carter, *From George Wallace to Newt Gingrich* (Baton Rouge: Louisiana State University Press, 1996), 14. See also Heale, *McCarthy's Americans*, 216–17, 278–88.

9. Carter, *From George Wallace to Newt Gingrich*, 9; Roy Reed, *Faubus: The Life and Times of an American Prodigal* (Fayetteville: University of Arkansas Press, 1997).

10. Glen Jeansonne, *Leander Perez: Boss of the Delta* (Lafayette: University of Southwestern Louisiana, 1995); Kenneth O'Reilly, *"Racial Matters": The FBI's Secret File on Black America, 1960–1972* (New York: Free Press, 1989), 358.

essential red- and black-investigating southern nationalist, Mississippi senator James Eastland, showed signs of both opportunism and true belief at different times. Like Joe McCarthy, Eastland fully recognized the political benefits of anti-Communism, but his persistence in denouncing black bolshevism suggests that he believed that his charges were generally true. Early in his career, the Mississippi senator announced that the civil rights movement was nothing less than a conspiracy directed by the Kremlin. Clearly these charges were disingenuous. Eastland was grandstanding. He was lying. But as time went on and the civil rights struggle intensified, Eastland argued with more careful conviction that Communists and integrationists promoted a set of values that ran directly counter to the traditional southern way of life. Of this he and most southerners had no doubt.[11]

Whether opportunists or ideologues, leaders of the southern red scare were able to compile a huge documentary record to support their contentions. Clearly there were elements of truth in their charges. Communists and radicals did work for the civil rights movement. Some, such as Paul Robeson, Victor Rabinowitz, Jack O'Dell, Stanley Levinson, and Doxey Wilkerson were devoted Marxists, dedicated as much to moving the proletariat toward revolution as they were to providing equal rights for blacks. Others, such as Robert Williams and Stokely Carmichael, adopted Communist ideology as a strategy to further the black struggle. Still others were popular fronters from the Southern Conference Education Fund, the Highlander Folk School, and the National Lawyers Guild who hoped to bring the fight for racial justice under the larger umbrella of class struggle. They included Carl and Anne Braden, Myles Horton, and James Dombrowski. Even mainstream movement figures such as Bayard Rustin and Fred Shuttlesworth had leftist political leanings.[12]

11. David Oshinsky, *A Conspiracy So Immense* (New York: Free Press, 1983), 285.

12. See Jervis Anderson, *Bayard Rustin: Troubles I've Seen* (New York: Harper Collins, 1997); Linda Reed, *Simple Decency and Common Sense* (Bloomington: Indiana University Press, 1991); John M. Glen, *Highlander: No Ordinary School* (Knoxville: University of Tennessee Press, 1996); David Garrow, *Bearing the Cross* (New York: William Morrow , 1986); Gerald Horne, *Communist Front? The Civil Rights Congress, 1946–1956* (London: Fairleigh Dickinson University Press, 1988); Robin D. G. Kelley, *Hammer and Hoe: Alabama Communists during the Great Depression* (Chapel Hill: University of North Carolina Press, 1990); Mark Solomon, *The Cry Was Unity: Communists and African Americans, 1917–1936* (Jackson: University Press of Mississippi, 1998); Timothy Tyson, *Radio Free Dixie: Robert F. Williams and the Roots of Black Power* (Chapel Hill: University of North Carolina Press, 1999).

But in the end, as historian John Earl Haynes has stated, the "campaign to link civil rights to communism failed chiefly because it was untrue." Southern red and black investigators simply ignored the mountains of evidence proving that the movement was fundamentally liberal and committed to working within the limits of capitalism and the American democratic system. As Martin Luther King put it, there were "as many Communists in the freedom movement," as "Eskimos in Florida." The clearly false accusations of southern red and black investigators ultimately only added to their reputations as hate-mongers and undermined their cause. Whatever legitimate concerns they might have addressed, they were easily linked to the abuses of McCarthyism. The money, time, and human resources devoted to the southern red scare ultimately constituted an enormous waste.[13]

The southern red scare's failure, however, did not mean that the civil rights movement went unscathed. Even those unjustly accused could be jailed, lose their jobs, endure physical abuse, and face ostracism in their communities. Southern segregationist anti-Communists also had an effect on the movement as a whole. They exacerbated an existing rift in the civil rights ranks by forcing the leaders to publicly declare whether or not the movement would accept the aid of Communists. For some movement activists, purging Communists meant alienating a valued ally and giving in to the concerns of red and black investigators. But for others, accepting Communist aid meant the destruction of an even more valued alliance—that with liberal anti-Communist politicians who controlled the fate of federal civil- and voting-rights legislation.

The decision was not an easy one. As historian Manning Marable has demonstrated, when civil rights groups such as the National Association for the Advancement of Colored People and the Congress of Racial Equality refused to work with Marxists, they lost many of "the most principled anti-racist organizers and activists" and to some degree "accepted the prevailing xenophobia of the times." Moreover, unjustly accused activists would have clearly been remiss had southern attempts to paint the movement red gone unchallenged. But Americans of the 1950s and 1960s regarded Communism

13. Numan Bartley, *The New South* (Baton Rouge: Louisiana State University Press, 1995), 364; John Earl Haynes, *Red Scare or Red Menace?* (Chicago: Ivan R. Dee, 1996), 186. See also Charles Cobb, interview by John Rachal, 21 October 1996, Mississippi Oral History Program, University of Southern Mississippi; Jan Handke, interview by John Rachal, 8 May 1996, Mississippi Oral History Program; Lawrence Guyot, interview by John Rachal, 7 September 1996, Mississippi Oral History Program.

as an even greater evil than southern racism. They found it hypocritical and untenable for movement advocates to defend the civil liberties of American blacks while accepting aid from Communists, whom they inevitably identified with totalitarian restraints on the same liberties. Thus the immediate movement goals were better met by distancing the cause from ties with overt Marxists. Without general public support and without help from liberals—who were far more powerful, numerous, and helpful than radicals—the movement might not have made the enormous gains that it did.[14]

In their attacks on blacks and reds, southern segregationists aided what historian Mary Dudziak referred to as "a narrowing of acceptable civil rights discourse." They helped limit possible social change in the civil rights era. But their effect on the movement should not be overstated. Dudziak also reminds us that anti-Communism was not per se detrimental to the civil rights movement. Indeed, she argues, "civil rights reform was *in part* a product of the Cold War." Racial oppression in the United States made the American claim to liberty and equality ring hollow in the emerging postcolonial nations of Africa and Asia. Americans who were otherwise unconcerned with the race issue supported civil rights reform as an effort to counter Communist appeals abroad. Thus anti-Communism worked as much to the movement's advantage as it did to the southern massive resisters'. The southern red scare for this reason and others—the memory of Joe McCarthy's abuses and the bumbling of Dixie's scare leaders, to name two—never had the devastating effect upon the cause of blacks' civil rights that its proponents had hoped it would have had. Perhaps historian Richard Fried put it best when he stated that, on balance, the "Communist issue operated as a retarding force" on the civil rights movement. Southern nationalists disrupted the struggle for black equality, but they could not prevent desegregation or the rise of black voters as a political force in the South.[15]

14. Manning Marable, *Race, Reform, and Rebellion* (Jackson: University Press of Mississippi, 1991), 21–26.

15. Mary Dudziak, *Cold War Civil Rights: Race and the Image of American Democracy* (Princeton: Princeton University Press, 2000), 12–13. See also Penny Von Eschen, *Race against Empire: Black Americans and Anticolonialism, 1937–1957* (Ithaca: Cornell University Press, 1997); Brenda Plummer, *Rising Wind: Black Americans against U.S. Foreign Affairs, 1935–1960* (Chapel Hill: University of North Carolina Press, 1996); Thomas Borstelmann, *Apartheid's Reluctant Uncle: The United States and South Africa in the Early Cold War* (New York: Oxford University Press, 1993); Thomas Noer, *Cold War and Black Liberation* (Columbia: University of Missouri Press, 1985); Marable, *Race, Reform, and*

By the late 1960s, the southern red scare had begun to fade away. The civil rights movement's new focus on urban centers in the North and improved relationships between the United States and the Communist world all but eliminated the social and political turmoil that had powered the southern red scare. Both antagonists could retreat and still declare victory. The civil rights movement had won guarantees for black voting rights and an end to legal segregation. Southern nationalists, meanwhile, took solace in the country's embracing of the Nixon administration's law-and-order conservatism. As the momentum behind the southern red scare slowed in the early 1970s, the federal and state agencies making up the red and black investigating network were phased out. Soon thereafter the scare's principal leaders were all dead or voted out of office.

Rebellion, 18; Richard Fried, *Nightmare in Red: The McCarthy Era in Perspective* (New York: Oxford University Press, 1990), 164–65.

RED AND BLACK

THE SOUTHERN RED SCARE'S CORE ASSUMPTION—THAT racial reform was a plot hatched by foreign radicals—had deep roots in the region's past. Dixie's defense of slavery before the Civil War and white supremacy during and after Reconstruction rested in large part on the idea that "outside agitators" veiled their intentions to strip the South of political and economic power with calls for emancipation, civil rights, and desegregation. The red scares of the early twentieth century nurtured a similar suspicion of subversive foreign agents on a national and international scale. That these concerns for regional and national security would form a common ideology in the South became evident by the 1930s. Southerners would regard Communists as carpetbagger revolutionaries duping unwitting southern blacks into service. They would fuse traditional fears of subversive racial reform to anxieties about Marxist revolution. Then as the cold war and civil rights struggles increasingly dominated public discourse after World War II, the charge that Communists were behind the struggle for black equality gained critical political and emotional significance. Southern-nationalist politicians who had hammered home the accusation in their home region for generations could begin to carry their message on to Washington as Dixiecrats and as congressional leaders of the national anti-Communist crusade.

Southern fears of black conspiracies can be traced back to the seventeenth century. Communities of runaway slaves, called maroons, inspired white fears of black revolt throughout the colonial era. Maroons at that time posed a legitimate threat to European slaveholders. Building armed camps throughout the West Indies, maroon settlements gained enough military might to ensure reasonably autonomous enclaves in Jamaica and Surinam. Although no maroon group came close to holding such power in the American South, white slaveholders in the region expressed concern that maroon communities might serve as strongholds for slave revolts. They understood, as historian Eugene Genovese pointed out, that maroons in fact "had a destructive impact on slavery and provided a spur to slave disaffection, desertion, and rebellion"; they "inspired slaves to challenge white authority and to rebel."[1]

In the 1670s authorities in Virginia were so moved by the concern over maroon-led slave revolts that they ordered soldiers in the area to attack what communities they could find. One hundred years later, little had changed. Virginians were still quashing maroon revolts in the Blue Ridge Mountains and in the Dismal Swamp area along the Virginia–North Carolina border. Slaveholding communities in Georgia, South Carolina, Tennessee, Louisiana, and Florida led similar actions well into the nineteenth century, some as late as the Civil War. [13

The region's response to maroon revolutionaries began a pattern of resistance that would be repeated time and again in southern history. Southern whites hoping to protect the status quo racial order habitually returned to the threat of a massive, violent black insurrection to aid their cause. In the early republic, slave intrigues led by Gabriel Prosser in Virginia and Denmark Vesey in South Carolina were cited in support of legal restrictions designed to keep blacks in their place and prevent further uprisings. Authorities uncovered and crushed the Prosser and Vesey insurrections in the planning stages, but they found good evidence that bloody rebellions were in the making. Prosser had gathered armories of swords and clubs for a force of more than one thousand slaves, while Vesey had stockpiled pikes, bayonets, and daggers and recruited hundreds of assistants. Moreover, the fresh memory of the successful rebellion of Toussaint L'Ouverture in Haiti inspired anxious comparisons.[2]

A similar reaction came as a result of Nat Turner's rebellion in 1831. Turner, a black preacher from Southampton, Virginia, led a small band of sixty slaves in a murderous rampage that left fifty-five whites dead. Turner proved that bloody slave revolts could be successfully carried out in heart of Dixie. The fear of like rebellions prompted southerners to expand their legal codes restricting black assembly.

The Turner incident marked another important trend in white southern reactions to black insurrection. That Turner's rebellion came just as William Lloyd Garrison's fiery rhetoric was beginning to gain prominence in

---

1. Eugene Genovese, *From Rebellion to Revolution: Afro-American Slave Revolts in the Making of the Modern World* (Baton Rouge: Louisiana State University Press), 55–56.

2. John Hope Franklin, *From Slavery to Freedom* (New York: Random House, 1969), 188, 210–12.

14]

the North did not escape notice in the South. In the tense decades leading up to the Civil War, southerners began speculating that "outside agitators" might inflame black anger and spur blacks to violence. President John Tyler and his secretary of the navy Abel Parker Upshur, both Virginians who supported slavery as a positive good, were among those that shared this fear. During their administrations, the pair would define outside influence on the southern slave population as a national-security threat. Like the subversive foreign radical, the domestic radical abolitionist who "invades our hearth, assails our domestic circles, preaches up sedition, and encourages insurrection," according to Tyler, could easily incite the region's large, concentrated black population to rebellion.[3]

John Brown's raid in 1859 all but confirmed Tyler's warnings. Brown, a white abolitionist who had worked on the Underground Railroad and fought for the antislavery forces in Kansas, seized the federal arsenal at Harpers Ferry, Virginia with fewer than fifty men. His plan was to secure sufficient ammunition to carry on a large-scale guerilla operation against Virginia slaveholders, but federal and state troops trapped his small band and killed several of its members. Brown was later hanged amid much fanfare. Abolitionists declared him a martyr while southerners demonized him as a radical, a madman, and a representative of those who would stop at nothing to destroy slavery and the "southern way of life."

Southern fears of outside agitators and black rebellion contributed significantly to the social, cultural, and psychological tension that gave rise to southern nationalism and a separate Confederate state. Confederates argued repeatedly that secession was necessary for the defense of their social systems and livelihoods in the absence of federal action against abolitionist incitement of the slave population. Other factors certainly provided as much or more to southern nationalist ideology, but entrenchment against outside forces bent on changing the racial status quo had become its most characteristic expression.[4]

3. Thomas Hietala, *Manifest Design* (Ithaca: Cornell University Press, 1985), 13–14.
4. See Drew Gilpin Faust, *The Creation of Confederate Nationalism: Ideology and Identity in the Civil War South* (Baton Rouge: Louisiana State University Press, 1988); David M. Potter, "The Historian's Use of Nationalism and Vice Versa," in *The South and the Sectional Conflict* (Baton Rouge: Louisiana State University Press, 1968); John McCardell, *The Idea of a Southern Nation: Southern Nationalists and Southern Nationalism, 1830–1860* (New York: W. W. Norton, 1979). See also Clifford Geertz, "Ideology as a Cultural System," in *Ideology and Discontent*, ed. David E. Apter (London: Free Press of Glen-

Traditional southern anxieties about black vengeance grew to new levels during the Civil War as social revolution became more reality than abstraction. When Union troops invaded their homeland, Confederates worried [15 that their slaves and former slaves would rise up against the soldiers' wives and children who were left at home to care for family estates. Then with the South's surrender, emancipation, and Reconstruction, many anticipated social chaos and the black revolution they had long feared.[5]

The war and Reconstruction certainly wrought tremendous changes in Dixie. Blacks gained their freedom. Radical Republicans took temporary control of the South's political destiny. And carpetbaggers paid for a partial rebuilding of Dixie in the North's image. But if these changes amounted to a revolution, it was of a weak and temporary variety. Former Confederates quickly regained control of the region's political and social institutions and managed to keep the traditional racial hierarchy intact. Southern whites forced blacks back to the bottom of the southern social ladder and, ironically, in the process, remade them into an oppressed underclass searching more and more desperately for social, political, and economic reform. The collateral fear of black rebellion naturally continued.

Indeed, the anxious lessons of the Civil War, emancipation, and Reconstruction molded a southern identity newly preoccupied with black revolutionaries and "outside agitators." Southern whites remained regional nationalists invested in the idea that southern order and stability depended on white supremacy. In the Social Darwinist vogue of the post–Civil War era, they argued that Anglo-Saxons were democratic by blood and culture, and nonwhites, especially blacks, were inherently undemocratic. By this reasoning blacks integrated into white society would corrupt America's heritage of pure Anglo-Saxon democracy. Blacks and whites should be separated to prevent intermarriage, the "mongrelization" of both races, and the diluting of white America's racially unique democratic instinct. Integration became the new revolutionary threat for post–Civil War southerners.[6]

---

coe, 1964) and Sheldon Hackney, "Southern Violence," *American Historical Review* 74 (February 1969).

5. See, for example, Reid Mitchell, "Perseverance of the Soldiers," in Gabor S. Boritt, ed., *Why the Confederacy Lost* (New York: Oxford University Press, 1992), 109–32.

6. See Reginald Horsman, *Race and Manifest Destiny* (Cambridge: Harvard University Press, 1981) and Michael Hunt, *Ideology and U.S. Foreign Policy* (New Haven: Yale University Press, 1987). Also see Robert Beisner, *Twelve against Empire* (New York: McGraw-Hill, 1968).

The South responded to this threat with Jim Crow laws that explicitly prevented blacks from entering the democratic process and fomenting racial revolution. Poll taxes and literacy requirements restricted the political participation of poor and illiterate blacks, while extralegal threats of violence and bribes kept other nonwhites from reaching the voting boxes. At the same time, the discriminatory practices of white government, business, and labor in the South forced blacks to the bottom rung of the economic ladder thus further eroding their political power.[7]

Many white southerners of the Jim Crow era, like their predecessors, assumed that blacks, because they were not blessed with inherited democratic instincts or because they had been denied the benefits of capitalism and democracy under Jim Crow, were antisouthern, anti-American, and susceptible to manipulation by foreign agents. When Soviet Communism emerged on the international scene as the world's most vocal enemy of capitalist democracy at the end of World War I, southerners again grew increasingly anxious about the revolutionary potential of the country's black population.

Yet southerners were certainly not the only ones worried about Communist designs on the United States. The Bolshevik victory in 1917, followed by Communist insurrections in Europe, Lenin's pleas to American workers—including blacks—to join the revolution, and the industrial unrest of the winter of 1918–1919 ushered in a national red scare. Across the country, anti-Communists launched campaigns to identify and eradicate the red menace, both real and perceived. Among those targeted nationwide as potential subversives were blacks.[8]

Southerners, thus, could not claim to be the only Americans worried about the revolutionary potential of African Americans. Indeed, it might be argued that the southern red scare had roots in New York. At the height of the first red scare in the spring of 1919, Clayton Lusk, director of the New York State Assembly's antiradical investigating committee, issued a report stating that radical activity had made significant progress among blacks and that a more active program of Communist indoctrination of Negroes was soon to come. Many Americans found confirmation of Lusk's contentions in that year's race riots in Washington, D.C., and Chicago. That July a *New*

7. See C. Vann Woodward, *Origins of the New South* (Baton Rouge: Louisiana State University Press, 1951) 361–65.

8. See Richard Gid Powers, *Not without Honor* (New York: Free Press, 1995), 117–52.

York Times editorial spread the charge that "Bolshevist agitation has been extended among the Negroes, especially those in the South." The author expressed disbelief "that in such widely separated cities as Washington and Chicago there could be an outbreak of violent racial animosity . . . without influence or suggestion from any outside source."[9]

With reports such as these, as well as some widely publicized statements in the radical press claiming Negro allegiance with bolshevism, large numbers of Americans inside and outside the South accepted the argument that the country's racial unrest was due in some part to Communist agitation. The charges were unquestionably exaggerated, especially by organizations such as the Ku Klux Klan. Housing discrimination and Negro-white competition for jobs as southern blacks moved North were infinitely more important in motivating riots in places like Chicago and Washington than Communist agitation. Nevertheless, for the first time black and red ran together in the American consciousness to paint a powerful and lasting portrait of a conspiratorial enemy.[10]

Southerners thus, despite their usual habit of tying black revolution to regional security, originally understood Communist and African American collusion mostly as a national problem. But in October 1919, the perceived danger again became tied to traditional regional concerns. Near Elaine, Arkansas, black tenant farmers formed a semisecret fraternal order called the Progressive Farmers and Household Union of America. The members of the union sought legal aid and greater control over their earnings, but local observers saw such manifestations of black self-reliance as conspiratorial and alarming. In response an armed party, hoping to uncover the group's secrets, initiated a bloody encounter with union members that eventually led to sporadic fighting across the southern end of Phillips County, Arkansas. White men from the state, as well as others from Mississippi and Tennessee, joined the fracas while Arkansas governor Charles Brough mobilized the National Guard to round up black militants.

At the end of the fighting, official reports counted five whites and twenty-five blacks dead. Newspapers credited the massacre to black insurrection, while a committee of local planters charged that the tenants' union

9. "Race Riots," *New York Times*, 28 July 1919, p. 10.

10. Robert K. Murray, *Red Scare* (Minneapolis: University of Minnesota Press, 1955), 178–79. See also Theodore Kornweibel Jr., *"Seeing Red": Federal Campaigns against Black Militancy, 1919–1925* (Bloomington: Indiana University Press, 1998).

had been "established for the purpose of banding Negroes together for the killing of white people." Although the Progressive Farmers and Household Union of America had its origins in Arkansas under the leadership of black resident Robert Hill, Governor Brough blamed the "damned rebellion" on northern "agitators." Elaine proved to many that the radical specter had come to the South.[11]

White southern reactions in Arkansas were certainly in part a response to a new spirit of resistance among blacks that was brought on by the war years. In Elaine, as in Washington, Chicago, Charleston, Longview, Knoxville, Tulsa, and Rosewood, blacks—many of whom had been soldiers in the Great War—were beginning to more vigorously pursue the promise of racial equality. The regional backlash was tremendous and drew strength, in part, from popular stereotypes about African American disloyalty. In Congress, Representative James F. Byrnes of South Carolina, for one, claimed that the disturbances in the nation's cities were the result of incendiary propaganda distributed by northern Negro magazines. He demanded that Negro editors be prosecuted under the Espionage Act. The Justice Department responded with a report that all but confirmed Byrnes's suspicions. It declared that "a well-concerted movement among a certain class of Negro leaders" had become "a determined and persistent source of radical opposition to the Government, and to the established rule of law and order." Along with promoting an "openly expressed demand for racial equality," the black leaders were, according to the document, identifying the Negro with "such radical organizations as the I.W.W." and advocating "Bolshevik or Soviet doctrines."[12]

Demonstrating their indigenous militancy, southern black newspapers rejected the notion that black protesters were the dupes of alien agitators. For example, an editor of the *Black Dispatch* in Oklahoma wrote to state leaders, "It does not take an I.W.W. to clinch the argument that the majority of Negroes in the United States cannot vote. It does not take an anarchist to ride with us on the railroad for us to know . . . we do not get what you get by paying the same identical amount. It does not take a Bolshevist to inform us that . . . a separate status as citizens is designed for the black man." Still, many white southerners insisted that amicable race relations

11. George Tindall, *The Emergence of the New South, 1913–1945* (Baton Rouge: Louisiana State University Press, 1967), 152–54.

12. Ibid., 155–57.

existed in the South and that whatever anxiety blacks expressed was forced on them by subversive alien influences.[13]

Through the 1920s, southern concerns about a Communist conspiracy [19 sporadically continued to occupy a place in the regional consciousness. Local conservatives in southern industrial towns became especially aware of Communist militancy in the embryonic southern labor movement. In Birmingham, Alabama, the industrial center of the South, black and red became inextricably intertwined. There in 1928 the mostly black Share Croppers' Union openly accepted the calls of the Moscow Congress of the Communist International for "self-determination of the black belt" in the United States. The union also adopted in 1930 a program for preparing blacks for revolutionary action under Communist leadership. The union's radical stance soon drew local protests. In July 1931, a Tallapoosa County sheriff and two deputies were called out to investigate a confrontation between protesters and Share Croppers' Union members. By the time the police arrived, the encounter had turned violent. One man would die in the fracas and a handful of others would be wounded. William Pickens, an official with the National Association for the Advancement of Colored People (NAACP), which investigated the case, announced in the aftermath that few of the croppers knew that the organizers of the union were Communists or what Communism meant. Local whites drew little comfort from this revelation. They considered blacks who unwittingly collaborated with the Communist Party to be as dangerous as those who knowingly adopted its radical dictates.[14]

The Birmingham affair aroused concern locally, but southerners would not confront Communist and African American cooperation as a pervasive problem until the events in Scottsboro unfolded one hundred miles to the north. Scottsboro would become one of the most widely publicized and dramatic events in the region's history and would pave the way for the southern red scare.

In March 1931, local police arrested nine black teenage boys in Scottsboro, Alabama. They were charged with the rape of two white women on a train traveling through northern Alabama en route from Chattanooga to Memphis. The same month four separate juries convicted eight of the boys and sentenced them to death. The Communist Party of the United States

13. Ibid., 156–57.
14. Ibid., 379–80.

immediately expressed its outrage at the verdicts. The party's legal branch, the International Labor Defense, subsequently announced that it would defend the boys on appeal. Through seven retrials and two Supreme Court decisions, the defendants spent no less than six and as many as nineteen years in jail.[15]

Throughout the proceedings, white southerners insisted on the guilt of the black youths and on the Communists' desire to use the incident to foment race war and revolution in the South. When streams of mail flowed into Alabama protesting the convictions, state officials quickly concluded that the uproar was the work of Communist propaganda. Chief Justice John C. Anderson of the Alabama Supreme Court denounced the letters and telegrams as "highly improper, inflammatory, and revolutionary in their nature." White Alabamians insisted that southern blacks were otherwise content. There had never been any trouble between the races until alien influences began instigating racial strife in the state. The state's white population concluded that ignorant and trusting blacks were simply being misled by "wolves that came in sheep's clothing." Open Communist support of the Scottsboro nine convinced the white South, more than any other event, of a regional red and black plot.[16]

Not surprisingly, the events in Scottsboro led civil rights advocates to begin to struggle with the question of whether or not to accept the help of Communists. The Communist Party had gained a great deal of prestige in black communities because of Scottsboro, and Communists were for the first time provided access to black churches and the black press. Moreover, the Angelo Herndon case in Atlanta, which developed at the same time as Scottsboro, demonstrated Communist solidarity with blacks as an oppressed underclass. A state court convicted Angelo Herndon, a black Communist organizer, for "inciting insurrection" while leading a biracial demonstration protesting unemployment in Atlanta. Herndon was sentenced to twenty years on the chain gang. Communists used the case, together with the Scottsboro trial in Alabama, to draw civil rights advocates into an alliance with the party.[17]

Civil rights leaders, however, were extremely cautious about accepting

15. James Goodman, *Stories of Scottsboro* (New York: Vintage, 1995) and Dan Carter, *Scottsboro: A Tragedy of the American South* (Baton Rouge: Louisiana State University Press, 1969).

16. Goodman, *Scottsboro*, 48–52.

17. Powers, *Not without Honor*, 97.

Communist aid. The NAACP, for one, learned the perils of cooperation with Communists when it joined the case in defense of the Scottsboro boys. By the end of the ordeal, association members had become as critical of Communist participation as they were of the verdicts. Throughout the proceedings the NAACP had fought with the Communist Party of the United States (CP) for control of the defense. Association leaders denounced the party's exploitation of the case for its own ends rather than for the benefit of the Scottsboro nine.[18]

Others in the black community were equally critical of Communist participation in the trial. Among the most vocal was George Schuyler, a black journalist and probably the most zealous black anti-Communist in the country. He feverishly lashed out at Communist aid to all African American causes, particularly those with worldwide attention such as Scottsboro. Blacks who accepted help from the party were being fooled, Schuyler argued, and the Scottsboro defense had "all the earmarks of a Communist plot." Schuyler and the NAACP agreed that African Americans had enough to worry about in reforming Jim Crow without the added stigma of disloyalty and revolution.[19]

Even so, the denunciation of capitalism and the promise of a socialist utopia devoid of poverty and discrimination were potentially appealing messages to blacks during the Great Depression. Just as the Herndon and Scottsboro cases were attracting the region's attention, the Depression was ravishing already vulnerable southern farms and industries. When jobs became increasingly scarce, racial discrimination increased. Blacks lost jobs first and received relief last. Unions made little headway against the entrenched southern business community, thus paving the way for even more radicalism among the working classes. Communists gained members among the destitute in textile towns while the *Southern Worker*, the party's regional mouthpiece published in Birmingham, promised hope for oppressed working classes, including blacks. The violent confrontations near Birmingham, the Scottsboro imbroglio, and the Angelo Herndon case were but manifestations of the increasingly class-conscious spirit of southern workers in general and southern black workers in particular. If ever there

18. Walter White, "The Negro and the Communists," *Harper's Magazine* (December 1931), 62–72. See also Wilson Record, *Race and Radicalism* (Ithaca: Cornell University Press, 1964), 61.

19. Powers, *Not without Honor*, 100–103. See also George Schuyler, *Black and Conservative* (New Rochelle: Arlington House, 1966).

was a time when the reality of a red and black alliance could be strong, it was during the Great Depression.

American Communists had only just begun to realize this. Though Karl Marx, V. I. Lenin, and Joseph Stalin had all recognized the plight of American blacks and their potential as a revolutionary cadre, the CP had trouble recruiting blacks before 1928. That year, however, the Soviet Union determined the CP's program for American blacks during its Sixth World Congress of the Comintern. The party decided at the congress that the CP would purge itself of "white chauvinism," actively recruit blacks into leadership positions, and promote "self-determination for the Black Belt." Under the self-determination plan, where blacks formed a majority of the people in southern districts, the party would promote black secession and independence.

Black numbers in the American Communist Party rose from around 7.2 percent of the total membership in 1931 to around 14 percent in 1946. Black representation in the American Communist Party's Central Committee for those years also increased rapidly, a trend that continued into the early 1960s. At least on the surface, the Communist Party had begun to assign African Americans a significant position in its plans from the early 1930s on.

Still, Communism in the United States, even at its height during the Depression, never gained a significant number of black converts. While blacks were overrepresented in the party leadership, the CP never had more than eight thousand African Americans on its rolls at any one time. The new CP program appealed to few blacks, even those within the party's ranks. For many the self-determination plan was too outrageous to be practical. Some argued that it might even promote the further segregation of the races. The party also suffered from devastating divisions after the Nazi-Soviet Pact in 1939. Black Communists were naturally leery of a Russian alliance with such a racist German regime. And finally most African Americans had come to understand that any cooperation with Communists meant drawing the criticism of the anti-Communist left as well as further abuse from white southerners.[20]

20. See Gerald Horne, *Black Liberation/Red Scare: Ben Davis and the Communist Party* (Newark: University of Delaware Press, 1994), 66–72, and Harvey Klehr, *Communist Cadre* (Stanford: Hoover Institution Press, 1978), 53–69. See also Mark Solomon, *The Cry Was Unity: Communists and African-Americans, 1917–36* (Jackson: University Press of

Members of the Southern Tenant Farmers' Union (STFU) learned the latter lesson all too well just as the Depression reached its nadir. Reacting to the failure of the Agricultural Adjustment Administration to address the needs of sharecroppers in the Arkansas Delta, two young socialists organized the STFU in 1934. The union membership grew over the next few years to more than thirty thousand, two-thirds of which was black. Although the STFU originally adopted separate white and black locals, the union founders consciously moved to integrate the membership in a united struggle against the economic exploitation of tenant farmers. Blacks increasingly served in union leadership positions.

That blacks played a prominent role in the union irked the racist sensibilities of some white southerners in the Delta, but the combination of a radical ideology with the racial makeup of the STFU intensified the animosity directed at the group. In a series of events in Marked Tree, Arkansas, in early 1935, local whites displayed acute anxiety over the mixing of red and black in the STFU. After spokesmen for the union addressed a gathering about the plans of Henry Wallace to reform the Agricultural Adjustment Administration, landlords and lawmen waiting in the crowd listened for their opportunity. Reacting to mentions of Russia and the plight of the Arkansas poor, the local prosecuting attorney ordered police to arrest Ward Rodgers, a white speaker at the rally, for "criminal anarchy." Confiscating Rodgers's letters and papers, policemen found mention of the Communist Party's United Front campaign. Newspapers in the area interpreted the find to mean that Rodgers was an agent for a "Socialist-Communist Combine." A local jury later listened to testimony that Rodgers was an organizer for the Communist Party and an advocate for "racial equality right here in Arkansas." It took ten minutes to find him guilty. Justice of the peace J. C. McCroy sentenced Rodgers to six months in jail and fined him five hundred dollars plus court costs.

Communists and socialists in the area, including many from radical Commonwealth College, where young Orval Faubus was studying, moved to support Rodgers and the STFU. When leaders of the Young Communist League, the League for Industrial Democracy, and other radical groups began holding rallies in the area, local whites responded with violence, beating

---

Mississippi, 1998) and Earl Ofari Hutchinson, *Blacks and Reds: Race and Class in Conflict, 1919–1990* (East Lansing: Michigan State University Press, 1995).

speakers and shooting into STFU members' homes. The *Marked Tree Tribune*, in an unintentionally comic understatement, reported, "Citizens Ask Reds to Leave."[21]

While white harassment chipped at the union from the outside, fighting among Communists and anti-Communists disintegrated it from within. Leaders H. L. Mitchell and Howard Kester had always been suspicious of Communist designs on the union. Although they agreed to accept the aid of any group helping to further the STFU's cause, they were leery of party orthodoxy and rejected allegiances with Communist-dominated unions. The rest of the union membership, however, did not share their concerns. When Mitchell and Kester fought against a merger with Congress of Industrial Organizations (CIO) affiliate the United Cannery, Agricultural, Packing and Allied Workers of America—a union headed by Communist Donald Anderson and rumored to follow Communist doctrine—the STFU membership defied their leaders and voted to join the union. The decision led to two years of bitter wrangling between Communists and anti-Communists within the merged organization. The infighting would contribute to the eventual demise of the STFU in the early 1940s.[22]

Because Communist affiliations offered as many negatives as positives to southern blacks during the Depression, an overwhelming majority of African Americans remained loyal to mainstream political organizations such as the Democratic Party. This was particularly true after the economic relief and recovery of World War II had renewed hope in American capitalism. For the most part blacks, like whites—especially in the South—turned to Washington and the liberal policies of President Franklin Delano Roosevelt rather than to the radical left.

Roosevelt was immensely popular in the South throughout the 1930s, even among racist and anti-Communist southern nationalists. Although they harbored doubts about the clash between states' rights and the New Deal, southern politicians could not help but recognize its benefits to the region or deny Roosevelt's appeal among the general electorate. The region's political collaborators with the New Deal thrived. Congressional

---

21. Donald Grubbs, *Cry from the Cotton: The Southern Tenant Farmers' Union and the New Deal* (Chapel Hill: University of North Carolina Press, 1971). See also H. L. Mitchell, *Mean Things Happening in This Land* (Montclair, N.J.: Allanheld, Osmun, 1979).

22. Grubbs, *Cry from the Cotton*, 83–84, 162–92. See also John Egerton, *Speak Now against the Day: The Generation before the Civil Rights Movement in the South* (New York: Alfred A. Knopf, 1994), 157.

leaders such as William Bankhead of Alabama, Sam Rayburn of Texas, Joseph T. Robinson of Arkansas, and James F. Byrnes of South Carolina all benefited from cooperation with and loyalty to the president and his programs.

But while Roosevelt drew significant support in the South, a hard core of white southern conservatism waited for its chance to reemerge. In the late1930s Eugene Talmadge, Harry Byrd, and others began openly expressing their concerns about the New Deal. They admitted the need for federal aid to the ailing economy but could not abide the chipping away at states' rights or the liberal social policies that threatened the region's racial and economic caste system. After the initial shock of Pearl Harbor began to wear off, a gathering storm of conservative discontent rose in the South. The 1942 congressional elections registered a national swing against the New Deal. That year, two southern conservatives who became among the most ardent red- and black-baiters of the era gained Senate seats—James O. Eastland of Mississippi and John L. McClellan of Arkansas. They represented an anti–New Deal, anti-Communist, and anti-black force in the South that hoped to reassert its power against Roosevelt's unionized, ethnic, and statist coalition.[23]

The resurgence of southern conservatism during and just after World War II came in large part as a reaction to potentially revolutionary changes brought to the South by blacks, civil rights groups, and the federal government. Black soldiers who supported a Double V campaign calling for victory over fascism abroad and racism at home drew attention to the fundamental inequities in southern society. Black workers who found jobs in the growing war industry empowered their communities as they helped reorient the southern economy away from the farm. The NAACP, meanwhile, began making significant gains in its legal battles to achieve equal rights for African Americans. And the Roosevelt administration created a Fair Employment Practices Commission to address racial discrimination in the federal workforce.[24]

Southern conservatives rightly anticipated a revolution in race relations, as did some southern liberals. In 1943 Virginius Dabney, the liberal editor

23. See James T. Patterson, *Congressional Conservatism and the New Deal* (Lexington: University of Kentucky Press, 1967).

24. See Patricia Sullivan, *Days of Hope: Race and Democracy in the New Deal Era* (Chapel Hill: University of North Carolina Press, 1996).

of the *Times-Dispatch* in Richmond, Virginia, wrote that "a small group of Negro agitators and another small group of white rabble-rousers are pushing the country closer and closer to an international explosion which may make the race riots of the First World War and its aftermath seem mild by comparison." The demands for an "overnight revolution in race relations" threatened faster and more dramatic change than even the liberal South was ready for.[25]

The more wartime changes challenged the racial status quo in the South, the more southerners homed in on the putative link between the black-liberation movement and international Communism. Martin Dies, a Democrat representing the hill country of east Texas and an emerging leader in the southern revolt against the New Deal, fought vehemently for white southern concerns. His suspicion of big cities, big capital, big labor, big government, foreigners, and foreign ideologies combined with his racism to make him a leader of southern reaction.

Dies institutionalized these concerns in the House Un-American Activities Committee (HUAC). Approved by Congress in 1938 to investigate extremists on both the right and the left, HUAC became the nerve center of counter-subversive anti-Communism during the 1940s and 1950s and a principal contributor to the southern red scare. With the help of his chief investigator, J. B. Matthews, Dies steered the committee to probe the labor, Jewish, popular-front, and black allies of Roosevelt's New Deal coalition.

Although Dies's chairmanship of the committee ended with the Texas representative's decision not to run for reelection in 1944, HUAC continued under southern leadership. In a canny political maneuver, Representative John Rankin of Mississippi used a conservative coalition of Republicans and southern Democrats to establish HUAC as a standing committee of the House on the opening day of the Seventy-ninth Congress in 1945. Rankin never chaired the committee because he continued as head of the Veterans' Affairs Committee, but he remained HUAC's spiritual leader. Rankin's foremost claim to Americanism was his hatred of Negroes, aliens, liberals, and Jews. Indeed, for the congressman, "to call a Jew a Communist was a tautology." He even attributed the horrors of the Russian Revolution to the Jewish-born Trotsky, while he saw Stalin as a kind of reformer. But although

25. Virginius Dabney, "Nearer and Nearer the Precipice," *Atlantic Monthly* (January 1943): 94–95. See also Morton Sosna, *In Search of the Silent South* (New York: Columbia University Press, 1977),121–39.

Rankin was a racist demagogue, he was also a shrewd politician and an effective anti–New Dealer. He used the committee in the spring of 1945 to investigate the Office of Price Administration, an agency that many businessmen saw as the New Deal incarnate.[26]

HUAC's rise as a political power was only beginning at the end of the Second World War. The cold war would bring a new sense of urgency to the anti-Communist cause and give its leaders a huge boost. The war had established the Soviet Union as the world's other great super power. Russian domination of Eastern Europe, and threatened Communist inroads in Greece and Turkey, convinced an increasing number of Americans that Moscow was prepared to employ whatever means necessary, especially subversion and espionage, to realize its dream of a global empire. That Soviet designs included America became clear in 1945 and 1946 after the *Amerasia* and Hiss cases uncovered rings of Communist agents operating at the highest levels of the United States government.

The following year anti-Communist zeal reached a new high both in Congress and in the Truman administration. In 1947 lawmakers proposed legislation that would outlaw the Communist Party, force the party and its fronts to register with the attorney general, and compel labor union officials to file non-Communist affidavits. Meanwhile President Harry S. Truman established a federal loyalty program that stipulated that government employees could be dismissed for, among other things, affiliation with any group "designated by the Attorney General as totalitarian, fascist, communist, or subversive."[27]

It was at this point that southern congressmen gave new life to the idea that a black and red conspiracy was the foremost threat to the southern and American way of life. They could protect the racial status quo by playing on the traditional southern fear of black rebellion and the growing national fear of Communist subversion. They could redirect southern nationalism in the cause of union rather than disunion. They could wrap their region's racial agenda in the American flag and tie southern security to national security. And they had the ideal platform from which to do it: HUAC.

Southerners had used HUAC to apply racist doctrines to the anti-

26. Walter Goodman, *The Committee* (New York: Farrar, Straus & Giroux, 1968), 19–58, 172–89.

27. See Richard Fried, *Nightmare in Red* (New York: Oxford University Press, 1990), 68, 73.

Communist cause since the committee's beginning. But under John Rankin's leadership in 1947, the committee began pursuing black radicalism in earnest. That year Rankin declared that all of the "racial disturbances you have seen in the South have been inspired by the tentacles of this great octopus, communism, which is out to destroy everything." The disturbances he referred to included those involving Henry Wallace's 1948 presidential campaign. Calling for major civil rights reforms and a less confrontational stand against the Soviet Union, the former vice-president had undertaken a campaign to speak before integrated audiences in the South. At several rallies his supporters were attacked, and the candidate himself was barraged with rotten vegetables and epithets of "Communist" and "nigger lover." According to the congressman, the confrontations could be blamed on Wallace and the Communists whose efforts at racial reform were but "a smoke screen" for Marxist subversion. In reality, he declared, the radicals "do not give a tinker's dam about the Negro."[28]

Many of Rankin's southern colleagues agreed with his assessments. As they saw it, Rankin's HUAC was preserving both democracy and the Anglo-Saxon way of life. Thus the Mississippian's charges and tactics, however crude, became mainstays of the southern red- and black-baiters who followed. The Communist Party's stated goal of creating an independent black state in the South, and the charge that all racial disturbances in the region were Communist inspired, would be repeated ad nauseam. The evidence backing the accusations was often meticulously researched and documented. The charges would be supported by reliable statements about Communist goals, Communist Party membership, and Communist-front affiliations and would list press statements regarding Communist support of particular civil rights campaigns along with membership histories of civil rights organizers who had worked or continued to work for Communist and Communist-front organizations. But the accusations were almost always coupled with unverifiable charges. All civil rights initiatives, even those carried out by avowed anti-Communists, would be carelessly lumped together with the efforts of a larger Communist conspiracy. Truth would be reduced to molehills while speculation was expanded into mountains.[29]

28. *Congressional Record*, 80th Cong., 1st sess., 1947, 93, pt. 1:551; *Congressional Record*, 80th Cong., 1st sess., 1947, 93, pt. 4:6896; *Congressional Record*, 80th Cong., 1st sess., 1947, 93, pt. 1:1012.

29. Goodman, *The Committee*, 172–89.

HUAC employed Rankin's charges and tactics even after Republican J. Parnell Thomas of New Jersey became HUAC's first nonsouthern head. Indeed, the Thomas committee manufactured ammunition used by leaders of [29 the southern red scare for the next two decades. With southern Democrats Rankin, John Wood of Georgia, Herbert C. Bonner of North Carolina, and J. Hardin Peterson of Florida still on the committee, HUAC issued two reports in 1947 that successfully cast a red cloud over popular-front groups that actively supported Henry Wallace and the southern civil rights movement. The first report, issued in June, called the Southern Conference on Human Welfare (SCHW) "perhaps the most deviously camouflaged Communist-front operation" of the day.

Middle-class, white New Dealers and pre-war liberal and leftist supporters of a united front against fascism had created the SCHW in 1938 to improve the economic lot of the South in general and African Americans in particular. More specifically, the SCHW was a response to the Roosevelt administration's "Report on Economic Conditions of the South." The report praised the South's contributions to the nation but also noted its numerous problems. The South had remained the poorest and least economically progressive section of the country through the Great Depression years, and the administration proposed immediate relief efforts as well as long-term improvements to the region's economy, including diversification and industrialization. While many southern elites objected to the spin of its conclusions, the report inspired a wave of regional economic discussion and a reinvigoration of New South ideology. The SCHW grew from these discussions, incorporating along the way a commitment to improving the lot of the South's vast unskilled black labor force.[30]

As an interracial organization committed to challenging the conservative traditions of the South, however, the SCHW was susceptible to the most damaging charges that could be levied by southerners at southerners. Conservatives from the region argued the SCHW leaders were the reincarnation of the evil overlords of Reconstruction. HUAC's Rankin claimed the group was full of scalawags, "local men . . . abusing and misrepresenting and undermining the people of the Southern States." With the coming of the cold war and the anti-Communist crusade, defenders of the status quo in the South were able to add powerful new ingredients to the mix: black

30. See Linda Reed, *Simple Decency and Common Sense: The Southern Conference Movement, 1938–1963* (Bloomington: Indiana University Press, 1991).

Communism and Soviet subversion. The charge that the group was full of "parlor pinks," and "left-wing fellow travelers," reinforced the notion that, while the SCHW claimed southern roots, its objective was to undermine the most sacred institutions of the South and the United States.[31]

Communist Party members did indeed participate in and influence SCHW activities, but they were hardly able to lead the conference toward an "unswerving loyalty" to Communist causes, as HUAC's report concluded. Written hastily for release prior to an SCHW rally featuring Henry Wallace, the report relied on logical fallacies, quotations taken out of context, and guilt by association. Nevertheless, it added political weight to the charges of Communist influence that had been levied against the conference since its founding. Moreover, it established one of the first government-documented links between civil rights activism and Communism. The report highlighted several SCHW members' ties to black organizations such as the National Negro Congress, which was cited as subversive by the U.S. attorney general. It also linked a black Communist vice-presidential candidate to the group and associated other SCHW leaders with the Communist-led Scottsboro defense.[32]

From this "evidence," the report wildly argued that the SCHW "wittingly or unwittingly" promoted a fundamental technique and a crucial goal of the Communist Party in "dealing with the Negro question." First, rather than having the "long-range welfare of the Negro" at heart, the Communists and the SCHW were using the race issue as "explosive and revolutionary tinder in destroying American democracy." And second, both the Communists and the SCHW favored "an independent Negro Soviet Republic in the southern Black Belt which in essence is a call to civil war." In fact, the SCHW leadership, while endorsing the notion of racial equality, could not decide how to deal with the region's racial problems. The leadership was equally split over whether to continue to accept members with radical political views. Many Americans, however, particularly in the South, considered HUAC's unjustified conclusions to be the truth.[33]

31. *Congressional Record*, 80th Cong., 1st sess., 1947, 93, pt. 4:7066. See also the *Charlotte Observer*, 15 June 1947, and the *Memphis Commercial Appeal*, 16 June 1946.

32. Thomas A. Krueger, *And Promises to Keep* (Nashville: Vanderbilt University Press, 1967), 176; Walter Gellhorn, "Report on a Report of the House Committee on Un-American Activities," *Harvard Law Review* 60 (1947): 1193–1234. See also Goodman, *The Committee*, 199–202, and Tindall, *Emergence of the New South*, 636–42.

33. *Report on Southern Conference for Human Welfare*, 80th Cong., 1st sess., House Report No. 592 (Washington: United States Government Printing Office, 1947); Reed, *Simple Decency*, 55–56.

Crippled by internal mismanagement and burdened by the increasing weight of the charges of Communist influence, the SCHW disbanded in November 1948. It survived, however, in a different form, as the Southern Conference Education Fund (SCEF) headed by James Dombrowski. In its new incarnation the group became even more fully committed to the struggle for black civil rights. It would thus continue to feel the wrath of southern red- and black-baiters and carry the scars of the 1947 report well into the 1950s and 1960s.[34]

The House Committee on Un-American Activities issued a second report dealing with Communist activity in organizations promoting black civil rights in late August 1947. Like the SCHW document, the second report provided federally endorsed ammunition to southern segregationists and anti-Communists. The report's title left no doubt as to its contents: "Civil Rights Congress As a Communist Front Organization." HUAC described the Civil Rights Congress (CRC) as a group solely devoted to the protection of Communist Party members who ran afoul of the law. The committee listed a number of luminaries as CRC members: Representative Vito Marcantonio, American Labor Party, of New York; Senator Glen Taylor, Democrat, of Idaho; Representative Adam Clayton Powell, Democrat, of New York; CIO general counsel Lee Pressman; Harvard professor Arthur M. Schlesinger Jr.; actor Edward G. Robinson; president of the National Farmers Union James G. Patton; Texas NAACP secretary Lulu White; and SCHW president Clark Foreman. HUAC did not specifically identify any of those listed as Communists, but the CRC's record of protecting Communists during America's second red scare made the entire membership suspect as far as conservative southerners were concerned.[35]

After HUAC published its report, some members, such as Schlesinger and Robinson, distanced themselves from an affiliation with the CRC while others attacked HUAC for its sweeping indictments. What could not be denied was that the CRC had Communist members. Like the SCHW, the CRC was made up of an amalgam of liberals and leftists; some of them, such as Lee Pressman, were closely associated with the Communist Party. The CRC had been formed in 1946 by members of the National Negro Congress, the International Labor Defense, and the National Federation for Constitu-

34. Ellen Schrecker, *Many Are the Crimes* (Boston: Little, Brown and Company, 1998), 391. See also Reed, *Simple Decency,* 127, and Goodman, *The Committee,* 199–202.

35. *Report on Civil Rights Congress as a Communist Front Organization,* 80th Cong., 2nd sess. (Washington, United States Government Printing Office, 1948).

tional Liberties, all groups with strong Communist ties. Indeed, although originally sponsored by the NAACP, the National Negro Congress had been the undisguised civil rights wing of the Communist Party since 1940, along with its offspring the Southern Negro Youth Congress. The kernel of truth that the HUAC report contained was that the CRC defended Communists and had Communist members.[36]

The HUAC investigation of the CRC drew special attention from Mississippians. Just two years before the 1947 report, the CRC had been involved in the Willie McGee trial. In November 1945, a white housewife from Laurel, Mississippi, Wilmetta Hawkins, had charged Willie McGee, a black resident of the town, with rape. The local police arrested McGee, who admitted to having consenting sex with the woman but denied the rape charge. After a Laurel jury convicted him and the judge sentenced him to death, McGee turned his appeal over to the Civil Rights Congress (CRC) and a young New York attorney named Bella Abzug.

The CRC was already well known for having several Communist members and for having defended Communists in court cases throughout the 1940s. But the connection among McGee, the CRC, and Communism was massively reinforced in the public mind when the Comintern took official notice of the case and promoted it around the world as a cause celebre. The Communist press described southern blacks as a vast underclass of low-paid laborers subjugated by a racist society. In various third-world countries, the party used the McGee case to expose Jim Crow, revealing what in fact was the Achilles heel of American cold-war policy. Rallies and protests erupted throughout Africa, Asia, and the Communist-bloc countries denouncing the racism of the Mississippi courts.

Despite the facts that blacks had been systematically excluded from the juries, and that the defense presented sworn statements maintaining Hawkins had been having an affair with McGee well before the alleged rape, the CRC and McGee lost all subsequent appeals. HUAC's report on the CRC, although not decisive, surely contributed to those defeats. It was convenient for Mississippi juries and judges, who were already racially biased, to convince themselves that a government-documented report linking the McGee defense to Communism was accurate. It was also easy for them to

36. "Civil Rights Group Called Red 'Front'" *New York Times*, 31 August 1947, p. 2; Record, *Race and Radicalism*, 93–100; Gerald Horne, *Communist Front?* (Rutherford, N.J.: Fairleigh Dickinson University Press, 1988).

believe that Communists on the defense team, in promoting their own interests, had manufactured evidence and falsely represented the events under consideration. McGee was executed on May 7, 1951.[37]

HUAC's treatment of the SCHW and CRC was but a manifestation of a much larger phenomenon. A developing anti-Communist consensus in the country, coupled with an increasingly assertive coalition of southern conservatives, was able to crush liberal causes in the South during the late 1940s. "Operation Dixie," a 1946 project of the Congress of Industrial Organizations (CIO), was a case in point. Working closely and sharing leadership responsibilities with the Southern Conference for Human Welfare, the CIO launched the drive to unionize traditional southern industries such as textiles, lumber, and tobacco. The drive immediately faced a range of opponents, including business leaders and politicians who "almost invariably linked the unions with racial integration, Communism, un-Christian values, and outside control of local affairs." The CIO integrated its campaign to organize southern workers and openly appealed to blacks. This fact, combined with long-held southern suspicions of unions and their Communist influences, led the conservative political establishment to bait the labor group as a red and black conspirator. The antiunion *Militant Truth* summed up these suspicions when it claimed that the CIO's principal aim was "to arouse class-hatred and race-hatred for the purpose of creating strikes, riots, bloodshed, anarchy, and revolution."[38]

Coupled with the divisive politics among southern liberals who argued over the goals and leadership of "Operation Dixie," red- and black-baiters' torments had an especially strong impact on the CIO's drive. Although it originated in the North, the South experienced the full effects of a fundamental ideological split in the CIO. The issue was Communism. Many in the union realized that their political power stemmed from their participation in Harry Truman's liberal coalition and that anti-Communist sentiment was increasingly strong within that coalition. The CIO had evolved from its militant roots into a more moderate and therefore publicly accept-

37. Horne, *Communist Front?* 14 and 73–90; John Dittmer, *Local People: The Struggle for Civil Rights in Mississippi* (Urbana: University of Illinois Press, 1995), 21–22.

38. Numan Bartley, *The New South 1945–1980* (Baton Rouge: Louisiana State University Press, 1995), 41; Dittmer, *Local People*, 23; Barbara S. Griffith, *The Crisis of American Labor: Operation Dixie and the Defeat of the CIO* (Philadelphia: Temple University Press, 1988), 109. See also Donald Mosely, "Holt Ross, The Second President of the Mississippi State Federation of Labor," *Journal of Mississippi History* 34 (August 1972): 239–40.

able institution during World War II. The continued stigma of radicalism, concluded the organization's leadership, had become counterproductive. Not coincidentally, right-wing unionists became increasingly prominent within the CIO and had begun an intraorganizational anti-Communist crusade. They focused on purging the union of left-wingers, some closely tied to the Southern Conference for Human Welfare, who refused to abandon the commitment to popular-front cooperation with Communists. Southern Conference head Clark Foreman tried to hold off right-wing attacks by arguing that red-baiting had begun to "divide us, to make us attack each other instead of getting on with the job of democracy" but to no avail. "Operation Dixie" felt the impact of this right-wing surge directly. Its primary organizer, Van Bittner, sided with the right when he declared in Atlanta, "No crowd, whether communist, Socialist, or anybody else is going to mix up in this organizing drive. That goes for the Southern Conference for Human Welfare."[39]

By 1948 the rift between right and left had become full blown within the unionization movement in the South and was increasingly exacerbated by racial antagonisms. In 1947 the left-wing food and tobacco Local 22 launched a strike at what was reputed to be the world's largest tobacco factory in Winston-Salem, North Carolina. The five thousand black employees who constituted half the work force generally supported the strike, while their white counterparts continued to report to work. The *Winston-Salem Journal* immediately launched an attack on the local headlined "Communist-Union Collusion Is Exposed in City." This in turn provoked another investigation by HUAC into Communist activity in the cigarette industry. The black community eventually rallied behind the strikers, elected black candidate Kenneth Williams city alderman, and negotiated a positive settlement, but the taint would remain.

Increasingly, right and left in the union movement in the South divided into white and black. While unions had been one of the few integrated institutions in the South, CIO affiliates by the late 1940s increasingly met on a segregated basis. The unions also continued to be at odds over Communist membership. The CIO carried on its purge of Communists from the unions

39. See Alonzo L. Hamby, *Beyond the New Deal: Harry S. Truman and American Liberalism* (New York: Columbia University Press, 1973) and Harvey A. Levenstein, *Communism, Anticommunism, and the CIO* (Westport, Conn.: Greenwood Press, 1981); Bartley, *New South*, 45; "CIO Stands Alone Organizing South," *New York Times*, 19 April 1946.

in 1947 and 1948, finally officially expelling left-wing internationals at the 1949 national convention. Combined with the already persistent red- and black-baiting from southern conservatives and the rival American Federation of Labor, the CIO's internal difficulties with black and red issues doomed "Operation Dixie."[40]

Conservative harassment of leftist elements in the CIO, CRC, and SCHW was indicative of a growing movement in the South to halt liberal reforms associated with the Truman administration and the left wing of the Democratic Party. Southern Democrats, while accepting the need for aid during the Depression, had long been critical of the economic and social liberalism of the New Deal. But it was the racial policies of Truman that finally moved them into open rebellion against the party. In December 1946, the president issued Executive Order 9008 creating the President's Committee on Civil Rights. A year later the committee offered a formal report titled "To Secure These Rights," which argued for a permanent nationwide system of guardianship for civil rights. With the 1948 election at hand, Truman gambled that his open support of the proposal would win more votes than he would lose by appeasing the white South. Consequently, in February 1948, the president called for action, giving his support to a permanent Fair Employment Protection Commission, anti-lynching legislation, anti–poll tax laws, and measures to end discrimination in interstate transport facilities.

The southern reaction to Truman's racial policies was a clear indication that red and black fears had become a defining element of the region's ideology; the southern red scare was under way. Mississippi congressman John Rankin replied to the president's announcement by suggesting that the South choose independent electors for the upcoming Democratic convention that would "stop these smearing Communists who creep into every bureau and every commission that is appointed and attempt to undermine and destroy everything our people have fought for and everything we hold dear." Southerners flooded the White House with letters supporting the rebellion Rankin hoped to lead. They called the Truman proposals Communistic and unconstitutional, arguing that they violated states' rights and promoted the mongrelization of the white race. One letter was typical: "You have advocated and asked Congress for a lot of good legislation both Domestic and Foreign but when you down the Crown of Thorns on the

40. Bartley, *New South*, 59–61.

South's brow and crucify the South's people on a Communistic Cross disguised in Negro equality, that was the straw that broke the Camel's back."[41]

The Truman administration held firm to its policies, knowing the worst of the southern reaction was yet to come. When the Southern Governor's Conference sent a five-man committee led by South Carolina governor Strom Thurmond to meet with Truman, the White House turned it away, declaring that there would be no compromise on any point. Shortly thereafter southerners in the House of Representatives led by Mississippi representative William Colmer condemned Truman's civil rights program, putting red and black issues at the forefront of their criticisms. Colmer argued that the president's initiatives encouraged racial agitation and divided Americans at a time when national survival depended on a united front against the international Communist menace. He told his colleagues that the administration's civil rights policies had "inflicted an apparently fatal blow, not only to the unity of the party, but to the unity of the country, at a time when that unity is so highly desirable in a fight to the death with the enemy of free men—Communism." Furthermore, he proclaimed, Truman's policies had "encouraged the arrogant demands of these minority groups to whom it was designed to appeal."[42] Colmer's home-state colleague John Bell Williams was even more blunt, declaring that the "so-called civil-rights movement," which Truman supported, was "a Communist movement."[43]

In early July the president again challenged southern nationalists when he established through Executive Order 9981, the Committee on Equality of Treatment and Opportunity in the Armed Forces, later called the Fahy Committee. The committee put into motion army, navy, and air force policies that would eventually desegregate military service. But the final break came when the Democratic National Convention voted to adopt Minneapolis mayor Hubert Humphrey's liberal civil rights plank later that month. All of Mississippi's delegates and about half of Alabama's walked out of the convention. Two days later disgruntled southerners convened their own meeting in Birmingham. There they formed the States' Rights Party, which was subsequently dubbed the Dixiecrats by the press. They chose Strom

41. Monroe Lee Billington, *The Political South in the Twentieth Century* (New York: Scribner, 1975), 94–106.

42. *Congressional Record*, 80th Cong., 2nd sess., 1948, 94, pt. 4:4312.

43. John Bell Williams, "The President's Infamous Civil Rights Program" (Washington: United States Government Printing Office, 1948). See also *Congressional Record*, 80th Cong., 2nd sess., 1948, 94, pt. 4:4361.

Thurmond as their presidential candidate and Mississippi governor Fielding Wright as their vice-presidential candidate.[44]

Thurmond and Wright carried out a campaign that made black bolshevism a primary issue facing southerners and all white Americans. A virtuous republic depended on those traditions and institutions the South held most dear, they argued. Inherently democratic Anglo-Saxon leadership and decentralized power based on states' rights would ensure that America remained resistant to hostile leftists and integrationists. Truman's promise to renew the Fair Employment Practices Commission (FEPC) would both centralize federal control and chip away at the South's racial caste system. The FEPC, according to Thurmond, was "made to order for communist use in their designs upon our national security."[45]

The Dixiecrats' case for putting red and black at the center of the debate came largely from *Whither Solid South?* by Alabama lawyer Charles Wallace Collins. In many ways this book, published in 1947, was the political and ideological manual for the States' Rights Party. It depicted a black, red, federalist, and unionist enemy bent on destroying southern civilization. According to Collins, influential admirers of the Soviet system—including federal bureaucrats, liberal politicians, African Americans, the CIO, and northern church groups—had focused their crusade for black equality and socialism on the South. But there the forces of conservatism and southern culture, if vigilant, would defeat the red and black foe.[46]

The Dixiecrats' appeals to segregationists and anti-Communists never made the electoral impact the States' Rights Party hoped they would make. Southerners generally remained loyal to the Democratic Party. The Dixiecrats did, however, make significant showings in the plantation counties of Alabama, Mississippi, South Carolina, and Louisiana. These were areas where the potential mobilization of relatively large populations of nonvoting blacks posed the greatest challenge to the social and political status quo. There the Dixiecrats were able to articulate the concerns of white southerners most threatened by the specter of liberal change. Not coincidentally,

44. Billington, *Political South in the Twentieth Century*, 94–106. See also William Barnard, *Dixiecrats and Democrats* (Tuscaloosa: University of Alabama Press, 1974).

45. See Wayne Addison Clark, "An Analysis of the Relationship between Anti-communism and Segregationist Thought in the Deep South, 1948–1964" (Ph.D. diss., University of North Carolina, 1976), 33–35.

46. Charles Wallace Collins, *Whither Solid South? A Study in Politics and Race Relations* (New Orleans: Pelican Press, 1947).

over the following two decades these areas became the established centers
of the southern red scare.

While not to the degree that those from the Deep South were, moderate
white Americans were also concerned about the tactics black Americans
would adopt in their quest for political and social equality. Hoping to address their worries more fully, HUAC—this time under Georgia congressman John Wood—launched in 1949 its most ambitious effort to date to
certify the loyalty of black Americans. HUAC's "Hearings Regarding Communist Infiltration of Minority Groups" had an even more lasting impact
on southern red- and black-baiters than the 1947 reports. As a summary of
Communist influence among minority groups, specifically African Americans, at the height of the Dixiecrat revolt and the second red scare, these
hearings became sacred scrolls for those hoping to paint the maturing civil
rights movement red.

The proceedings began on a moderate note. Even before the testimony
of the first witness, a letter from Dwight D. Eisenhower set the "historical
record" straight by claiming "irrefutable evidence of the loyalty of our
Negro troops." HUAC investigator Alvin W. Stokes followed up on Eisenhower's letter with his own declaration that, despite the Communists' re-
lentless propaganda campaigns to indoctrinate African Americans, only
"one-tenth of 1 percent of the entire Negro population of the United States,
are members of the Communist Party." The NAACP, the Urban League, religious leaders, and Negro women, according to Stokes, deserved special
mention as combatants against Communist influence within the race. But
setting up a typical "good Negro–bad Negro" dichotomy, Stokes continued
by arguing that the headway made by Communists among a small minority
of blacks was distorting the picture white America had of black loyalty.
Prominent black entertainers caught in the Communist web were throwing
into question African American patriotism. Paul Robeson was one example.

Here the committee had come to the crux. During the spring and early
summer of 1949, Robeson had repeatedly stated that it was unthinkable
"that American Negroes or Negroes anywhere would go to war on behalf of
those who have oppressed us for generations." His reiteration of this theme
at a Civil Rights Congress fund-raising concert in Peekskill, New York, had
provoked violent reactions from a group of World War II veterans led by the
American Legion. Southerners on the committee saw the hearings as a perfect opportunity to alert the nation to the potential threat that Communism
posed in indoctrinating oppressed minority groups. They also unwillingly

provided civil rights leaders a forum for asserting their patriotism and responding to Robeson's position.[47]

Rabbi Benjamin Schultz and Catholic Interracial Council head George Hunton took the stand. Both reaffirmed Stokes's statements concerning the overall loyalty of blacks and the questionable stature of Paul Robeson as a spokesman for his people. The next witness, Fisk University president Charles S. Johnson, questioned whether he could actually speak to the loyalty of an entire race of people but ventured an opinion anyway. Blacks, Johnson declared, were remarkably loyal given "the price of their citizenship." The fact that they desired the elimination of racial inequalities in the United States did not mean they wanted "to subvert the Government." Indeed, he added, few blacks knew what Communism was, and most believed profoundly in the promises of democracy and capitalism. The conditions under which black loyalty was even questioned, Johnson said as he glared at southerners on the committee, had come from those who had used the term "communism" with "malevolence to prejudice the public against the objects of their personal hostility and aversion." African American veteran C. B. Clark then took the stand and told the committee of his ancestors who had fought for the United States in every war since the Revolution. Finally baseball giant Jackie Robinson called Robeson's statements "silly," denounced Communism, and promised to continue the fight against racial discrimination.

Although Clark and Robinson captured the attention of the press and the popular imagination, red- and black-baiters in subsequent years proved to be more interested in the testimony of two state witnesses. The first was Manning Johnson, a black Communist Party member turned conservative labor leader after the Nazi-Soviet Pact. Johnson outlined the CP's efforts to foment black revolution in the South and destroy the American government. As evidence he offered testimony that a Communist training school he attended in New York City taught legal and illegal methods of operation toward these goals. The party, he claimed, was using the civil rights movement as a means to an end, not an end itself. When the Bill of Rights "serves our purposes," he said, speaking for fellow Communists, "we use it; when it does not serve our purposes, we denounce it." Regardless, he warned, once the "Communists come to power the Constitution will be burned,"

47. John Earl Haynes, *Red Scare or Red Menace?* (Chicago: Ivan R. Dee, 1996), 187–88.

and the nation will be controlled, like the Communist Party of the United States, by direct instructions from Moscow.

Johnson went on to openly indict Paul Robeson as a major subversive voice of the international movement. As a secret member of the Communist Party, the popular singer and actor had allegedly used his fame to subtly indoctrinate American blacks and promote himself as the black Stalin. Johnson declared that functionaries such as Robeson and the Southern Sharecroppers Union, invoking Leninist principles concerning self-determination for national minorities and the Sixth World Congress declarations, would help establish an autonomous republic in the Black Belt, formerly known as the Cotton Belt. Communist fronts in the South would organize the black masses for action, "including demonstrations, riots, and so forth, leading to armed rebellion in that area and the seizure of governmental power."

For racially conservative southerners experiencing the civil rights movement of the 1950s and 1960s, Johnson's words would seem prophetic. He reaffirmed that Communist plans for black self-determination continued to threaten the South, and he confirmed suspicions that the Communist Party used front groups involved with the civil rights movement to inspire racial antagonism. Southern nationalists were convinced that such antagonism would escalate into armed conflict and socialist revolution if left unchecked. Johnson's message was thus a powerful stimulant for defeated Dixiecrats hoping to justify continued diligence against a red and black menace challenging segregation and the southern way of life.

A surprise witness reinforced the buzz a year later when he requested that his statement be entered as part of the HUAC hearings. Joshua Daniel White, an African American singer, actor, and musician who had once shared the stage with Paul Robeson, told the committee that he might have been an unwitting dupe of the Communist Party. He had performed in support of groups claiming to be fighting Jim Crow only to find out that the attorney general had labeled them "subversive." White had voluntarily come before the committee to declare his allegiance to the U.S. and announce that he was devoting himself to erasing Communism from the American landscape.

White's testimony demonstrated to reactionary southerners that their anti-Communist investigations could discourage black participation in civil rights activities. African Americans were generally sensitive to the charges of disloyalty and hoped to reinforce their image as "good," law-abiding, anti-Communists. If civil rights activities and popular-front support could be publicly linked to Communism, "good" blacks might be prevented from joining the movement. Chairman Wood seemed to understand this as he concluded the hearing: "I hope that others who have been similarly imposed upon by Communist-front organizations will wake up to that fact."[48]

With the HUAC hearings on Communists and minority groups, southern blacks and whites entered the age of McCarthyism. The proceedings concluded just as Senator Joseph R. McCarthy launched his four-year crusade against alleged Communists in the highest ranks of the United States government and military. A series of trials exposing Soviet espionage, the detonation of the first Russian atomic bomb, and the outbreak of the Korean conflict focused the nation's attention on Communist subversion with an intensity not seen since 1919. Frustrated by Communist advances abroad and faced with nuclear annihilation, Americans searched for excuses and scapegoats. Convinced of their global preeminence, they blamed their inability to win a complete victory over Communism on traitors burrowing from within.

Republicans used this mood to defeat the Democratic administration. The threat of Communist subversion was the perfect political issue, reconciling what Bertrand Russell once called the two principal fears of Americans—taxes and Communism. If American reverses abroad were due to betrayal at home, there was no need for huge new expenditures on defense and foreign aid. All that was required was a domestic house cleaning. The Republican McCarthy made the most of the moment, charging the Truman administration with Communist collusion and helping pave the way for an Eisenhower victory in 1952. While the country would ultimately come to denounce McCarthy's reckless accusations, in the early 1950s it was markedly unconcerned about the issue of civil liberties and was willing to give the inquisitor the benefit of the doubt.

While McCarthy personally enjoyed less support in the South than in other regions of the country, his anti-Communist convictions and flamboyant political style resonated with the doctrines and political techniques of southern conservatism. In the spring of 1954 the senator from Wisconsin drew favorable ratings from those interviewed in a nationwide Gallup poll.

---

48. *Hearings Regarding Communist Infiltration of Minority Groups before the Committee on Un-American Activities House of Representatives, 81st Congress, First Session* (Washington: United States Government Printing Office, 1949).

The poll revealed, however, that the South was the only region where more people opposed McCarthy than supported him. But the Democratic, Protestant, and pro-military South objected as much to McCarthy's Republicanism, Catholicism, and attempted purge of the army as to his exaggerated charges that Communists had overrun the federal government. Indeed, the South contained pockets of McCarthy's most ardent supporters, especially in Texas. In Houston, for example, red- and black-baiters warmly welcomed McCarthy's crusade in the fall of 1950 and were inspired to initiate Houston's own local red scare. Moreover Texas oil barons Clint Murchison, Hugh Roy Cullen, and H. L. Hunt were among McCarthy's most enthusiastic financial backers. Fearing Communism's threat to their newly acquired empires abroad as well as creeping socialism and integration at home, these men applauded McCarthy's attacks on the New and Fair Deals. They also deeply appreciated the senator's pro-industry vote on oil legislation. According to historian David Oshinsky, McCarthy had become by the mid-1950s "something of a 'third senator' to the state of Texas."[49]

McCarthy also appealed to many Dixiecrats. While States' Righters generally shied away from any open alliance with McCarthy, they agreed with his anti-Communist convictions and some even adopted his tactics. One Dixiecrat in particular even launched a McCarthyite crusade of his own. Senator James O. Eastland, dubbed the "Mississippi McCarthy" by journalist I. F. Stone, mirrored the Wisconsin senator's style while carrying on the traditional southern struggle against a perceived black revolutionary movement. It was Eastland, more than any other person, who brought the red scare south.[50]

James Eastland grew up in a small town near Jackson. As a young lawyer, Mississippi state representative, and cotton-plantation owner, he adopted the lifestyle and worldview of the conservative southern white ruling elite. But it was as a United States senator that he became known as one of the nation's leading segregationists and anti-Communists. Eastland had his first taste of national politics in 1941 when Mississippi governor Paul Johnson appointed the young politician to a temporary position in the U.S. Sen-

49. *U.S. News and World Report*, 19 March 1954, p. 20; Daniel Bell, ed., *The New American Right* (New York: Criterion Books, 1955), 160; Don Carleton, *Red Scare* (Austin: Texas Monthly Press, 1985), 136–38; David Oshinsky, *A Conspiracy So Immense* (New York: Free Press, 1983), 302–303.

50. Robert Sherrill, "James Eastland: Child of Scorn," *The Nation* 201 (October 1965): 184.

ate to replace the recently deceased Pat Harrison. Eastland subsequently won election to a full term in 1942 with strong support from the state's agricultural community. He would remain in office for more than thirty years as a leading supporter of farmers and an opponent of black civil rights.

Eastland was a virulent racist. He called the use of black troops in Europe during World War II "an utter and dismal failure." He repeated the southern racist mantra that all nonwhites were inherently un-American. According to Eastland, blacks were lazy, irresponsible, "of very low intelligence," of an "inferior race," and incapable of acquiring Anglo-Saxon civilization. The senator made the prevention of racial reform his main issue during the 1948 campaign season. Among the first to break with the national Democratic Party over the civil rights issue and join the States' Rights faction, he vowed to stop the organization of "mongrel minorities" in government and the "harlemization" of the country. Eastland's racist rhetoric was so extreme that it even drew frowns from Dixiecrat presidential candidate Strom Thurmond, but in his home state it helped him win reelection.[51]

Back in the Senate, Eastland remained committed to blocking civil rights legislation and at the same time began building his anti-Communist credentials. Sharing McCarthy's and the Dixiecrats' belief that the Truman administration was advancing subversive causes, he joined fellow renegade Democrat Pat McCarran of Nevada in calling for the resignation of secretary of state Dean Acheson, whom Eastland accused of sympathizing with pro-Soviet advisers in the State Department. In 1950 his alliance with McCarran earned Eastland membership in the Nevadan's new Senate Internal Security Subcommittee (SISS), where the Mississippian would hold court on black and red issues for almost twenty years.

Eastland would become the quintessential southern red- and black-baiter. "Just as Joseph McCarthy saw a Red behind every government door," one witness called before SISS commented, "Eastland saw a Red behind every black." That Eastland's main concern was to serve the segregationist cause cannot be in doubt. He shared this concern with all of the leaders of the southern red scare. He fully understood the opportunity to harass the

51. Dittmer, *Local People*, 18; Bartley, *New South*, 82–83. See also Dan W. Smith, "James O. Eastland: Early Life and Career, 1904–1942" (master's thesis, Mississippi College, 1978) and Nick Walters, "The Repairman Chairman: Senator James O. Eastland and His Influence on the U.S. Supreme Court" (master's thesis, Mississippi College, 1992).

civil rights movement and win political points with his racist constituents by labeling the movement red. Also, like many leaders of the southern red scare, he was not beyond using exaggerations, and even lies. A Citizens' Council and John Birch Society supporter, leading senatorial filibusterer, and lifelong Mississippi racist, he at various points in his career denounced any organization that promoted prejudice, hatred, and bigotry; claimed he never engaged in a filibuster; and declared that not a single Ku Klux Klan chapter existed in Mississippi. He also certainly exaggerated and lied about Communists in the civil rights movement.[52]

Yet while Eastland might be called a cynic, a fool, a boob, a simpleton, and even slightly insane, he was also a product of his time and place. He was committed to a segregationist cause that engrossed the South at the midpoint of the twentieth century. He was also a sincere and devoted anti-Communist, like his contemporaries nationwide. He shared the view that Communism's aggression abroad and potential subversion at home was a legitimate threat to the United States. As with all those caught up in the southern red scare, his criticism of Communism was rooted in his beliefs about centralized authority, atheism, and totalitarianism as well as in his belief that Communist promotion of racial integration endangered the southern way of life. His anti-Communism was not simply a convenient front for his racism, it was part of a world view that fused cold-war concerns with the southern struggle over segregation.

Eastland's commitment to thwarting the red and black enemy, even if it meant bending the truth, became evident in the Senate Internal Security Subcommittee's first significant hearing under the Mississippi senator's leadership. In the early spring of 1954, the SISS investigated the Southern Conference Education Fund, an offshoot of the Southern Conference for Human Welfare. The Southern Conference for Human Welfare had initiated the tax-exempt Southern Conference Education Fund (SCEF) in 1946. James Dombrowski became executive director of SCEF in 1947 and kept the fund going despite the parent organization's demise. SCEF focused from the beginning almost exclusively on racial segregation and discrimination, portraying the racist caste system as the root of the South's economic problems.[53]

In view of the damage HUAC investigations had done to the SCHW, Sen-

52. Frank Adams and Myles Horton, *Unearthing Seeds of Fire: The Idea of Highlander* (Winston-Salem: John F. Blair, 1975), 194–200; Sherrill, "Eastland: Child of Scorn," 187, 194.
53. Reed, *Simple Decency,* 127–45.

ator Eastland saw its offspring, SCEF, as a relatively easy target. Through the late 1940s and early 1950s, Dombrowski and SCEF had gained the support of an impressive list of liberal New Dealers, leftist southerners, and civil rights activists, including former National Youth Administration head Aubrey Williams, anti–poll tax advocate Virginia Durr, U.S. senator Frank Graham, and Highlander Folk School director Myles Horton. It would not be difficult to link this group to popular-front causes, and its fame would certainly make the case high profile.

In early March 1954, the subcommittee served SCEF board members Williams, Dombrowski, Horton, Durr, and professor Alva Taylor of the University of Tennessee Divinity School with subpoenas. All were ordered to present themselves at a hearing in New Orleans and defend their organization against charges that it was Communist controlled.

The accused immediately responded with formal press statements denying SCEF's connection to Communism or any other subversive cause. They also sought the support of some powerful allies. Durr and Williams in particular asked their mutual friend senate minority leader Lyndon Baines Johnson for help. Johnson had been a longtime admirer of Mrs. Durr and had worked with Williams on the National Youth Administration in Texas. The Texas Democrat promised Durr in a phone conversation that he would try to persuade subcommittee members John McClellan of Arkansas and Pat McCarran of Nevada to stay in Washington. The outlandish Eastland, Johnson said comfortingly, could do them little damage on his own.

McClellan's and McCarran's absence from the hearing testified to Johnson's powers of persuasion, but Eastland was not entirely disarmed. Government informers Paul Crouch and John Butler, as well as the subcommittee's special counsel Richard Arens, accompanied him. Former Communist Crouch especially, like Manning Johnson in 1949, was to be the star government witness tying SCEF to the forces of international Communism.

The hearing began with the testimony of the Anti-subversive Committee of the Young Men's Business Club of New Orleans. The group's representatives traced SCEF's lineage to the SCHW and charged Dombrowski with "a record of continually supporting the Communist Party Line." Next up came Leo Sheiner, an attorney with no formal connection to SCEF but who had once worked with Dombrowski in Miami. Sheiner, when questioned about his Communist Party activity, invoked the Fifth Amendment. Paul Crouch then took the stand and identified Sheiner as an "undercover" Communist Party member and testified that the only function of the

SCHW and SCEF was "to promote Communism" by dividing "race against race" in the South.

Eastland then called James Dombrowski. The senator from Mississippi and counsel Arens probed the SCEF head about his Communist and Communist-front connections. Dombrowski admitted he had been a socialist but denied ever having been a Communist Party member. Crouch again pounced. He and John Butler identified Dombrowski as a "topflight operator" and party member.

Crouch would make similar allegations against Virginia Durr and Aubrey Williams before Eastland allowed Clifford Durr—Aubrey William's counsel, Virginia Durr's husband, former Reconstruction Finance Corporation lawyer, and one-time Federal Communications Commission director—to cross-examine Crouch. Durr showed that Crouch's recollections were disturbingly imprecise, even coaxing Crouch to admit that he was unsure if Williams was still a Communist. Durr made Crouch further admit that he could not provide any details about the Durrs' activities at party meetings. At that he declared that Crouch's claims were "absolutely false." "One or the other of us," Durr argued, "should be indicted for perjury."

The hearings all but broke down the next day when Myles Horton took the stand. When questioned about his work at the Highlander Folk School—itself a heavily red-baited institution in Monteagle, Tennessee—Horton asked to make a statement of principle. Eastland denied his request, but Horton began speaking and refused to stop. The Mississippi senator ordered the witness forcibly ejected from the room; as he was dragged through the doors, Horton shouted that he was being treated "like a criminal."

A frustrated but persistent Eastland closed the hearings with a pledge to continue his "general investigation" into the activities of the Communist Party in the South. But the drama was not over. As the crowd filed out of the room, Crouch and Durr found themselves face to face and exchanged harsh words. Federal marshals hurried Crouch away while Durr proceeded to have a mild heart attack.

The hearings were a disaster for Eastland. At the post-hearing press conference, even the subcommittee head had to admit that Crouch had not convinced him that either Durr or Williams was a Communist. In the end only the most conservative journalists supported Eastland's handling of the hearings, even in the South; indeed, a majority of the region's journals criticized it. The *St. Petersburg Times* equated the Mississippi senator's tactics with Joe McCarthy's while the *Montgomery Advertiser* called the hearings a blight on "Southern honor." Most observers agreed that the type of character assassination carried out by Eastland's subcommittee was far more dangerous to American ideals than any posed by the leaders of SCEF. Again under pressure from Lyndon Johnson, the SISS cancelled a proposed Birmingham probe of Communism in Alabama. And Crouch never testified for the government again.

With some justification James Dombrowski claimed that the hearings amounted to a positive good for SCEF. Horton's dramatic exit prompted press reports that portrayed him as a victim of the subcommittee's heavy-handedness. But Dombrowski could not have predicted the long-term effects the hearings would have on the fund and its leadership. Leo Sheiner's professional life in Florida came to an end, Virginia and Clifford Durr lost friends and supporters in Montgomery, and Williams's journal the *Southern Farmer* lost revenue. But the most enduring blow came from the Eastland subcommittee's final report. Despite the bungled testimony of Crouch and the overall lack of evidence, the report emphasized SCEF's association with the former SCHW "a mass organization to promote Communism throughout the Southern states." SCEF, the report implied, was a key thread in the web of liberal-left, Communist-front organizations promoting black revolution. For the next several years, red- and black-baiters would use the subcommittee's findings to denounce SCEF's efforts in the South.[54]

Two months after Eastland's botched hearings in New Orleans, the Supreme Court delivered its ruling in the landmark *Brown v. Board of Education* case. Seven months later, the Senate censured Joe McCarthy. McCarthy's excesses had given his brand of reckless anti-Communism a bad name. But while Eastland's tactics might have fallen into disfavor alongside McCarthy's, there was a renewed interest among racially conservative southerners in attributing the civil rights movement to alien influences. Southern segregationists would carry the red scare into the looming battle against school integration.[55]

54. John A. Salmond, "The Great Southern Commie Hunt," *South Atlantic Quarterly* 77 (Autumn 1978): 433–52. See also John Salmond, *A Southern Rebel: The Life and Times of Aubrey Willis Williams, 1890–1965* (Chapel Hill: University of North Carolina Press, 1983), 229–46 and *Southern Conference Education Fund Inc. Hearings before the Subcommittee to Investigate the Administration of the Internal Security Act and Other Internal Security Laws of the Committee of the Judiciary, United States Senate, 83rd Congress, Second Session* (Washington: United States Government Printing Office, 1955).

55. Powers, *Not without Honor*, 235. See also Oshinsky, *Conspiracy So Immense*.

The southern red scare had taken shape in the years between 1948 and 1954, but it rested on traditions stretching back to the antebellum period. Massive resisters, like their conservative southern predecessors, equated dramatic social reform, particularly in race relations, with the conspiratorial designs of outsiders. The long-held racist assumption that African Americans were easily duped into supporting un-American causes served as a linchpin to their argument. Reacting to the changing social and political conditions of the early cold war, they counted black and red cooperation among the greatest threats to domestic tranquility. Responses to the menace ultimately found expression in national politics with the Dixiecrats and the southern leadership of the House Un-American Activities Committee and the Senate Internal Security Subcommittee.

Working through these congressional entities, red- and black-baiters refined their tactics in the early cold-war years. They intertwined elements of truth and speculation to support accusations that might otherwise have been discounted. So while they certainly exaggerated the influence of Communists in the civil rights movement, they backed their contentions with reliable evidence that SCEF, the SCHW, CRC, CIO, and sharecroppers' unions all had Communist members and that the Communist Party did indeed support "self-determination in the Black Belt" as a step toward the ultimate overthrow of the United States government. But both baiters and baited understood the power of anti-Communist charges, regardless of their merits, to influence public opinion. On the national scene the anti-Communist consensus remained intact despite McCarthy's censure, and at the regional level the white public still overwhelmingly supported segregation, even more so in the wake of *Brown*. Certain that red-baiting was an answer to the Supreme Court's decision and the proper foundation for massive resistance, southern segregationists redoubled their search for evidence that the civil rights movement was closely allied with the Communist Party and its goals. Indeed, the experiences of the CRC, SCHW, and SCEF before congressional committees had proven that organizational ties to Communism could be used to harass and defame the movement as a whole. Civil rights organizations were coming to understand that if they did not want to encumber their already difficult task, they would have to purge Communist influences and hope that this would redeem the struggle for black equality in the eyes of the public.

DESIGNED TO HARASS

2

IN THE YEARS IMMEDIATELY FOLLOWING *BROWN,* THE southern red scare reached full strength as part of the region's massive-resistance campaign against integration. Conservative white southerners found anti-Communist legislation and litigation particularly useful in harassing the civil rights movement. State assemblies across Dixie revived anti-Communist measures that jailed, fined, and denied employment to red civil rights activists. Like other interposition measures, the laws invoked the rights of states, but they also appealed to broader national-security interests. This added to their legal durability. With *Brown* the Supreme Court had effectively declared all overtly segregationist laws produced by the states unconstitutional, but it had not yet made any such definitive statement concerning anti-Communist measures. For a few crucial years in the late 1950s, the southern red scare grew as massive resisters relied on anti-Communist laws to bully the civil rights movement.

Segregationists' anti-red laws primarily targeted the National Association for the Advancement of Colored People (NAACP). Between 1918 and the early 1950s the NAACP had grown to become the largest and most important organization for the promotion of racial change in the South. As early as World War II, the group's litigation and education campaigns had begun dismantling Jim Crow and the white power structure while inspiring middle-class blacks, and some working-class blacks, to join the struggle. By the 1950s the group had attracted the full attention of segregationists. Southern reactionaries charged that Communists had infiltrated the group and were beginning to control its movements.[1]

Responding early and often to these accusations, the NAACP, like the Congress of Industrial Organizations (CIO) around the same time, purged Communists from its ranks and reiterated its commitment to anti-Communism. The group's efforts, however, were lost on segregationists. The

1. See Aldon Morris, *The Origins of the Civil Rights Movement* (New York: Free Press, 1984), 26–33.

NAACP's leadership in litigating the *Brown* case left southern nationalists convinced that the association was the vanguard of revolution in Dixie. The region's segregationists and anti-Communists dug deep to find evidence of Communist-NAACP collusion and assembled long lists of NAACP officials with former Communist-front affiliations. These lists activated southern loyalty oaths and security measures. Texas officials used such evidence to charge the NAACP with violating foreign-corporation and Communist-registration laws. South Carolina's legislature used the same lists to pass a law forbidding state employment of association members and mounted an initiative to have the NAACP added to the federal attorney general's list of Communist fronts. And Alabama leaders cited the lists in banning all of the association's activities in their state.

While not the most extreme, Arkansas's Act 10 was the last and most representative of the southern antisubversive laws targeting the NAACP. Passed in the wake of the Little Rock crisis of 1957–58, it required state employees to list their organizational affiliations from the previous five years. The law had been originally designed to expose Communists on the state's payroll, but legislators understood that it worked equally well to reveal members of the NAACP. Along with an act similar to South Carolina's law banning state employment of NAACP members, Arkansas's segregationists adopted the anti-Communist legislation to leverage association acquiescence. After two years of legal battles, the Supreme Court would rule Act 10 unconstitutional, but while it and similar legislation across the South remained on the books, the southern red scare grew.

Southern state governments had been combating Communists, foreign and domestic, real and imaginary, since World War I. Mimicking existing state and national programs, they employed loyalty oaths and Communist-control laws in their crusade to fend off red subversion. Indeed, almost every southern state had adopted a loyalty oath of some kind by 1953. The most common of these required that state employees swear their allegiance to the Constitution of the United States and disavow any advocacy of the overthrow of the government or membership in a group with that as its objective. Others required that state employees list their organizational affiliations. Especially harsh loyalty requirements, like those in Georgia, demanded that workers list family members who were affiliated with subversives or front organizations. Federal courts ultimately annulled Georgia's loyalty requirement along with Florida's and finally Arkansas's in the early 1960s. While the courts were not bothered by the notion that state governments could question their employees' affiliations, the breadth of information required of citizens under certain loyalty laws disturbed them. Nevertheless at midcentury it remained generally safe and prudent for state [51 politicians to support loyalty oaths.[2]

While mandatory pledges of allegiance were more common, southerners also put great stock in Communist-control laws. These measures came in various forms. The most common required Communist-front groups to register with state attorneys general, restricted CP members' voting in state elections, and prohibited the employment of Communists by public agencies. But some went even further. In 1947, provoked by the CIO's Operation Dixie and Communist activities in Birmingham, the Alabama legislature adopted a law authorizing the dissolution of the Communist Party if it was found guilty of advocating the forcible overthrow of the government. Moreover in 1950 Mississippi used "clear and present danger" legal doctrines to make participation in any foreign subversive organization illegal. A few years later the state legislature's Legal Education and Advisory Committee would move to establish a permanent list of subversive organizations. Texas legislators even briefly considered the death penalty for Communists around the same time.[3]

It was no coincidence that the South developed and implemented more loyalty and security measures as the massive-resistance campaign against integration gained momentum. Massive resistance, like the fight against Communism, was a cold, defensive, ideological campaign. It required more than just providing deterrents to physical danger; it required containing the enemy on all fronts. It meant the winning of minds. It was also, strangely enough, a campaign waged in the name of democracy. Segregation, massive resisters argued, protected democracy by eliminating racial conflict and preserving democratic instincts that southern racial conservatives associated with pure Anglo-Saxon heritage. Loyalty to southern racial institutions, for them, was loyalty to Americanism.

Under this logic racially conservative southerners could also fuse state sovereignty to national security. The southern brand of Americanism was grounded in states' rights. Southerners defended decentralized, state-based

2. See Walter Gellhorn, *The States and Subversion* (Ithaca: Cornell University Press, 1952) and M. J. Heale, *McCarthy's Americans* (Athens: University of Georgia Press, 1998).

3. See Heale, *McCarthy's Americans*, 28–75, and John Herbers, "Mississippi Prepares New Subversive List," *Jackson Daily News*, 18 December 1955.

government—and its prerogative to determine racial policy—as the bedrock of democracy. They easily and often quoted Thomas Jefferson and John C. Calhoun in the same sentence. America's halcyon days were under an agrarian, yeoman society, according to southern conservatives, where local government superseded federal authority. States, moreover, had surrendered to the national government only those powers enumerated in the Constitution. Federal integration efforts were unsouthern, un-American, and a step toward the creation of a centralized, autocratic, socialist government. Massive resisters thus considered their efforts to be patriotic endeavors, helping to ensure the region's and the nation's loyalty and security.[4]

By the early 1950s, conservative southerners had effectively used combined interposition and anti-Communist legal initiatives to cripple civil rights organizations, intimidate individuals, and eradicate vestiges of political radicalism. To an extent they also succeeded in making liberalism politically and even socially dangerous. Registration laws in Alabama, Arkansas, Louisiana, Texas, North Carolina, and South Carolina were particularly effective in this regard. These states obliged Communists and members of Communist-front organizations, which included a number of the most prominent civil rights advocates, to register with state officials. Those failing to do so could be fired, fined, and even jailed. In 1952, for example, Louisiana officials arrested two African Americans for failing to register as Communists, and in 1954 Alabama policemen jailed a sixty-four-year-old black janitor, Matthew Knox, for having Marxist literature in his room. As litigation challenging segregation increased after *Brown*, southern conservatives used the same registration requirements to harass civil rights organizations deemed to be Communist fronts.[5]

Anti-Communist measures in the South targeted the National Association for the Advancement of Colored People (NAACP) more than the Communist Party itself. The NAACP posed an open and real threat to segregation in the South throughout the 1940s and 1950s and had been the driving legal force behind *Brown*. Massive resisters would have considered the group subversive based on its integration efforts alone, but the fact that the group shared membership and occasional partnership with organizations labeled subversive by various national authorities only added to segre-

4. See Numan Bartley, *The Rise of Massive Resistance* (Baton Rouge: Louisiana State University Press, 1969), 126–49.
5. Heale, *McCarthy's Americans*, 76–77.

gationist and anti-Communist scrutiny. Southern conservatives were able to assert that, because of the affiliations of its members, the NAACP was in cahoots with Moscow. The association, they maintained, was a potential threat to national security.

Southerners never found any good evidence that Communists had a perceptible influence in the NAACP. Indeed, much of the evidence pointed to the contrary. At its national convention in Boston in 1950, the NAACP, like the CIO a year earlier, had officially declared its devotion to anti-Communism. There the group adopted a resolution empowering the national office to expel any unit the board of directors determined to be under Communist control. The NAACP enforced this policy throughout the 1950s and 1960s. In addition, although Communists and the NAACP sometimes worked together for the eradication of racial discrimination in the United States, the association's goals were for the most part in direct opposition to those of the party. Where Communism sought the destruction of private property through revolutionary means, the NAACP for the most part sought to make the capitalist system its ally as it pushed for the repeal of racially discriminatory laws. As historian Wilson Record put it, "the principal goal of Negroes and other traditionally underprivileged groups has been to get into the supermarket rather than to burn it down." Because of its efforts to work with and through liberal democracy, the NAACP actually competed with the Communist Party for members. All in all the association was as anti-Communist as any civil rights group in the United States.[6]

Southern blacks generally were as leery of Communists as the NAACP was. The American Communist Party had experienced difficulty recruiting African Americans to its cause since its formation. Even before the centralization of the Communist movement around a party, Communists in the United States failed to rank the "Negro question" as a high priority. Although the international arm of Soviet Communism, the Comintern, occasionally called for the infiltration and usurpation of the American movement for black equality, the party's efforts were generally lacking. In many ways this failure was a direct result of Marxist doctrine that dictated that the real divisions among men were economic rather than racial. It was also a result of the absence of an organized black proletariat in the poorly industrialized South. Although socialism gained some headway in New

6. Wilson Record, *Race and Radicalism: The NAACP and the Communist Party in Conflict* (Ithaca: Cornell University Press, 1964), 94–97, 100–102, 153–56, and 222.

York and among black intellectuals and trade-unionists, Communism
never captured the imagination of the African American masses.[7]

Yet despite strong evidence that the NAACP and black Americans in
general were not the pawns of Communists, massive resisters gathered
enough research and had a strong enough national voice to arouse suspicions. They laid the foundations of their charges only ten days after the Supreme Court's decision in *Brown.* Mississippi senator James Eastland stood
before the Senate and accused the Court of pandering to Communism and
its allies when it handed down the "Black Monday" *Brown* decision. "Our
Court," Eastland argued, "has been indoctrinated and brainwashed by left-
wing pressure groups." Justice Hugo Black, he charged, had exhibited an improper bias by accepting an award from the Southern Conference for Human
Welfare, a "Communist-front organization." And Justice William O. Douglas had in Eastland's words "become virtually the protégé of the CIO," an
organization that had recently contributed $75,000 to the NAACP. Douglas
had also shown his pinkish colors, according to Eastland, when he proposed
that the United States recognize Red China.[8]

In this and other Eastland speeches delivered in the months following
Brown, the Mississippi senator outlined a conspiracy that linked the
NAACP, the CIO, the SCHW, and the Supreme Court to the forces of international Communism. The conspiracy's overriding goals were racial integration, the destruction of American democracy, and the elimination of the
southern way of life. Eastland's arguments echoed traditional southern fears
of black revolution and embodied the ideological forces driving the southern red scare. "Everyone knows," the senator maintained, "that the Negroes
did not themselves instigate the agitation against segregation." They were
the dupes of a leftist program "designed to mongrelize the Anglo-Saxon
race." Quoting Benjamin Disraeli, Eastland explained that democratic society was determined by blood, blood that rendered "an island [Britain] . . .
the arbiter of the world." "The white people of the South do not have race
prejudice," he continued, they have "race consciousness." The region's
awareness that civilization was a matter of race and race a matter of blood
had kept southern, Anglo-Saxon, democratic civilization from being "mon-

7. See Harvey Klehr et al., *The Soviet World of American Communism* (New Haven:
Yale University Press, 1998); John Haynes, *Red Scare or Red Menace?* (Chicago: Ivan R.
Dee, 1996),186; and Richard Gid Powers, *Not without Honor* (New York: Free Press, 1995),
57.
8. *Congressional Record,* 83rd Cong., 2nd sess., 1954, 100, pt. 5:7251–57.

grelized" and "destroyed." The future greatness of America, Eastland concluded, depended "upon racial purity and the maintenance of Anglo-Saxon
institutions, which still flourish in full flower in the South." In its struggle
with godless Communism, the senator implied, the United States should
look to the South and its customs as the essence of Americanism, the
touchstone of democracy.[9]

[55

Eastland contended that the Court's decision in *Brown* had pushed the
South to the precipice of a slope at the bottom of which lay racial "mongrelization," the destruction of democracy, and the triumph of Communism;
this contention drew its power from facts that could not be easily disproven.
That the Court had fallen to Communist and integrationist discipline, Eastland argued, could be found in the "partisan books on sociology and psychology" it cited. The Court in particular referred heavily to Gunner
Myrdal's famous work *An American Dilemma.* Myrdal, according to Eastland, was a Swedish socialist who accepted money from the Carnegie Foundation, a group that was then under investigation by HUAC for radical
control. In addition the Court cited a number of books that espoused leftist
and integrationist views, including works by Kenneth B. Clark, a black social scientist occasionally employed by the NAACP.[10]

Eastland's "evidence" was far from definitive. None of the tracts he
cited directly proposed the overthrow of democracy or capitalism. Myrdal
had even argued in *An American Dilemma* that "*the Communists have not
succeeded in getting any appreciable following among Negroes in America
and it does not seem likely that they will* [Myrdal's emphasis]." Myrdal's
work had even come under vicious attack by Communists in the mid-
1940s. Southern conservatives, nevertheless, agreed with Eastland implicitly that there was little difference between socialism and Communism and
that the works in question had sown the seeds of destruction that were
flowering with the *Brown* decision.[11]

Senator Eastland made his accusations in 1955, just as his power to support them broadened. He, Senator Olin Johnston of South Carolina (Eastland's protégé in the SISS), and other segregationists sponsored a resolution

9. Ibid.; ibid. pt. 8:11522–27.
10. James O. Eastland, "The Supreme Court's 'Modern Scientific Authorities' in the Segregation Cases" (Washington: United States Government Printing Office, 1955).
11. Gunner Myrdal, *An American Dilemma: The Negro Problem and Modern Democracy* (New York: Harper and Row, 1944), 508. See also Herbert Aptheker, *The Negro People
in America* (New York: International Publishers, 1946).

to investigate the sources of materials used by the Court in *Brown*. The resolution never made it out of committee, but the Senate appeased Eastland with the chairmanship of the Senate Internal Security Subcommittee (SISS). Under his direction, the subcommittee continued to probe civil rights organizations, paying special attention to the NAACP, the group the Mississippi senator increasingly held responsible for the school-integration decision. Eastland dug deeply into the extensive House Un-American Activities Committee (HUAC) files, collecting reports on high-ranking NAACP leaders Roy Wilkins and Clarence Mitchell in the fall of 1955. He also sought the help of like-minded friends in southern state politics.[12]

One such friend was Eastland's philosophical and political soul mate Leander Perez. At the local level, few politicos in the South could match the power of Perez. As judge, district attorney, Citizens' Council leader, and oil tycoon, he ruled Plaquemines Parish, Louisiana. He became a popular speaker in segregationist circles after gaining regional recognition as an outspoken Dixiecrat insider in 1948. The "boss of the delta" was a rabid anti-Semite and an experienced red- and black-baiter. Jews, according to Perez, were the link between the Kremlin and the civil rights movement. They dominated the NAACP and used the organization to promote racial strife through integration and intermarriage. Miscegenation, Perez maintained, would lead to a mongrelized, lazy race that lacked the ability to resist international bolshevism. Like Eastland, Perez considered the *Brown* decision "Communist trash" and the NAACP a "Communist-front infested hybrid organization."[13]

While Eastland empowered the southern red scare in Washington, Perez and others expanded its scope in the South. In the early 1950s, Perez helped draft legislation that would protect Louisiana from *Brown*, miscegenation, and Communism. He worked closely with Willie Rainach, a senator from Claiborne Parish, founder of the state's Citizens' Council, and head of Louisiana's newly formed Joint Legislative Committee on Segregation. Perez met a like-minded legislator in Rainach, one willing to take the red and black issue before the state legislature. And Rainach, not a lawyer himself,

12. Johnston to Eastland, 15 March 1956, Box 53, Folder Civil Rights General 1956, Johnston Papers, South Caroliniana Library, University of South Carolina, Columbia; Subject Mitchell and Subject Wilkins, 13 October 1955, 3N160, Folder 5, Texas v. NAACP Collection, Center for American History, University of Texas, Austin.

13. Glen Jeansonne, *Leander Perez: Boss of the Delta* (Lafayette: University of Southwestern Louisiana, 1995), 226–28.

depended on Perez's legal knowledge to compose bills that would pass the state's scrutiny. Together the two constructed several segregationist measures that were eventually enacted by the 1954 Louisiana legislature. One, a constitutional amendment ratified overwhelmingly by the public in November, directly defied the Supreme Court's ruling, establishing police-enforced segregation in the state's schools. In campaigning for the passage of the amendment, Rainach directly attacked the "arrogant, alien" NAACP. He argued that the people of Louisiana deeply resented "the carpetbag NAACP so cynically exploiting our colored people only as an instrument to an end, to be discarded when their ignoble purpose is served." According to Rainach the NAACP was trying to replace southern institutions with a "foreign way of life." It was little wonder, he mused, that "white control has receded all over the world while Communism has advanced."[14]

In the months immediately following "Black Monday," Rainach and Perez provided little additional evidence that individual NAACP members were Communists. Their accusations were based almost completely on preconceived notions. In 1956, however, they received some help from two fellow massive resisters from Georgia. On March 24, 1956, before a packed crowd of eight thousand people at the New Orleans Municipal Auditorium, Eugene Cook and fellow Georgian Roy V. Harris shared the podium with Willie Rainach and Leander Perez. Harris, the "king-maker" of Georgia, was among the strongest advocates of segregation and anti-Communism in the South. The man whom Eastland called a "correct" and "sound thinker" had served as a lawyer, state speaker of the house, state board of regents member, Georgia Citizens' Council president, and editor of the *Augusta Courier*. Echoing Eastland's outrage at the *Brown* decision, Harris was determined to give substance to the Mississippi senator's contention that the Supreme Court and Chief Justice Earl Warren were "catapulting" the United States toward socialism. Harris had for months been using the *Courier* to warn the South about the red and black menace. The newspaper frequently assaulted the Southern Regional Council (SRC) as a "haven for known communist fronters," even though the SRC was among the most conservative liberal organizations in the South.[15]

---

14. Ibid., 231–32; *Southern School News*, 4 November 1954, p. 2.

15. "A 'King-Maker' Rates the 'Kings,'" Series IV, Box 2, 56–60, Harris Collection, University of Georgia Special Collections; *Congressional Record*, 83rd Cong., 2nd sess., 1954, 100, pt. 8:11524; Heale, *McCarthy's Americans*, 248. Also see Numan Bartley, *The New South* (Baton Rouge: Louisiana State University Press, 1995), 29–30.

Harris, like Perez, was an extremely popular speaker in southern conservative circles. Louisiana was only one of several stops he would make on a post-*Brown* tour of the South. But in New Orleans, it was Eugene Cook, the lesser-known attorney general from Georgia, who stole the show with his report on the NAACP. Cook used the occasion to label as Communists the executive secretary and fifty-two other high-ranking officials of the NAACP.[16]

Cook's address was identical to a speech he had given before the Peace Officers Association of Georgia in October 1955 titled "The Ugly Truth about the NAACP." A letter the attorney general received from a prominent black educator, Dr. J. W. Holley, had originally inspired the speech. Holley had warned Cook that the National Council of Churches, the CIO, and the NAACP were "putting into effect the seven points promulgated by the Communist Party in 1929." Cook spent "many weeks" investigating the NAACP, aided to a large degree by Congressman James C. Davis of Georgia as well as Senator Eastland. The result was a diatribe that cited government sources documenting Communist influence within the organization. Segregationists hailed these revelations as a means to slow down if not halt the desegregation effort. Just a few months earlier, the Supreme Court had endorsed the South's gradual implementation of *Brown.*[17]

Cook's speech would have been more accurately titled "The Ugly Half-Truth about the NAACP." It once again wildly exaggerated Communist influence over NAACP policies. "The Communist-inspired doctrine of racial integration" in the South was, he said, among "the most ominous . . . threats to arise during our lifetime." The NAACP, Cook added, was a white-dominated revolutionary body designed to "dupe naive do-gooders, fuzzy-minded intellectuals, misguided clergymen, and radical journalists." The NAACP, of course, was nothing of the kind, but Cook had done some homework. The association, he reported, had begun in New York as the brainchild of "Russian-trained revolutionary" William E. Walling. Walling was indeed a Progressive Era socialist who had inspired the creation of the NAACP with an article on the Springfield, Illinois, race riots in 1908. When Walling wrote the piece, he had just returned from czarist Russia, where his wife had been imprisoned for alleged revolutionary activities. A number of

16. "Crowd Rocks Auditorium with Its Tumultuous Demonstration," *Plaquemines Gazette,* 24 March 1956.

17. Heale, *McCarthy's Americans,* 251–52.

the founders of the civil rights organization, Cook went on, had been the "descendants of the rabble-rousing abolitionists." The grandson of William Lloyd Garrison, Oswald Garrison Villard, also a socialist, was in fact an NAACP founder.[18]

For objective observers the few threads of reliable research woven into Cook's speech in no way supported the argument that the NAACP was a Communist pawn. But for a conservative southern audience predisposed to accept a black and red conspiracy, the Georgia attorney general confirmed their worst fears. Cook reinforced his argument with House Un-American Activities Committee reports. Covering one hundred and twenty-one pages of single-spaced, typewritten copy, the documents revealed the front and fellow-traveling affiliations of NAACP leaders. The only black man among the group's founders, W. E. B. DuBois, took up eight pages. Other prominent figures listed included Arthur Spingarn, Channing Tobias, Roy Wilkins, Thurgood Marshall, Clarence Mitchell, A. Philip Randolph, Eleanor Roosevelt, Walter Reuther, and Herbert Lehman.

Cook had made the presentation of incomplete evidence from HUAC's files the foundation of his case against the NAACP. Listing the former Communist-front affiliations of civil rights organizations, although grossly misleading, was common practice among massive resisters. Channing Tobias, one of those listed in Cook's speech, had been on the executive board of the Southern Conference for Human Welfare while another, Thurgood Marshall, served on the board of the National Lawyers Guild, a group described by HUAC as "the foremost legal bulwark of the Communist Party." The two NAACP leaders, however, were far from Communist supporters. In fact, Marshall would prove to be one of the most devoted anti-Communists in the civil rights movement. Also, while HUAC had its own biases, it was aware that its statements could be misinterpreted and exaggerated. The committee was always careful to include a warning with its reports that a named individual was "not necessarily a Communist, a Communist sympathizer, or a fellow-traveler unless otherwise indicated." Neither Marshall, Tobias, nor any of those listed was specifically named as a Communist in any HUAC documents.[19]

18. Mary White Ovington, *The Walls Came Tumbling Down* (New York: Harcourt, Brace & Co., 1947), 102; Charles Flint Kellogg, *NAACP: A History of the National Association for the Advancement of Colored People* (Baltimore: Johns Hopkins University Press, 1967), 5, 286–90.

19. Linda Reed, *Simple Decency and Common Sense: The Southern Conference Movement, 1938–1963* (Bloomington: Indiana University Press, 1991), 123, 139; Juan Williams,

Among the most outrageous and thinly supported charges that Cook made was that NAACP executive secretary Roy Wilkins was a subversive. Citing HUAC documents, Cook reported that Wilkins had voted for Negro Communist Benjamin J. Davis to replace Adam Clayton Powell on New York's city council in 1943. At one point, according to Cook and HUAC, Wilkins had even stated that the Communist Party's racial program had "a very wholesome effect" in the United States. Wilkins had indeed publicly supported Davis but not because he was the Communist candidate. He supported Davis because he believed the candidate's devotion to racial causes was more genuine than Powell's. Wilkins, in fact, was among the group's most extreme anti-Communists. HUAC and Cook failed to note statements such as those made by Wilkins in the *New York Amsterdam News*. While hailing Davis's victory, the NAACP leader had criticized his party, writing that it was a "great crime" for "Communists to use racial appeals."[20]

Clearly Cook, Eastland, and the other red- and black-baiters were less concerned with conducting a fair investigation of subversives in the NAACP than promoting the massive-resistance cause. The primary focus was preventing segregation in the South by discrediting the NAACP. That individual members and the NAACP as a group had openly rejected Communism did not matter; Cook insisted they were unwitting dupes of Moscow. It was enough, he declared, that according to "former Negro Communist Foster Williams, Jr.," who testified before HUAC in 1954, "the Communist Party very sneakily manipulated the Negro people for their purposes"; the NAACP had made clear its role in "this trouble." The Georgia attorney general concluded that "the NAACP is being used as a front and tool by subversive elements. . . . Either knowingly or unwittingly, it has allowed itself to become part and parcel of the Communist conspiracy to overthrow the democratic governments of this nation and its sovereign states." He finally advised the members of subversive civil rights organizations to "disavow their programs and leaders before they, their friends, and

---

Thurgood Marshall: American Revolutionary (New York: Random House, 1998), 105; Subject Wilkins, Subject Mitchell, Subject Tobias, Subject Randolph, 13 October 1955, 3N160, Folder 5, Texas v. NAACP Collection; *Congressional Record*, 84th Cong., 2nd sess., 1956, 102, pt. 3:3215–59.

20. See Gerald Horne, *Black Liberation/Red Scare: Ben Davis and the Communist Party* (Newark: University of Delaware Press, 1994), 116.

their congregations are exposed to the anguish and embarrassment which exposure of these groups will necessarily mean."[21]

Not surprisingly, the original release and subsequent regional distribu-
tion by the Citizens' Council of "The Ugly Truth" drew the attention of the NAACP. Roy Wilkins, NAACP executive secretary, accused Cook of partic- ipating in the South's own "conspiracy" to oppose the Supreme Court's order to desegregate. Wilkins declared "the NAACP is not a Communist or- ganization or a Communist-front organization. . . . Neither the attorney general of the United States, the House Un-American Committee, nor any other official federal body has ever branded the NAACP as a Communist or Communist-front organization." The executive secretary also cited FBI director J. Edgar Hoover, who once wrote that the NAACP had done much to preserve "equality, freedom, and tolerance," essential components of democratic government. Cook's speech, the NAACP charged, was full of "distortions, word-juggling, free translations, and untruths." The civil rights organization had always worked "within the framework and with the tools of democratic government."[22]

Nevertheless the NAACP leadership recognized the threat posed to the civil rights movement by "The Ugly Truth." In mid-February 1956, Wilkins wrote to the NAACP branch and youth-council officers that they should be leery of Communists hoping to be elected as delegates to the National As- sembly for Civil Rights to be held in Washington, D.C., in early March: "Be- cause left-wing publications and organizations already have urged their members to 'support' the civil rights rally in Washington, many Washington officials and numerous daily newspapers and wire services are making in- quiries because they have heard that our rally in Washington will be 'cap- tured' by left-wing individuals and groups. If this should happen the whole civil rights movement will receive a black eye, and we will get very little attention, if any, by the Congress." A year later the executive secretary de- nied black Communist leader Benjamin Davis's request to join the NAACP.[23]

---

21. Eugene Cook, "The Ugly Truth about the NAACP" (Greenwood, Miss.: Lawrence Printing, 1955), found in Folder 11, Citizens' Council Collection, Mitchell Memorial Li- brary, Mississippi State University.

22. *Southern School News*, November 1955, p. 15.

23. See "NAACP Backs Wilkins, Under Fire by Reds," *New York World Telegram*, 16 February 1950, p. 15; Wilkins to Branch and Youth Council Officers, 14 February 1956, RG46, Subject Files, NAACP 1956, Senate Internal Security Subcommittee Papers, Na-

Exposed!

The NAACP "Exposed!" Cartoon by *Jackson Daily News* cartoonist Bob Howie for *The Citizens' Council*, October 1956.
Mississippi Department of Archives and History

At the same time, Thurgood Marshall, the group's powerful lead attorney, expressed his concerns about radicals in the movement to J. Edgar Hoover and worked with the director to remove Communists from the NAACP. At the NAACP's 1956 convention, he stated his position quite publicly, declaring "there is no place in this organization for communists or those who follow the communist line."[24]

Despite Wilkins's and Marshall's best efforts, Cook's charges continued to gain in popularity and power. Back in Georgia he expanded his already extensive mandate to investigate the NAACP under the state's Communist-control program. Cook employed the state's Floyd Act, which required state employees to list "all" groups to which they had ever belonged, and empowered the attorney general to investigate suspected cases of subver-

---

tional Archives; "American Communist Leader's Bid for NAACP Membership Rejected," *Washington Post*, 12 November 1957, p. 13. See also "The NAACP Continues Its Red-Baiting Policy," *The Worker*, 5 September 1965, p. 3.

24. Williams, *Thurgood Marshall*, 253–58

sion. Under this act the attorney general gained the authority to raid NAACP offices, which he did in November 1956. Cook cited his findings when he called for a legislative inquiry into the NAACP as well as a total ban on NAACP activity in Georgia.[25]

The diligence of Cook, Perez, Harris, Eastland, and others stimulated a wave of anti-NAACP efforts both in the South and in the nation's capital. Massive resisters focused on measures to reassert state control over race and security issues. The message was often repeated as southern states launched investigations of the NAACP. By the end of 1956, anti-Communism had become among the most popular tools used by segregationists to harass the NAACP.

While several national representatives from southern states voiced their concerns about subversive influences in the NAACP, E. C. Gathings of Arkansas called the United States House of Representatives to action. On February 23, 1956, Gathings stood before the House to remark on the "subversive character of the NAACP." He entered into the record more than sixty HUAC reports on NAACP leaders, taking up some forty pages of the *Congressional Record*. Out of 177 NAACP officers, board members, executive staff members, and affiliates, according to Gathings's count, 78 had been cited by HUAC. Based on these findings the representative from Arkansas called for a congressional probe into the financial and membership records of the NAACP. Such an investigation, Gathings argued, was "necessary to protect the southern Negro and others who have been duped, victimized, and exploited by and through the promotion schemes of the NAACP." Many southern representatives, including Davis of Georgia, Williams of Mississippi, Ashmore of South Carolina, and Grant of Alabama, immediately supported the resolution, although the House as a whole declined further action.[26]

While the national legislature did not respond to Gathings's call to arms, state governments did. Like Eugene Cook's Georgia, Texas began investiga-

25. Heale, *McCarthy's Americans*, 245–46; *Southern School News*, December 1956, p. 10; *Race Relations Law Reporter* 1 (1956): 956–58. See also *Southern School News*, September 1956, p. 5, and February 1957, p. 9.

26. *Congressional Record*, 84th Cong., 2nd sess., 1956, 102, pt. 2:3215–59; *Congressional Record*, 84th Cong., 2nd sess., 1956, 102, pt. 2:3206–11; *Congressional Record*, 84th Cong., 2nd sess., 1956, 102, pt. 3:4444–45; *Congressional Record*, 84th Cong., 2nd sess., 1956, 102, pt. 8:12944–47; *Congressional Record*, 85th Cong., 1st sess., 1957, 103, pt. 7:8657–58.

tions of Communist influence in the NAACP in 1956. In April of that year, state attorney Phil Sanders discussed with Texas attorney general John Ben Sheppard the "possibility of keeping the NAACP out of Texas through the use of the Texas Communist Control law." "To keep the NAACP out of Texas," Sanders argued, "it would be necessary to prove that it engages in or advocates, advises, etc., any activities where the intent behind the activities is to overthrow, destroy, etc., the government by force or violence." Thus if it were possible for the state to show that "the NAACP is connected with any Communistic front organization," it would be a "prima facie case." To that end, the state employed investigators for the sole purpose of determining the Communist-front affiliations of the NAACP.[27]

The pursuit of reds in the civil rights movement was nothing new to Texans. Racial conservatives in the state had used a Communist Control Act to harass the NAACP in the early 1950s, and in communities such as Houston they vigorously pursued integrationists with charges of subversion. But with a growing number of cases brought by the NAACP after 1954, the red and black campaign took on new significance. State leaders in Texas drew heavily from internal sources as well as those provided by Senator Eastland and HUAC. They also relied on Cook's findings and on investigative resources from other states.[28]

Among the most important documents influencing anti-NAACP action in Texas were letters from L. E. Faulkner, the president of the Mississippi Central Railroad, who moonlighted as a segregationist and an anti-Communist researcher. In early October 1955, Faulkner began an extended correspondence with the U.S. Treasury Department. He requested that the body investigate the tax-exempt status of the NAACP's Legal Defense and Education Fund. In support of this case, he listed several publications including Cook's speech that charged the NAACP with Communist affiliations. Faulkner hoped to suggest that money raised for the Legal Defense and Education Fund supported the integrationist and thus Communist cause in the South. H. T. Schwartz of the Tax Rulings Division of the Treasury Depart-

27. Sanders to Sheppard, 30 April 1956, 3N159, and Fulmore to Sheppard, 11 September 1956, 3N160, Folder 4, Texas v. NAACP Collection.

28. Subject Wilkins, Subject Mitchell, Subject Tobias, Subject Randolph, 13 October 1955, 3N160, Folder 5, Texas v. NAACP Collection; "NAACP Probe Asked," 15 August 1956, 3N164, Folder 8, Texas v. NAACP Collection. See also Don Carleton, *Red Scare: Right-wing Hysteria, Fifties Fanaticism, and Their Legacy in Texas* (Austin: Texas Monthly Press, 1985).

ment informed Faulkner that while the NAACP itself was not a tax-exempt organization, its Legal Defense and Education Fund was. The Mississippian nevertheless insisted that since the activities and objectives of the NAACP and its Legal Defense and Education Fund were the same, and were together the same as those of the Communists, the tax-exempt status of the Legal Defense and Education fund meant that the United States was in effect subsidizing the NAACP and the Communist Party.[29]

In the spring of 1956, Faulkner sent copies of his correspondence to Senator Eastland, Congressman Rainach, and Congressman Gathings. These offices passed the letters on to southern state prosecutors. While the United States Treasury refused to accept Faulkner's reasoning, officials in Texas did accept it, as did officials in Alabama, Georgia, Louisiana, and North Carolina. Using Faulkner's letters as well as supporting evidence from Eastland, Cook, and its own investigations, Texas accused the NAACP of failing to gain a permit from the Texas secretary of state to operate as a foreign corporation and a profit-making body. The NAACP, prosecutors argued, was guilty of failing to pay franchise taxes in Texas. A Texas district court issued a temporary injunction in 1956 after finding that continued NAACP operations would "tend to incite racial prejudice, picketing, riots, and other unlawful acts which are contrary to public peace and quietude." The judge in the case also ordered the NAACP to pay accrued franchise taxes, plus interest and penalties, and allowed the state attorney general to inspect the group's records.[30]

The NAACP decided not to press an appeal in Texas but vowed to con-

29. Faulkner to Schwartz, 7 October 1955, 3N160, Folder 3, Texas v. NAACP Collection; Faulkner to Schwartz, 10 October 1955, 3N160, Folder 3, Texas v. NAACP Collection; Rainach to Brooks, 7 October 1955, 3N160, Folder 3, Texas v. NAACP Collection; Faulkner to Eastland, 10 October 1955, 3N160, Folder 3, Texas v. NAACP Collection; Faulkner to Pennington, 14 October 1955, 3N160, Folder 3, Texas v. NAACP Collection; Schwartz to Faulkner, 31 October 1955, 3N160, Folder 3, Texas v. NAACP Collection; Faulkner to Schwartz, 3 November 1955, 3N160, Folder 3, Texas v. NAACP Collection; Faulkner to Schwartz, 20 October 1955, 3N160, Folder 3, Texas v. NAACP Collection; Pace to Faulkner, 3 November 1955, 3N160, Folder 3, Texas v. NAACP Collection; Faulkner to Gathings, 21 March 1956, 3N160, Folder 2, Texas v. NAACP Collection; Faulkner to Stennis, 22 March 1956, 3N160, Folder 2, Texas v. NAACP Collection.

30. *Race Relations Law Reporter* 2 (1957): 177, 181, 185, 448, 678, and 892–93; Walter F. Murphy, "The South Counterattacks: The Anti-NAACP Laws," *Western Political Quarterly* 12 (June 1959): 377–78.

tinue filing lawsuits if asked to do so by citizens whose civil rights had been violated. In cases brought during the next two years, however, court-ordered delays, many based on Faulkner's reasoning, stifled the NAACP's legal efforts in Texas. Indeed, a Smith County district court issued a permanent injunction against the NAACP that would bind the group into the 1960s. The NAACP was not completely without court support in defending itself against charges that it was controlled by foreign radicals. A U.S. Supreme Court ruling on Alabama's foreign-corporation and registration laws, for example, made Texas's comparable laws unenforceable in 1958. The high court found in *NAACP v. Alabama* that "the immunity from state scrutiny of membership lists which the Association claims on behalf of its members is here so related to the right of the members to pursue their lawful private interest privately and to associate freely with others in so doing as to come within the protection of the Fourteenth Amendment."[31]

But the number and diversity of legal means by which the leaders of the southern red scare harassed the NAACP taxed the organization's resources. At the same time Texas pursued the association, South Carolina moved to have the NAACP officially listed as a Communist front, and the attorney general went after subversive civil rights advocates on the state payroll. In February 1956, South Carolina representatives introduced legislation to forbid the employment of NAACP members by state and local governments. The same month both the state house and senate acted favorably on a resolution requesting the attorney general of the United States to place the NAACP on the list of subversive organizations. Taking a cue from Eugene Cook's numbers, the resolution listed fifty-three NAACP officials with HUAC files and affiliations among Communist and Communist-front organizations.[32]

South Carolina's resolution rallied whites in the state against the NAACP at a moment when the massive resistance against integration was quickening under southern congressional leadership. State leaders delivered the resolution to the United States Senate on March 12, 1956, the same day congressional segregationists released their Southern Manifesto denouncing the Supreme Court's decision in *Brown*. Among other promises, the Manifesto's signers vowed to stop "outside agitators" by lawful means and to pre-

---

31. *Southern School News*, November 1956, p. 8; *NAACP v. Alabama*, 91 U.S. 78 (1958); *Race Relations Law Reporter* 3 (1958): 611–12.

32. *Southern School News*, March 1956, p. 9.

vent the federal courts from bringing about revolutionary change in the South. Three days later Olin Johnston, a New Dealer but a committed segregationist from South Carolina, wrote a letter to James Eastland, his colleague on the Senate Judiciary Committee and SISS. Johnston called for the Judiciary Committee chairman to begin actions on the year-old Resolution 104 calling for an investigation into the "communistic sources" behind the *Brown* decision.[33]

Johnston had come under increasing pressure from his conservative constituents for his New Deal voting record. One sarcastic critic even called the senator's "anti-communist record . . . clinically indistinguishable from Vito Marcantonio's or Paul Robeson's." Johnston, aware of the concerns of South Carolina conservatives, used the increased interest in the red and black question in his own state, and the heightened national awareness of the issues addressed in the Southern Manifesto, to reassert his anti-Communist and segregationist credentials. He capitalized on similar conditions again after the Little Rock crisis in the fall of 1957. In late September, he called on the governors of the southern states to contribute to a national probe of the NAACP and subversive forces in the integration crisis.[34]

The South Carolina legislature, meanwhile, had begun investigating subversive members of the civil rights movement at a number of South Carolina colleges and universities. This action drew the direct support of Governor George Bell Timmerman and the state's attorney general, T. C. Callison, who charged the NAACP with "carrying out the real program which was mapped out by Communists 25 or 30 years ago." South Carolina's legislative investigations led to several state-employee resignations and dismissals. And it cast a pall over free speech. Students at the South Carolina State College for Negroes at Orangeburg, for example, tried to protest investigations on campus only to be labeled subversive themselves. Moreover, while the legislature did eventually repeal its anti-NAACP statute in

33. Southern Manifesto, 12 March 1956, Series III, Subseries A, Box 27, Russell Papers, Richard Russell Memorial Library; *Congressional Record*, 84th Cong., 2nd sess., 1956, 102, pt. 3:4444–45; Johnston to Eastland, 15 March 1956, Box 53, Civil Rights Folder, Johnston Papers.

34. Alderson to Johnston, 28 September 1957, Box 60, Judiciary Committee NAACP Folder, Johnston Papers; Collins to Johnston, 4 October 1957, Box 60, Judiciary Committee NAACP Folder, Johnston Papers; Alderson to Johnston, 28 September 1957, Box 60, Judiciary Committee NAACP Folder, Johnston Papers. See also "Red Influence of Decision Is Charged," *Charleston News and Courier*, 2 June 1955.

April 1956 after the NAACP challenged the law in federal court, legislators immediately replaced it with an act requiring state workers to list their or-

ganizational affiliations.[35]

By the end of 1956, Virginia, Georgia, Florida, South Carolina, North Carolina, and Mississippi had all instituted laws and investigations designed to harass the NAACP while Alabama, Louisiana, and Texas succeeded in banning the organization's actions outright. In making their cases against the NAACP, each of these states drew on HUAC and SISS material as well as the Cook report indicting the group's Communist associations. Thus did half-truths and innuendo become the basis for legal action by southern nationalists in their war against Communists and integrationists. As the region's red and black scare reached a crescendo, events shifted attention from the Deep South to the region's periphery.[36]

Until the integration crisis in Little Rock in the fall of 1957, Arkansas's response to the civil rights movement in general and the *Brown* decision in particular had been moderate. The NAACP was able to operate relatively freely. A series of events convinced Governor Orval Faubus that he must play the race card. His decision to defy the Supreme Court, and to figuratively stand in the schoolhouse door at Central High, focused the attention of civil rights activists and massive resisters on Little Rock. Coupled with the Soviets' successful launching of the unmanned satellite *Sputnik* in October 1957, Little Rock fused southern anxieties over Communism to the country's race question.

Events in Little Rock, however, did not necessarily play out in a manner to suit southern red-scare leaders. When at 9 P.M. on Tuesday, September 24, President Dwight Eisenhower announced on national television that he had federalized the Arkansas National Guard to enforce a court order allowing blacks to attend Little Rock's Central High School, he maintained that segregation, not integration, had aided the Communist cause. The president declared that "demagogic extremists" preventing the Court's orders in Arkansas had pushed the issue to a showdown at a time "when we face grave situations abroad because of the hatred that Communism bears toward a

35. *Southern School News*, June 1956, p. 14, and September 1956, p. 4; *Southern School News*, November 1956, p. 13; *Southern School News*, May 1957, p. 3; *Southern School News*, June 1958, p. 15; *Race Relations Law Reporter* 1 (1956): 600–601, and *Race Relations Law Reporter* 2 (1957): 852–53.

36. *Southern School News*, January 1957, p. 1; Murphy, "South Counterattacks," 371–90.

system of government based on human rights." He continued: "It would be difficult to exaggerate the harm that is being done to the prestige and influence, and indeed to the safety, of our nation and the world. Our enemies are gloating over this incident and using it everywhere to misrepresent our whole nation." Eisenhower was echoing the concerns of his secretary of state, John Foster Dulles, who had reported to Attorney General Herbert Brownell earlier in the day that the situation in Little Rock "was ruining our foreign policy." The effect in Africa and Asia, Dulles predicted, would be "worse for us than Hungary was for the Russians."[37]

A few weeks later, Clare Boothe Luce, a former playwright, journalist, and congresswoman who had recently resigned as U.S. ambassador to Italy, expanded on the integrationist, anti-Communist argument. At the Alfred E. Smith Memorial Dinner in New York, Luce delivered an address entitled "Little Rock and the Moscow Moon: Challenges to America's Leadership." Both the Little Rock crisis and the Soviet satellite were symbols of the fundamental challenges facing the United States, according to Luce. Where Little Rock was a moral challenge, *Sputnik* was a material one. Launch of the Russian satellite had proved Soviet technological superiority while lending credence to Communist contentions that its prowess in ballistics was tied to its moral superiority. Little Rock, meanwhile, had undermined the United States' claim that its democracy ensured the equality of man. Both challenges, according to Luce, had to be addressed by the United States before the uncommitted nations of the world decided "to hitch their wagon to her [Russia's] Beeping Star."[38]

Not surprisingly, the notion that they rather than the integrationists were allies of the international Communist conspiracy provoked cries of outrage from massive resisters. Federal intervention in the Little Rock crisis reinforced the southerners' claims that the states' right to determine their

37. White House Press Release, 24 September 1957, Administration Series, Box 23, Little Rock (2) File, Ann Whitman Files, Eisenhower Presidential Papers, Dwight D. Eisenhower Library; Dulles to Brownell, 24 September 1957, Telephone Series, Box 7, Memo–General, September 2, 1957 to October 31, 1957 (3), Dulles Papers, Dwight D. Eisenhower Library. See also Neal Stanford, "Moscow Exploits Little Rock Fight," *Christian Science Monitor*, 18 September 1957, and "Red Press Gloats over Little Rock," *New York Times*, 26 September 1957, p. 14.

38. "Little Rock and the Moscow Moon," Box 46, 1957–1958 Civil Rights, Little Rock Folder, William Jennings Bryan Dorn Papers, South Caroliniana Library. See also Herbert Philbrick, "Little Rock Used As Basis for Party Attack on U.S.," *New York Herald Tribune*, 29 September 1957.

own racial destiny was being undermined by outsiders; but attacking the Supreme Court and a popular president threatened the segregationists' strategy of convincing the populace at large that the southern way was the American way. For some, however, there seemed to be little choice. In October 1957, the police jury of Caddo Parish, Louisiana, sent a resolution to the White House denouncing the Supreme Court and the president as tentacles of "the growing octopus of government." The Louisianans analyzed the Little Rock situation in mixed but clear metaphors: the "octopus" had been playing "political football" with "professional rabble-rousers and paid integrationists" instead of taking care of the country's security. As a result Russia had been able to "pass the United States in the field of earth satellites and guided missiles." All indications were, the jury argued, that the Communist Party had made the press and the federal government unwitting accomplices in its effort to "take America from within by setting race against race."[39]

In January 1958, Georgia's house and senate passed a resolution that mirrored the sentiments of the police jury. Georgia's resolution was decidedly more professional and representative but no less caustic. It denounced the president's order enforcing integration in Arkansas, a "sovereign state." Eisenhower's actions, according to the document, "sacrificed the honesty and integrity of our highest executive office on an altar of political expediency to appease the NAACP and other radical, communist-sympathizing organizations." The document concluded with a formal censure of the president of the United States.[40]

It was the tendency among southern conservatives to equate Communism with socialism, socialism with liberalism, and liberalism with an assertive federal power. Thus it was natural for them to portray events in Little Rock as a long stride toward the development of a Soviet-style, collectivist police state in America. In mid-September 1957, just prior to the showdown at Central High, Martin Dies, congressman-at-large from Texas and former chairman of the House Un-American Activities Committee, reported to an audience in east Texas that the federal government was "moving steadily toward a Communist state." The government's support of civil

39. Caddo Parish Resolution, 16 October 1957, School Arkansas, Box 921, Folder 7, White House Central File, Eisenhower Presidential Papers.

40. Georgia Resolution, 22 January 1958, School Arkansas, Box 921, Folder 9, White House Central File, Eisenhower Presidential Papers.

rights and its increasingly intrusive regulation of business along with its Gestapo-like enforcement of integration was in no small part the product of Communist propaganda, according to Dies. Once the Communists had [71 concentrated political and economic power in the federal government, he concluded, "establishing a Communist government will be easy." Little Rock was the warning knell.[41]

Dies's rhetoric resonated with his audience of mainly east Texas oilmen hoping to ward off regulation of their industry. But many southern conservatives recorded similar concerns in private correspondence. A letter written by South Carolina congressman William Jennings Bryan Dorn to P. M Archibald echoed Dies's sentiments:

The communists stir up racial trouble, then launch their satellite and move into Syria. . . . [A] communist named Cohen wrote in a book as far back as 1913 that America must be divided with racial strife before the United States will be ripe for communism. Arch, here is another danger in this civil rights business. The national socialists' and communists' real objective in America is the free enterprise system. In the last twenty years the free enterprise system has been vigorously defended in Congress by men like Harry Byrd, Dick Russell, and other southern and western leaders. Now before they start their real all-out campaign against American business, they feel that they must discredit southern leadership with this civil rights business.[42]

Dies, Dorn, and like-minded conservatives all over the South used the symbolic red and black enemy in the wake of Little Rock as a scapegoat for the region's economic, political, and social problems. This strategy contributed to the siege mentality already apparent among massive resisters and reflected a growing southern nationalist reaction against "outside agitators." Indeed, Little Rock motivated heretofore quiescent southern nationalists across the region to join the red and black campaign in earnest.

Nowhere was the crisis more catalytic than in the state where it occurred. Arkansas before the crisis had been known for its relative modera-

41. "Federal Government Playing into Reds' Hands," *Dallas Morning News*, 13 September 1957. See also Communism Does Away with Privilege, Box 395, Faubus Opposing Ike R–Z, Johnson Senate Papers, Lyndon Baines Johnson Library.

42. See Dorn to Archibald, 28 October 1957, Box 46, 1957–58 Civil Rights Infamy, Dorn Papers.

tion on racial and anti-Communist issues. But Little Rock changed things. Forced to accept the immediate desegregation of the capital city, Arkansas's political leaders became hardened massive resisters. Digging in against the federal onslaught, they passed a series of laws designed to harass integration efforts generally and handcuff the NAACP specifically.

At the center of the Little Rock crisis was Arkansas governor Orval Faubus. Prior to the fall of 1957, most observers considered Faubus a moderate. During the bitterly fought gubernatorial election of 1954, his opponents suggested that he was an outright leftist. In fact Faubus's father had been a socialist, and Faubus himself had briefly attended Commonwealth College, an institution designated by the U.S. Justice Department as a Communist front. When in March 1957 Pulaski County senator Artie Gregory introduced Senate Bill 28, a measure designed to root out subversives in the state's educational institutions, Faubus vetoed it. The governor declared both the intent and scope to be flawed. No such measure, he said, could "make people be patriots."[43]

But the ambitious young politician was not about to let his heritage or ideological predilections affect his future. As governor he decided that the path to power in Arkansas lay to the right. In quick succession Faubus decided to resist integration in Little Rock and then to back Gregory's bill. As biographer Roy Reed makes clear, following the Little Rock crisis the governor adopted a "blend of coded white supremacy and McCarthyism." In directly defying federal enforcement of the *Brown v. Board of Education* decision at Central High, Faubus was seeking to reinvent himself as the king of massive resistance and a card-carrying southern nationalist. Demagoguery, it appeared, was the better part of valor.[44]

Throughout 1958, an election year, the governor strengthened his ties with state conservatives. Aware that his reelection in the overwhelmingly Democratic and segregationist state would depend on a primary victory, Faubus devoted a third of his campaign to the desegregation issue and drew support from such groups as the Capital Citizens' Council by promising a special session of the state legislature to address the race issue. With this

43. Roy Reed, *Faubus: The Life and Times of an American Prodigal* (Fayetteville: University of Arkansas Press, 1997), 25–40, 284; Timothy Donovan and Willard Gatewood, *The Governors of Arkansas* (Fayetteville: University of Arkansas Press, 1981), 218; "Act 10's Author Keeps Calm while Storm Rages," *Arkansas Democrat*, 3 March 1959; Author's interview with Orval Faubus, Fort Smith, Ark., 5 February 1994.

44. Roy Reed, *Faubus*, 260; *Brown v. Board of Education*, 349 U.S. 294 (1955).

strategy he was able to undercut his more right-wing opponents and win the primary handily.[45]

In preparation for the fall general election, and as a payoff to his conser- vative supporters, the governor called the special session he had earlier proposed. The Arkansas legislature convened in late August 1958. In the course of the extraordinary session, the body enacted sixteen interposition bills. These included laws that would allow the governor to shut down integrated schools and withhold state funds from them, permit student transfers to schools of their own race, ensure a student's right to refuse to attend integrated classes, outlaw sit-ins, and strengthen laws curtailing "frivolous" lawsuits. The state's segregationist attorney general, Bruce Bennett, introduced the most ominous of these measures. The bills, according to the author, were "designed to harass" and "to keep the enemies of America busy." At the top of Bennett's "enemies" list was the NAACP. Other Bennett measures passed during the session prevented the NAACP from providing legal counsel or funding for lawsuits and allowed the attorney general access to NAACP membership and personnel records.

Bennett reintroduced Gregory's affidavit law as part of his anti-NAACP package. With its passage along with the other massive-resistance bills, the attorney general had an important new weapon in his arsenal. Indeed, Gregory's law cut a wide swath. Requiring state employees to list all of their organizational affiliations from the previous five years, it gave the attorney general unprecedented access to state workers' personal information. Those who were members of civil rights organizations or groups listed as Communist fronts could no longer hide their affiliations. Most important, the law would expose members of the NAACP, a group Bennett was convinced had Communist ties. So convinced and convincing was he that the legislature enacted a statute making it illegal for state employees to be members of the NAACP. The circle was complete.[46]

Arkansas's special session adopted Gregory's affidavit law as Act 10 and

45. *Southern School News*, January 1958, p. 1. See also Walter E. Rowland, *Faubus, Arkansas and Education* (Conway, Ark.: River Road Press, 1989), 79; Roy Reed, *Faubus*, 239–51; Donovan and Gatewood, *Governors of Arkansas*, 221.

46. *Southern School News*, March 1959, p. 2; *Southern School News*, September 1958, pp. 2 and 4; Numan Bartley, *The Rise of Massive Resistance* (Baton Rouge: Louisiana State University Press, 1972), 274. See also Jeff Broadwater, *Eisenhower and the Anticommunist Crusade* (Chapel Hill: University of North Carolina Press, 1992), 180–82, and Richard Gid Powers, *Secrecy and Power: The Life of J. Edgar Hoover* (New York: Free Press, 1986).

the measure outlawing public employment of NAACP members as Act 115. Both laws replicated those already passed in other southern states. They mirrored, for example, Mississippi's, Louisiana's, and South Carolina's laws exposing state employees' subversive affiliations and barring NAACP members from state employment. The last laws of their kind passed in the South, Arkansas's legislation was in many ways the culmination of southern red scare leaders' legal efforts to restrict the actions of the NAACP.[47]

Conservative Arkansas lawmakers considered Act 10 and Act 115 to be legally durable because the legislation focused on security issues involving state employment. The right to public employment was poorly protected under constitutional doctrine in the late 1950s, especially for those deemed subversive. Lawmakers generally took the position that, while due process protected a citizen's right to make a living, no one had a constitutional right to government employment. States could not be denied the right to keep out of their employ those seeking to overthrow the government or members of organizations engaging in such endeavors. As long as the state could establish that the NAACP was subversive, it had every right to bar its activities.[48]

This legal reasoning was suspect. Even if massive resisters in Arkansas could prove that the NAACP advocated the overthrow of the government, this was no guarantee that the court system would allow Act 10 and Act 115 to stand. The statutes in many ways defied the spirit of a host of recent Supreme Court rulings. Both measures, for example, challenged the Court's decisions in *Slochower v. Board of Higher Education* and *Brown v. Board of Education* by asserting that states, not the federal government, held sovereignty in making sedition and segregation laws. The affidavit law also indirectly challenged rulings such as *Jencks v. United States*, and what critics of the Court referred to as the "Red Monday" decisions, *Service v. Dulles*, *Yates v. United States*, *Watkins v. United States*, and *Sweezy v. New Hampshire. Jencks, Service, Yates, Watkins,* and *Sweezy* all restricted commonly used state antisubversive statutes.[49]

47. Murphy, "South Counterattacks," 379–80. See also Ernest Vandiver Oral History, Richard Russell Memorial Library, 38–39.

48. Murphy, "South Counterattacks," 381–83.

49. *Brown; Slochower v. Board of Education*, 350 U.S. 551 (1956); *Jencks v. United States*, 353 U.S. 657(1957); *Service v. Dulles*, 354 U.S. 363 (1957); *Yates v. United States*, 354 U.S. 298 (1957), 355 U.S. 66 (1957), and 356 U.S. 363 (1958); *Watkins v. United States*, 354 U.S. 178 (1957); *Sweezy v. New Hampshire*, 354 U.S. 234 (1957). See also Peter H. Buckingham, *America Sees Red* (Claremont, Calif.: Regina Books, 1988), 104, and "Court-

Protesters march from the state capitol to Little Rock Central High School on the day integration resumes. Photograph taken by I. Wilmer Counts, August 12, 1959.
Courtesy Arkansas History Commission

Regardless of the constitutionality of Act 10 and Act 115, they were extremely popular among Arkansas conservatives and meshed conveniently with Governor Faubus's move to the right. In September 1958, a few hours after the U.S. Supreme Court overruled an appeal to delay integration in Little Rock, the governor signed all of the special-session bills, including Act 10 and Act 115, into law. Faubus closed the Little Rock schools a day later and went on to win the November election by a landslide.[50]

Civil rights activists and intellectuals immediately moved to defend their rights. Two Arkansas organizations were particularly conspicuous for their opposition to the red- and black-baiters. Not surprisingly, the NAACP was the first to file suits testing Act 10, Act 115, and the state's other new laws. B. T. Shelton, a Little Rock teacher whose 1958–59 contract was not renewed because of his membership in the NAACP, became the first plaintiff in cases challenging Act 10 and Act 115. The second group to move

Commies-Congress," 19 June 1957, C46, B173, F6, Willis Papers, University of Louisiana at Lafayette.

50. *Southern School News*, October 1958, p. 7. See also C. Vann Woodward, *The Strange Career of Jim Crow* (New York: Oxford University Press, 1957), 167.

against the special-session laws was the University of Arkansas's chapter of the American Association of University Professors (AAUP). The AAUP specifically challenged Act 10 in the courts with its own plaintiff, Max Carr. A professor of music at the Fayetteville campus, Carr refused to sign the required affidavit listing his organizational affiliations. Although several groups in the state joined in challenging the 1958 legislation, the NAACP and AAUP, backed by their national affiliates, were the most powerful.

The NAACP and AAUP initially fought Arkansas's special-session laws independently. The NAACP rightly identified all the Bennett measures as instruments to block the achievement of civil rights for blacks in the South. The local chapters tied Acts 10 and 115 in particular to Arkansas's massive-resistance campaign and to attempts to specifically block the integration of Little Rock's public schools. With these issues at stake, the state NAACP was able to enlist the aid of national legal counsel Thurgood Marshall. The AAUP, meanwhile, fought Act 10 specifically as an infringement on a teacher's ability to do his or her job. The organization listed among its most basic functions the defense of academic freedom. Education, according to the organization, necessitated the free expression of ideas in the classroom, even if those ideas were controversial. Act 10, they complained, restricted academic freedom by creating an atmosphere in which teachers were unwilling to explore controversial topics.[51]

Although there was not at first overt collaboration between the organizations, the NAACP and AAUP shared the opinion that Act 10 and Act 115 violated fundamental rights outlined in the First and Fourteenth Amendments. Both argued that rights to privacy and free association were curbed by the legislative assembly's enactments. They feared that the tandem intimidated those with unpopular affiliations and prevented racial and political minorities from organizing, acting, and speaking freely.

The struggle over Act 10 and Act 115 quickly became part of a larger public-relations battle in Arkansas and the rest of the South. Liberal and conservative forces in the region during the 1950s were really struggling for

51. "Faculty Will Seek Stay from Court on Act 10," *Arkansas Traveler*, 30 April 1959; "Two School Men Who Fought Affidavits Not on Renewal List," *Arkansas Democrat*, 5 May 1959; *Arkansas Alumnus*, July 1959. See also John A. Kirk, "The Little Rock Crisis and Postwar Black Activism in Arkansas," *Arkansas Historical Quarterly* 56 (Autumn 1997): 273–293; Daisy Bates, *The Long Shadow of Little Rock* (Fayetteville: University of Arkansas Press, 1987); Ellen Schrecker, *No Ivory Tower* (New York: Oxford University Press, 1986), 10–25.

the hearts and minds of southern moderates, a population crucial to the cause of civil rights. Which end of the political spectrum moderates supported meant the difference between preserving a "traditional southern way of life" and achieving a greater degree of social equality. The battles over these measures, therefore, were initially fought as much in the press as they were in the courts.[52]

Anti-Communist and segregationist forces in the state leveled some familiar charges in the winter of 1958–59. State attorney general Bennett continued to hammer away at the "subversive threat" aimed at the heart of Arkansas. As head of the Arkansas Legislative Council's Special Education Committee, Bennett opened public hearings on the "alleged Communist subversion behind the racial trouble in Arkansas." Testifying before the committee, J. B. Matthews, a former investigator and expert witness for the House Committee on Un-American Activities, charged that several schools in the state, including the University of Arkansas, had been penetrated by Communist agents who were involved in the Southern Conference Educational Fund, a civil rights organization listed by the Arkansas attorney general's office as subversive. Red- and black-baiters all over the South used the findings of the Special Education Committee to reassert that the Little Rock crisis had as its "motivating factor the international Communist conspiracy of world domination." Measures like Act 10 and Act 115 were necessary, they argued, as barriers against the tide of liberalism washing over Arkansas and the South.[53]

Forces challenging Acts 10 and 115 counterattacked. Although anti-Communism and segregation were extremely popular in the state, teachers and citizens all over Arkansas publicly sided with the AAUP and NAACP. Letters to the editors of major newspapers published articles such as "Who's a Red?" which, after the obligatory denunciation of Communism, argued that democracy could not work without the free interchange of ideas. The

52. See David Chappell, *Inside Agitators: White Southerners in the Civil Rights Movement* (Baltimore: Johns Hopkins University Press, 1994); Tony Badger, " 'The Forerunner of Our Opposition': Arkansas and the Southern Manifesto of 1956," *Arkansas Historical Quarterly* 56 (Autumn 1997); Tony Freyer, "The Little Rock Crisis Reconsidered," *Arkansas Historical Quarterly* 56 (Autumn 1997).

53. "College Heads Discount Slap from Witness," *Arkansas Gazette*, 18 December 1958; *Southern School News*, January 1959, p. 14; *Southern School News*, February 1959, p. 14. See also Bartley, *New South*, 187, and Linda Reed, *Simple Decency and Common Sense*.

Arkansas Education Association also joined the protest, contributing time and funds to challenge Act 10. University professors from Arkansas A & M, Arkansas Tech, and Hendrix College added their public support as well. Several others supported the movement privately. Marie King, a teacher at Little Rock Central, for instance, sent money to the University of Arkansas's ReAct 10 fund, an account set up to support AAUP litigation against Act 10. Act 10 opponents at the University of Arkansas also rallied behind their most influential and vocal leader, Guerdon Nichols. Nichols, the dean of Arts and Sciences at the university, used an address before Phi Beta Kappa initiates to echo the sentiments of many of his fellow teachers by claiming the Arkansas affidavit law contributed "to an atmosphere of fear and insecurity" and constituted a "belated McCarthyism."[54]

Some protesters against the special-session acts worried that their pronouncements might do more harm than good. Vocal condemnation of the Arkansas laws might "stir up the fanatics." Their concerns were warranted. In the summer of 1959, Clyde L. Barr, director of the right-wing All American Club, distributed a pamphlet supporting an amended form of Act 10 prohibiting the employment of "all teachers and professors who hold or subscribe to left-wing policies, United Nations–UNESCO ideologies, world citizenship plots, and prointegration views." Taking only a slightly softer stance, the Little Rock–based Capital Citizens' Council under the leadership of Dr. Malcolm Taylor spoke out in support of Acts 10 and 115. Taylor argued that both laws were effective in throwing "consternation" into the opposition's ranks. Citizens' Council attorney Amis Guthridge added his own indictment of Arkansas teachers: "Communists and their camp followers have great influence in the public education field all over the United States. . . .They have a beachhead in Arkansas education." Rounding out its remarks, the Capital Citizens' Council proposed that the school boards and

54. "Who's a Red?" 1:2, McNeil Papers, University of Arkansas Special Collections; Rozzell to Trapp, 17 December 1959, 1:3, Trapp Papers, University of Arkansas Special Collections; News Release, 1 May 1959, 1:3, McNeil Papers; Trapp to Ely, 28 May 1959, 1:1, Trapp Papers; Griner to Trapp, 15 May 1959, 1:1, Trapp Papers; Yates to Trapp, 15 May 1959, 1:1, Trapp Papers; King to Trapp, 1:1, Trapp Papers; Senate Unanimously Rejects Act 10 in Special Session, 1:2, McNeil Papers. See also "Eleven A and M Teachers Call Act 10 Wrong," *Arkansas Gazette*, 26 May 1959; "Faculty Members, Students Draft Protest Petitions," *Arkansas Traveler*, 1 May 1959; "Monday Strike Called by Group," *Arkansas Traveler*, 1 May 1959; "The Flexible Mind and the True University," *Arkansas Alumnus*, July 1959.

boards of trustees retain the option to publicize the Act 10 affidavits. Although "fanatics" such as Barr and Taylor were few compared to those in Mississippi and Alabama, their rhetoric could stir suspicions in a state where anti-Communist and moderate racial sentiments were prevalent.[55]

The NAACP filed the first legal suits challenging Acts 10 and 115 in late April 1959. J. R. Booker represented B. T. Shelton and J. O. Powell in the Act 10 and Act 115 cases. Shelton, a teacher at Horace Mann High and Dunbar Junior High School for Negroes, and Powell, an assistant principal at Central High School, both refused to sign the Act 10 affidavit. After losses in the lower courts, Booker and the NAACP appealed Shelton's and Powell's cases to a federal district court in June 1959 with the addition of another plaintiff, T. W. Coggs of the Arkansas Negro Teachers' Association. The district court upheld Act 10. The court ruled that the affidavit law "simply requires the local school boards and the government bodies of institutions of higher learning to ascertain the affiliations of their respective faculties. Once that information has been furnished, so far as Act 10 is concerned, the local board or governing body of a college is free to take any action it may choose with respect to the employment status of a given individual."[56]

Act 115, however, was overturned. The three-judge federal court stated that the measure outlawing state employment of NAACP members violated the Fourteenth Amendment of the Constitution. Association alone, they declared, could not be used to determine disloyalty or disqualification. The ruling was an important one for opponents of anti-NAACP laws in the South. South Carolina's identical 1956 law banning the public employment

55. McNeil to Joughin, 28 November 1958, 1:3, McNeil Papers; The Miracle of Act 10, 1:7, Trapp Papers; Who Will Clean Up This Subversive Mess, 1:3, McNeil Papers; Board of Trustees Minutes, 18 April 1959, University of Arkansas Special Collections; "Citizens' Council Calls Act 10 Good Because of 'Consternation'" *Arkansas Traveler*, 27 April 1959; "Act 10 Is Not a Mere Abstraction," *Arkansas Gazette*, 2 May 1959; "Faculty Group Seeks Legal Advice," *Arkansas Traveler*, 23 April 1959; "Affidavits Private," *Arkansas Traveler*, 28 April 1959. See also Badger, "'The Forerunner of Our Opposition,'" 354; Willard B. Gatewood, "School Desegregation in Fayetteville: A Forty-Year Perspective," in Julianne Lewis and Thomas A. DeBlack, *Civil Disobedience: An Oral History of School Desegregation in Fayetteville, Arkansas, 1954–1965* (Fayetteville: University of Arkansas Press, 1994), 1–11; Neil McMillen, *The Citizens' Council: Organized Resistance to the Second Reconstruction, 1954–64* (Urbana: University of Illinois Press, 1971), 94–95.

56. "Two School Men Who Fought Affidavits Not on Renewal List," *Arkansas Democrat*, 5 May 1959; "Faculty Will Seek Stay from Court on Act 10," *Arkansas Traveler*, 30 April 1959.

of NAACP members had never been formally tested in the federal court system. The ruling against Act 115 set a legal and traceable precedent that could be used against similar laws in the future.[57]

With Act 115 out of the way, the University of Arkansas's branch of the AAUP focused exclusively on Act 10. Attorney Edwin Dunaway argued, like Booker, that the Supreme Court had limited an employer's right to require from an employee information not directly associated with his or her job. Dunaway's case also challenged Act 10 on the same constitutional principles that Booker's had in preceding trials. In every case, the plaintiffs against Act 10 maintained that the law denied First and Fourteenth Amendment rights. Outside of these general arguments, however, the suit brought by the AAUP differed in an important way from *Shelton*. Unlike the NAACP, the AAUP attempted to separate Act 10 from the race issue. Dunaway claimed that Act 10 did not fall under "the purview of the governor's proclamation calling the Second Extraordinary Session of 1958" and that the act was really aimed at intimidating teachers. Dunaway argued the affidavit law infringed on a teacher's right to academic freedom by noting that the threatened publication of affidavits by the Capital Citizens' Council created an atmosphere in which teachers were afraid to exercise their professional rights.[58]

The lower courts granted stays of execution preventing the implementation of Act 10 throughout the early stages of litigation. After repeated decisions affirming the law's constitutionality, however, the higher courts refused to grant further postponements. Filing deadlines were set for July 1959. Most state employees opted for quiet acquiescence and filed their affidavits without protest. Others, however, submitted protests with their signatures. Only a handful flatly refused to sign the affidavits.[59]

The state supreme court approved Act 10 unanimously in early January 1960. Justice George Rose Smith wrote that school boards had every right to inquire into the backgrounds of teachers. Smith also echoed the sentiments of Arkansas's assistant attorney general Bill J. Davis, who declared

57. "Affidavits Law Blocked 10 Days," *Arkansas Gazette*, 5 May 1959; *Southern School News*, May 1959, pp. 6–7; *Southern School News*, July 1959, p. 8.

58. U of A Teacher Contests Act 10, 10 June 1959, 1:2, McNeil Papers; Act 10: The Case against It, 1:3, McNeil Papers; Act 10 Faces New Challenge, 1:2, McNeil Papers.

59. Notes from H. Wilcoxon, 15 July 1959, 1:5, Trapp Papers; 14 July 1959, 1:1, Hantz Papers; Wilcoxon to Fidler, 17 July 1959, 1:3, Hantz Papers; Wilcoxon to Fidler, 22 July 1959, 1:2, Trapp Papers.

that public employers should enjoy the same rights as private employers. Smith opined:

> We have no doubt that a school board might ask an applicant whether he belonged, specifically, to the Communist Party, to any organization dedicated to the violent overthrow of the government, to a nudist colony, to a drag-racing club, to an association of atheists, or to other organizations that might be listed almost without number, membership in which might shed light upon applicant's fitness to guide young minds in the classroom. . . .
>
> We are not persuaded that the Constitution compels the board to ask scores of hundreds of permissible questions one by one, instead of making blanket inquiry required by Act 10.

But the court also courageously voiced a warning: "In reaching this conclusion we are not unmindful of the settled principle that a statute, even though fair on its face, may become invalid if it is administered 'with an evil eye and an unequal hand.' " Specifically citing the threats of the Capital Citizens' Council, the court warned that, if used "in a discriminatory fashion," the law would become unconstitutional.[60]

After losses in Arkansas's courts, the NAACP and AAUP both appealed to the U.S. Supreme Court. The Court granted a hearing to a unified Shelton-Carr case in the early spring of 1960. A date was tentatively set for the fall of the same year. Although many in the state predicted that the affidavit law would pass muster with the Court, the fate of a separate case brought by Arkansas NAACP head Daisy Bates encouraged the Act 10 opposition. In the *Bates* case, the Court ruled against local ordinances requiring the NAACP to list its members and contributors. The majority declared that "it is now beyond dispute that freedom of association for the purpose of advancing ideas and airing grievances is protected by the Due Process Clause of the Fourteenth Amendment from invasion by the states."[61]

Nevertheless the *Bates* case could not be considered a reliable predictor for the Act 10 litigation. The Court had recently decided several cases involving issues pertinent to *Shelton-Carr,* but as a whole the decisions did

---

60. *Southern School News,* February 1960, p. 5; "State Court Approves Teacher Affidavits," *Arkansas Democrat,* 8 January 1960; "State Tribunal Upholds Teacher Affidavit Law," *Arkansas Gazette,* 9 February 1960.

61. *Bates v. Little Rock,* 361 U.S. 516 (1960); *Southern School News,* May 1960, p. 8.

not reveal a consistent pattern. In *Slochower v. Board of Higher Education of the City of New York*, the Supreme Court ruled that the automatic dismissal of a professor who had invoked the Fifth Amendment before a congressional inquiry violated the Constitution. The inquiry, the Court decided, was not directly concerned with the professor's qualifications for employment. This seemingly confirmed the assumption of the opposition to Act 10 that a government body could not legally ask questions of an employee if those questions were not directly related to his or her job. In *Schware v. Board of Bar Examiners of the State of New Mexico* and *Konigsberg v. State Bar of California*, the Court ruled against state administrators who disallowed Communist Party members' becoming certified to practice law. These cases upheld the dictum that a state employee's fitness to serve could not be judged merely by his or her political affiliations. Finally *Sweezy v. New Hampshire* implied that academic freedom was protected by the First and Fourteenth Amendments against encroachments by either federal or state governments.[62]

Two other decisions, however, were not encouraging for the Act 10 opposition. In *Barenblatt v. United States*, the Supreme Court ruled that a House Committee on Un-American Activities investigation did not violate the Constitution when it held Lloyd Barenblatt, a graduate student and teaching fellow at the University of Michigan, in contempt for failing to answer questions relating to his Communist Party membership. Justice John Marshall Harlan wrote for the majority that the Supreme Court "has consistently refused to view the Communist Party as an ordinary political party" and has let the government behave in ways that "in a different context would certainly have raised Constitutional issues of the gravest character." Harlan's opinion implied that if the Court considered Act 10 to be an anti-Communist law, the legislation had a much greater chance of surviving than if the Court considered it an anti-NAACP or anti-integration bill. Ralph Fuchs, an AAUP attorney and contributor to the Act 10 opposition's case, concurred. The Court's attitude toward racial discrimination in cases such as *NAACP v. Alabama* had been to support "organizational freedom against official scrutiny into membership," but as *Barenblatt* had proved,

---

62. *Slochower;* "Texts of the Majority Opinion and Dissents in Slochower Case," *New York Times,* 10 April 1956; *Schware v. Board of Bar Examiners,* 353 U.S. 232 (1957); *Konigsberg v. State Bar of California,* 353 U.S. 252 (1957); *Sweezy;* "Academic Freedom, the AAUP and the U.S. Supreme Court," *American Association of University Professors Bulletin,* March 1959.

the Court was less tolerant of Communists. In *Beilan v. Board of Education,* a case similar to *Barenblatt,* the Court sustained a Philadelphia school superintendent's dismissal of a teacher who had refused to answer questions about his political affiliations. Justice Harold H. Burton wrote for the majority, "By engaging in teaching in the public schools, petitioner did not give up his right to freedom of belief, speech, or association. He did, however, undertake obligations of frankness, candor, and cooperation in answering inquiries made of him by his employing Board."[63]

On December 12, 1960, the Supreme Court handed down its decision in the Act 10 case. Reflecting the particularly divisive nature of the issues involved, the Court overturned the Arkansas affidavit law by a slim five-to-four margin. Justice Potter Stewart wrote for the majority, "Act 10 deprives teachers in Arkansas of their rights to personal, associational, and academic liberty, protected by the Due Process Clause of the Fourteenth Amendment from invasion by state action." Justice Stewart cited two main postulates in deriving this conclusion. First, he stated, "there can be no doubt of the right of a state to investigate the competence and fitness of those whom it hires to teach in its schools." Stewart's second postulate, however, limited the first: "It is not disputed that to compel a teacher to disclose his every associational tie is to impair that teacher's right of free association, a right closely allied to freedom of speech and a right which, like free speech, lies at the foundation of a free society." "Public exposure," Stewart continued, "bringing with it the possibility of public pressures upon school boards to discharge teachers who belong to unpopular or minority organizations, would simply operate to widen and aggravate the impairment of constitutional liberty." Stewart and the majority recognized that Act 10 required teachers to list "every conceivable kind of associational tie—social, professional, political, avocational, or religious." "Many such relationships," they declared, "could have no possible bearing upon the teacher's occupational competence or fitness." The majority opinion ended with a resounding endorsement of freedom of association: "The statute's comprehensive interference with associational freedom goes far beyond what might be justified in the

---

63. *Barenblatt v. United States,* 360 U.S. 109 (1959); "Experts from the High Court," *New York Times,* 8 June 1959; *NAACP v. Alabama,* 360 U.S. 240 (1959); "The Barenblatt Decision of the Supreme Court and the Academic Profession," *American Association of University Professors Bulletin,* March 1959; *Beilan v. Board of Education,* 357 U.S. 399 (1958); "Academic Freedom, the AAUP and the U.S. Supreme Court." See also Schrecker, *No Ivory Tower,* 3.

exercise of the State's legitimate inquiry into the fitness and competency of its teachers. The judgments in both cases must be reversed."[64]

When the AAUP censured the University of Arkansas for not voluntarily reinstating four faculty members fired under Act 10, Governor Faubus and other conservatives in the state declared victory. They welcomed the AAUP's action, maintaining that the censure stopped "the wrong kind of teachers" and "undesirables cold at the state line." Arkansas segregationists were further heartened that Act 10 and Act 115 had drawn legal and monetary resources from the NAACP; had thrown "consternation into the ranks" of potentially disloyal teachers; and had, through the AAUP's censure, inadvertently defended Arkansas from creeping liberalism from the "Northern" universities. And, in fact, in most southern states the NAACP's legal campaigns had been temporarily frustrated. NAACP members lost their jobs and lost time defending themselves against red and black charges rather than continuing the struggle for black equality.[65]

Viewed from a wider perspective, southern liberals had gained two important federal rulings that would protect them against massive resisters. Act 10 and Act 115 were among the last of the anti-NAACP statutes to be erased from southern judicial codes. As such they became lasting precedents that closed the debate over similar state interposition measures. Specifically the NAACP succeeded in making it more difficult for its enemies to justify legal restrictions on anti-Communist grounds. The NAACP also held its own in the public-relations battle. For every piece of evidence brought by Eastland, Gathings, Cook, Perez, Harris, Johnston, Rainach, or Bennett, the NAACP was able to counter with proof of its anti-Communist position. Under Roy Wilkins's leadership, the NAACP became more staunchly anti-Communist than ever. Nevertheless, conservative perceptions of a red and black conspiracy continued to flourish. Indeed, the Southern Manifesto and white-majority reactions to the Little Rock crisis revealed a deepening southern nationalism that thrived increasingly on both segregation and anti-Communism. The southern red scare had only just begun.

64. *Shelton v. Tucker*, 364 U.S. 479 (1960); Supreme Court of the United States: Shelton v. Tucker and Carr v. Young, 12 December 1960, 1:3, McNeil Papers.

65. "Freezing 'em Out," *Arkansas Gazette*, 12 April 1964.

LITTLE HUACs AND LITTLE FBIs

3

WHILE THE UBIQUITOUS NATIONAL ASSOCIATION FOR the Advancement of Colored People (NAACP) battled segregation in the courts, local black activists took the movement to the streets of southern towns and cities. Black community leaders, many of them returning World War II veterans, initiated school-desegregation and voter-registration campaigns in every southern community, even in the Deep South. Mississippi blacks created local institutions such as the Mississippi Progressive Voters' League and the Regional Council of Negro Leadership to bring an end to racial discrimination. Local blacks in Georgia, meanwhile, capitalized on the Supreme Court's ruling in *Smith v. Allwright* , a Texas case invalidating the so-called white primary, to begin loosening the one-party, Democratic grip on state politics. Their effort led directly to the defeat of red-baiting, segregationist candidates such as Roy Harris. And in Louisiana local black-registration initiatives increased the number of African American voters in the state from 7,000 to 161,000 between 1946 and 1956 and pressured Louisiana State University to become the first state university in the Deep South to admit a black student.[1]

The guardians of white anti-Communist Dixie saw revolution in the groundswell of local black activism. They responded by institutionalizing the southern red scare. Using the House Committee on Un-American Activities (HUAC) and the Federal Bureau of Investigation (FBI) as models, southern nationalists in every state in the region converted and constructed law-enforcement and legislative agencies to pursue subversives in the civil rights movement. These "little HUACs" and "little FBIs," together with the

1. John Dittmer, *Local People: The Struggle for Civil Rights in Mississippi* (Urbana: University of Illinois Press, 1995), 25–37; John Egerton, *Speak Now against the Day* (New York: Knopf, 1994), 380–83; Adam Fairclough, *Race and Democracy* (Athens: University of Georgia Press, 1995), 106. See also David Colburn, *Racial Change and Community Crisis* (New York: Columbia University Press, 1985); William Chafe, *Civil Liberties and Civil Rights* (New York: Oxford University Press, 1980); and Richard Kruger, *Simple Justice* (New York: Knopf, 1975).

federal agencies they emulated, formed the beginning of a network of red and black investigators.

FBI director J. Edgar Hoover inspired the network of red and black investigators more than any other individual. He had much in common with southern nationalists. Hoover had grown up in a southern city, Washington D.C., where segregation was the norm and had come of age at a time when Jim Crow was accepted as a respectable social standard. He shared the opinion of his fellow southerners that civil rights activism was revolutionary in nature and threatened an ideal American way of life. This predilection had a profound effect on his career as the country's preeminent crusader against domestic subversion. He became the most powerful, aggressive, and obsessive investigator of Communist influence among African Americans in the country's history, a fact that earned him tremendous popularity and respect in the segregationist and anti-Communist South.[2]

It was during the nation's first red scare that Hoover began a fifty-year campaign to uncover Communist influence in the African American community. A pioneer in red and black investigations, Hoover developed the Bureau's earliest policies on the subversive potential of black Communists. Along with men like Clayton Lusk, he saw Communists as having "done a vast amount of evil damage by carrying doctrines of race revolt and the poison of Bolshevism to the Negroes." In 1924 Hoover rose to the top position in the FBI and intensified the Bureau's investigation of red agents attempting to subvert black causes. Throughout the 1930s and 1940s, the FBI scrutinized Communist influence in the Civil Rights Congress, the Southern Conference for Human Welfare, the National Negro Congress, and the National Association for the Advancement of Colored People. By the 1950s Hoover's Bureau had become the country's foremost expert on Communist relationships with black Americans. At the same time movies, magazines, and television honored FBI agents as the national keepers of truth and integrity.[3]

A 1953 private FBI report on "The Communist Party and the Negro" outlined Hoover's and the FBI's perception of the red and black menace in the United States just as the southern red scare began to coalesce. The re-

2. See Richard Gid Powers, *Secrecy and Power: The Life of J. Edgar Hoover* (New York: Free Press, 1987).

3. See Theodore Kornweibel Jr., *"Seeing Red": Federal Campaigns against Black Militancy, 1919–1925* (Bloomington: Indiana University Press, 1998); James D. Williams, "A Communist under Every Bed," *Baltimore Afro-American*, 2 May 1964.

port covered Communist positions on the "negro question" from 1919 to 1953 and drew conclusions that mirrored those emanating from HUAC's 1949 hearings. Citing a number of instances of red and black cooperation, including Scottsboro and the Angelo Herndon Case, the document concluded that the Communist Party of the United States (CP) had "devoted an inordinate portion of its time, funds, propaganda, and personnel to recruiting . . . Negroes." The report, however, admitted that the Communist Party had failed "to attract even a significant minority of the Negro population to its program." Hoover understood that the party "line" was determined by the needs of the Soviet Union and not necessarily by American Negroes. Yet while Hoover held that African Americans generally had worked for equality within the American system, he maintained that the potential for subversion among civil rights protesters was real.

Indeed, the FBI's 1953 report concentrated more on the potential threat of a red and black conspiracy than any actual subversive activity. Always protective of the Bureau's interests, Hoover saw the report partly as another opportunity to demonstrate the indispensability of the FBI to American patriots then caught up in the most intense days of the national red scare. Yet the report also wove in elements of truth that meshed well with Hoover's and southern white prejudices concerning black revolutionaries. The result, like HUAC's 1949 hearings, was a report with an alarmist tone. It outlined the Communist Party's cynical bid to exploit naive blacks with appeals to "equal rights" and "self-determination" in the Black Belt. To this end, the report continued, the Communist Party had enlisted Negro support in its united front for peace, elected or appointed blacks to positions of authority in the party, and used Negro front groups like the American Negro Labor Congress and the Civil Rights Congress to promote its agenda. Furthermore the CP had also successfully gained control of "non-Communist organized Negro improvement organizations." The Communists may have failed thus far with the NAACP, the report concluded, but they had made significant headway in other groups and were determined to continue their infiltration of civil rights organizations.[4]

A year after Hoover delivered the 1953 report to the White House, the *Brown* decision put the director in the precarious position of meshing his

---

4. "The Communist Party and the Negro," Special Assistant for National Security Affairs Records, FBI, Box 16, Communist Party and the Negro Folder, White House Office Files, Eisenhower Presidential Papers, Eisenhower Library.

investigations of the red and black conspiracy with his responsibility to investigate violations of federal law. Hoover and the FBI came under increasing pressure to see that the civil rights of blacks were protected, but their suspicions that Communists had heavily influenced the civil rights movement made succumbing to this pressure problematical. Hoover's solution was to keep the FBI on the sidelines in the battle between the white South and the civil rights movement by limiting the Bureau's involvement in civil rights matters. At the same time, he continued quietly to supply HUAC and the Senate Internal Security Subcommittee with information on red and black collusion. FBI reports on Benjamin J. Davis, Paul Robeson, and the NAACP found their way to the offices of James Eastland, E. C. Gathings, and James C. Davis and through them to southern state investigators.[5]

Hoover's suspicions that the civil rights movement was Communist controlled increased markedly during the mid-1950s as his relationship with black leaders pushing the FBI to act on behalf of African Americans became more and more confrontational. A second confidential FBI report on Communism and blacks, delivered to the White House in 1956, reflected the director's willingness to accept views closer to those of southern massive resisters. Taking up where the 1953 report left off, the 1956 summary focused on civil rights cases in the South leading up to and following the Supreme Court's school-integration decision. It revealed an FBI more concerned with Communist infiltration of the civil rights movement and Communist slandering of southern political figures such as Hoover's friend James Eastland than with human rights abuses.

The report examined the Communist Party's support of the Montgomery Bus Boycott and of Autherine Lucy's bid to enter the University of Alabama, but more than these, the case of Emmett Till highlighted the FBI's priorities. Till, a fourteen-year-old Chicagoan visiting relatives in Money, Mississippi, had allegedly whistled at a white woman. The woman's husband and his half brother had abducted Till, shot him in the head with a .45 caliber pistol, tied him to a cotton-gin fan, and dumped him in the Tallahatchie River. Hoover and the FBI refused to investigate the murder, claiming that "no violation of federal civil rights statutes" had occurred. While he easily could have claimed federal jurisdiction over the case as a kidnapping,

---

5. Kenneth O'Reilly, *"Racial Matters": The FBI's Secret File on Black America, 1960–1972* (New York: Free Press, 1989), 9–47. See also Kenneth O'Reilly, *Black Americans: The FBI Files* (New York: Carroll and Graf, 1994).

the director instead left it to a racist Mississippi judicial system. Ultimately a state court acquitted both suspects of murder, and a federal grand jury refused to issue indictments.[6]

While Hoover and the FBI neglected to assign agents to examine the civil rights or kidnapping implications of the Till case, the 1956 report revealed that the Bureau had committed several agents to investigate Communist protests against the verdict. The Bureau produced an internal party memorandum uncovering what it claimed was an agreement reached by the Communist Party and the NAACP on a "plan of work" for the Till case.

International events, the 1956 report explained, had spurred the Bureau to redouble its diligence in investigating Communist influence among black Americans. Communists, according to the FBI, had come to consider the American movement for Negro freedom as part of the international struggle of colonial peoples. The Bandung conference of so-called neutralist nations held in April 1955 had encouraged the Communist Party to help unite African and Asian peoples against "the common enemy—Wall Street imperialism." Moreover, in light of Khrushchev's secret speech in February 1956, the American Communist Party's "self-determination" directive on American blacks had changed. While the ultimate goal of the Communists remained the establishment of a socialist America, the push for an independent black region had softened. According to the report, the "struggle for Negro rights and freedom . . . has emerged as a general, national democratic task," including advances in voting rights, black representation in government, education, and agricultural reform. This change mirrored the Soviet Union's own reinterpretation of the nationalities question. In his secret speech, Khrushchev had condemned Stalin's abuse of the nationalities under the Soviet umbrella. "Love of one's motherland," according to Khrushchev, did not contradict "socialist internationalism." In the United States, according to the Bureau, this change in Soviet policy translated into active CP support of short-term civil rights goals rather than an immediate black nationalist revolution.[7]

The changes abroad and at home, the FBI thus concluded, had ushered in a new alliance of the civil rights movement and international Communism. Those African Americans who had been put off by the calls of Communists

6. Powers, *Secrecy and Power*, 328.

7. Bohdan Nahaylo and Victor Swoboda, *Soviet Disunion: A History of the Nationalities Problem in the USSR* (New York: Free Press, 1990), 118–19.

for immediate revolution, the FBI implied, would now be brought back into the fold under softer Communist policies advocating black civil rights. Once covert red colonization of the civil rights movement was complete, movement goals could then be directed toward revolutionary action. The report warned that Communists were already usurping the concerns of blacks, particularly in terms of fair housing and black representation in government. While Communists still struggled with "white chauvinism" in their ranks and had yet to make much headway with American blacks, the party's efforts had intensified and were dovetailing neatly with the goals of the burgeoning civil rights movement. The movement itself, Hoover's report suggested, was a threat to American democracy. All bureau investigations of civil rights matters, thus, would be subsumed by the search for black bolsheviks.[8]

The 1956 report was just one of many that reflected Hoover's and the FBI's determination to focus on Communists in civil rights groups. Like southern segregationists and anti-Communists, the director and his beloved agency proved particularly interested in the NAACP. FBI agents reported that while the Communist Party had yet to dominate the national organization, it had succeeded in establishing control over isolated chapters, acted jointly with the NAACP, and "engaged in parallel activities," as in the Till case. In March 1956, the FBI maintained heavy surveillance of an NAACP-sponsored national conference on civil rights. Party functionaries were spotted attending various sessions, although Roy Wilkins and his lieutenants had rejected Communists as official delegates. Hoover realized that the NAACP remained strongly anti-Communist, even noting that the group had reaffirmed these convictions at its annual convention in San Francisco in June of that year. But the NAACP, with the White Citizen's Councils and the Nation of Islam, he believed, had contributed to a growing tension in the South that could at any time erupt into violence. The Communists, meanwhile, were gaining converts amid this racial strife.[9]

8. "The Communist Party and the Negro, 1953–1956," Special Assistant for National Security Affairs Records, FBI, Box 10, Communist Party and the Negro Folder, White House Office Files, Eisenhower Presidential Papers.

9. Hoover to Anderson, 3 January 1956, Special Assistant for National Security Affairs Records, FBI, Box 3, FBI L–N (3), White House Office Files, Eisenhower Presidential Papers; "The Communist Party and the Negro, 1953–1956," Special Assistant for National Security Affairs Records, FBI, Box 10, Communist Party and the Negro Folder, White House Office Files, Eisenhower Presidential Papers; Hoover to Anderson, March 6, March 7, June 22, and June 29, 1956, Special Assistant for National Security Affairs Records, FBI, Box 2, FBI

J. Edgar Hoover's investigations of the NAACP and reports on red and black cooperation flooded the president's offices between 1954 and 1957. To a degree they had the effect Hoover desired. They redirected the debate on the Eisenhower administration's civil rights bill. While Eisenhower himself favored voting-rights stipulations in the 1957 civil rights bill, his cabinet was generally sympathetic to FBI warnings about Communist influence in the civil rights movement. Hoover briefed the cabinet in March 1957 on recent protests brought by "some overzealous but ill-advised leaders of the NAACP and by the Communist party, which seeks to use incidents to further the so-called class struggle." The FBI director was no longer able to conceal his segregationist convictions. In keeping with the racist assumptions of southern whites, he invoked "the specter of racial intermarriages" and "mixed education." For many cabinet members, Hoover had successfully linked a national consensus concerning the threat of Communism to the more problematic one concerning the threat of the civil rights movement to American and particularly southern institutions. Eisenhower's chief of staff Sherman Adams concluded from Hoover's reports that the "Communist influence" in race issues was "tremendous." Eisenhower eventually approved the civil rights bill, but his endorsement came over the objections of a number of cabinet members and the legislation enacted was weak, to say the least.[10]

The FBI investigations had an even more profound impact as a moving force behind the southern red scare. The Bureau's duty to uphold federal law, its reputation as the country's most elite investigative agency, and Hoover's understanding that an overt alliance with Dixie's racists would corner the agency politically certainly limited his ability to publicly support southern massive resisters. Still, Hoover overtly and covertly aided the southern segregationist and anti-Communist cause. He frequently revealed to the press that he was continuing to investigate Communist influences in the civil rights movement and maintained a steady flow of confidential reports and leaked file information to HUAC and the SISS. Most important,

L–N(2) Folder, White House Office Files, Eisenhower Presidential Papers; Hoover to Anderson, January 16, March 2, March 5, and March 6, 1956, Special Assistant for National Security Affairs Records, FBI, Box 3, FBI L–N (3) Folder, White House Office Files, Eisenhower Presidential Papers. Also see Juan Williams, *Thurgood Marshall: American Revolutionary* (New York: Times Books, 1998), 253–54.

10. Numan Bartley, *The New South* (Baton Rouge: Louisiana State University Press, 1995) 232–33; O'Reilly, *"Racial Matters,"* 41.

he provided a general model and specific guidance to local and state law-enforcement officials conducting red and black investigations.

In June 1955 the American Civil Liberties Union (ACLU) raised the alarm over potential abuse in Hoover's relationship with the states. In a letter to the governors of all forty-eight states, the ACLU requested that FBI data be used carefully so as not to invade the civil liberties of individual citizens. The group expressed concern about J. Edgar Hoover's sharing of "confidential FBI file information" with state agencies in the South and across the nation. ACLU leaders had recently become aware of an arrangement between state governors and the FBI to share files on state and municipal employees who might pose security risks. This information, the civil-liberties advocates warned, should "never be revealed except in appropriate forums." There were no guarantees, to the ACLU's knowledge, that due process would be observed when state officials used the FBI data. In fact the *Denver Post* had already reported abuses in this regard. Local school authorities in Colorado had fired teachers based on FBI reports listing their Communist affiliations. While security checkups were proper for those in sensitive positions, the ACLU continued, national-security concerns did not justify the "dragnet approach" now used by the nation's loyalty-security programs. Moreover, FBI file information was profoundly dangerous in the hands of state officials who did not understand that the material contained mostly "unproven allegations against individuals." The letter finally asked that the states ensure the accuracy of the information in the files and take care to guarantee accused individuals due process.[11]

While the ACLU's letter expressed concern about the risk to civil liberties posed by the prevailing arrangement between the states and the FBI, it observed that things could be worse. While the status quo was far from perfect, it was much preferable to the creation of forty-eight "little FBI's" manned by those without the same training and experience as federal agents. Soon all of the ACLU's fears would become reality in the South. Not only would the FBI continue to share information with southern massive resisters, the South would develop its own special investigative bodies. If the FBI could only selectively support the southern red scare, the "little FBIs" could offer their full attention to the cause.[12]

---

11. ACLU to Allan Shivers, 1 June 1955, 1977/81–79, Public Safety Department Papers, Texas State Archives.

12. ACLU to Allan Shivers, 1 June 1955, 1977/81–79, Public Safety Department Papers.

Southern state law-enforcement agencies mirrored the activities of the Federal Bureau throughout the 1950s and 1960s. The North Carolina State Bureau of Investigation and the Georgia Bureau of Investigation took their names as well as their tactics from the FBI, while other state and local police departments created investigative divisions. The Louisiana State Police, for example, maintained a Criminal Bureau of Identification while the New Orleans Police housed an Intelligence Division. Investigative divisions of the departments of public safety in Texas and Alabama and the department of state police in Virginia also kept their own tabs on enemies of the state.

Like Hoover's FBI each of these state and local agencies collected data and established files on Communists real and suspected in the civil rights movement. Virginia's investigative division initiated a special study of "civil disturbances" stemming from racial unrest and Communist subversion, as did Alabama's. Indeed, Alabama's largest industrial city, Birmingham, had a long history of investigating the connection between black and red. The police department in that city maintained a network of informants from its old "Red Squad" of the 1930s and 1940s that continued to contribute data on black bolsheviks and white subversives well into the 1960s. In 1963 alone, the Birmingham antisubversive squad infiltrated and tape-recorded more than fifty civil rights meetings. Texas's investigative division, meanwhile, focused on "subversive activities" and "racial agitation" as crucial areas of research. North Carolina's bureau, moreover, looked for Communists involved in the state's youth protests. Georgia's bureau shared its findings on Communists with the state's most virulent red-and black-baiters. And Louisiana Criminal Bureau of Identification supervisor Billy Joe Booth relied on a constant stream of information on Communists and civil rights organizers from Louisiana's HUAC representative Edwin Willis. Reciprocating, the New Orleans Intelligence Division contributed information to HUAC as it continued its own red and black investigations in the South.[13]

13. "Individuals Active in Civil Disturbances" SG22394, Wallace Papers, Alabama Department of Archives; Racial Matters, February 1965, SG22394, Wallace Papers; Suthard to Terry, 5 July 1965, Box 138, Harrison Executive Papers, Library of Virginia; Bradley Investigation, 7 May 1965 Box 138, Harrison Executive Papers; Bradley Investigation, 12 May 1965, Box 138, Harrison Executive Papers; "Intelligence," 27, Box 74, 6M48g, DPS 1963–1967, Connally Papers, Lyndon Baines Johnson Library; Civil Rights and Youth Protest Folders, Boxes 4, 5, and 6, State Bureau of Investigation Series, North Carolina State Archives; Booth to Willis, 23 October 1961, C46, B174, F11, Edwin Willis Papers, University

94]   Not only were state investigative agencies supported by a steady stream of information from federal bodies, they also maintained close contact with one another. Through the Southern Association of Investigators (SAI), for example, officers in Georgia, Texas, Mississippi, Louisiana, Alabama, Arkansas, North Carolina, South Carolina, Tennessee, Florida, and Oklahoma shared their findings. The SAI digested and distributed scores of intelligence documents to its members on "subversive influences" among the "far left and militant civil rights groups" active in the region. By the early 1960s, state police departments through umbrella groups like the SAI had begun building networks of informers.[14]

"Little FBIs" generally used their investigations of red and black activities to directly support massive resistance in the South. Because of this, FBI agents and local police were sometimes at odds when investigating civil rights violations. Still, federal and state investigators agreed that the threat of Communists in the civil rights movement was real. The FBI privately continued to share information with state law enforcement about Communist influence in black protests. The state agencies then used this information to undermine the credibility of the civil rights movement. Despite his obligation to defend the constitutional rights of African Americans, Hoover instituted a policy that bolstered the southern red scare and the segregationist ends it sought.[15]

While the "little FBIs" were well equipped to gather information on the alleged red and black conspiracy in the South, they were stifled to some ex-

of Louisiana at Lafayette; Tavenner to Willis, 20 September 1961, C46, B174, F12, Willis Papers; Booth to Willis, 14 September 1961, C46, B174, F12, Willis Papers; Tavenner to Booth, 16 April 1961, C46, B174, F13, Willis Papers; Candler to Booth, 4 January 1962, C46, B175, F1, Willis Papers; Tavenner to Willis, 2 January 1962, , C46, B175, F1, Willis Papers; Booth to Willis, 12 September 1961, C46, B175, F1, Willis Papers; Willis to Banister and Badeaux, 21 February 1957, C46, B169, F8, Willis Papers. See also Dan Carter, *The Politics of Rage: George Wallace, the Origins of the New Conservatism, and the Transformation of American Politics* (New York: Simon and Schuster, 1995), 229; Robin Kelley, *Hammer and Hoe: Alabama Communists during the Great Depression* (Chapel Hill: University of North Carolina Press, 1990), 72–73; M. J. Heale, *McCarthy's Americans* (Athens: University of Georgia Press, 1998), 261.

14. SAI New Officers, SG21074, Alabama Legislative Commission to Preserve the Peace Papers, Alabama Department of Archives and History; Strickland to Goss, 26 October 1966, SG21074, Alabama Legislative Commission to Preserve the Peace Papers, Alabama Department of Archives and History.

15. Powers, *Secrecy and Power*, 327–31.

tent, like their federal counterpart, by their law-enforcement duties. While the "little FBIs" could gather information alongside the "big" FBI, they rarely found enough evidence to make arrests. They did dig up enough material, however, to bring into question the loyalty of certain civil rights groups. Again following the lead of federal bodies, southern states created "little HUACs" to process and use the information for the segregationist cause. Given broad powers to subpoena witnesses and material evidence, they became the primary investigative tools of the southern red scare. In almost every state in the South, the committees would use the national anti-Communist consensus to promote state sovereignty and the regional racial cause.[16]

Mississippi was among the first states in the South to establish legislative agencies that bolstered segregation by investigating Communist influence on its opponents. In 1955 the Mississippi legislature created the Legal Educational Advisory Committee "to preserve and promote the best interests of both races" by maintaining separate educational facilities. Among its other duties, the committee would hold hearings on the subversive nature of the integration movement. But it was a year later, on the heels of the Southern Manifesto in March 1956, that the Mississippi assembly created the State Sovereignty Commission (SSC), a body given enormous power to expose the red and black conspiracy. Mississippi legislators granted the commission the ability to "do and perform any and all acts and things deemed necessary and proper to protect the sovereignty of the state of Mississippi, and her sister states" against federal integration efforts. The governor led the commission as ex-officio chairman with the president of the state senate, the state attorney general, and the state speaker of the house acting as supporting ex-officio members. Other members of the state legislature as well as citizens appointed by the governor would also serve on the commission.[17]

16. See " 'Little HUACs' in the South Harassing Integration Groups," RG46, Subject Series, SCEF 1956–1963, Senate Internal Security Subcommittee Papers, National Archives; Heale, *McCarthy's Americans*, 7–27.

17. "Mississippi Reveals Dark Secrets," *New York Times*, 18 March 1998; Anne Braden, "House Un-American Activities Committee: Bulwark of Segregation," id# 6-44-0-11-1-1-1, p. 26, State Sovereignty Commission Files, Mississippi Department of Archives and History; *General Laws of the State of Mississippi*, 1956, Chapter 365, pp. 520–24. See also Neil McMillen, *The Citizens' Council: Organized Resistance to the Second Reconstruction, 1954–64* (Urbana: University of Illinois Press, 1971), 16.

The Mississippi SSC in some ways set the standard for state legislative commissions across the South. Its basic make-up was typical. The daily tasks of the commission were left to a small staff that included a general director, a public-relations director, a few investigators, and clerical workers. The commission's directors and investigators came mostly from state law-enforcement agencies, although its primary investigator in the late 1950s, Zack Van Landingham, was a former FBI agent. As in other states, the commission regularly reported to the legislature about, among other things, socialists, subversives, and revolutionaries allegedly driving the civil rights campaigns in the South.

In other ways, however, the Mississippi SSC was extreme in its view of its own objectives and in its power to carry out those objectives. It took literally the comparison to the FBI and to armed-services intelligence agencies. Like those federal bodies, the SSC would seek out "the enemy" and gather information about "what the enemy proposes to do." The State Sovereignty Commission thus became Mississippi's secret police, wiretapping, bugging, and infiltrating civil rights organizations. The commission's files would ultimately contain thousands of reports on individuals suspected of "subversive activities."[18]

Under the Mississippi SSC's definition, "subversive activities" included any and all challenges to the state's racial hierarchy. After a frantic mother wrote to Governor Paul Johnson in early 1965 that the boyfriend of her daughter, a freshman at the University of Southern Mississippi, might be "part Negro," Johnson had the commission conduct a background check. Erle Johnston, then head of the SSC, had agents inquire about the young man's family tree and his age. Had proper evidence of his black ancestry been found, and had the young man been at least twenty-two years old, Johnston suggested, the SSC would have had him drafted. In another investigation SSC agent Tom Scarbrough checked into the ethnic heritage of a baby born in Grenada, Mississippi, after locals informed the agency that the baby's mother might have had a sexual relationship with a black man. After looking closely at the child's fingernails, presumably under the theory that African ancestry could be detected by the presence of half-moons at the cuticles, Scarbrough declared that he could not determine if the child was part black but could say with certainty that "it was not 100 percent Caucasian."

18. SSC Speech, 13 July 1958, , id# 7-0-1-56-2-1-1, State Sovereignty Commission Files; Dittmer, *Local People*, 60.

Noted for its fanaticism in protecting the racial status quo, the Mississippi SSC became the most infamous and powerful body of its kind in the South.[19]

Other southern states followed Mississippi in establishing investigative committees that would focus on "subversive activities." None was as extreme as the Mississippi SSC, but they all took seriously a mandate to protect segregationist institutions and suggest legal methods to sidestep federal integration efforts. On the heels of Eugene Cook's revelations about the NAACP, the "Red Monday" decisions, and the formation of the Mississippi SSC, two southern legislatures in particular broadened their committees' duties in early 1957 to include public hearings on, and propaganda campaigns against, subversive activity in the civil rights movement.

Eugene Cook's home state was the first to expand the powers of its segregation committee. With the *Brown* decision looming on the horizon in late 1953, the state established the Georgia Commission on Education (GCE). That year, along with measures designed to preserve segregated schools and the state's Floyd Anti-Subversion Act, Georgia passed the bill establishing the commission. From its beginnings the GCE leadership lashed out at an alleged red and black conspiracy. In the fall of 1954, GCE executive director Durwood T. Pye, an Atlanta attorney, helped lobby for a state constitutional amendment privatizing Georgia's schools in order to keep them segregated. In calling for this amendment, Pye told one correspondent that the "Communists and their dupes are on the march." It was their purpose to destroy "all standards set by laws such as those providing for separate education." Anti-Communism had a strong appeal among Georgians, especially among the state's large fundamentalist Christian community. The constitutional amendment passed in November 1954.[20]

That fall one of the South's most dedicated anti-Communists and segregationists was elected governor of Georgia. Marvin Griffin turned the GCE into a major agency of the state government, approving interposition recommendations and asking the commission to submit regular reports to the legislature. Over the next two years, the GCE established itself as a fixture in Georgia's campaign against integration.[21]

19. "Documents Outline How State Fought Desegregation," *Mississippi Clarion-Ledger*, 28 January 1990; Calvin Trillin, "State Secrets," *New Yorker*, 29 May 1995, pp. 54–64.
20. Heale, *McCarthy's Americans*, 246–47.
21. Ibid., 249–50.

It was in early 1957, though, that Governor Griffin helped increase the GCE's power to the extent that it could very literally act as a "little HUAC." That year Griffin asked legislators to give the GCE the authority to employ investigators, hold hearings, and subpoena witnesses. Despite objections from more liberal urban representatives, the bill swept through the state assembly. With a new mandate for the commission, the governor formulated plans to extend its propaganda campaign. Using Eugene Cook's office as well as the resources of powerful commission members such as Roy Harris, the GCE immediately printed "Ten Directors of the NAACP," an exposé on the alleged Communist associations of several NAACP leaders.[22]

While the GCE was augmenting its power, a second state broadened its committee's mandate to pursue red and black subversives. Like the GCE, Louisiana's Joint Legislative Committee on Segregation (JLCS) came about as a response to the rising tide of black protest. Part of Louisiana's framework of resistance against integration adopted by the legislature in 1954, the JLCS suggested ways to preserve the traditional racial order. Under its chairman, the state's leading legislative red- and black-baiter, senator Willie Rainach, the JLCS would make exposure of the conspiracy linking bolshevism and equal rights its top priority.

In March 1957 Louisiana's committee conducted hearings that would constitute the broadest scrutiny of a perceived red and black menace since HUAC's 1949 hearings on Communist infiltration of minority groups. The JLCS incorporated information from the usual sources to justify its hearing, including the GCE, the Senate Internal Security Subcommittee (SISS), and HUAC. It also employed the support of locals. New Orleans Police Intelligence Division head Hubert Badeaux and Rainach's mentor Judge Leander Perez provided testimony about red and black agents in and around New Orleans. Seasoned government informers including FBI agent W. Guy Banister and former Communists Joseph Kornfeder and Leonard Patterson bolstered their reports. The most compelling declarations, however, came from another pair of experienced government witnesses who worked closely with HUAC and the SISS, Manning Johnson and Martha Edmiston.

As he had been in HUAC's 1949 hearings, Manning Johnson was the Louisiana committee's star witness. The black ex-Communist reinforced and expanded on the message he had delivered eight years earlier. Johnson explained the Communist Party's Black Belt thesis to his audience and re-

22. Ibid., 256–58.

peated his contention that many African Americans had become pawns of the Kremlin. This time, however, Johnson added specific charges against civil rights groups. He claimed that the Southern Conference for Human Welfare (SCHW), the Southern Regional Council (SRC), the Southern Christian Leadership Conference (SCLC), and the NAACP were all "Communist transmission belts, all fronts." The NAACP especially, he declared, had been "successfully infiltrated" and converted into a "national liberation organization" helping to bring about a "Negro republic" in the South. And individuals such as Martin Luther King, Johnson concluded, were unwittingly leading blacks to follow the Communist "party line."

Johnson's message inspired a new surge of activity among regional red- and black-baiters, particularly those in Georgia. Eugene Cook proposed the circulation of transcripts of Johnson's testimony, "since several Georgia groups" were involved. Of special interest was the Atlanta-based Southern Regional Council (SRC). This organization seemed an unlikely target for Georgia red-baiters. The membership of the Southern Regional Council consisted overwhelmingly of moderate liberals, and its goals had been relatively conservative. It had been created in 1944 largely by white and black educators, journalists, and religious leaders, almost all of whom cautioned against rapid racial reform in the South. Indeed, under the human-rights councils it directed in many southern states, the SRC sought to improve race relations *within* a segregated society. It had also consistently declared its opposition to Communism and other totalitarian doctrines.[23]

Nevertheless the SRC had been a target of red and black investigators in Georgia for years. With the help of Roy Harris and the U.S. representative from Georgia Jimmie Davis, Cook had already produced pamphlets on the SRC's supposed Communist ties in 1956, but the Johnson testimony labeling the group as a red "transmission belt" gave him and his allies another opportunity to publicly lash the organization. While Cook saw that Johnson's testimony was spread far and wide, Jimmie Davis produced HUAC files on SRC leaders, and the American Legion's newsletter the *Firing Line* published an exposé on the SRC which was in turn distributed by the GCE.[24]

Citing Johnson's testimony extensively, the *Firing Line* article reported that the SRC was "formed by James E. Jackson, a southern organizer of the

23. Ibid., 263; Bartley, *New South*, 29–30.
24. Heale, *McCarthy's Americans*, 252–53, 261.

Communist Party." The story also revealed that several SRC officials were members of the SCHW and SCEF—evidence, it claimed, of Communist collusion. Highlighting this point, the article looked to SRC director and SCEF president Aubrey Williams. Williams, it noted, had been named as a member of the Communist Party by witnesses before the SISS's 1954 hearings on the SCEF.[25]

Alarmed over the damage that might be done to the group by Johnson and the American Legion, the SRC put together a refutation of the charges. The group claimed that the *Firing Line* article's accusations ranged from "outright falsehoods" to "cunning distortions." The founding of the SRC, for one, had been "a matter of public record." The incorporators had included Methodist bishop Arthur Moore, Atlanta University president Rufus Clement, Fisk University president Charles S. Johnson, University of North Carolina sociologist Howard Odum, and *Atlanta Constitution* editor Ralph McGill. Neither James E. Jackson, who was indeed a Communist Party official, nor "any other person of Communistic persuasion," the SRC claimed, had ever played any part in the founding of the SRC. Second, the *Firing Line* article had failed to mention that Aubrey Williams had vehemently denied any Communist Party affiliation. This denial, the SRC reported, had even been backed by SISS head James Eastland, who admitted to reporters after the 1954 hearings that he did not think Williams was a Communist. Finally, the SRC argued, the red and black investigator's "connection-by-association" logic was ridiculous. By the *Firing Line*'s reasoning, the Catholic Church, because of its members' association with the SCEF and SCHW, might also be considered a Communist front. Even South Carolina governor James F. Byrnes, who had attended an SCHW dinner honoring Hugo Black in 1945, might by the same reasoning be labeled a fellow traveler.[26]

While attacking the logic and documentation underlying the southern red scare, the SRC counterattack targeted Manning Johnson in particular. The council revealed that Johnson's testimony in other cases had been repudiated by the Department of Justice and the Subversive Activities Control Board. Since 1949 Johnson's career as a HUAC witness and FBI confidant

25. *The Firing Line*, 15 May 1957.

26. "An Analysis of the Attack on SRC," Box 56, Folder 23, McGill Papers, Woodruff Library Special Collections, Emory University; "Wright Defends Regional Group," *New Orleans Times-Picayune*, 15 May 1957.

had deteriorated. His standing among sympathetic liberal anti-Communists had been permanently damaged in 1954 when he accused Ralph Bunche of being a Communist. Even more important, Johnson's reliability as a witness [101 had been seriously undermined when he testified before the Subversive Activities Control Board that he would lie under oath in a court of law, if necessary "a thousand times," rather than run counter to his instructions from the FBI. His testimony had even spurred a Justice Department perjury investigation.[27]

Sensing Johnson's vulnerability, NAACP officials, like those from the SRC, saw their chance to discredit the red and black investigators' star witness. Executive secretary Roy Wilkins sent a letter to Herbert Brownell informing the attorney general that several southern newspapers had falsely described Johnson as a research director at the Justice Department. His branding of the NAACP as a "vehicle of the Communist Party" before the JLCS, Wilkins explained, had thus been interpreted in the South as an official Justice Department position. Wilkins warned the attorney general that a public backlash would result if he did not correct the record.[28]

While she was not as obviously suspect a witness as Johnson, Martha Edmiston's testimony before the JLCS also drew the scorn of the NAACP. Edmiston appeared before the 1957 hearings of the JLCS to reiterate her charge that Lee Lorch, the white secretary of the Tennessee chapter of the NAACP, was a Communist Party member. Martha and her husband John Edmiston, both former FBI informants, had long hounded Lorch. The two had testified before HUAC in the summer of 1950 concerning alleged Communist Party activities of Lorch, who was then a mathematics professor at Fisk University. The 1950 hearings, according to Lorch, had come on the heels of his dismissal from Penn State after that university's inquiry into his participation in an integrated-housing-project campaign. Although no other source confirmed the charge that he was a Communist, southern red scare leaders cited HUAC in charging that the liberal educator was not only a key civil rights activist but a Communist to boot. In 1954 the committee had again called Lorch to testify at a hearing on Communist activities in the Dayton, Ohio, area. There he refused to answer questions concerning his

27. Kenneth O'Reilly, *Hoover and the Un-Americans: The FBI, HUAC, and the Red Menace* (Philadelphia: Temple University Press, 1983), 237.

28. Wilkins to Brownell, 28 March 1957, III: J3, Justice Department File, NAACP Papers, Library of Congress.

political views or affiliations, arguing that such matters were not the legitimate concern of Congress. Lorch was subsequently charged with contempt of Congress, and Fisk University terminated his contract.[29]

Lorch had long suspected that his harassment by Edmiston and the committees had more to do with his views on integration than with any affinity for Communism he might have had. He had publicly denounced the investigation of the Southern Conference Education Fund by the Senate Internal Security Subcommittee, an act that in itself was sufficient to draw the scrutiny of James Eastland. But Lorch's position as an educator and a white NAACP activist made him particularly vulnerable. Lorch ventured to say that it was not his association with any Communist front that had precipitated his subpoena before HUAC in 1954 but his attempt to enroll his daughter in an all-black public school near his home in Nashville. Edmiston's testimony before the JLCS seemed to confirm these suspicions. Martha Edmiston declared, with no apparent concern for the inherent prejudice in her statement, that Lorch had indeed tried to pull a "switcheroo" when he attempted to enroll his daughter in a Negro school. She assumed that, on its own merits, this action constituted "another form of agitation."[30]

Edmiston's testimony, like Johnson's, was replete with bias but was accepted by the JLCS as hard proof of the red and black conspiracy. Indeed, Willie Rainach declared that the testimony given by Edmiston, Johnson, and the others had made "history." It was "the first time in the United States," Rainach declared, that a hearing had as its "sole purpose" the "racial aspects of the subversion problem." Rainach also criticized U.S. congressmen for avoiding the question because they had been "afraid to face the bloc vote in the north, in the cities of the north that have been dominated by the NAACP."

In some ways Rainach's claims were valid. The JLCS hearings had indeed addressed general concerns about black loyalty for the first time since HUAC had held its hearings in 1949. Moreover the scope of red and black

29. My Pending Trial, 21 September 1956, III:J1, Communism File, NAACP Papers; *Congressional Record*, 86th Cong., 1st sess., 1959, 105, pt. 2:2318; Lee and Grace Lorch, 10 March 1958, RG46, Name File 1, Lorch, Senate Internal Security Subcommittee Papers; Ellen Schrecker, *Many Are the Crimes: McCarthyism in America* (Boston: Little, Brown, 1998), 344–45.

30. My Pending Trial, 21 September 1956, III: J1, Communism File, NAACP Papers; Lee and Grace Lorch, 10 March 1958, RG46, Name File 1, Lorch, Senate Internal Security Subcommittee Papers.

activity alleged before the JLCS in some ways exceeded what was presented
to HUAC. Witnesses before the Louisiana committee were much more specific about their charges against the NAACP, SRC, SCHW, and individuals
involved both in civil rights and Communist-front activity. The committee
could indeed attack Communist-inspired integration without worrying that
political opponents—Rainach's so-called northern-bloc vote—might question the credibility of its sources. It spoke primarily to a like-minded southern audience that included, by invitation, groups such as Mississippi's
Legislative Investigation Committee. And it focused on building state institutions such as a Louisiana "Red Squad" that could thwart local red and
black schemes.[31]

In other ways, however, Rainach overstated the significance of the JLCS
hearings. They were not as new as he made them out to be. All of the accusations leveled had been heard before in HUAC and SISS hearings and in
Eugene Cook's "The Ugly Truth about the NAACP." Also, the acceptance
of questionable testimony by Edmiston and Johnson revealed the proceedings to be less about getting at the truth than about buttressing segregation
by whatever means necessary. Rather than being the "historic" undertaking
Rainach claimed, the JLCS hearings were actually another vehicle for those
hoping to preserve southern segregation. Their appeal would be limited
mainly to racial conservatives in the South.[32]

The public exposure of red and black conspirators became the primary
tool for the South's "little HUACs." Where the JLCS used public hearings
to out the Communist, integrationist menace, the GCE chose written propaganda. A few months after the JLCS heard the testimony of Manning
Johnson and Martha Edmiston, the Georgia commission's propaganda campaign accelerated. By the end of the year, the GCE would mail some 515,000
pamphlets and papers. Of the pieces it published, none was more famous
than the commission's "exposé" of the Highlander Folk School. Even more
than the JLCS hearings, the GCE investigation of Highlander encouraged
the belief among southerners that the civil rights movement was a tool of
Communism.

Headed by Myles Horton, Highlander was an adult-education center in

31. Phil Stroupe, "Race Unrest Probe Opens in Louisiana," *Jackson Daily News*, 7
March 1957; "Reds Infiltrate NAACP, Hearing Told by Police," *New Orleans Times-Picayune*, 10 March 1957.

32. *Subversion in Racial Unrest, Public Hearings of the State of Louisiana Joint Legislative Committee, March 6–9 1957* (Baton Rouge: 1957).

Monteagle, Tennessee, that trained, among others, the South's most prominent civil rights leaders. Horton had founded the school in 1932 with the purpose of educating "rural and industrial leaders for a new social order." Throughout the 1930s, the school had aided the emerging southern labor movement, particularly the Congress of Industrial Organizations (CIO). Highlander's relationship with organized labor diminished in the late 1940s and 1950s, but the school filled the void with a new interest in civil rights for southern blacks. Aiding desegregation efforts, sit-in protests, and voting campaigns, Highlander became a training center for civil rights activists in the 1950s and 1960s.[33]

From the beginning Highlander's and Horton's militancy drew the attention of anti-Communists. Horton and many of his co-founders, including Christian Socialist Reinhold Niebuhr and Socialist Party leader Norman Thomas, hoped the school would educate a "radical labor leadership" in the South. The school's open embrace of socialist philosophies drew the attention of local American Legionnaires, conservative unionists, and religious leaders who considered the school "a thoroughly Communistic enterprise." Highlander board member James Dombrowski considered such charges "absurd" and insisted that the school's policy was to remain "non-factional in fact and spirit." Still, suspicious observers kept up a drumbeat of accusations. Even the CIO, which worked closely with Highlander in the 1940s, split with the school after it refused to follow the labor group's policy of purging Communists from its ranks.[34]

Not surprisingly, as the school increased its civil rights activities in the early 1950s, Highlander and Horton drew even greater attention from southern red- and black-baiters. In September 1953, HUAC informer Paul Crouch charged that several people connected to the school were affiliated with the Communist Party. Two months later Tennessee congressman Pat Sutton made Highlander an issue in his campaign to defeat Senator Estes Kefauver in the Democratic primary. In a November 1953 speech, Sutton labeled Highlander, Horton, and James Dombrowski, Communists. A few months later, Senate Internal Security Subcommittee head James Eastland subpoenaed Horton and Dombrowski to appear before the committee's

---

33. John M. Glen, *Highlander: No Ordinary School* (Knoxville: University of Tennessee Press, 1996), 2–3. See also Myles Horton, *The Long Haul: An Autobiography* (New York: Teachers College Press, 1998).

34. Glen, *Highlander*, 40, 51, 144–146.

hearings on the Southern Conference Education Fund (SCEF) and answer charges that Highlander and the SCEF were part of the Communist conspiracy in the American South. In fact, by the time the GCE began its campaign against Highlander, the school was already awash in the southern red scare.[35]

The GCE became interested in Highlander after it and the Georgia Bureau of Investigation (GBI) looked into the activities of the interracial Koinonia Farm near Americus, Georgia. Koinonia leaders drew the attention of the GCE and the GBI after they took part in an attempt to desegregate Georgia State College in 1956. Through paid informants Georgia's red and black investigators learned that the Koinonia activists planned an interracial children's camp for the same year. When legal obstacles and violence against the farm by racist vigilantes marred the plans for the children's camp, Highlander stepped in and offered to cosponsor the operation in Tennessee. The GBI and GCE took due note. (In April 1957 a Georgia grand jury would declare that Koinonia was a Communist front and that racial violence at the farm had actually been committed by the organization against itself in order to get publicity and insurance money.) As a result of their surveillance in 1956 and 1957, the GBI and GCE learned that Highlander was planning a twenty-fifth anniversary celebration and that it anticipated the attendance of prominent civil rights leaders, including Martin Luther King Jr.[36]

On Labor Day weekend 1957, Highlander held its anniversary celebrations. The GCE ordered undercover agent Edwin Friend to register for the anniversary seminar and observe the proceedings. Friend returned with material that confirmed in the minds of many southern segregationists the link between Communism and the civil rights movement.[37]

Using Friend's findings, the GCE published a newspaper-like pamphlet with the headline "Highlander Folk School: Communist Training School, Monteagle, Tenn." According to the main article, "the leaders of every major race incident in the South" had attended the Labor Day assembly at Highlander. There, "in the company of many known Communists," specialists on "inter-racial strife" had furnished training and tactics to fellow "agitators." Citing the testimony of government witnesses Paul Crouch and

35. Ibid., 208–16.
36. "Georgia Grand Jury Blames Koinonia for Shootings, Violence," *Peacemaker* 7 (22 April 1957), Box 31, Communism Folder, South Carolina Council on Human Relations Papers, South Caroliniana Library, University of South Carolina; Glen, *Highlander*, 216–17.
37. Heale, *McCarthy's Americans*, 258–60.

John Butler as well as HUAC and SISS hearings—while ignoring the fact that Crouch had been declared a "tainted" witness by the Supreme Court—the pamphlet went on to outline the alleged Communist affiliations of Myles Horton, James Dombrowski, Aubrey Williams, and others. Although none of the articles identified these Highlander leaders as Communist Party members, the pamphlet did outline their membership in Communist-front organizations, including the Southern Conference for Human Welfare and the Civil Rights Congress. The pamphlet also identified the participation of the Southern Regional Council, founded, according to the text, by SCEF leader "Jim Jackson, Negro Communist." The NAACP, the article went on, which had provided leadership for many of the "major incidents of interracial strife" and whose membership had amassed some "400 incidents of Communist Front Affiliation" was also well represented at Highlander.[38]

What made the GCE pamphlet most compelling to massive resisters, however, was its reproduction of Friend's photographs from the Labor Day assembly. The pictures revealed a "day and night life" at Highlander that was "integrated in all respects." Blacks and whites were shown swimming, dancing, and eating together. Pictures also revealed that Montgomery Bus Boycott leaders Rosa Parks, Ralph Abernathy, and Martin Luther King Jr. had participated in the Highlander conference. But it was the photograph of the " 'four horsemen' of racial agitation" that was most disturbing to southern conservatives. The picture showed King, Williams, Horton, and conference attendee Abner Berry of "the Central Committee of the Communist Party" seated together. The photograph was for many southerners proof that the leaders of a red and black conspiracy had come together at Highlander to plan continued "tension, disturbance, strife, and violence" in the advancement of "the Communist doctrine of 'racial nationalism.' "[39]

Berry, in fact a longtime and high-ranking member of the Communist Party, had indeed registered for the conference and attended as a freelance reporter. He had apparently failed to inform Horton that he was a correspondent for the *Daily Worker*. This oversight had significant ramifications for the school and the civil rights movement in the South. The GCE used Berry's presence at the assembly as evidence of the direct participation of Com-

38. See O'Reilly, *Hoover and the Un-Americans*, 237.

39. "Highlander Folk School: Communist Training School, Monteagle, Tenn.," Series IA, Box 11, Segregation General Folder, Vandiver Papers, Richard Russell Memorial Library.

munists at Highlander civil rights functions. The commission circulated some 250,000 copies of the paper on its own. Governor Griffin also author- ized reprints "with or without credit being given to this Commission." Cir- culation of the exposé reached more than one million by the end of 1959. Together with the GCE's pamphlets on "Communism and the NAACP" and "CORE and Its Communist Connections," the Highlander paper en- sured the commission's place as the leading propaganda machine in the southern red scare.[40]

The Highlander exposé set off a bitter public debate in Tennessee that ultimately led to the closing of the school. But it had regional implications as well. Along with the GCE, legislative committees in Louisiana, Florida, Mississippi, and Arkansas would use the Highlander findings as the basis for their depictions of a broad red and black conspiracy in the South. With the Little Rock crisis and the launching of the Soviet satellite *Sputnik* in the fall, these accusations took on a new significance for southerners. Most important, at the height of the growing fear, Georgia's findings on High- lander and Louisiana's investigations buttressed an effort by Eastland's SISS to resurrect the doctrine of states' rights and use it to persuade Congress to arm the South legislatively against subversion and, indirectly, integration.

In the last few days of October, with the Little Rock confrontation and *Sputnik* very much on the minds of Americans, Senator Eastland's SISS again focused on red and black issues at its hearings on the mid-South. Op- erating from Memphis the subcommittee gathered testimony about individ- uals and groups considered key mediators between the Communist Party and the civil rights movement. The SISS hoped to use the evidence gathered in the states to persuade Congress to adopt measures reestablishing states' rights to outlaw sedition.

The bulk of the initial testimony dealt with Carl Braden. Braden, a jour- nalist, and his wife Anne had been active in the union and desegregation movements in Louisville, Kentucky. Friends in the civil rights movement also remembered that the two had at one time espoused Communist beliefs rather openly. In 1954 Carl Braden was charged with violating Kentucky's antisedition laws. His wife was implicated by association. The Bradens had purchased a house in a white neighborhood for Andrew Wade, a black elec- trical contractor. Local vigilantes harassed the Wade family from the mo- ment they moved in, even burning a cross in the yard and shooting at

40. Heale, *McCarthy's Americans*, 263; Glen, *Highlander*, 218–19.

windows. When an explosion destroyed the house, however, local authorities concluded that it was not the work of racists. Rather, under FBI and
HUAC guidance, they indicted Carl Braden along with other suspected
Communists for dynamiting the house in an attempt to gain publicity and
provoke a broader racial incident. Prosecutors called in professional witnesses, among them Manning Johnson, to bolster their case. Braden testified
in his own defense that he was interested in socialism but had never been a
member of the Communist Party and had never advocated the overthrow of
the government of the United States or of the state of Kentucky. Nevertheless he spent eight months in jail and lost his job; eventually a Supreme
Court case, *Pennsylvania v. Nelson*, stripped states of the ability to enforce
their criminal-sedition statutes and nullified the indictment in *Commonwealth v. Braden*.[41]

At the outset of the 1957 probe, the SISS questioned Kentucky attorney
general Jo Ferguson and *Commonwealth v. Braden* prosecutor Scott Hamilton about the campaign to use states' rights to protect their state against
sedition and subversion. Both supported the idea that these rights should be
guaranteed by federal legislation. And both hammered away at the charge
that Braden was a Communist who had been working for civil rights in the
South. In fact, prosecutor Hamilton revealed that since the incident in Louisville, the Bradens had continued to be active members of the alleged Communist-front SCEF. Another witness, FBI undercover agent Alberta Ahearn,
testified before the subcommittee that the Bradens had recruited her into
the CP and had encouraged her to infiltrate church and labor groups working for integration.[42]

The subcommittee then brought in Don West. With Myles Horton, West
had been the founder of the now infamous Highlander Folk School. He was
an avowed socialist and to some at Highlander a bit too "radical," even a

41. Author interview with Bob Zellner, 12 February 2002; *Commonwealth v. Carl Braden*, 20 November 1954, Box 1, Kentucky v. Braden 1954 Folder, Braden Papers, University
of Tennessee Special Collections; Summary of Evidence, 29 November 1954, Box 1, Kentucky v. Braden 1954 Folder, Braden Papers; *Pennsylvania v. Nelson*, 350 U.S. 497 (1956).
See also Griffin Fariello, *Red Scare: Memories of the American Inquisition, An Oral History* (New York: W. W. Norton, 1995), 469–506; Kenneth O'Reilly, *"Racial Matters"* (New
York: Free Press, 1989), 41–44; Anne Braden, *The Wall Between* (New York: Monthly Review Press, 1958); Shrecker, *Many Are the Crimes*, 392.

42. Frank T. Adams, *James Dombrowski: An American Heretic, 1897–1983* (Knoxville:
University of Tennessee Press, 1992), 241.

little "unstable." Horton and West had split in the early 1930s, but West had remained a target of speculation as head of the defense committee for Angelo Herndon in Atlanta. He had remained in Georgia since. When the subcommittee asked West whether he had ever been a Communist, he replied that he had not and pled the Fifth Amendment. Not satisfied with his testimony, the subcommittee read into evidence statements by government informers Paul Crouch and Martha Edmiston, who claimed West had been an active Communist Party member in North Carolina, Kentucky, and Ohio. The SISS also offered as an exhibit a GCE report listing West as a Communist Party and SCHW member.[43]

After a series of additional witnesses joined West in pleading the Fifth Amendment, the frustrated subcommittee moved to end its hearings by calling Grace Lorch, the wife of the same Lee Lorch who had been repeatedly scrutinized by HUAC and Louisiana's Joint Legislative Committee on Segregation. The Lorches had been on the minds of red and black investigators since the spring. About the same time the JLCS heard Martha Edmiston's testimony about Lee Lorch, the couple had moved to Arkansas, where Professor Lorch had accepted a position at all-black Philander Smith College. The job had been created in part by public funding from the National Science Foundation, a fact that had irked southern conservatives. But even more significant to those looking for a black and red conspiracy was the fact that the Lorches had arrived in Little Rock just as the conflict over integration erupted there. Indeed, amid the furor, Grace Lorch had gained national fame when she comforted a weeping black girl at a bus stop in Little Rock. The fifteen-year old girl, Elizabeth Eckford, had just been refused admittance to Central High School by the Arkansas National Guard and was surrounded by a mob of taunting whites.[44]

The gray-haired, middle-aged Grace Lorch had already created more than a little havoc during the otherwise calm proceedings in Memphis. On the first day, when subcommittee chief investigator Frank Schroeder asked Lorch to meet briefly in executive session with the subcommittee staff, she loudly refused. Lorch said she would see subcommittee member William Jenner (the Republican senator from Indiana and a former ally of Joe McCar-

43. Ibid., 68; Glen, *Highlander*, 21–25 and 44–45.

44. *Congressional Record*, 86th Cong., 1st sess., 1959, 105, pt. 2:2318; Lee and Grace Lorch, 10 March 1958, RG46, Name File 1, Lorch, Senate Internal Security Subcommittee Papers; Communism and Racial Agitation, 29 October 1957, RG46, Name File 1, Lorch, Senate Internal Security Subcommittee Papers.

thy) "up a tree" before she would attend any executive session. She also asked for legal representation and the opportunity to testify with "a whole room full of people listening." As Lorch verbally jabbed at subcommittee chief counsel Robert Morris, reporters overheard Lorch's thirteen-year-old daughter Alice comment that she'd like to throw a brick at Jenner.[45]

A day after her first exchange with SISS members, Lorch delivered her testimony as the hearing's final witness in front of a packed house. Before the subcommittee, she answered every question with the statement, "I am here under protest." Not a man to take such affronts to the subcommittee lightly, Jenner pounded the table, clenched his fist, and shouted, "You're a troublemaker, aren't you?" Responding to Lorch's claims that she had only been called before the SISS because she had comforted a black girl in Little Rock, Jenner said, "We don't care about Little Rock. We are concerned with the threat of communism to this nation. We want to know if you were a member of the Communist Party in Boston." Turning to the crowd, Jenner then exclaimed, "This woman came here to try to disrupt this proceeding. If she's not going to answer questions I think she should be excused and cited for contempt." The crowd broke into applause mixed with Rebel yells.[46]

Grace Lorch was never charged with contempt, but the Communist label followed the Lorches thereafter wherever they went in the South. Immediately following Grace's appearance before the SISS in Memphis, the Lorches were pursued under the state's Communist Registration Act by Bruce Bennett, Arkansas's segregationist and anti-Communist attorney general. This 1951 law required that Communists register with the state police or face a thousand-dollar fine and/or two years in prison. But the case never panned out, nor did Eastland's efforts to promote federal legislation ensuring states' rights to enforce antisedition laws.[47]

45. "Georgia Farmer Defies 20 Queries at Red Probe," *Atlanta Constitution*, 29 October 1957, p. 11; "Chief Investigator Is Dealt Surprise by Irate Arkansan," *Memphis Commercial Appeal*, 29 October 1957, p. 1.

46. *Communism in the Mid-South, Hearings before the Subcommittee to Investigate the Administration of the Internal Security Act and other Internal Security Laws of the Committee of the Judiciary, United States Senate, 85th Congress, First Session* (Washington: United States Government Printing Office, 1957). Also see "Mrs. Lorch Gets Contempt Threat," *Nashville Banner*, 30 October 1957, p. 1.

47. "Dr. Lorch to Leave Little Rock," *Arkansas Democrat*, 28 May 1958, p. 17; Bennett to Jenner, 31 October 1957, RG46, Name File 1, Lorch, Senate Internal Security Subcommittee Papers; *Congressional Record*, 85th Cong., 2nd sess., 1958, 104, pt. 14:18925–30.

Nevertheless, with its hearings on Communism in the mid-South, SISS had begun to entrench in the public's mind accusations that red and black conspirators were at work in the region. Targeting key figures such as the Lorches, the Bradens, and Don West, along with key organizations such as the SCEF, the SRC, the NAACP, and the Highlander Folk School, SISS focused the efforts of "little HUACs" and "little FBIs" on ferreting out allegedly subversive activities in southern states. Indeed, cooperation between federal and state agencies such as the FBI, SISS, HUAC, GCE, JLCS, and state law-enforcement bodies led to the creation of a network of red and black investigators equal to the conspiracy they envisioned. Over the next decade, the network would continue to grow as southern nationalists reacted to civil rights activism and took advantage of growing cold-war tensions.

J. Edgar Hoover had helped fuel the southern red scare by sharing the FBI's extensive files on civil rights officials with SISS and HUAC. These committees in turn provided the basic lists of names and affiliations used by the states to reveal the red associations of civil rights workers. But Hoover and the committees offered more than information to the states; they provided an institutional example. Southern red and black investigating groups took great pride in the "little HUAC" and "little FBI" labels. They successfully applied FBI and HUAC tactics to the state and local level. While the "little FBIs" gathered information about activists with ties to Communist fronts, "little HUACs" used it publicly to undermine the civil rights movement. At stake was southern state security against Communist subversion and integration, issues southern nationalists associated with national security. GBI, SSC, GCE, and JLCS officials who sought out red and black conspirators convinced themselves they were g-men searching out a subversive enemy that was destroying the southern way of life. But civil rights activism would not cease. As the Second Reconstruction threatened to become a reality in every southern state, reaction, in the form of a southern red scare continued to intensify. Those southern states that had not yet joined the campaign against red and black would do so, just as the FBI would institute a counterintelligence program (COINTELPRO) targeting leading black activists in the country, including Martin Luther King.[48]

48. O'Reilly, *"Racial Matters,"* 41–44.

CONSPIRACY SO IMMENSE

4

IN EARLY 1959 ROBERT H. W. WELCH JR., A FUDGE AND candy manufacturer from Massachusetts, gathered eleven of his friends in an Indianapolis hotel and founded the John Birch Society. Named for a Christian missionary and American serviceman who had been killed by Red Chinese soldiers in 1945, the organization spread rapidly in its first two years. It was a semisecret network of "Americanists" dedicated to fighting Communists and avenging Birch's death. Ironically, the group adopted some of Communism's own clandestine and ruthless tactics, including the curtailment of civil liberties and the repression of dissent. For Welch and the Birchers, most domestic programs were socialistic "welfarism" and a Communist plot to destroy the Republic. He reviled Earl Warren, telling his followers that their campaign to impeach the chief justice would deliver a crippling blow to international Communism. In the same vein, Welch portrayed the *Brown* decision as a product of "radicalism" within the Supreme Court that aided Russia's attempt to "absorb" the United States. To his disciples, Welch was a hero who was bravely rallying the true believers for the decisive battle against Communism.[1]

The Birch Society was to be the cutting edge of the new radical right. The 1960s would begin not only with the political triumph of a young, activist, progressive president, but also, and perhaps not coincidentally, with the emergence of a new American reactionary movement whose members *Time* magazine labeled the ultras. By the close of the 1950s, Americans worried about the problems of the cold war—Cuba, Berlin, Laos, and the H-bomb—but those problems seemed so distant and massive to individual citizens that they despaired of being able to do anything about them. Those frustrations provided the breeding ground for the ultra movement, whose leaders offered ready-made solutions to apparently insoluble problems. Like fundamentalists who promise to make a remote, transcendent God imma-

1. George Barrett, "Close-up of the Birchers' 'Founder,'" *New York Times Magazine*, 14 May 1961, pp. 13, 89, 91–92.

nent, leaders of the radical right promised to make Communism a tangible problem with which the average American could come to grips. As had the McCarthyites of the previous decade, they argued that the real threat to the nation's security resided not so much in Sino-Soviet imperialism overseas but in Communist subversion at home. Appealing to the American penchant for action, they urged their followers to fight this subversion by keeping a close eye on their fellow citizens, scrutinizing voting records, writing letters, and generally raising a hue and cry across the land. If they could not fight the Communists in Cuba or Laos, at least they could smite the ones alleged to be at their elbow.[2]

It was in this environment that southern nationalism and the southern red scare flourished. Not all ultras were southern nationalists and not all southern nationalists were ultras, but at times their goals and tactics were indistinguishable. The Little Rock crisis and the Soviet Union's launching of *Sputnik* had created a nexus within which southerners could claim that the twin evils of Communism and integration were on the rise. Over the next few years, the civil rights movement's direct-action efforts and the continuing tense relationship between the cold war superpowers only strengthened their hand. State and federal investigators responded by casting a broad net that snared a number of preachers, teachers, and activists thought to be using integration to promote the larger Communist cause. Their efforts, however, produced mixed results. While the network of southern red and black investigators continued to grow and gain significant victories over its enemies, its powers were limited.

In at least one state, concerns for civil liberties limited investigators' abilities to pursue Communists in the civil rights movement. South Carolina set up a body to scrutinize red and black collusion but remained leery of granting it the power given to similar institutions elsewhere in the South. Of all the "little HUACs" and "little FBIs," South Carolina's was in many ways the least destructive.

The South Carolina General Assembly created the Committee to Investigate Communist Activities (CICA) in early 1958. The body was principally the brain child of Governor George Bell Timmerman. Like many segregationists in the South, Timmerman assumed that subversives would use the racial turmoil in the region to foster their own agenda. Acting on

2. "The Ultras: Ultraconservative Anti-Communism," *Time*, 8 December 1961, pp. 22–25.

this assumption in 1956, the governor pushed through legislation outlawing the state's employment of NAACP members. A year later Timmerman supported the firing of faculty members at two all-black institutions in Columbia—Allen University and Benedict College—for alleged Communist ties. The faculty members and their comrades, according to Timmerman, were "looking toward an ultimate Communist goal of creating civil and racial disorder." In January 1958, the governor finally authorized the creation of the state's own little HUAC. Although Timmerman lost the 1958 election, the investigative committee he created carried the battle against a red and black menace into the next administration.[3]

In its initial report, the state legislative investigating committee made clear its ties to similar federal and state agencies. The committee employed George Bishop, a former FBI agent, as general counsel and established official ties with the Senate Internal Security Subcommittee (SISS) and House Un-American Activities Committee (HUAC). It also declared its intention to work closely with South Carolina Law Enforcement Division personnel and with Stanley Morse of Charleston.

Morse was in many ways the state's foremost southern nationalist. A Harvard-educated agricultural expert, he had come to South Carolina in 1926 as a freelance consultant to inspect farms for Judge J. H. Marion near Chester. A year later he purchased a plantation in Sumter County and a home on Wadmalaw Island. In 1944, at the age of sixty, Morse moved to Morocco to serve with the Foreign Economics Administration as chief of the American Food Mission to French North Africa. When he returned to Wadmalaw Island after World War II, he became president and co-founder of the states' rights–oriented, anti-Communist Charleston County Citizens' League. From this organization Morse went on to build the Grass Roots League in the early 1950s.

The Grass Roots League was ostensibly a nonprofit, nonpolitical, patriotic organization devoted to civic fact-finding and furnishing information to the public. Its newsletters could be found in the mailboxes of every prominent segregationist in the South. As its main editorialist, Morse wrote and

3. "Bearcoats Says He Has Never Been Communist," *The State*, 8 February 1958; "S. C. College Controversy Spotlighted," *Southern School News*, March 1958, p. 4; "Body to Probe Communist Activity in State Is Set Up," *Charleston News and Courier*, 19 April 1958. Also see Joyce Johnston, "Communism vs. Segregation: Evolution of the Committee to Investigate Communist Activities in South Carolina," *Proceedings of the South Carolina Historical Association* (Columbia: University of South Carolina, 1993).

spoke tirelessly about the destructive forces of Communism at work in all aspects of society and particularly in race relations. In one of the league's more widely distributed pamphlets titled "Negroes Menaced by Red Plot," he argued that "intelligent, loyal" Americans would recognize the Communist drive among blacks and work to "preserve our free American heritage" against the forces promoting integration. As the league's leader, Morse also lobbied state politicians, HUAC, and other friends in government including U.S. senator Strom Thurmond of South Carolina, whom he warned about an "aggressive pro-negro drive . . . instigated and directed by Red Plotters against the U.S."[4]

But despite a close relationship with Morse and others clearly convinced of Communist influence in the civil rights movement, the South Carolina Committee to Investigate Communist Activities was relatively inactive. Like a host of state and federal agencies, CICA concluded in its first report that Communist doctrine had "failed to take widespread root among the colored race in South Carolina." But unlike many agencies, CICA never acted on the potential threat of reds in the movement. Although it was empowered to recommend legislation to combat Communism in the state, the committee failed to have any measure enacted during its first five years of existence. Moreover, at the height of what was developing into a full-blown red and black hunt in other southern states in 1961, CICA restricted itself to a relatively innocuous program designed to educate the state on Communism.

Individual members of the South Carolina Committee acted to moderate the group's activities. J. P. Strom, head of the State Law Enforcement Division and CICA's principal liaison with the state police, vowed to limit the committee's power after he had visited Mississippi. He considered the Mississippi Sovereignty Commission's tactics to be reckless and ill advised. Moreover the committee as a whole agreed that the use of a government agency for what might be called propaganda was improper. While these committeemen and white South Carolinians in general were devoted segregationists and anti-Communists, many understood that an unrestrained

4. "Chronology," "Biographical Sketch," and Morse to Thurmond, 17 December 1954, Box 9, Morse and Thurmond Correspondence 1952–1968 Folder, Morse Papers, South Caroliniana Library, University of South Carolina, Columbia. Also see "Negroes Menaced by Red Plot," Folder 18, Citizens' Council Collection, Mitchell Memorial Library, Mississippi State University.

anti-red and anti-black crusade in the state could hinder as much as help the southern nationalist cause.[5]

But the South Carolina Committee was an aberration. Most red and black investigating committees did not exhibit its caution. More typical was the Florida legislature's "little HUAC." With few self-imposed limitations placed on its investigative and communicative powers, the committee's achievements were ultimately confounded by its inability to prove that Communists had significantly influenced the civil rights movement. Even after acquiring the testimony of one of the country's most famous anti-Communist investigators, and scrutinizing dozens of members of groups supposedly influenced by Communists, the committee could not produce sufficient evidence of a red and black conspiracy.

Florida joined the southern red and black investigating network in the summer of 1956 when a bus boycott in Tallahassee led a special session of the Florida legislature to set up an interim committee to study the NAACP's role in "racial agitation." Inspired by the anti-NAACP investigations of the Texas legislature and the Georgia Commission on Education, the committee identified Communists as the instigators of the NAACP's efforts in the state and set out to eradicate the influence of both. The legislature would eventually renew the original interim committee as the Florida Legislative Investigation Committee and make representative Charley Johns of Starke its head. By the end of 1957, Johns wielded so much influence over the group that it became known simply as the Johns Committee.[6]

True to form, the Johns Committee held hearings in early 1958. On February 10, the committee and red and black investigators all over the South were treated to the testimony of one of the country's foremost experts on Communist fronts, J. B. Matthews. In the 1920s Matthews had been a Christian pacifist and a socialist. During the Depression he became the executive secretary of the Fellowship of Reconciliation, a leader of the Lovestoneite faction of the Communist Party, and a member of some fifteen Communist-front organizations. Historian Richard Gid Powers called him a "one-man front coalition, a microcosmic red network." In the late 1930s, Matthews eventually became disenchanted with Communist plotting and

5. Johnston, "Communism vs. Segregation."
6. "Anti-NAACP Committee Hires Tampan," *Tampa Tribune*, 19 October 1956; "Collins Lets NAACP Probe Pass," *Tampa Tribune*, 22 August 1956; M. J. Heale, *McCarthy's Americans* (Athens: University of Georgia Press, 1998), 263.

frustrated at the realization that the left would never be reunited. He denounced his front associations and turned to a life in business.[7]

Matthews emerged as an anti-Communist activist when the Communist Party of the United States tried to use a strike at Consumers' Research,
a product-testing organization he directed, to capture the company's workers for the party. He became convinced that the Communists were destroying the country's chances for any real progress for the masses. In 1938 he
wrote *Odyssey of a Fellow Traveler*, an alarmist memoir of his days with
the left. The same year, Martin Dies learned of Matthews through conservative columnist George Sokolsky. Between 1938 and 1945, Matthews served
as director of research for the House Un-American Activities Committee.
By the late 1940s, he was selling his files on fronts to anyone who would
buy them.

Like his southern counterparts, the venerable countersubversive was
prone to exaggeration. At no time was this more evident than in 1953 when,
working for Joe McCarthy as director of his Permanent Subcommittee on
Investigations, Matthews wrote "Reds and Our Churches." Appearing in
the *American Mercury*, the article advanced the controversial thesis that
"the largest single group supporting the Communist apparatus in the
United States today is composed of Protestant clergymen." This improbable
accusation immediately drew repudiation from all sides, including from
President Eisenhower. The president claimed such attacks weakened the
church, "the greatest American bulwark against atheistic materialism and
Communism," and, with Vice-President Richard Nixon, pressured McCarthy to fire Matthews.[8]

No longer employed by the federal government, Matthews nevertheless
continued his career as a Communist-front expert for hire. Indeed, just as
his star fell in Washington it rose in the South. His targeting of Protestant
clergymen actually furthered his credentials among conservatives in the region, particularly the religious right. Southern nationalists were often at
odds with church liberals. They considered Protestants who embraced racial and social change to be dangerous deviants, wittingly and unwittingly
supporting the Communist cause. Manning Johnson and another popular
black Communist turned anti-Communist for hire, Leonard Patterson, had

---

7. Richard Gid Powers, *Not without Honor* (New York: Free Press, 1995), 104.

8. Kenneth O'Reilly, *Hoover and the Un-Americans* (Philadelphia: Temple University
Press, 1983), 85; and Powers, *Not without Honor*, 267.

already profited from this notion during Louisiana's Joint Legislative Committee on Segregation hearings in March 1957. The state witnesses charged that religion was a principal tool of Communists hoping to win black converts and listed Reverend Martin Luther King; Reverend T. J. Jemison, a black Baptist minister from Baton Rouge; and Reverend A. L. Davis Jr., a minister from New Orleans, as religious leaders/civil rights activists under the spell of Communists.[9]

Matthews was a close associate of Myers Lowman, also an established red investigator for hire, who had contributed information on Highlander, Martin Luther King, and Tuskegee activist Charles Gomillion to the SISS for its October 1957 hearings. Matthews and Lowman sympathized with the view that churches involved in the civil rights struggle were vulnerable to Communist influence. In 1955, Lowman wrote to Matthews that anti-Communist midwesterners and southerners must lead the country toward a better spiritual life, one devoid of "materialistic matters, such as socialism, wages and hours, cooperatives, race, and other subjects."[10]

Information the pair had gathered about the National Council of Churches (NCC) would prove particularly appealing to southern conservatives. The NCC constituted a group of representatives from many of the nation's Protestant and Orthodox Christian denominations. Among its other activities, the National Council had issued resolutions denouncing racial prejudice and enacted programs designed to end segregation. Since its "Statement on the Churches and Segregation" in 1952, the NCC had officially taken a stand against segregation, maintaining that it was "diametrically opposed to what Christians believe about the worth of men." In keeping with this policy, the NCC had supported the *Brown* decision and Eisenhower's handling of the Little Rock crisis.

More important for segregationists, the NCC actually joined the activist ranks of the civil rights movement. It began to pressure its members to integrate their churches and in December 1955 set up a "Southern Project" to ameliorate interracial tensions where conflicts over the implementation of

9. Jay Hall, "Ex-Red Blasts Negro Pastors," *New Orleans Times-Picayune*, 9 March 1957. See also Samuel S. Hill Jr., *Southern Churches in Crisis* (New York: Holt, Rinehart, and Winston, 1966) and Samuel S. Hill Jr., *Religion and the Solid South* (Nashville: Abingdon Press, 1972).

10. Lowman Telephone Statement, 15 August 1957, RG46, Name File 3, King 56–59, Senate Internal Security Subcommittee Papers, National Archives; Lowman to Matthews, 20 May 1955, Box 83, Folder 6, J. B. Matthews Papers, Duke University.

the *Brown* decision were taking place. Through the project's efforts, the NCC made lasting contacts with groups that southern massive resisters had labeled subversive, including the Southern Regional Council (SRC), the Southern Christian Leadership Conference (SCLC), and the National Association for the Advancement of Colored People (NAACP).

These ties would have been more than enough to raise southern nationalists' suspicions, but the added scrutiny of the Citizens' Council, right-wing preachers Carl McIntyre and Billy James Hargis, and J. B. Matthews heightened their paranoia. Most significant, Matthews and McIntyre had participated in HUAC and FBI investigations of G. Bromley Oxnam, a Methodist bishop of Washington and president of the World Council of Churches, a group closely associated with the National Council. Oxnam had been a bona fide fellow traveler in the 1930s but had turned anti-Communist in the late 1940s. Matthews used his information about Oxnam's Communist ties and a 1935 Naval Intelligence report calling the NCC a Communist-front to label the NCC leadership red. The subsequent red and black investigation of the NCC would ultimately have an effect. According to historian James Findlay, efforts to link the NCC with Communism would contribute to a general "go-slow" environment in the organization throughout the late 1950s.[11]

In 1957 as mini-HUACS redoubled their efforts in the South, Matthews's interest in the NCC and other groups as part of the supposed red and black conspiracy proved profitable. With Lowman often serving as a go-between, Matthews sold his information about the NCC, NAACP, SCLC, Southern Conference Education Fund (SCEF), Highlander Folk School and other groups to southern red and black investigating commissions. He also shared notes directly with former Communist Party member and HUAC researcher Benjamin Mandel, who had been the research director for Eastland's SISS since 1950. The report Matthews delivered to Florida's Johns Committee in February 1958 was the culmination of his own efforts to uncover Communists in the civil rights movement.[12]

11. James Findlay Jr., *Church People in the Struggle: The National Council of Churches and the Black Freedom Movement, 1950–1970* (New York: Oxford University Press, 1993), 11–28; O'Reilly, *Hoover and the Un-Americans*, 82–86. Also see Neil McMillen, *The Citizens' Council: Organized Resistance to the Second Reconstruction, 1954–64* (Urbana: University of Illinois Press, 1971), 177–78.

12. "$960 Payment Goes to Witness at Red Hearings," *Arkansas Gazette*, 19 December 1958; Lowman to Matthews, 16 January 1957, Box 671, Folder Lowman 1957, Matthews Papers; Matthews to Lowman, 6 February 1957, Box 671, Folder Lowman 1957, Matthews

Appearing before the Johns Committee, Matthews drew familiar conclusions from his research. Communists, he argued, had agitated among African Americans in the South for thirty years, making "Negro liberation" or self-determination in the Black Belt their primary goal. Moreover, while Communists continued to seek violent revolution and the confiscation and redistribution of white wealth, they were joining protests against public-school integration to build associations with black leaders and stir racial conflict in the South. Finally, Matthews concluded, Communists were promoting a popular front and manipulating southern liberal organizations to further the goal of racial amalgamation and world conquest.

In reaching these conclusions, Matthews highlighted the activities of a number of non-Communist organizations "penetrated" by Communists, including the NCC, Highlander, the SRC, SCEF, and the NAACP. James Dombrowski, Aubrey Williams, Martin Luther King, and Rosa Parks all drew special mention for their affiliations with these groups. More for comparison than contrast, Matthews listed them alongside "sputnik" organizations, which included undisputed Communist fronts such as the African Blood Brotherhood, the American Negro Labor Congress, and the National Negro Congress.[13]

Matthews actually had little new to offer in the search for a red and black conspiracy. He addressed the usual suspects in the usual way. His friendship with Mandel had clearly been put to good use. His report was loaded with references to SISS hearings, particularly the 1954 investigation of SCEF. His observation that SCEF had the same leadership and purposes as the Communist-front SCHW came directly from James Eastland. Matthews's view of the NAACP was almost identical to J. Edgar Hoover's. He concluded that while the NAACP had fought openly against Communist infiltration, "prominent individuals connected with the NAACP have suc-

Papers; Matthews to Lowman, 14 February 1957, Box 671, Folder Lowman 1957, Matthews Papers; Lowman to Matthews, 18 February 1957, Box 671, Folder Lowman 1957, Matthews Papers; Matthews to Lowman, 27 February 1957, Box 671, Folder Lowman 1957, Matthews Papers; Lowman to McIntire, 9 April 1957, Box 671, Folder Lowman 1957, Matthews Papers; Lowman to Matthews, 23 August 1957, Box 671, Folder Lowman 1957, Matthews Papers; Matthews to Lowman, 5 December 1957, Box 671, Folder Lowman 1957, Matthews Papers; Matthews to Mandel, 8 December 1957, Box 692, Folder Mandel to JBM 54–69, Matthews Papers. See also Ellen Schrecker, *Many Are the Crimes: McCarthyism in America* (Boston: Little, Brown, 1998), 393.

13. "Communists, Negroes, and Integration," Box 714, Folder Communists, Negroes, and Integration, Matthews Papers.

cumbed to the appeals of the Communist-front apparatus." In sum Matthews claimed that "Communists or Communist influence were directly involved in every major race incident of the past four years since the Supreme Court 'legislated' on the subject of integration."[14]

While he could not add a smoking gun to the case against the civil rights movement, Matthews successfully summarized the findings of national and southern-state investigative agencies. He also put his reputation as a longtime red investigator behind the charges that Communists and blacks were in cahoots, and he tied these accusations to the idea that religious organizers associated with the civil rights movement were also subversive. For these reasons, the testimony eventually drew a great deal of attention from southern conservatives.

In the months following the hearing, the Georgia Commission on Education (GCE) distributed Matthews's testimony before the Johns Committee in a two-volume pamphlet titled "Communism and the NAACP." Like the Highlander article, the Matthews diatribe drew an enormous response from southern groups, including American Legion posts, conservative church organizations, and law-enforcement offices.[15]

Southern liberals, meanwhile, were outraged at the Johns Committee investigations and particularly at its targeting of the Tallahassee Council on Human Relations. In December 1957, the committee had employed the same cloak-and-dagger techniques the GCE had used at Highlander. A photographer hired by the committee poked his camera into a council meeting room, snapped pictures, and fled.[16]

The harassment of the council continued at the February hearings. There the organization's treasurer, who was appearing as a witness, declared that "when the committee called me, it cast aspersions on me and the organization I represent." He was ordered from the stand. The American Civil Liberties Union (ACLU) denounced the committee and its actions, calling the hearings "cynical political opportunism" and labeling Charley Johns

14. "Communists, Negroes, and Integration," Box 714, Folder Communists, Negroes, and Integration, Matthews Papers; "Communism and the NAACP," Box 671, Folder Lowman 1958, Matthews Papers; and "Florida Legislative Group Probes 'Communist' Role," *Southern School News*, March 1958, p. 5.

15. Lowman to Matthews, 12 February 1958, Box 671, Folder Lowman 1958, Matthews Papers; "Communism and the NAACP," RG46, Subject Files, NAACP Pamphlets, Senate Internal Security Subcommittee Papers; Heale, *McCarthy's Americans*, 263.

16. "Race Probe Hinted," *Miami News*, 15 December 1958.

"politically irresponsible." For their outspoken opposition, ACLU and NAACP representatives were questioned by the committee in Miami later that month.[17]

The Johns Committee hearings in Miami followed J. B. Matthews's lead in pursuing the Communist affiliations of religious leaders involved in the civil rights struggle. The committee subpoenaed some thirty witnesses, including the Reverend Theodore Gibson. An African American, an Episcopal minister, and a leader of the Miami NAACP, Gibson had been involved in litigation attacking school segregation and pupil-assignment laws in Florida.

While waiting to testify, Gibson listened to representative W. C. Herrell of Dade County declare that any person refusing to cooperate with the committee and answer all questions "was not fit to be a citizen of this state." Following the Tallahassee hearings, Gibson had promised that NAACP officials called before the committee would answer questions and not invoke the Fifth Amendment, but Herrell's statement struck a nerve. Gibson decided to refuse to submit to Johns Committee questioning. Herrell's attempt at intimidation, Gibson said, had shown the committee to be lacking in the necessary objectivity to conduct a fair hearing. "I am not a Communist, a Communist sympathizer or otherwise," the activist priest declared before he stalked out of the hearing room. He and fourteen others who also refused to testify were cited for contempt. Although the hearings ended with no testimony from key witnesses entered into the record, Charley Johns remained determined to link the NAACP with the Communist conspiracy.[18]

The committee's report to the state legislature reflected that determination. Relying primarily on J. B. Matthews's testimony, the report declared that Gibson's organization had been "the prime target of communist penetration for the past 30 years." Moreover, Communists had registered "a degree of success in penetrating the NAACP which is not paralleled in the case of any other non-communist organization of comparable size." The Johns Committee alleged that, of the 256 officers of the civil rights group, 145, or 61 percent, had recorded affiliations with Communist organizations.

17. "Florida Legislative Group Probes 'Communist' Role," *Southern School News*, March 1958, p. 5.

18. "Florida Lawmakers Push Probe of Racial Affairs," *Southern School News*, April 1958, p. 9; "10 More Cited in Reds Hunt," *Miami Herald*, 28 February 1958, p. 1.

While these individuals were not necessarily Communists, the committee made clear, they had "knowingly or unknowingly aided the Communist cause in this country."

The committee admitted, however, that while it was convinced of the NAACP's ties to Communist causes, it was unable to determine the degree to which Communists had penetrated the Florida group. Gibson's and the other witnesses' refusal to testify in Miami had severely hampered the investigation as had court action initiated by the priest. Hoping to overturn his contempt conviction, Gibson charged that the committee had violated its mandate, was prejudiced, and was only seeking to embarrass and harass the civil rights movement. After the Florida Supreme Court found that the committee had not abused its power, Gibson's lawyers appealed. Eventually the case reached the United States Supreme Court. The Court issued a stay order while it considered *Gibson v. Committee*. According to the committee, the central legal issue before the Court involved the preservation of states' rights against an encroaching federal power. Once and for all, the committee hoped, the case would put an end to "federal control of state action" in pursuing subversives.[19]

While the Court reviewed *Gibson*, the House Un-American Activities Committee became involved in a case that ran parallel to the Florida conflict. In hearings held in Atlanta in late July 1958 on "Communist Infiltration and Activities in the South," HUAC again pursued some familiar characters in the alleged red and black conspiracy. Once more the committee put Carl Braden and SCEF at center stage. Although the committee, along with other federal and state agencies, had had ample opportunity to specify Braden's activities in hearings between 1954 and 1958, HUAC insisted there was more to reveal about Braden's and his wife's roles as alleged liaisons between the Communist Party and the civil rights movement. This time though, Braden, like Gibson, had had enough. While Gibson would test a state legislative committee's ability to question witnesses, Braden would test a federal committee's.

HUAC justified its continuing scrutiny of Braden with the assumption that, because Communists worked continuously and surreptitiously, there would always be more to know. Georgia governor Marvin Griffin delivered

---

19. "Part II: Report of the Florida Legislative Investigation Committee to the 1959 Session of the Legislature," Series 1486, Carton 1, Florida Legislative Investigation Committee Papers, Florida State Archives.

the opening statement at the hearings and outlined the problems confronted by the committee in this regard: "We know that the Communist conspiracy in our country has gone underground during recent years; that there is no such thing as a card-carrying Communist." Griffin also outlined the conservative political motive of the hearing from a southern nationalist's perspective. The committee's task, as the governor saw it, was to protect the South from those "who would exchange the great American system of States Rights and local self-government for totalitarian dictatorship."

On July 30 HUAC's presiding officer in Atlanta, Edwin Willis, the segregationist representative from Louisiana, called Carl Braden to testify. Braden identified himself as "a worker in the integration movement in the South" and an employee of SCEF. When asked about his associations with Harvey O'Connor (chairman of a Communist front called the Emergency Civil Liberties Committee and himself a "hard-core" member of the Communist conspiracy, according to HUAC staff director Richard Arens), Braden refused to answer, claiming that the question fell outside the committee's scope. Arens explained that "responsible witnesses" had identified Braden as a Communist "masquerading behind a facade of humanitarianism." Braden replied that Arens was misinformed and that his own beliefs and associations were "none of the business of this committee."

In refusing to answer, Braden, like Theodore Gibson, cited his First Amendment rights to free speech and free association rather than his Fifth Amendment right not to reveal evidence that might incriminate him. He and the committee knew full well the consequences of this distinction. A decade earlier, the famous Hollywood Ten had refused to answer HUAC's questions on the same grounds and had been held in contempt of Congress. Their convictions would be upheld in the federal courts, and each of the ten would spend from six months to a year in jail. Braden hoped for another contempt citation and legal challenge. Chairman Willis immediately understood the significance of Braden's tactics and asked him again, for the record, about his refusal to testify. Again the SCEF worker insisted that he challenged the committee's right to question him about his affiliations based on the First Amendment's protection of free belief and association.

At this point the hearing became a battle of two visions of American freedom that contrasted the southern conservative's view with the liberal integrationist's philosophy. Arens interjected that if HUAC could not "solicit from a citizen information respecting the operation within the confines of the border of this Godless, atheistic conspiracy, God help this country."

Braden replied with a glance at Willis: "Are you saying integration is communism like they do in Louisiana?" Answering his own question Braden continued: "Integration is what you are investigating. All the people here are integrationists." Indeed, most of those called were active in some way in the civil rights movement. Representative Donald Jackson of California retorted that the committee was not interested in integration or segregation but in the Communist conspiracy. What the committee wanted to know was whether Braden had agitated for civil rights "out of American principles" or "out of any sympathy for the Communist cause." Braden answered, "Anything I do is done by American principles," and presented the committee with a petition signed by two hundred black leaders in the South protesting the Atlanta hearings. Jackson looked at the list and stated for the record that a number of the signers of the letter were "closely associated with the Communist Party."[20]

The petition, whose signers included a reluctant Martin Luther King, posed a risk to its supporters. Braden was a lifelong proponent of liberal and leftist causes. He had grown up in Louisville, the son of a railroad-shop worker. His father had been an ardent follower of Eugene Debs. In 1922 the elder Braden had been fired after joining a strike, leaving the family temporarily hungry and eight-year-old Carl permanently scarred. Because of that traumatic experience, young Braden had come to identify himself with the have-nots; he saw the lost strike as a symbol of the world's injustices. Like his father, he became a devout socialist. With his wife Anne, a committed integration activist, he also worked for a range of groups, some of which appeared on the attorney general's list of subversive organizations and others that were decidedly less radical. The pair's affiliations included Henry Wallace's Progressive Party, the NAACP, the Negro Labor Council, and SCEF. Although only hearsay evidence pointed to the Bradens' membership in the Communist Party, it was safe to say that they held radical political beliefs while working as civil rights activists. The black leaders who signed the petition were thus in danger of validating the claims that the movement was influenced by Marxists.[21]

20. *Communist Infiltration and Activities in the South: Hearings before the Committee on Un-American Activities, House of Representatives, 85th Congress, Second Session, July 29, 30, and 31, 1958* (Washington: United States Government Printing Office, 1958).

21. David Garrow, *Bearing the Cross* (New York: William Morrow, 1986), 155; Richard Fried, *Nightmare in Red* (New York: Oxford University Press, 1990),174–76; Anne Braden, *The Wall Between* (New York: Monthly Review Press, 1958).

Frank Wilkinson's testimony immediately followed Braden's. Wilkinson, too, was a member of a number of radical organizations and refused to answer questions on the same grounds as Braden. The committee then called Hunter Pitts O'Dell. O'Dell had been identified as a Communist by Arthur Eugene at a February 1957 HUAC hearing in New Orleans. Committee members questioned him in Atlanta about his association with the National Maritime Union and other Communist fronts, but he refused to answer citing "the First and Fifth Amendments, and any other amendment of the Constitution that offers me support and protection from not [*sic*] being prosecuted." For his invocation of the Fifth Amendment, O'Dell, who would later work for the SCLC and draw the further scrutiny of red and black investigators, escaped contempt charges. Braden and Wilkinson did not. The House cited the two for contempt on August 13, 1958. On December 2, a federal grand jury in Atlanta indicted Carl Braden and Frank Wilkinson. Like Gibson they both appealed their cases to the Supreme Court.[22]

The cast would be larger still. In December 1958, just as federal prosecutors were indicting Wilkinson and Braden, Arkansas's segregationist and anti-Communist attorney general Bruce Bennett joined the fray, issuing his own charges against Braden, SCEF, and others he associated with a red and black conspiracy.

In the build-up to the integration crisis in Little Rock, Arkansas conservatives had begun to institutionalize their anti-red and anti-black efforts, with Bennett leading the way. He and other Arkansas segregationists convinced the governor to sign off on the state's own Sovereignty Commission in the spring of 1957. Governor Orval Faubus acquiesced to the bill legalizing the Arkansas SSC, despite warnings that it might become an "Arkansas Gestapo." The governor had already made his own move to the right and was wary of Bennett's political ambition. Arkansas's commission never amounted to anything like Mississippi's SSC, but Bennett was able to use

22. *Communist Infiltration and Activities in the South: Hearings before the Committee on Un-American Activities, House of Representatives, 85th Congress, Second Session, July 29, 30, and 31, 1958* (Washington: United States Government Printing Office, 1958); SCEF News, 2 December 1958, MS425, Box 1, Braden Papers, University of Tennessee; SCEF News, 11 December 1958, MS425, Box 1, Braden Papers; SCEF News, 21 January 1959, MS425, Box 1, Braden Papers; SCEF News, 10 March 1960, MS425, Box 1, Braden Papers; SCEF News, 11 April 1960, MS425, Box 1, Braden Papers; SCEF News, 6 May 1960, MS425, Box 1, Braden Papers; SCEF News, 24 May 1960, MS425, Box 1, Braden Papers; SCEF News, 22 November 1960, MS425, Box 1, Braden Papers.

another body, the Education Committee of the Arkansas Legislative Council, to publicly expose an alleged Communist conspiracy in the civil rights movement.[23]

On December 16, 17, and 18, 1958, Bennett and the Legislative Council held televised hearings to prove that "Communists are behind racial unrest in Arkansas." The first day of the hearings focused on state NAACP leaders L. C. and Daisy Bates. Bennett presented photographs showing the Bateses having breakfast with former vice-president Henry A. Wallace and two white men identified by state witnesses as Communists, Leonard Farmer and Ladislav Pushkarski. Leonard Farmer had indeed been an active Communist until 1947, when he moved from Connecticut to Arkansas and set up a law practice. He subsequently became a minor celebrity in the state when an Arkansas court awarded his ex-wife custody of their two children, citing Farmer's Communist past. Pushkarski, according to his brother's testimony, had moved to Poland years earlier and could not be reached for questioning. At the close of the day, however, Farmer's and Pushkarski's link to the Bateses, other than sharing space in a photograph, remained a mystery.[24]

On the second day, Bennett called J. B. Matthews as a state witness. Borrowing from his Florida text, Matthews referred to a "bridge" between southern liberals and Communism. Among the groups crucial to the Communists, Matthews repeated, were the SCHW/SCEF and Southern Regional Council, groups that shared some fifty members. L. C. Bates, Matthews continued, had been a board member of SCEF, while Daisy Bates had served on the board of the Southern Regional Council. The state's key witness also brought up the now familiar names of Lee and Grace Lorch, who had been identified the day before by Arkansas representative Oren Harris, as among some forty-one persons involved in Communist-front groups working in Arkansas. Indeed, Matthews reported, when Grace Lorch had comforted Elizabeth Eckford before the cameras during the Little Rock crisis, she had acted on instructions from "her Communist masters." After the lunch recess, Bennett joined Matthews and identified the Communists and Communist

23. "'Public Opinion' Bennett Target," *Arkansas Gazette*, 15 December 1958; Roy Reed, *Faubus: The Life and Times of an American Prodigal* (Fayetteville: University of Arkansas Press, 1997), 186–88.

24. "Attack Threat Made against Probe Witness," *Arkansas Gazette*, 19 December 1958; "Names, Groups Listed As Red Probe Opens," and "Two Linked to Communism at Probe," 17 December 1958, *Arkansas Gazette*, pp.1 and 8a.

sympathizers highlighted in a film made of the May Day, 1957, meeting at the Highlander Folk School. Groups to which the Bateses, Lorches, and Bradens belonged were all represented.[25]

On the final day of the hearings, other familiar faces appeared. Bennett called Manning Johnson to testify. Johnson again attacked the NAACP as "Communist dominated" and declared his support for Governor Faubus's action in blocking the Little Rock nine from entering Central High. Bennett also called former FBI agent W. Guy Banister, who had testified in the JLCS hearings in New Orleans. Banister confirmed Johnson's claims that Communism was indeed behind the racial unrest in Arkansas.[26]

Two months later, in February 1959, Arkansas attorney general Bennett offered his services to Tennessee officials if they brought legal action against Highlander. The Tennessee legislature immediately responded to Bennett's proposal and began its own probe of subversive activities at Highlander. Armed with GCE material, the 1954 SISS hearings, and Bennett's findings from the 1958 Arkansas Legislative Council, the Highlander investigating committee held the first of its hearings later that month. The closed session heard the testimony of local witnesses who expanded on their suspicions that Highlander participated in "Communist activities." A second hearing a few days later echoed the first but also included some testimony that Highlander had violated its tax-exempt charter. The final round of hearings, which closely followed the first two, focused on the statements of Myles Horton and Bruce Bennett. Horton testified that neither he nor any Highlander student, teacher, or official was a Communist, subscribed to Communist publications, or solicited contributions from Communist groups. Bennett scoffed at this and diagramed on a blackboard Arkansas's version of the southern red and black conspiracy. Highlander was at the center, connected by arrows to SCEF, Carl and Anne Braden, Lee and Grace Lorch, and Charles Gomillion, a Tuskegee Institute dean who was associated with SCEF and had been involved in a court battle to prevent the discriminatory gerrymandering of his home district in Alabama. When asked by the committee what he thought Bennett's diagram proved, Horton re-

25. "Reds, Integration Linked by Ex-aide to McCarthy," *Arkansas Gazette,* 18 December 1958, p. 1.

26. "Hearings End; Red Probers See Success," *Arkansas Gazette,* 19 December 1958, p. 1, and "Little Rock a Red Plot, Negro Says," *Atlanta Constitution,* 19 December 1958, p. 1.

plied that it proved Bennett could "write a name and write other names and draw lines between them."[27]

Following up on Horton's testimony, Highlander published a more [129 lengthy response to the state's charges. In "Who Is a Subversive?" Marion Wright, vice-president of the Southern Regional Council and a former attorney in South Carolina, argued that red- and black-baiters, not the advocates of black civil rights, were the true subversives. While the civil rights movement upheld the Constitution's guarantes of free speech and equality under the law regardless of race, segregationists were advocating disrespect for federal law. Southern politicians may not have committed violent acts against blacks in the South, but they had advocated them. Indeed, their words and deeds followed "patterns devised in Moscow." Southern politicians had given their people something to fear and then attempted to rescue them from the fictitious peril. They had throttled "opposition so that it cannot be heard." While denouncing Communism, "they imitate it," harassing and persecuting the opposition. They had finally succumbed to the "orgy of McCarthyism." Indeed, Wright charged, southern states had created committees on subversive activities that relied on "professional witnesses" manufactured by McCarthy and his underlings. Their "inquisitions" were helping to rear a generation of white children who believed the "federal government is something foreign, alien, hostile."[28]

Wright's powerful argument, that southern nationalism had in it the seeds of totalitarianism, fell on deaf ears in Tennessee. In its final report, the Tennessee legislature's Highlander committee recommended the revocation of the school's charter for legal and financial transgressions. While circumstantial evidence pointed to Highlander as a "meeting place for known Communists or fellow-travelers," the committee actually indicted the school on technicalities involving restrictions for nonprofit institutions and welfare corporations. Still, the final reckoning was yet to come. The local district attorney obtained warrants from the Eighteenth Judicial Circuit Court to raid the Highlander campus. There he found evidence that alcohol was being sold and distributed on the school grounds, an illegal act

27. Myles Horton, *The Long Haul: An Autobiography* (New York: Teachers College Press, 1998), 108–109.

28. "Who Is a Subversive?" 23 May 1959, Box 19, Highlander FS Folder, Yarmolinsky Papers, John F. Kennedy Library.

Arkansas Attorney General Bruce Bennett diagrams the connections between the Highlander Folk School and alleged subversives. Photograph taken in Tennessee, 1959. *Wisconsin Historical Society*

given that the school did not have a liquor license. The judge overseeing the case ordered Highlander's doors padlocked in September 1959. Six months later he revoked the school's charter. Although Highlander leaders reopened a research-and-education center in Knoxville, southern anti-Communist segregationists had achieved a significant victory in helping to bring down one of the South's pioneering civil rights institutions.[29]

The revocation of Highlander's charter came just as the civil rights movement was expanding its direct-action efforts to include sit-ins. The Greensboro protests inspired a new generation of activists who were committed to employing confrontational, nonviolent means to highlight the injustices of segregation. But it also elicited accusations that the movement's tactics promoted increased "racial hatred" and thus furthered the divide-and-conquer tactics of the Communists. Indeed, for those concerned about

29. John M. Glen, *Highlander: No Ordinary School* (Knoxville: University of Tennessee Press, 1996), 230–50. See also "The Trouble at Highlander," Box 19, Highlander FS Folder, Yarmolinsky Papers.

red and black subversion, the sit-ins seemed a prime vehicle for Communist infiltration of the civil rights movement. J. Edgar Hoover called them "made-to-order" for the Communist Party. Even former president Harry S. Truman claimed that Communists were exploiting the sit-ins. Student Nonviolent Coordinating Committee leaders, including young Marion Barry Jr, denied both charges.[30]

Largely in response to the sit-in movement in Texas, the state's General Investigating Committee joined the list of "little HUACs" in 1960. The Texas house of representatives formed the committee in hopes of determining the extent to which "outside influences" were violating property rights, fomenting breaches of the peace, and conducting economic boycotts. Explicit in the committee's objectives was the goal of revealing members of the "Communist Party, known Communist Agents, underground Communist Agents, subversives not officially connected with the Communist Party, and professional agitators" who were active in sit-in demonstrations. It was also specifically concerned with "racial agitation" stirred by the NAACP. In 1960 that organization was still banned under a 1957 Smith County permanent injunction from practicing law—which included encouraging, instigating, financing, or soliciting lawsuits—and engaging in lobbying activities in the state.

The General Investigating Committee outlined the extent of its investigations in a report to the Texas legislature in 1961. It focused primarily on the late March 1960 sit-in demonstrations protesting the segregation of local businesses in and around Marshall, Texas. The committee charged "known Communists, Communist-fronts, and the NAACP" with aiding the demonstrators. It further held them responsible for creating the disorder that forced local authorities to arrest some protesters and disperse others with fire hoses.[31]

The featured villain in the committee's revelations was Doxey Wilkerson, a Bishop College professor of education, who trained and led students

30. "Sit-ins Made-to-Order for Reds, Hoover Says," *Birmingham Post-Herald*, 22 May 1961, p. 26; "Truman Links Reds to Sit-ins," *Florida Times-Union*, 13 June 1960; Vernon Louviere, "Red, Sit-in Link Charge Denied," *Nashville Tennessean*, 21 July 1960. See also "Fowler Urges Probe of Reds in Sitdowns," *Atlanta Journal*, 20 April 1960; David Lawrence, "Is Communism behind the Southern Lunch Counter Demonstrations?" *Atlanta Journal*, 21 April 1960; "Reds behind Sit-in Move, Group Told," *Montgomery Advertiser*, 22 February 1961.

31. Witt Memo, 3N160, Folder 8, Texas v. NAACP Papers, Center for American History, University of Texas.

from Bishop and from Wiley Negro College in the demonstrations around Marshall. According to the findings of the Intelligence Section of the Texas Department of Public Safety and "other official agencies"—including HUAC, the SISS, the FBI, and the Subversive Activities Control Board— Wilkerson had "reluctantly" resigned from the Communist Party in November 1957. But, the report added, he remained an advocate of its goals at the time of the sit-ins. Indeed, the Investigating Committee suggested that Wilkerson had resigned only to "go underground" to achieve Communist objectives in the racial field.

The Texas committee was mostly correct about Wilkerson's background, although it missed a few interesting points. Wilkerson had been one of the best-educated and most experienced black men in the Communist Party. He held a master's degree from the University of Kansas and had taught at Virginia State College and Howard University. He had also been an assistant to Gunner Myrdal when that prominent social scientist wrote *An American Dilemma.* By the early 1950s, his experience and education had made him a national committee member of the CP and one of its most respected theorists on racial questions.

Wilkerson's musings on black America, however, would ultimately contribute to his split with the Communists. As early as 1945 he began criticizing the Black Belt thesis, claiming it isolated the CP from the masses who were fighting for black equality. Nevertheless he remained committed to Communist discipline and acquiesced to the party's race policy for almost a decade. With Stalin's death in 1953, Wilkerson gained the opportunity to help change the party's stance on African Americans. For the next two years, he encouraged the CP to adopt a new tactic of "mass policy" on the race question. African Americans, he argued, were unimpressed with the Black Belt thesis. Moreover, the party's exaggerated estimates of "white chauvinism" within its ranks had also driven blacks away. For Wilkerson, repairing the fracture with the larger black community meant a policy of working "within the mass organizations" such as the NAACP to help bring about civil rights reform. Although many CP members who associated Stalin's reign with racial intolerance expressed their agreement in 1955, Wilkerson's stance put him at odds with the powerful Stalinist wing of the party.[32]

32. David A. Shannon, *The Decline of American Communism* (Chatham, N.J.: Chatham Bookseller, 1959), 63, 247, 262–65,

This came at a time when the Communist Party was beginning to disintegrate. In early 1956, Khrushchev's secret speech denouncing Stalin's regime fractured the CP within the Soviet Union and in other countries, including the United States. The invasion of Hungary a year later divided the party even further. Compounding this internal rift in the U.S. was J. Edgar Hoover's Counterintelligence Program (COINTELPRO). Under the program FBI agents successfully infiltrated the party and exacerbated the feuds that were already festering. By the time it held its 1957 convention, the American Communist Party was in complete disarray.[33]

Wilkerson's goal of a more democratic party that cooperated with other groups working for common goals, such as black equality, put him solidly in the camp of *Daily Worker* editor John Gates. Gates's group of unorthodox Communists ran headlong into William Z. Foster's Stalinists during the convention elections. When the Fosterites retook control of the party, the Gates faction, including Wilkerson, resigned its Communist Party membership.[34]

As the Texas report suggested, although Wilkerson was no longer a CP member he remained committed to Marxist-Leninist philosophy as a civil rights activist in the South. The Texas committee thus had real reason to suspect that Wilkerson was working to align movement goals with those of a radical proletariat. It had further reason to speculate that he was working for the Communist "underground." Wilkerson, like Whittaker Chambers, could have renounced his public affiliation with the Communist Party while secretly continuing to work for its hidden apparatus. Still, the committee had little evidence to support the accusation that his immediate job was to act as a liaison among "Communist controlled" groups, "fellow-travelers," and other "dupes" in Marshall. While Wilkerson did participate in a "definite conspiracy" (to use the Investigating Committee's words) to plan and execute demonstrations in Marshall, his comrades included mem-

33. Guenter Lewy, *The Cause That Failed: Communism in American Political Life* (New York: Oxford University Press, 1990), 116–17; Richard Gid Powers, *Secrecy and Power* (New York: Free Press, 1987), 339–40. See also Ellen Schrecker, "McCarthyism and the Decline of American Communism, 1945–1960," and Gerald Horne, "The Red and the Black: The Communist Party and African-Americans in Historical Perspective," in Michael E. Brown et al., eds., *New Studies in the Politics and Culture of U.S. Communism* (New York: Monthly Review Press, 1993).

34. Shannon, *Decline of American Communism*, 277–87, 345.

bers of the Southern Conference Education Fund and the NAACP, groups in no way directly controlled by the Communist Party.[35]

Nevertheless, student and movement workers, some connected to polygraph machines, testified to committee investigators that Wilkerson had instructed them in demonstration techniques in secret meetings at Wiley and Bishop Colleges in January 1960. Furthermore, according to the committee, Wilkerson had presided at organizational meetings for the sit-in movement before and after the Marshall incident. At an open meeting of the NAACP at Prairie View A&M College in December 1959, he had outlined procedures for forthcoming regional student sit-in demonstrations in Texas, Arkansas, Louisiana, Mississippi, and Tennessee. Wilkerson later organized students for demonstrations in Shreveport, Louisiana. The techniques of protest proposed by Wilkerson at each of these meetings, according to the report, were "highly organized and completely disciplined." The committee associated these qualities with "Communist Policy" and argued that the evidence contradicted claims that the sit-ins were "spontaneous."

In fact, by the time Marshall hit the headlines, the region-wide sit-ins were showing signs of becoming highly organized. By February and March, the demonstrations were increasingly influenced by national organizations such as the NAACP, CORE, and the SCLC, as the Texas report revealed. Lawyers, organizers, advice, and money from these groups helped channel the civil rights movement into a direct-action effort. The vast network of protest groups working together constituted, by definition, a conspiracy, and the General Investigating Committee hoped to prove, through Doxey Wilkerson's participation, that it was a Communist conspiracy.[36]

That Wilkerson was a Communist who had worked with many of the groups involved in the movement was undeniable. Phone taps ordered by the committee revealed that Wilkerson and his cohorts in the NAACP contacted leaders of the Highlander Folk School and SCEF, including Fred Shuttlesworth and James Dombrowski. Further investigations connected the sit-ins to the Congress of Racial Equality, the Fellowship of Reconciliation, and the Southern Christian Leadership Conference. All of this was only the "visible part of an iceberg," according to the report. The committee argued

35. Gerald Horne, *Black Liberation/Red Scare* (Newark: University of Delaware Press, 1994), 140 and 277.

36. Martin Oppenheimer, *The Sit-in Movement of 1960* (New York: Carlson Publishing, 1989), 44–46. See also Taylor Branch, *Parting the Waters: America in the King Years, 1954–1963* (New York: Simon and Schuster, 1988), 272–311.

that the ranks of those joining with known Communist fronts working for the civil rights movement were swelling to enormous proportions. The committee's extensive files allegedly revealed only a "small portion of the total conspiracy." The committee, however, never produced this evidence or showed how Wilkerson, or any other past or present Communist, had controlled civil rights protests or engaged in any illegal activity. Its conclusions rested entirely on the faulty logic of guilt by association.

The committee employed similarly poor reasoning when it claimed that the demonstrations were timed to aid international Communist goals. Taking a cue from accusations that had been recently issued by South Carolina governor James F. Byrnes, the report maintained that the sit-ins were coordinated with demonstrations abroad to influence the Eisenhower-Khrushchev summit conference. Race riots resulting from the demonstrations, the report elaborated, would place the United States on the defensive at the conference table. The protesters in the United States and abroad, the report concluded, actually sought "violence to achieve publicity and martyrdom."[37]

A public martyrdom of sorts was certainly a goal of the civil rights movement, but the suggestion that it was conceived as part of a global Communist plot was again highly exaggerated. The Texas committee, like so many in the South, hindered its own efforts with spurious logic and overt racial biases. In one of its more ridiculous moments, the report on the Marshall sit-ins implied that Wilkerson, the Communists, and their civil rights comrades imposed discipline through wild combinations of coercion and enticement. The report maintained that protesters found to be leaking information about tactics were actually beaten by other demonstrators. The committee also revealed its racist assumptions when it argued that some black participants were drawn "along the road of racial agitation" because Communists had given them the "red carpet" treatment, which included "invitations to predominantly white functions, liquor, and a selected group of white women."

Despite the committee's faulty reasoning, apparent racial bias, and lack of solid proof that movement actions were in any way directed by Moscow, it was able to use some of its findings in the Wilkerson case to justify ongoing legal harassment of the civil rights movement in Texas. Wilkerson

37. General Investigating Committee Report, Vol. III, 1961, 3N160, Folder 9, Texas v. NAACP Papers.

worked closely with black attorney Romeo Williams who, the committee discovered, had promised to help procure money and legal aid for arrested demonstrators from the NAACP. When the NAACP delivered thirty-five thousand dollars to Wiley and Bishop College protesters in mid-March 1960, committee investigators were sure it constituted a violation of the Smith County injunction banning NAACP aid to state lawsuits.

Just as the sit-ins in Texas and across the South were inspiring increasingly irrational fears among conservative whites that blacks were joining with Communists to foment racial strife, the country was also dealing with the excruciating loss of Cuba to Fidel Castro. While the civil rights movement alarmed segregationists by engaging in mass direct action on a regional scale, red and black investigators looked to Cuba as the new leader of the Communist plan to bring an independent Black Belt to the South. The White Citizens' Council, for example, made much of Castro's public wooing of American blacks. Fighting the red and black conspiracy thus took on new significance just as the cases against Carl Braden and Theodore Gibson came to a head.[38]

In many ways the litigation marked a showdown between the leaders of the southern red scare and those they accused of conspiring to change the southern way of life. Southern red and black investigators anticipated that the suits would reestablish both state and federal rights to create and enforce antisubversive laws. Braden, Gibson, and the groups they represented, meanwhile, hoped the litigation would end federal and state harassment of the civil rights movement. The outcome, all parties were convinced, would define or redefine the southern campaign against reds and blacks at the height of the civil rights struggle and the apex of the cold war.

From the outset Braden and his attorneys—who included John M. Coe of the National Lawyers Guild, a longtime resident on the U.S. attorney general's list of Communist fronts, and Conrad J. Lynn of the NAACP—understood the significance their case held for other victims of the southern red scare. They realized that Braden's conviction, if upheld, would open the way for widespread harassment of those who advocated civil rights for blacks. Their hope was that Braden's refusal to answer HUAC questions might be protected under rules limiting the questioning of congressional committees and by the First Amendment. If the Court decided with Braden, accused Communists jailed for refusing to cooperate with congressional and

38. "Castro Woos Negroes," *The Citizens' Council*, August 1960.

state committees would be freed, including Gibson and three other NAACP leaders in Florida.[39]

The *Braden* and *Gibson* cases also had very real implications for two diametrically opposed campaigns focusing on the red and black issue. The first was James Eastland's campaign to reverse *Pennsylvania v. Nelson*, the 1956 case which held that the Smith Act preempted state sedition measures. Eastland had been obsessed with *Nelson* since the 1957 SISS hearings in Memphis and had specifically gone after Braden to challenge the ruling. His efforts in 1959 and 1960 to usher through legislation protecting the rights of states to maintain their antisubversive laws had produced a forum for red- and black-baiting rhetoric but no laws. Eastland and his supporters still hoped, however, that what the Citizens' Councils referred to as the "seditious sit-downs" might have an effect on the Court's ruling in the *Braden* and *Gibson* cases.[40]

An opposing political movement that was equally interested in the cases centered around a growing campaign to eliminate HUAC. The Emergency Civil Liberties Committee (ECLC), which was listed by the U.S. attorney general as a Communist-front organization, had been working to dismantle the federal, state, and local internal-security apparatus since the mid-1950s. Its efforts had been stifled after HUAC issued a report in 1957 titled "Operation Abolition" which charged that the ECLC's campaign was Communist directed. Many liberals had distanced themselves from the ECLC because of the report, but the campaign to eliminate HUAC had continued. On May 8, 1960, just as the *Braden* case was being considered, the campaign had come to a head. The ECLC and other anti-HUAC activists protesting HUAC hearings in San Francisco grew unruly and were turned back with fire hoses.[41]

Among those protesting in California were not only the ECLC, but NCC and SCEF supporters of Carl Braden and his codefendant Frank Wilkinson. Indeed, the Braden case actually had direct ties to the San Francisco hearings. HUAC had called Vernon Bown, an integrationist and a key figure in Braden's 1954 sedition case in Kentucky, to testify in San Francisco. Bown, a Communist, had been among those, along with Braden, who had helped

39. SCEF News, 10 March 1960, 8 November 1960, MS425, Box 1, Carl Braden Press Releases Folder, Braden Papers.

40. SCEF News, 11 April 1960, MS425, Box 1, Carl Braden Press Releases Folder, Braden Papers.

41. Powers, *Not without Honor*, 306–307.

Andrew Wade, a black man, buy a home in a white neighborhood. After spending months in jail awaiting trial, Bown had been released with Braden after the *Nelson* case overrode their convictions under state sedition laws.[42]

138]

When they discovered Communist Party members in films taken of the crowd protesting HUAC in San Francisco, red- and black-baiters assumed that the clashes that followed were Communist inspired. The anti-HUAC forces, meanwhile, claimed police brutality and insisted that their persecution constituted evidence of a burgeoning totalitarian police state committed to stifling the voices of American citizens. It seemed to many that the *Braden* case offered the high court the opportunity to decide if HUAC or its opponents were seditious.

The San Francisco imbroglio also had an impact on the *Gibson* case. In the wake of the disturbances in California, the Johns Committee in Florida once again called Theodore Gibson and Edward Graham, another NAACP official who had refused to testify about his organizational affiliations at the committee's February 1958 hearings. The committee hoped to persuade Gibson and Graham to testify in exchange for dropping the contempt charges against them. Florida no doubt hoped to avoid a repeat of the San Francisco protests. Gibson reiterated that any Communists found in NAACP ranks would be expelled but again refused to answer questions or open the group's membership records. Graham also rejected the committee's requests for further information. Graham's case went before the Florida Supreme Court a few days before Christmas. His conviction was reversed but Gibson's stood. The activist priest's six-month prison sentence and twelve-hundred-dollar fine were commuted, however, pending an appeal to the United States Supreme Court.[43]

Hoping to create some solidarity between his and Gibson's camps, Carl Braden went to Florida in early 1961. On January 25, he met with NAACP members in Volusia County to discuss strategy. As he addressed the crowd, John's Committee officials served him with a summons to appear before

42. SCEF News, 6 May 1960, MS425, Box 1, Carl Braden Press Releases Folder, Braden Papers. See also Jerold Simmons, *Operation Abolition: The Campaign to Abolish the House Un-American Activities Committee, 1938–1975* (New York: Garland Publishing, 1986).

43. "Supreme Court Dismisses Contempt Charge," *Pensacola Journal*, 26 March 1963; "Report of the Florida Legislative Investigation Committee to the 1961 Session of the Legislature," Series 1486, Carton 1, Florida Legislative Investigation Committee Papers; SCEF News, 11 January 1961, MS425, Box 1, Carl Braden Press Releases Folder, Braden Papers.

that body in early February. At the subsequent hearing, Braden told the committee his name but refused to answer any further questions, silently challenging the committee to add his name, beside Gibson's, to the list of those cited by the state of Florida for contempt.[44]

Before the committee could take further action against Braden, however, the Supreme Court delivered its decision in the *Braden* and *Wilkinson* contempt-of-Congress cases. On February 27, 1961, the Supreme Court voted five to four to sustain the convictions and the one-year prison terms given to both men. Citing the recent *Barenblatt* decision, Justice Potter Stewart, writing for the majority, declared that HUAC's questioning of the two was pertinent to their inquiry and was constitutional. The petitioners' First Amendment rights had not been violated. Dissenting justice Hugo Black declared that the majority opinion "may well strip the Negro of the aid of many of the white people who have been willing to speak up in his behalf," a sentiment shared by those involved in the campaign to abolish HUAC.[45]

In early May 1961, as a light drizzle fell, Braden and Wilkinson entered the jailhouse in Atlanta to begin serving their year-long terms. Looking on, Martin Luther King commented that their conviction was evidence that "McCarthyism" was again on the rise in the South. "I have no doubt," the civil rights leader announced "they are being punished—particularly Mr. Braden—for their integration activities." Making it clear that he was "not upholding communism in any way," King insisted that anti-Communism had become one of the only remaining viable weapons for segregationists, and HUAC was being used by its southern members "to thwart integration," a practice, he declared, that had to stop. Southern anti-Communist segregationists, however, were only getting started.[46]

Later that month the Johns Committee underscored Braden's conviction with its own findings on SCEF and the alleged red and black conspiracy. Linking Braden and SCEF to NAACP officials in Florida, including Edward Graham and state NAACP president Leon Lowry, the committee justified its pursuit of Theodore Gibson in a report delivered to the state assembly.

44. "Report of the Florida Legislative Investigation Committee to the 1961 Session of the Legislature," Series 1486, Carton 1, Florida Legislative Investigation Committee Papers; SCEF News, 26 January 1961, 4 February 1961, MS425, Box 1, Carl Braden Press Releases Folder, Braden Papers.

45. *Braden v. United States*, 365 U.S. 431 (1961); SCEF News, 1 March 1961, 10 October 1961, MS425, Box 1, Carl Braden Press Releases Folder, Braden Papers.

46. "King Sees 'McCarthyism,'" *Atlanta Journal*, 2 May 1961.

Despite Gibson's and other witnesses' "attempts to obstruct and destroy the Committee's investigations . . . the Committee's record of sworn testimony shows conclusively that Communist Party members and Communist-front organizations are presently very active in Florida agitating racial issues." Undercover agents working for the Johns Committee, the report went on, had infiltrated and confirmed Communist activity among several groups working for civil rights in the state including SCEF, the Florida Civil Liberties Union, the Florida Council on Human Relations, the NAACP, the Congress of Racial Equality, the Fellowship of Reconciliation, and the Emergency Civil Liberties Committee. None other than Carl Braden, according to the committee, had led a joint meeting of these groups in Orlando on March 12, 1960. There and in other meetings in the state he had advocated the abolition of HUAC, SISS, and the Johns Committee. Those associated with SCEF in Florida, the report concluded, were "knowingly or un-knowingly lending aid to the subversive thrust of the Communist Party."[47]

In its 1961 analysis, the Johns Committee outlined an updated version of the red and black conspiracy. It put SCEF at the center with the NAACP, SRC, ECLC, CORE, and other groups in orbit around it. In doing so the committee linked the Gibson and Braden cases to the anti-HUAC protests in San Francisco and the sit-in movement, as well as the freedom rides that had just begun in the South. Extending the matrix even further, the committee also outlined the beginnings of a "lavender scare" that linked homosexuals to Communist activity in state-supported schools and universities.

Aubrey Williams, president of SCEF and an active participant in the anti-HUAC campaign, responded to the report, declaring that the Florida committee equated "subversive activity with working for integration, and communism with advocacy of equal treatment under law." Carl Braden's wife joined in charging that the committee was less afraid of Communism than of democracy. The Johns Committee, like HUAC and the SISS, according to Anne Braden, had not "one scintilla of proof" that her husband was a Communist. Indeed, all of the accusations had been hearsay. "This is the way committees of this kind scratch each other's back," Braden declared.

47. "Report of the Florida Legislative Investigation Committee to the 1961 Session of the Legislature," Series 1486, Carton 1, Florida Legislative Investigation Committee Papers; "Proof Is Claimed of Red Agitation," *Florida Times-Union*, 28 May 1961; "Investigation Report Has Some Disturbing Detail on Commies in Florida," *Fort Lauderdale News*, 10 October 1961.

"They label as 'communist' everything liberal in America, and then one committee quotes the report of another as supposed documentation of unfounded charges." With this technique, she argued, they had destroyed "many efforts for progress and good." Despite recent setbacks, however, Braden still held out hope that "right will prevail" and the freedoms of belief and association would be revived.[48]

[141

On March 25, 1963, Anne Braden's hopes were partially fulfilled. In a five-to-four decision, the Supreme Court held that Theodore Gibson's contempt conviction violated his First Amendment right of free association. According to the majority, compelling the NAACP, a "concededly legitimate and nonsubversive organization," to provide information to the state about its members was not akin to compelling the Communist Party, which was not an "ordinary or legitimate political party," to do so. The state had not shown a sufficient connection between the NAACP and Communist activities or that the NAACP was acting contrary to the state interest.[49]

While Carl Braden's conviction confirmed that federal red and black investigators were not violating the First Amendment rights of witnesses when they asked about Communist Party affiliations, the Gibson case denied state committees the right to question those belonging to clearly nonsubversive civil rights groups about their members. The Supreme Court thus further defined the tactics that could be employed by the red and black investigating network. Without direct evidence that civil rights groups were closely connected to the Communist Party, answers concerning their memberships and associations could not be compelled. But the Court allowed in the same rulings that both federal and state committees could continue to investigate and question individuals about their Communist and Communist-front affiliations. More important, perhaps, they could continue to publish and distribute their conclusions, however misleading. Thus the red and black investigating network, while not entrusted with the powers its more zealous contributors might have hoped for, could continue to exist and expand, particularly as a public-relations vehicle.

In the years stretching from Little Rock to the early sit-ins, southern segregationists had redoubled their efforts to stem the rising tide of federally

48. SCEF News, 26 June 1961, MS425, Box 1, Carl Braden Press Releases Folder, Braden Papers.

49. *Gibson v. Florida Legislative Investigating Committee*, 372 U.S. 539 (1963); "Supreme Court Dismisses Contempt Charge," *Pensacola Journal*, 26 March 1963.

enforced integration. Red and black investigations constituted a key tool in this struggle. Though South Carolina employed a less aggressive style of pursuing the alleged conspiracy, little HUACs and little FBIs in the region generally fought their red and black enemies with increasing zeal. The Johns Committee in Florida, the Legislative Council in Arkansas, and the General Investigating Committee in Texas were particularly effective. Together with the help of HUAC and anti-Communists-for-hire such as J. B. Matthews and Myers Lowman, these state agencies did real damage to those whom they pursued. Arkansas's attorney general Bruce Bennett and Tennessee's courts closed Highlander's doors; Texas's committee found real evidence of a well-known Communist leading sit-ins in the South; and the Florida legislature and HUAC fought key public-relations and legal battles against Carl Braden. At the same time, red and black investigators damaged their own cause with blatant racism, brutality, and reckless accusations about the political motives of the civil rights movement as a whole. Moreover, civil rights workers and their allies on the left became increasingly effective in defending themselves against the charges leveled by southern reactionaries. In the press, civil rights activists used incidents in San Francisco and Marshall, Texas, to associate defenders of anti-Communism and segregation with violence and fascism, while in the courts movement supporters succeeded in limiting southern states' questioning of alleged Communists working for the civil rights movement. Still, their greatest challenges were yet to come. While civil rights activists might discredit unsupported attacks of segregationists at the state level, they could not as easily defend the movement against nationally publicized charges that their best known spokesman and spiritual leader, Martin Luther King, had employed and worked closely with known Communists.

BLACK, WHITE, AND RED ALL OVER

5

THE ULTIMATE SUCCESS OF THE CIVIL RIGHTS MOVE-
ment depended in large part on public opinion. Changing minds about the
condition of blacks under segregation meant reaching the ears of those with
the moral conscience to listen. At the same time, it meant defending the
movement against damaging publicity. The network of red and black investigators had devoted itself, through open hearings and piecemeal propaganda, to publicly linking civil rights advocates to Communism. In
addition, the backers of segregation developed their own channels of com-
munication for reaching wide audiences. Newspapers, radio programs, and
television shows barraged southerners with warnings about a black and red
conspiracy. To counter the negative publicity, civil rights advocates initiated their own public-relations campaigns. In the process individuals and
groups in the movement were forced to decide whether to deny the charges
leveled against them and denounce Communist influence or to deny that
the charges were relevant and protect their right to maintain left-wing political affiliations.

The Citizens' Council was perhaps the loudest and most influential
voice linking the black revolution to a Communist conspiracy in the South.
Formed in Indianola, Mississippi, in reaction to the *Brown* decision, the Citizens' Council denounced "race-mixing" and advocated an unrelenting defense of segregation. It differed from more radical groups such as the Ku
Klux Klan in its upper-middle-class make-up and its stated intention to preserve Jim Crow through open, legal means. Many of the South's most prominent political and economic leaders joined the Councils, making them
among the most influential groups in the region.[1]

From its inception the Citizens' Council used every mode of communi-
cation it could muster to charge that reds had infiltrated the civil rights
movement. In pamphlets the organization popularized Eugene Cook's "The

1. Neil R. McMillen, *The Citizens' Council: Organized Resistance to the Second Reconstruction, 1954–64* (Urbana: University of Illinois Press, 1971), 18–19, 192–204.

Ugly Truth about the NAACP." In its paper *The Citizen,* the Council's most persistent editorialist on red and black issues, Medford Evans, repeatedly maintained that integration was "Communism in action." And on its national television and radio program "The Citizens' Council Forum," notables such as Senator Strom Thurmond of South Carolina "exposed" the Communist conspiracy behind the civil rights movement.[2]

The Citizens' Council's information about Communists in the civil rights movement came from many of the usual sources across the nation. Myers Lowman's Circuit Riders, Inc., based in Cincinnati, Ohio, added stacks of "evidence" to the Council's pile. Lowman had long provided information to the House Committee on Un-American Activities (HUAC) and the Senate Internal Security Subcommittee (SISS), but along with J. B. Matthews, Manning Johnson, and others, he and his group had found a new market for their data in the South during the late 1950s and 1960s.[3]

Although personality and policy conflicts occasionally marred the relationship, the State Sovereignty Commissions also maintained direct ties to the Citizens' Council. The governors of Alabama and Mississippi, who acted as their Commissions' nominal heads, were almost invariably Citizens' Council supporters, especially during election time. The Sovereignty Commissions even subsidized the Councils' radio and television series and funneled hundreds of thousands of taxpayer dollars into Council coffers. Moreover both the Commissions and the Council maintained close ties to national representatives, especially Mississippi's James Eastland.[4]

Furthering the southern nationalist message, other Council-like organizations added to southern fears of a red and black conspiracy. The Grass Roots League in South Carolina, for example, distributed a research bulletin to regional subscribers that frequently reported on red infiltration of the civil rights movement. The Defenders of State Sovereignty and Individual

2. Ibid., 197; "The Ugly Truth about the NAACP," Folder 11, Citizens' Council Collection, Mitchell Memorial Library Special Collections, Mississippi State University; Reel 007, Citizens' Council Forum Films, Mississippi Department of Archives and History.

3. See Reels 033, Citizens' Council Forum Films; 037, Citizens' Council Forum Films.

4. McMillen, *Citizens' Council,* 335–50; Report, "Citizens' Council Grant," ID# 99-30-0-46-1-1-1 to 2-1-1 Mississippi State Sovereignty Commission Files, Mississippi Department of Archives and History; Memo, "Coordinating Committee for Fundamental American Freedoms," ID# 6-70-0-102-1-1-1 to 2-1-1, Mississippi State Sovereignty Commission Files. See also Simmons to Howell, 24 March 1965, SG13842, Alabama State Sovereignty Commission Papers, Alabama Department of Archives and History.

Liberties in Virginia, moreover, made radio broadcasts declaring the "truth" about Communist support of integration efforts. Like the Councils, these groups principally represented upper-middle-class southerners promoting the open and legal defense of segregation.[5]

An even more extremist press also closely supported the southern red scare. The American Nazi Party's "Rockwell Report" reproduced the "shocking record" of Martin Luther King's Communist affiliations. And the Ku Klux Klan's *Fiery Cross* connected black civil rights disturbances to a supposed Jewish-Communist conspiracy. Radical periodicals such as the *Mid-South Informer* and the *Dixie American* also warned that civil rights organizations were Communist fronts. Meanwhile Joseph Kamp, Dan Smoot, and other commentators published articles warning against a plot to "sovietize the South."[6]

These propagandists did little to convince moderates to join the segregationist cause. The racist and recklessly anti-Communist right drew heavy criticism from political centrists. Conservatives especially denounced the exaggerated charges of red and black hunters. When the John Birch Society claimed in its publication *American Opinion* that the United States was "60-80 per cent" Communist dominated, *National Review* editor William F. Buckley Jr. took issue with the Birchers and their message. Among the most active right-wing propaganda machines in the 1960s, the John Birch Society had been among the groups distributing the Georgia Education Commission's (GCE) "exposé" on Highlander. The society had in fact funded a number of billboards along southern highways featuring the GCE photograph of Martin Luther King Jr. and Communist publicist Abner Berry at a Highlander meeting. *American Opinion*, moreover, frequently declared

5. Research Bulletin No. 1 and Research Bulletin No. 3, Folder 18, Citizens' Council Collection; Broadcast #12, 8003-A, -B, Box 21, Folder 1957, Defenders of State Sovereignty Collection, University of Virginia Library; Broadcast #22, 8003-A, -B, Box 21, Folder 1957, Defenders of State Sovereignty Collection.

6. "Is Martin Luther King a Communist?" 1 August 1963, Box 337, Lister Hill Papers, Hoole Special Collections, University of Alabama; "Negro Ex-Red Admits NAACP Is Most Powerful 'Front' Communists Have Left in US," Box 022, John Bell Williams Papers, Mississippi Department of Archives and History; "The Fiery Cross," Ku Klux Klan Folder, Segregation and Integration Collection, Mitchell Memorial Library Special Collections, Mississippi State University; "The Lowdown on Little Rock and the Plot to Sovietize the South," Box 022, John Bell Williams Papers; "Communism in the Civil Rights Movement," Box 142, Mississippi State Sovereignty Commission Papers, McCain Library and Archives, University of Southern Mississippi.

Billboard claiming to identify Martin Luther King Jr. at a Communist training school. Photograph taken en route from Selma, Alabama to Montgomery, March 25, 1965.
Corbis-Bettmann

civil rights activism to be Communist inspired. The publication would call the 1964 Civil Rights Act "part of the pattern for the Communist takeover of America" and the 1965 civil rights protests in Selma, Alabama, "a typical demonstration of Communist activism." In a series of articles for the *National Review*, Buckley called such claims "paranoid and unpatriotic drivel." The other contributing editors of the review concurred, arguing that the Birchers were "cultivating points of view whose bearing on the anti-Communist struggle is harmful."[7]

The accusations of overtly racist and extremist publicists that Communists controlled the civil rights movement did little to convince even conservatives to join the segregationist cause, but they did sway the undereducated and they solidified the support of those already committed to segregation. They also contributed to an atmosphere of fear that was beginning to engulf the South as violent responses to civil rights protests came to dominate the headlines. Many southern state and local newspapers gave the alleged red and black conspiracy equal space alongside stories of white-on-

7. Alabama Billboard, 1962, Citizens' Council Collection; "The John Birch Society and the Conservative Movement," *National Review*, 19 October 1965.

black brutality. Some featured the extremists' charges. The Herderman newspapers in Mississippi, the *Mississippi Clarion-Ledger* and the *Jackson Daily News*, offer a radical example. Thomas and Robert Herderman had gained control of the state's two most widely circulated newspapers by the early 1950s. They and their columnists were unquestioning supporters of segregation, James Eastland, and the Citizens' Council. Typical of their newspapers' frequent articles on the red and black menace was commentator Tom Etheridge's "Mississippi Notebook" column. Etheridge reiterated often that "it appears to be more than coincidence that racial disorders always seem to develop somewhere in the South at the very time Communism takes another forward step." Mississippi's most popular newspapers thus reinforced the fears that fed the southern red scare.[8]

Few newspapers in the South reported on Communists in the civil rights movement as often as the Mississippi papers, but fewer still passed on the opportunity to make red and black front-page news. The Highlander exposé, for example, drew enormous attention from the southern print media, particularly in the school's home state of Tennessee. While state newspapers such as the *Nashville Tennessean* denounced the Highlander investigation as a "witch hunt" and a return to McCarthyism, others such as Chattanooga's *News–Free Press* lauded the closing of the "notorious, disgraceful, left-wing, integrationist" Highlander. The southern press printed the red and black investigators' charges whether the newspapers supported segregation or black civil rights.[9]

This had a ripple effect nationally. Journalists who had come to the South to report on racial conflicts there took the accusations of southern segregationist anti-Communists back to their home regions. In the wake of the Little Rock crisis, for example, Edward Simmons, a correspondent for the *Standard Times* in New Bedford, Massachusetts, wrote a five-part series of articles on Communist influence in the southern racial struggle. He drew information from the range of investigations covered by the southern press, including witness testimony from the Louisiana Joint Legislative Committee on Segregation, the Georgia Commission on Education, the Johns Com-

---

8. Tom Etheridge, "Is It More than Just Coincidence?" *Mississippi Clarion-Ledger*, 28 May 1963; John Dittmer, *Local People: The Struggle for Civil Rights in Mississippi* (Urbana: University of Illinois Press, 1995), 65.

9. See *Birmingham Independent*, 18 August 1965; Hugh Davis Graham, *Crisis in Print: Desegregation and the Press in Tennessee* (Nashville: Vanderbilt University Press, 1967), 205–206.

mittee in Florida, the Senate Internal Security Subcommittee, and the House Un-American Activities Committee. Simmons's reports then re-echoed in the South. The *Jackson Daily News*, the *Richmond Times-Dispatch*, and several other southern papers reprinted Simmons's series.[10]

While journalists outside the South were relatively free to interpret events in the South as they wished, southern journalists who were critical of segregation risked being labeled red themselves and losing readers. Indeed, many of the most prominent southern editors giving sympathetic coverage to the struggle for black equality were pilloried. In front of the Mississippi General Legislative Investigating Committee on Un-American Activities in 1959, J. B. Matthews questioned the loyalty of Greenville's Hodding Carter III, the editor of the *Delta Democrat-Times*. Carter, Matthews revealed, was a member of the Southern Regional Council (SRC) and a supporter of the Southern Conference Education Fund (SCEF), both identified by Matthews as Communist-infiltrated allies of the civil rights movement. Although no friend of the civil rights movement himself, Carter had been a harsh critic of the Citizens' Councils and had won a 1946 Pulitzer Prize for "distinguished editorial writing against racial and religious intolerance."[11]

Other Pulitzer Prize–winning editors with links to the SRC also drew jabs from red and black hunters. Harry Ashmore of the *Arkansas Gazette* won his prize in 1958 for editorials criticizing Orval Faubus's handling of the Little Rock crisis and the governor's defense of segregation. State government officials and the conservative press called Ashmore a Communist sympathizer. They had received cues on Ashmore from Circuit Riders, Inc., which claimed the journalist was a director of the Fund for the Republic, which contributed some half million dollars to the SRC. Finally, Myers Lowman and J. B. Matthews supplied southern segregationists with material on liberal *Atlanta Constitution* editor, racial moderate, and 1959 Pulit-

10. See Edward Simmons, "U.S. Reds Planned Racial Strife 40 Years before Troubles Began," *Jackson Daily News*, 4 August 1958; Edward Simmons, "Red Propaganda Spurs Race Strife," *Richmond Times-Dispatch*, 5 August 1958. See also Edward Simmons, "Commie Authored Books Were Listed As Basis for Supreme Court's 1954 Integration Order," *Jackson Daily News*, 5 August 1958; Edward Simmons, "American Commies Urged Federal Intervention Two Years before Troops Stormed Little Rock," *Jackson Daily News*, 6 August 1958.

11. Charles Hills, "Commie Front Groups Listed," *Mississippi Clarion-Ledger*, 19 November 1959; Dittmer, *Local People*, 66–67.

zer winner Ralph McGill. McGill was among the many critics of segregation who understood that racial and religious prejudice only undermined American moral leadership abroad. He was also a founding member of the SRC and a contributor to the Southern Conference for Human Welfare (SCHW). In part to defend himself and the SRC against the attacks of anti-Communist segregationists, the editor had become a critic of Communist influences in the SCHW and other groups.[12]

The southern red scare's propaganda machine was well established by the time John F. Kennedy took office in 1961. The wealthy Catholic Massachusetts senator's candidacy, however, seemed to create within it a new sense of urgency. Kennedy had made clear during the election that he would devote more federal support to racial equality than President Eisenhower or Republican presidential candidate Richard Nixon. Linking the need for racial progress with the battle against Communism abroad, Kennedy promised to make the presidency a "symbol of the moral imperative upon which a free society is based," placing at the top of the agenda the issue of civil rights. He then made a symbolic gesture to this end by lending support to Martin Luther King soon after King was arrested in Georgia on questionable charges. Although Arkansas, Georgia, Louisiana, North Carolina, South Carolina, and Texas eventually threw their support behind Kennedy, it was only by the narrowest of margins and only after vice-presidential candidate Lyndon Johnson, a Texan, had lobbied frantically on his behalf. Nixon carried Florida, Kentucky, Oklahoma, Tennessee, and Virginia. States righters, still the most ardent opponents of red and black influence in the South, carried Mississippi, won a majority of electors in Alabama, and made a strong showing in Louisiana. Kennedy became president by one of the narrowest margins in history. Disappointed segregationists waited for their chance to strike.[13]

That opportunity came in the early days of the Kennedy administration.

12. "Southwide Rift Charged to Reds," *Nashville Tennessean*, 19 December 1958; "Names in the News, 1938–1958," July 1958, Box 671, Lowman 1958 Folder, Matthews Papers; Ralph McGill, "Little Helpers of Communism," *Atlanta Constitution*, 12 January 1960. See also Roy Reed, *Faubus: The Life and Times of an American Prodigal* (Fayetteville: University of Arkansas Press, 1997), 239–42, 262; Numan Bartley, *The New South, 1945–1980* (Baton Rouge: Louisiana State University Press, 1995), 54; Barbara Barksdale Clowse, *Ralph McGill: A Biography* (Macon, Ga.: Mercer University Press, 1998), 136–37, 150.

13. Bartley, *New South*, 238–39.

The freedom rides in the spring of 1961 followed closely on the heels of the botched U.S.-backed invasion of Cuba at the Bay of Pigs. A wave of criticism against the president and his advisers from the southern right followed closely after the news of the failed landing in mid-April 1961. Less than a month later, the southern right again blasted the administration for its handling of the freedom rides. On the first leg of the campaign against segregated interstate busing, led by the Congress of Racial Equality (CORE), protesters riding integrated buses through the Deep South attracted angry white mobs. In Anniston, Alabama, a group smashed freedom-bus windows and slashed tires. Another mob firebombed a vehicle carrying freedom riders to Birmingham. Finally, in Montgomery, Alabama, white supremacists again attacked freedom buses; the assault left one rider paralyzed from the neck down. Television footage and news photos of the scene shocked the nation. After the Montgomery incident, Kennedy intervened, providing federal marshals to ensure safe conduct for the riders. For liberals federal intervention came much too late, but for southern conservatives it conjured up images of a second Reconstruction and black revolution.

As the story unfolded, the White House and the attorney general's office received a flood of telegrams from southern politicians denouncing the federal government's support of the freedom riders. They argued that the riders were bent only on plunging the region into turmoil. Governors Orval Faubus of Arkansas and Ernest Hollings of South Carolina called for the president to investigate the professional "agitators" who were allegedly leading the rides. And Mississippi attorney general Joe Patterson declared that not only would he not protect "trouble makers," "fanatics," and "radicals" who were fomenting riots in the South, he would do his best to prevent the riders' "darned Communist conduct."[14]

Meanwhile, conservative commentators played up the Communist angle. In June 1961 the front page of the *Citizens' Council* reported links between the Congress of Racial Equality's "rider invasion" and the Communist Party. An article titled "Communists Mount Soapboxes in NYC to Back 'Riders'" described a Communist-led New York City protest against

14. Faubus to Robert Kennedy, 21 May 1961, Attorney General Collection, General Correspondence, Box 66, Civil Rights Alabama Folder, Robert Kennedy Papers, John F. Kennedy Library; Hollings to Robert Kennedy, 22 May 1961, Attorney General Collection, General Correspondence, Box 10, Civil Rights Alabama Folder, Robert Kennedy Papers; Marshall, Patterson Conversation, 22 May 1961, Attorney General Collection, General Correspondence, Box 10, Civil Rights Alabama Folder, Robert Kennedy Papers.

violent southern reactions to the freedom rides. Representatives of the Communist Party of the United States and its publication *The Worker,* according to the article, led the meeting and called for President Kennedy to defend the freedom riders against violence. Just below the column, a cartoon with a man pointing at a press clipping saying "accumulated evidence of subversive ties" and sporting a set of luggage labeled "CORE" summed up the red and black investigators' position. The man asked a member of the House Un-American Activities Committee, "Hadn't you better look into that luggage?"[15]

When the head of the Mississippi Highway Patrol, General T. B. Birdsong, declared that two jailed riders had recently attended a seminar led by Soviet officials in Cuba, the charges against the freedom riders were reproduced in several southern newspapers, including the *Jackson Daily News,* the *Memphis Commercial Appeal,* and the *Nashville Tennessean.* The accusations moved quickly beyond the South as journalists and conservative publications linked the freedom rides to Communist causes. A radio station in Providence, Rhode Island, aired an editorial arguing that the freedom riders "brought nothing but violence to the area," and in so doing added "much fuel to the communist sparked hate America campaign." The Citizens Anti-Communist Committee of Connecticut, meanwhile, charged in a newsletter that CORE was "aiding Communism in creating discord and unrest in the South." Many of the freedom riders, the letter continued, had long Communist-front histories.[16]

Red and black hunters outside of the South depended heavily on southern sources for their information. The Citizens Anti-Communist Committee, for one, cited as its main source a May 1961 speech delivered to the Senate by James Eastland. Senator Eastland used several HUAC reports linking CORE advisory-committee members A. Philip Randolph, Earl Dickerson, Algernon D. Black, Allan Knight Chalmers, Charles Zimmerman, and others to Communist organizations. He cited these reports to make the broad claim that the freedom riders were "part of the Communist move-

15. "Agitators Land in Mississippi Jails," Citizens' Council Collection.

16. "Reds in Havana Planned Rides," *Jackson Daily News,* 29 June 1961; "CORE Disputes Patrol Charge," *Jackson Daily News,* 30 June 1961; "Birdsong Says Known Reds behind Protest Riders," "CORE Disputes Patrol Charge," *Memphis Commercial-Appeal,* 30 June 1961; "Patrol Charges Riders Red-Led," "CORE Disputes Patrol Charge," *Nashville Tennessean,* 30 June 1961; WICE Editorial, 23 May 1961, Box 388, Colmer Papers, McCain Library, University of Southern Mississippi.

'Hadn't You Better Look
Into That Luggage?'

CORE under suspicion. Cartoon by *Nashville Banner* cartoonist Jack Knox for *The Citizens Council*, June 1961.
Mississippi Department of Archives and History

ment in the U.S." Eastland argued that under the leadership of New Yorker James Peck, a racial agitator, nuclear protester, and conscientious objector against the World War II draft, CORE brought the people of Mississippi "face to face with this world conspiracy." According to the senator, outside agitators, not grass-roots activists, were upsetting "the mutual love and affection that today exists there between the white and colored races." Mississippi representative John Bell Williams simultaneously delivered the same message to the House, claiming that the freedom riders were "doing Khrushchev's work" and were "deliberately seeking violence hoping to embarrass our people in the eyes of the rest of the nation and trying to foment strife on which Communism thrives."[17]

Alabama attorney general McDonald Gallion revisited Eastland's find-

17. *Congressional Record*, 87th Cong., 1st sess., 1961, 107, pt. 7:8957–69; "Eastland's Speech Hits 'Riders' Chief," *Mississippi Clarion-Ledger*, 26 May 1961; "Williams Praises

ings to further publicize the alleged Communist conspiracy behind the freedom rides and pressure the White House to end its support of CORE. In a
May 23, 1961, letter to President Kennedy, Gallion inquired "officially" if
the administration was "aware of the record of . . . James Douglas Peck as
a communist associate and the demonstrated enemy of America?" Gallion
reviewed SISS records linking Peck to several alleged Communist fronts including the Committee for Non-Violent Action, which had "demonstrated
against construction of our Polaris Submarines." He then called on the president to make available "the full record on Peck and on any others who have
participated in the events leading up to the serious breach of state sovereignty by federal forces." Surely, he argued, the administration would pursue agents in this country who hoped to "present America from a position
of weakness to the rest of the world" as energetically as he had committed
aid "to stop Communist aggression in Laos, Cuba, Africa and many other
parts of the world." Gallion sent the letter, which was designed for public
consumption, to newspapers throughout Alabama. They invariably published it as front-page news.[18]

A little over a year after the Bay of Pigs and the freedom rides, racial
clashes in Mississippi and a cold-war confrontation in Cuba erupted almost
simultaneously. As the Soviets installed a nuclear arsenal just ninety miles
off the coast of Florida, red and black hunters once more linked the growing
power of Communism with intensifying conflicts over segregation at the
University of Mississippi. It was no coincidence, they argued, that these cri-
ses had occurred simultaneously; both were part of a coordinated plan directed by Moscow.

A battle between Mississippi segregationists and liberal educators had
been building long before the eventual showdown at Ole Miss in early October 1962. Months before the riots in Oxford, Governor Ross Barnett had the
ears and eyes of the state when he addressed a television audience about the
dangers of Communism: "We have seen the centralization of government.
We have seen dangerous encroachments of socialism and communism grad-
ually but surely creeping into our government and our way of life—foreign

---

State: Says Agitators Doing Work for Khrushchev," *Mississippi Clarion-Ledger*, 25 May
1961.

18. Gallion to President, 23 May 1961, Box 376, Hill Papers; "Gallion Charges 'Freedom
Rider' Leader Red," *Mobile Journal*, 26 May 1961, p. 1; "Ala. Attorney General Reveals
Leader of 'Freedom Riders' As a Communist," *Fairhope Courier*, 25 May 1961.

ideologies—crackpot theories—corruption—left-wing and subversive groups gaining high favor—efforts to divide and change our way of life."[19]

When federal forces moved to desegregate the University of Mississippi, Barnett's words came to seem prophetic to many of his white fellow citizens. Black Mississippian James Meredith's lengthy battle to legally register at Ole Miss culminated in a September 13 decision of the Fifth Circuit Court mandating his immediate enrollment. From that day until September 30, the day Meredith was to move onto the Oxford campus, white Mississippians prepared for a showdown. On campus, a circular asked students to avoid violence but "not allow yourself to be intimidated by any leftist school administrators and officials." And on the front page of the *Jackson Daily News*, a headline warned Mississippi citizens: "On Your Guard: Commies Using Negro As Tool."[20]

Despite back-room negotiations between the Kennedy administration and Governor Barnett to orchestrate the peaceful admittance of Meredith, whites rioted in protest on September 30, making page-one news all over the world. Little more than two weeks later, the nuclear build-up in Cuba became public. Anti-red and anti-black anxieties rose to new levels in the South.[21]

Mississippi editorial pages competed with each other in warning their readers that the Communist integrationist plot was reaching a climax. Some argued that reds were directly to blame; but a much more prevalent view held that if the riots were not inspired directly by Communists, they reflected a dictatorial federal intervention that was furthering the cause of the international Communist Party. Popular commentators Tom Etheridge and Charles Hills echoed these sentiments in their weekly columns for the *Clarion-Ledger*, as did Medford Evans in *The Citizen* and Dan Smoot in *The Dan Smoot Report*. Moreover, on the Ole Miss campus a Citizens' Council–supported publication called *The Rebel Underground* chastised the "Left-wing professors" who supported Meredith's admission and thus further advanced the cause of the Communist-led NAACP.[22]

---

19. "Anti-communist Address of Governor Ross R. Barnett," Box 93, Russell Davis Papers, Mitchell Memorial Library Special Collections, Mississippi State University.

20. *Jackson Daily News*, 18 September 1962, p.1; *Jackson Daily News*, 19 September 1962, p. 1.

21. Dittmer, *Local People*, 139–41.

22. See "The Wages of Socialism," *Dan Smoot Report*, 15 October, 1962; "Forced Communism Is Communism in Action," *The Citizen*, September 1962; "Affairs of State," *Mis-*

Accepting the general links among federal intervention, the threat of So-viet-Cuban military aggression, and racial conflict in the region, white Mis-sissippians and much of the segregated South blamed President Kennedy, not Ross Barnett, for the Ole Miss riot. A Southern Baptist pastor from Jack-son, Edwin Quattlebaum, summed up his state's concerns in a letter to the president condemning his appointment of Robert Kennedy as attorney gen-eral, his use of federal troops in Mississippi, and his betrayal of Cuba to the Communists. Other writers acted on a Citizens' Council call for its mem-bers to sign letters requesting that Washington pay more attention to "the Communist menace and our Cuban problem" rather than waging "unnatu-ral warfare" on the "sovereign State of Mississippi." State congressman Wil-liam Colmer, meanwhile, distributed his own form letter showing his support for Mississippi's stand against Ole Miss's integration. It warned against "the ever increasing centralization of power in the federal govern-ment . . . [of which] the end result will be a totalitarian state not unlike Russia itself."[23]

Linking the Kennedy administration, Cuba, and desegregation became quite common in a wide range of printed media by the late fall. The Citi-zens' Councils distributed bumper stickers reading "The Castro brothers have moved into the White House," "Battle of Ole Miss: Kennedy's Hun-gary," and "Brotherhood by Bayonet." And the *Birmingham News* ran a typ-ical editorial cartoon that depicted the president and his advisers frantically looking over law books and a map with arrows pointing at Ole Miss. A sin-gle adviser stood across the room gesturing at a newspaper headline reading "Critical Cuban Problem." The president showed his palm to the lone fig-ure as if to say the Cuban crisis would have to wait. As the cartoon sug-gested, many southerners believed that clashes over the race issue were distracting attention from efforts to curb the more serious problem of ex-panding Communist beachheads near America's borders; whether civil rights workers and the Kennedy administration were directly involved or

sissippi *Clarion-Ledger*, 2 October 1962; "Mississippi Notebook," *Mississippi Clarion-Ledger*, 2 October 1962; "Mississippi Notebook," *Mississippi Clarion-Ledger*, 10 October 1962; "Mississippi Notebook," *Mississippi Clarion-Ledger*, 15 October 1962; *Rebel Under-ground* 1 (October 1962); Propaganda and Newspapers, University of Mississippi File, Seg-regation and Integration Collection.

23. "Quattlebaum to President," 16 October 1962, Box 395, Colmer Papers; "Colmer to Kaye," 16 October 1962, Box 388, Colmer Papers.

not, they agreed, Communists were using the race issue to further their revolutionary cause.[24]

The constant public barrage against the civil rights movement by the red and black hunting press had a significant effect on the movement's operations. More conservative civil rights groups such as the NAACP had long been cognizant of the threat that anti-Communist smear campaigns posed to the movement. The NAACP's formal declaration that it would purge its ranks of Communist members in 1950 had been a direct reaction to the charge that radicals controlled the group. Other organizations involved in direct-action campaigns after *Brown*, however, were just beginning to cope with the public-relations problems posed by anti-Communist segregationists. Since the Highlander exposé, Martin Luther King and the Southern Christian Leadership Conference (SCLC) had been prime targets of the red and black investigating network. King subsequently worked to minimize the damage done to his organization by these charges. When police arrested SCLC volunteer Robert Moses for picketing an Atlanta supermarket that refused to hire black clerks, King expressed his concern. He knew that the protest had been sponsored by the Southern Conference Education Fund, the group many believed was the keystone of the red conspiracy in the South. Whether the charges were true or not, King told Moses, "I advise against any more demonstrations with the SCEF people. Some people think it's Communist, and that's what matters. We have to be careful." Foreshadowing future conflicts within the SCLC and the movement in general, Moses did not agree, although he bowed for the moment to King's wishes.[25]

SCEF had long been aware that other groups working for black civil rights saw the red and black accusations as a liability to the movement. SCEF's Committee on Relationships chair Albert Barnett wrote to NAACP head Roy Wilkins in December 1956 that his membership in the NAACP's Committee of One Hundred "might be personally costly in view of the campaign in Southern states to brand NAACP as subversive." Given the same "scurrilous charges" against SCEF, the connection might be used against both organizations. Barnett suggested, however, that the organizations

24. White Citizens' Council Files, Cox Papers, Mitchell Memorial Library Special Collections, Mississippi State University; "First Things First," *Southern School News*, October 1962, p. 15.

25. Taylor Branch, *Parting the Waters: America in the King Years 1954–1963* (New York: Simon and Schuster, 1988), 328. See also "Savannah's Negroes Severing Ties to Union Linked to Reds," *Atlanta Constitution*, 27 August 1963.

unite and "share the heat of battle." He asked Wilkins to allow SCEF leader James Dombrowski to be included in the Leadership Conference on Civil Rights and to allow SCEF to be added to the list of Constituent Organizations of the National Community Relations Advisory Council. Wilkins, a committed anti-Communist who was supported by the executive committee, rejected Barnett's request.[26]

Despite pressure from others in the movement who hoped that SCEF would distance itself from the campaign for black civil rights, officials in the group were never discouraged. Jailed, publicly chastised, and even harassed with death threats, Anne and Carl Braden continued to goad anti-Communist segregationists and to appeal to others in the movement to accept the group's aid. Despite the fact that SCEF had been "hampered in its work for integration" by "constant attacks and charges of communism," Anne Braden wrote in a brief promotional history of the organization, the group would "continue, without wavering" and "do its bit to attempt to change the atmosphere both in the South and in the nation so that the cry of 'communist' cannot be used so effectively." Where other organizations like the NAACP would deal with similar attacks by "trying to get the smear off" themselves, SCEF decided not to appease the red and black investigators by adopting loyalty oaths or initiating "formal policies that exclude communists from membership." The group would promote an "America where 'communist' is not a scare word but an ideology to be discussed and judged rationally by intelligent, informed citizens."[27]

Perhaps better than any other civil rights advocates working in the South in the 1960s, the Bradens understood that the Communist label had the potential to significantly weaken the movement. After Carl Braden was convicted of contempt in 1958 for refusing to answer HUAC questions, he and Anne had even offered to resign from SCEF if the organization decided they were "more of a liability than an asset." SCEF decided that the Bradens were too good at organizing to let them go. But the couple continued to draw the fire of southern red-scare leaders who used their connection to the movement to label the entire civil rights cause Communist.[28]

In July 1962 Carl Braden made a trip to Mississippi as a SCEF representa-

26. Barnett to Wilkins, 4 December 1956, Box 4, SCEF Committee on Relations with Other Agencies Folder, Braden Papers, University of Tennessee; Morsell to Barnett, 3 April 1957, Box 4, SCEF Committee on Relations with Other Agencies Folder, Braden Papers.

27. History of SCEF Memo, Box 2, Dombrowski (1) Folder, Braden Papers.

28. Braden to Barnett, 29 December 1958, Box 3, HUAC Folder, Braden Papers.

tive of the Voter Education Project, a group that funded campaigns for black voting rights in the state. The *Jackson Daily News* labeled the project red after discovering its association with the now notorious Braden. SCEF head Aubrey Williams wrote to the editor of the *Daily News* suggesting that the newspaper had supported a "monolithic state" that would not tolerate any view that deviated from that laid down by "the White Citizens Council." Williams, who read a reprint of the article in the *Montgomery Advertiser*, understood that the story was making the rounds in the southern press and might damage the organization's credibility. His concerns were well founded.[29]

Members of the Southern Inter-Agency Conference, a precursor to the Council of Federated Organizations (COFO) and the leader of the Voter Education Project, turned on Braden when they learned about the story. At a September 1962 meeting, some suggested that Braden had deliberately sent copies of a confidential report concerning his July trip to the *Daily News*. Others implied that Braden had been irresponsible in making the trip at all, given the widely held belief that he was a Communist. Some even suggested that he had meant to sabotage the project by attracting negative publicity.

The Bradens attempted to set the record straight with a memo to the Inter-Agency Conference members. Bob Moses, they explained, had asked Anne Braden to conduct workshops on civil liberties in Mississippi. She told him that she was unable to go but her husband Carl would take her place. Moses agreed. Carl Braden subsequently traveled to Mississippi and led several workshops. Contrary to the *Daily News* reports, though, Braden had not "sponsored" workshops in Mt. Beulah, nor had he distributed questionnaires asking if a transition to Communism would improve the lot of Mississippi blacks. And Braden had never made his report on his Mississippi trip available to any news agency. The *Daily News* had acquired the report through a leak in the SCEF offices.

The Bradens did acknowledge that the resulting press attacks had hurt the movement, but they believed the blame should be placed on those who made the accusations, not on those who might have provoked them. To blame Braden for the attacks, they said, was the equivalent of segregation-

29. "Commie Crusader Active over State," *Jackson Daily News*, 31 August 1962; " 'Seminar' Registration Form," *Jackson Daily News*, 1 September 1962; James Ward, "Application Form at 'Workshop' Cited," *Jackson Daily News*, 1 September 1962; Williams to Editor, *Jackson Daily News*, 3 September 1962, Box 3, Mississippi 1962 Folder, Braden Papers.

ists blaming brutality against nonviolent civil rights protesters on the protesters themselves. Did the inter-agency group, they asked, actually "give
credence to the charges of subversion" leveled against Braden and SCEF by
James Eastland and HUAC? Did members fear an association with SCEF
would draw accusations against other participating groups? Or did the
groups think that they could escape the charges if they did "a little implied
red-baiting themselves?" "McCarthyism," the Bradens suggested, thrived
in a climate of fear. By "joining the pack or remaining silent," those who
gave credence to the red and black charges were contributing to the "mon-
ster's" growth. Liberals must stand up against the irrational charges of reckless extremists or acquiesce to the same kind of repressive "atmosphere"
that kept Mississippi a closed, brutally segregated society.[30]

The incident in Mississippi made it clear that the participation of controversial figures such as the Bradens had exposed a rift in the movement.
The various groups promoting black civil rights in the South faced a serious
dilemma: should they, like SCEF, accept the help of Communists and fellow
travelers, or should they, like the NAACP, avoid the red-baiting charge by
purging Communist influences? The decision was not an easy one. Many
movement activists with popular-front ties were energetic organizers and
willing protesters. Also, for many liberals, protecting the civil liberties of
Communists went hand in hand with protecting the civil liberties of blacks.
But Communist repression of dissent and totalitarian governance were
anathema to the democratic ideals of the movement. Consensus-era Americans were perplexed by the idea that those who advocated voting rights for
blacks could support a one-party, dictatorial Communist state. Given the
damage the red label had done to the movement in a society with a strong
anti-Communist sentiment, it was impossible for many groups in the
movement to accept any real or alleged Communist help.

One such group was Martin Luther King's SCLC. By the time southern
anxiety over a red and black menace reached new heights with the Ole Miss
riots and the Cuban Missile Crisis in October 1962, FBI director J. Edgar
Hoover was already investigating suspected links among Communism, the
civil rights movement, and the Kennedy administration. Communists
highly placed in the SCLC, according to Hoover, had influenced Martin Luther King and, through King, Communists had gained "access" to the attor-

---

30. Memo for the Southern Inter-Agency Conference, 11 March 1963, Box 3, Mississippi
1963 Folder, Braden Papers.

ney general and the White House. King, the director noted, had already met personally with both Kennedy brothers on several occasions.[31]

Hoover's charges centered primarily on Stanley Levinson, a white New York lawyer introduced to King by Bayard Rustin. Levinson helped organize and raise money for the SCLC and in this position hired a black financial manager, Jack O'Dell, to help with the group's direct-mail campaign. Levinson had been a leftist radical since his college days but, ironically, had made his mark as a capitalist. He had grown rich from real-estate investments and car dealerships. Levinson spent most of his time, however, raising money for leftist causes, including funds to save the Rosenbergs, abolish the McCarran Act, and aid the Smith Act defendants. Indeed, Levinson had secretly served as a fund-raiser for the Communist Party in the 1940s and 1950s and even acted as a courier of funds from Moscow. O'Dell, meanwhile, had his own record of radicalism. He had been an organizer for the National Maritime Union in New Orleans. The union and O'Dell openly followed the dictates of the Communist International. In 1950 an anti-Communist purge within the group had left him without a job. But O'Dell maintained his ties to his Communist friends in subsequent years as he worked for Rustin's 1959 Youth March on Washington and eventually for the SCLC.[32]

Martin Luther King found nothing particularly objectionable about his allies' Communist connections. Although he largely rejected Marxist doctrine himself, King felt that Communists had been diligent in their defense of black rights and he supported their right to speak freely and to organize. But the preeminent civil rights leader was constantly reminded that the Communist affiliations of his co-workers were potentially damaging to the movement's public image. Indeed, Levinson himself warned King about O'Dell's involvement with the Communist Party and the public-relations hazard it posed.[33]

J. Edgar Hoover alerted Attorney General Robert Kennedy about Levinson's ties to King in a January 8, 1962, confidential memo. Hoover's suspicions were backed by old information from questionable sources, and the director more than exaggerated the threat posed by King, a man he consid-

31. Branch, *Parting the Waters*, 564.

32. See David Garrow, *Bearing the Cross* (New York: William Morrow, 1986), and Branch, *Parting the Waters*.

33. Garrow, *Bearing the Cross*, 200–201.

ered "no good." The Justice Department, however, took Hoover at his word without demanding evidence. By early March Robert Kennedy had granted the FBI authority to place wiretaps in the office of Stanley Levinson, an of- fice the Bureau had already bugged without approval. When the FBI listened in on a King-Levinson phone call about the appointment of O'Dell, in which Levinson warned King about O'Dell's Communist affiliations and King responded that he would be hired anyway, the Bureau's interest sharpened. Surveillance over the next few months revealed little that confirmed Levinson's ties to Communism; more important, Hoover's accusations remained confidential, passed only to the White House, the attorney general's office, and a few select congressmen.

Among the congressmen, however, were the southern leaders of the SISS, James Eastland and John McClellan. In April the SISS subpoenaed Levinson, a move that would bring to light FBI suspicions of SCLC ties to Communism. Bureau officials feared the subpoena was premature, that it would drive Levinson into hiding before damning information could be uncovered. They asked the subcommittee to keep quiet whatever information it gained. The SISS grudgingly agreed. Levinson gave the subcommittee nothing worth revealing at the hearing anyway. He testified that he was "a loyal American" and "am not now and never have been a member of the Communist Party." He then invoked the Fifth Amendment and refused to answer further questions.[34]

The SISS had better information on Jack O'Dell, also known in southern segregationist circles as Hunter Pitts O'Dell. The subcommittee had a relationship with O'Dell that dated back to its 1956 hearings in New Orleans. Investigating subversive activities in the region, the SISS had uncovered O'Dell's relationship with the National Maritime Union. Expanding its investigation the subcommittee, with the help of the local Anti-Subversive Squad, searched O'Dell's room in New Orleans in late March 1956. The SISS found, among a number of Communist publications, letters from the party addressed "To all Districts: Proposals on Southern Party Organization—1955–1956." From this evidence the subcommittee concluded that O'Dell was a district organizer for the CP in New Orleans. They then subpoenaed him to appear before the SISS in early April. Unable to find O'Dell in New Orleans, the subcommittee eventually tracked him down and had

34. Branch, *Parting the Waters*, 586.

him testify in Washington. The witness invoked the Fifth Amendment, refusing to state whether or not he was a member of the Communist Party.[35]

O'Dell did, however, publicly defend himself. The day of the hearing he
issued a press release claiming that Senator Eastland led the real conspiracy
in the South. Eastland and the Citizens' Councils, according to O'Dell, had
"created the soil in which racist crimes of just about every description have
been allowed to flourish." In leading the rebellion against the *Brown* decision, Eastland was "leading a rebellion against the Constitution" and was
promoting a "McCarthyized press that would spread hate and confusion."
The Mississippi senator, O'Dell charged, "denies Americans the right to
read literature representing different viewpoints." The union activist then
called for the expulsion of Eastland from the Senate and for free elections in
Mississippi.[36]

Two years later, O'Dell appeared before HUAC. The committee subpoenaed him to answer accusations that he was a Communist made by two
former Communist leaders in the South. O'Dell again proved to be an unco-
operative, even confrontational witness. He redirected the committee's
questions asking "Do you know as much about the subversive activities in
this country that began with the slavery of the Negro people, and has [*sic*]
been going on for 300 years, including the Jim Crow system?" When the
committee confronted him again with the documents the SISS had confis-
cated from his room in 1956, O'Dell denied having seen the documents before and again pleaded the Fifth.[37]

Given the already extensive public investigation of O'Dell's Communist
ties by red and black investigators at the federal and state levels, King and
the SCLC might have been more cautious in taking him on. O'Dell was an
effective fund-raiser, but his association with the Communist Party could
have potentially undermined King's movement at a time when the need for
public support was most crucial. During the summer of 1962, the Albany

35. SISS to Thorman Draft, Southern Party Organization, 1955–1956, RG 46, Name File
1, O'Dell, Senate Internal Security Subcommittee Papers, National Archives; Papers Found
in the Room of H. O'Dell, 29 March 1956, RG 46, Name File 1, O'Dell, Senate Internal
Security Subcommittee Papers.

36. O'Dell Press Release, 12 April 1956, RG 46, Name File 1, O'Dell, Senate Internal
Security Subcommittee Papers.

37. *Communist Infiltration and Activities in the South: Hearings before the Committee on Un-American Activities, House of Representatives, 85th Congress, Second Session*
(Washington: United States Government Printing Office, 1958).

protests had failed to draw local sheriff Laurie Pritchett into acts of brutality against protesters. He quietly and peacefully filled the jails in the county, winning the praise of national newsmen and weakening the argument that [163 segregation could only be maintained through violent suppression. Observers in the movement, including King and Birmingham civil rights leader Fred Shuttlesworth, learned that they would have to better pick their battles. What they needed were graphic symbols of southern-segregationist brutality that would attract national attention and play on the moral sensibilities of an otherwise indifferent public. In Birmingham's Eugene "Bull" Connor, King and Shuttlesworth knew they had a representative of the segregationist cause who would react violently to protesters. But they also knew that they would have to keep the movement's image free of the taint of subversion. A proven Communist in their ranks might reverse whatever gains they had made in highlighting the moral differences between those struggling for and against black equality.

All of this was not lost on Robert Kennedy. On orders from the attorney general, Kennedy aide John Seigenthaler contacted SCLC board member Rev. Kelley Miller Smith. Smith relayed the message to King that the movement should sever all ties with O'Dell and in no case allow the alleged Communist to work on the Birmingham campaign. King found the request a nuisance but nevertheless acquiesced. He called O'Dell and informed him that he would have to stay behind in Atlanta; his scheduled workshops in Birmingham in September 1962 would be taken over by others.[38]

Just as King opened the SCLC's Birmingham convention, news about the Ole Miss riots and the Cuban Missile Crisis flashed across the country. As the nation focused on racial violence in Mississippi and nuclear weapons in Cuba, southern red and black hunters saw a perfect opportunity to publicize O'Dell's Communist ties. On October 26, the *New Orleans Times-Picayune*, the *St. Louis Globe-Democrat*, and several conservative newspapers ran almost identical front-page stories declaring O'Dell to be a "Communist who has infiltrated the top administrative post in the Rev. Martin Luther King's Southern Christian Leadership Conference," citing a "reliable source." In fact, the FBI had provided the information to the press.

King and the SCLC finally had to act. Instead of trying to deny O'Dell's connection to the Communist Party, King decided to minimize the former radical's connection to the SCLC. The conference leader told the press that

38. Branch, *Parting the Waters*, 646–47.

O'Dell's work had been limited to the mailing campaign in the North. King was lying. O'Dell had been working in the South for the SCLC for some time, coordinating a number of programs in the region and playing a major role in the SCLC's voter-registration campaign. King then accepted O'Dell's resignation, "pending further inquiry and clarification." This too was false. King assured O'Dell that the resignation was for public consumption only. O'Dell remained on the staff, despite the objections of many in and around the SCLC. Through existing wiretaps, the FBI was aware of the ruse and used it as evidence that the SCLC was covertly protecting subversives. The attorney general subsequently signed an FBI request to bug Stanley Levinson's home.[39]

Robert Kennedy had been acting as a middleman between King and Hoover as the distance between the two grew broader after the Levinson-O'Dell affair. In early 1963 he told King that the FBI knew O'Dell still worked for the SCLC and that the FBI's case was building. King attempted to cover his bases, asking O'Dell to provide him with a written record of his Communist affiliations as well as a written oath of allegiance to nonviolence and the American form of government. O'Dell wrote that even before joining the SCLC, he had concluded that his belief that lasting reform required "a Communist movement in the South" had been mistaken. About the same time, Stanley Levinson also decided the time had come to break his connections to the American Communist Party. Levinson met with CP financial functionary Lem Harris to break the news. The FBI overheard Levinson's declaration that he was through, but the Bureau continued to consider the SCLC fund-raiser a Soviet agent.[40]

On June 30, 1963, O'Dell's name again hit the papers. Relying once more on FBI leaks, the *Birmingham News* reported that the union radical was still on the SCLC payroll. Through attorney general for civil rights Burke Marshall, the Justice Department again pressed King to cut ties with O'Dell and Levinson. King finally gave in. In a letter copied to Marshall, he wrote to O'Dell that even though the SCLC had not uncovered "any present connection with the Communist party," the accusations against him were too damaging, and "in these critical times we cannot afford to risk such impressions." The SCLC would finally remove O'Dell from the payroll.

But King resisted giving up Levinson. He and Andrew Young asked Mar-

---

39. See *New Orleans Times-Picayune*, 26 October 1962, p. 1, and *St. Louis Globe-Democrat*, 26 October 1962, p. 1. Also see Garrow, *Bearing the Cross*, 222, and Branch, *Parting the Waters*, 675–79.

40. Garrow, *Bearing the Cross*, 235.

shall for specific evidence against Levinson. The attorney general for civil rights could only relay vague allegations but assured the civil rights leaders that Levinson had not just been scrutinized for some loose affiliation with Communists but had been implicated in espionage activity. King was not convinced.

Levinson, however, understood that he had become a liability to King and the movement. With the March on Washington approaching and the administration's civil rights bill under consideration in Congress, the White House had become less tolerant of the SCLC's protection of Levinson. Indeed, President Kennedy told King at a June 22 Rose Garden meeting that he must "get rid of" O'Dell and Levinson. "They're Communists," Kennedy said. Stanley Levinson realized that without Kennedy's support the movement's momentum would be stalled; on his own, the radical businessman ended any further direct contact with King. King grudgingly agreed to the break but continued to keep in touch with Levinson through New York attorney Clarence Jones.[41]

Red and black investigators gained perhaps their greatest victory to date with the withdrawals of Levinson and O'Dell from the SCLC. King's grudging dissociation from the two appeared to be tacit evidence that the civil rights leader had close ties to former Communists and was willing to protect them. Furthermore red and black hunters effectively used the King scandal to deliver their message to a larger national audience at a time when cold-war anxieties could be most successfully counterbalanced against concerns over racial conflict in the South. The civil rights movement was now on the defensive.

Not satisfied that King had truly broken ties with O'Dell, segregationists continued to publicly hound the civil rights leader about his former colleague. King sniped back that segregationists were using "McCarthy-like tactics" to thwart the movement and divert the public's attention. But he had to admit that for the SCLC "it became evident in Birmingham that the crusade for civil rights had reached the conscience of America and that Mr. O'Dell's employment could be used against the organization by segregationists."

King's reaction to the red and black charges, although not as acquiescent as the NAACP's, constituted a relatively conservative stance on the issue. Others in the movement, however, took an even harder line against the southern red scare. The Bradens in particular bristled at the SCLC's sacrifice

41. Ibid., 274–75, and Branch, *Parting the Waters*, 835–45, 850–53.

of O'Dell and Levinson. They would hold fast, publicly defending the rights of Americans to free association and free speech, even if the Americans in question were Communists.[42]

After the anti-HUAC riots in San Francisco, the Bradens worked closely with the National Committee to Abolish the House Un-American Activities Committee. Anne Braden in particular took on the committee with the zeal of a matriarch protecting her family. She delivered speeches appealing to liberal definitions of free speech and free association and to the American disdain for authoritarian demagogues. As a result of her work for the Committee to Abolish HUAC and with the sponsorship of SCEF, Anne Braden eventually wrote the most articulate and direct denunciation of the southern red scare that the era would produce.[43]

Braden's lengthy 1964 article, titled "House Un-American Activities Committee: Bulwark of Segregation," argued that the accusations of Communist affiliation directed against members of the civil rights movement had had a significant impact on whether southern whites joined the crusade for black equality. She wrote that while she and her compatriots knew many southern whites who were "willing to go to jail and to risk the physical danger" in the name of integration, "the word communist means 'traitor' to them, and they don't want to be called that." In Savannah, Georgia; Roanoke Virginia; Oxford Mississippi, and locations all over the South, direct-action efforts to end segregation and bring African Americans to the polls were smeared with the Communist charge. Braden quoted, among others, Georgia activist Hosea Williams: "It hurt us bad. Especially with the local white people. Last summer some of them were beginning to take an open stand with us and a lot more were quietly sympathetic. But when the communist business started, they all backed off. Now they won't touch us with a 10-foot pole."

Proving the charges false, however, was futile according to Braden. Most white southerners used Communism as a "nebulous scapegoat to which they can shift the guilt for the crimes of their society." The mere "feeling" that the movement was Communist-inspired was assumed to be fact, evidence to the contrary notwithstanding. Efforts to prove the accusations wrong, therefore, sapped the movement's energy and diverted workers from

42. "Martin Luther Admits Link," *Mississippi Clarion-Ledger*, 26 July 1963.

43. See for example Anti-HUAC Speech, December 1961, Box 3, HUAC Folder, Braden Papers.

the fight against racial oppression. Braden quoted Student Nonviolent Coordinating Committee worker Charles Sherrod's reflections on the sit-in movement in Richmond, Virginia: "We needed help and somebody suggested we get in touch with CORE. Then somebody else said no, CORE was communist and we'd better be careful. . . . I began to wonder whether the others were communists. We were all looking at each other, wondering, 'Which rock are they under?' We wasted months that way before we finally decided to forget it and go after segregation."

For Braden the only solution was to abolish the source of misleading and sometimes patently false accusations: state investigative agencies, Eastland's SISS, and their main source of information—HUAC. The movement groups that had made extensive efforts to prove the charges of subversion false and had purged their ranks of Communists, according to Braden, had accomplished nothing. None of their pleas, she declared, "had decreased the cries of communism against those groups." The "atmosphere" of accusation had to be broken. Southern nationalists should not be allowed to tie segregation to "the national issue of communism" and pose as "a guardian of the national security." Otherwise "Southern moderates," who were the key constituency to win over if the civil rights movement was to succeed, could also be labeled subversive if they so much as spoke out against segregation. This was a time of change, according to Braden, when the "world's have-nots, both here and abroad, have been coming into their own." "Invariably," she continued, the red- and black-baiters "worked to keep things pretty much as they have been," securing political power based on the repression of black voters. This conservative political chain had to be broken to allow for social progress.[44]

More than any other writer, Anne Braden connected anti-Communism with racism. She directly identified the leaders of the southern red scare and convincingly tied their efforts to the larger massive-resistance campaign. She also successfully mounted a public-relations effort that rivaled that of the segregationists. Braden's pamphlet eventually sold more than two hundred thousand copies. But while her writings were crucial in countering the charges of the red and black investigating network, her suggestion that the civil rights movement end its efforts to distance itself from the radical left served the interests of the popular front more than the direct interests of

44. "HUAC: Bulwark of Segregation," ID# 6-44-0-11-1-1-1, Mississippi State Sovereignty Commission Files, Mississippi Department of Archives and History.

southern blacks. Southern moderates, a group she understood to be key to the movement's success, were anti-Communists and needed to hear that the movement's goals were limited to ensuring an equal place for African Americans in a capitalist, democratic society.[45]

In the battle between the civil rights movement and massive resisters for the hearts and minds of southerners, public-relations management was crucial. Martin Luther King was right; success depended to a large degree on which side could reveal itself to be the moral keepers of American democratic and Christian traditions. While the civil rights movement increasingly aimed to highlight the brutality of segregation through direct-action campaigns in the Deep South, massive resisters looked to red and black accusations to throw into question the movement's claim to moral superiority. If it was Communist, segregationists could rightly argue, the movement would have no legitimate claim to Christian and democratic ideals. Communists were just as guilty of excluding whole classes of people from the political process as segregationists were.

The question for the movement was how to face the accusations. Should the organizations involved purge all those with Communist or popular-front ties from their ranks, or should they defend the civil rights of Communists as they had defended the rights of blacks and accept the aid of all those willing to help, regardless of their political affiliation? As King and the SCLC came to realize, philosophically and practically in terms of public relations, distancing the movement from current and former Communists was the only sure way to effectively counter the accusations. As Anne Braden had pointed out, the charges were difficult enough to fight even when untrue. In addition, the time and effort spent defending the civil rights of Communists would have drained resources from the struggle for black equality and weakened the moral claims of the movement. This did not mean, however, that the movement should acquiesce to an atmosphere of fear. It needed to challenge the poorly sustained conclusions of red- and black-baiters who capitalized on cold-war events to label the whole movement Communist. But for those with very real former or current ties to the Communist Party, such as Levinson and O'Dell, the costs of employing them outweighed the benefits. The key for the black civil rights movement was to denounce both Communism and the McCarthyite tactics of segregationists. Only then could it maintain a moral position that would resonate with moderate southerners and the majority of Americans.

---

45. Seth Cagin and Philip Dray, *We Are Not Afraid* (New York: Macmillan, 1988), 88.

THE SOUTHERN RED SCARE AND
THE CIVIL RIGHTS ACT OF 1964

6

WITH NEWS OF MARTIN LUTHER KING'S TIES TO COM-
munists all over the pages of the national press, the leaders of the southern
red scare moved to stall the revolutionary federal civil rights legislation
pending before Congress in 1963 and 1964. Their efforts convinced many
Americans that Communists had at least some influence over the civil
rights movement, but they failed to persuade a critical mass of their coun-
trymen that the movement's main goals and methods had been corrupted.
Moreover, just as the network of red and black investigators was beginning
to make its broadest and most politically potent appeal to date, the assassination of President John F. Kennedy stole the headlines. In the end the
southern red scare could do only limited damage to the movement's most
important legislative initiatives.

Shortly after he gained office, Alabama governor George Wallace's political rhetoric made him the nation's leading spokesman for the southern
right. In his January 1963 inaugural speech, Wallace wrapped his administration in segregation and anti-Communism. He lamented the increasing
role of the federal government in the lives of Alabama's citizens and the
diminishing power of white people from the Congo to Oxford, Mississippi.
"No wonder communism is winning the world," he shouted; white governments were no longer capable of defending against it. The "false doctrine of
communistic amalgamation" was taking its toll. The state's only defense
was "segregation forever."[1]

In the months following, thousands of demonstrators, many of them
black schoolchildren, took to the streets in Birmingham. Protests in "the
most segregated big city in America" had begun when local civil rights
leader Rev. Fred Shuttlesworth invited Martin Luther King to lead nonviolent demonstrations there. "Bombingham," so dubbed because of the numerous racially motivated bombings that had taken place in the city since
the mid-1950s, would not change easily. When protesters staged sit-ins at

1. Dan Carter, *The Politics of Rage* (New York: Simon and Schuster, 1995), 108–109.

local lunch counters and marched on city hall, Birmingham police under ardent segregationist and anti-Communist Eugene "Bull" Connor arrested the lot. City officials, meanwhile, secured injunctions barring racial demonstrations. King, Shuttlesworth, and their followers saw a chance for direct and public confrontation with segregationist brutality. Again taking to the streets, protesters met Connor's minions and were attacked by police dogs and riot-geared officers. The incident made national television and print news.

Arrested and jailed during the marches, Martin Luther King used his incarceration to make one of his most impassioned calls for nonviolent direct action against segregation. In his "Letter from Birmingham Jail," King challenged his critics in the movement (who had questioned his timing and tactics) not to wait for justice, and he made a plea to all Americans to support the effort to end segregation. Stirred by his vision, the Birmingham movement agreed to increase the pressure on the city government. King's followers decided to put their sons and daughters on the line. On May 2 a thousand black children, some as young as six years old, marched out of the Sixteenth Street Baptist Church into the city streets, where they were arrested. A day later another thousand children gathered to repeat the event. This time, however, Bull Connor's forces set upon them with nightsticks, dogs, and fire hoses. The violence continued over the next few days as some protesters retaliated against police attacks with stones and bottles.

Wallace seized the opportunity to appear before the state legislature and repeat his accusations that red agents were behind the black protests. The governor made public his view that the "troubles in Birmingham stem from a long history of outside agitation planned and directed by members of the communist party and their fellow-travelers." Suspected Communists— including Anne and Carl Braden, James Dombrowski, Myles Horton, and Leonard Holt, a National Lawyers Guild attorney—had been seen in the city at a conference on integration in the South. In view of this "evidence," Wallace found it reasonable to assert that Communists hoping to stir racial conflict had carried out many of the bombings in the city. He promised to stamp out the Communist-inspired and Communist-led revolutionaries who were paralyzing Birmingham.[2]

2. Ibid., 124. See also "The troubles in Birmingham . . ." Draft, SG22371, F15, and Wallace to Ford, 6 January 1964, SG12656, F1, Wallace Papers, Alabama Department of Archives and History. See also William D. Barnard, *Dixiecrats and Democrats: Alabama Politics 1942–1950* (Tuscaloosa: University of Alabama Press, 1974), 177 n. 30.

Days later the Alabama legislature established its Commission to Preserve the Peace, a body designed to help keep Wallace's pledge. Ben Allen, a state investigator who had worked with the Alabama state police's antisubversive squad, suggested to Wallace the idea for the Peace Commission just after the governor's inauguration. Allen argued that since 1938, when the Southern Conference for Human Welfare first set up shop in Birmingham, white liberals had been "confusing the minds of the Negro race." With its northern allies, he argued, this fifth column "sought to change our Southern way of life and integrate [*sic*] the races." The Peace Commission, under Allen's plan, would combat the red and black threat with broad subpoena powers, the authority to issue contempt citations, and the direct action of the state police.

Allen and the legislators who helped introduce his proposal drew their inspiration directly from the House Un-American Activities Committee (HUAC). Indeed, the commission requested the advice of HUAC founder Martin Dies, who assured the group that Communist plans for American blacks posed a very real threat to the South. The state would use the Peace Commission primarily to conduct public hearings exposing subversives in the civil rights movement. Under representative John Hawkins of Birmingham, the first head of the organization, the commission pledged to reveal "the entire scope of the subversive apparatus" in the state.[3]

Had Allen had his way, the Peace Commission would also have worked with the police to intimidate all who dissented from the state's position on segregation. Alabama legislators, however, refrained from issuing the commission subpoena powers and contempt authority. They decided to reserve these devices for a body more directly under the control of Governor Wallace. In the late summer, the general assembly created its own Sovereignty Commission (SSC). Structured after its forbears, the Alabama SSC wielded broad powers to investigate and make public its findings. The commission had the authority to subpoena, issue oaths, and examine witnesses and their papers. Its creators also added special sections to the SSC mandate that encouraged cooperation with similar state organizations. Governor Wallace welcomed the creation of the commission and looked forward to chairing it. Both he and Alabama SSC director Eli Howell would use the body in con-

3. Dies letter, 27 November 1963, SG21074, Legislative Commission to Preserve the Peace Papers, Alabama Department of Archives and History; Carter, *Politics of Rage,* 230–32.

junction with other state agencies to launch a "counter-offense" against civil rights activists. They argued that the Sovereignty Commission was justified by a "clear need to investigate communist infiltration" in Alabama.[4]

While demonstrations in Birmingham accelerated Alabama's efforts to expose a black and red conspiracy, they also had the effect of prompting President Kennedy to renew his commitment to national civil rights legislation. After network television flashed images of young protesters batoned and hosed by Bull Connor and Alabama law-enforcement officials, the young president felt he could no longer stand idly by. Before a national television and radio audience on June 11, 1963, Kennedy called for passage of a sweeping civil rights act. The administration's bill included provisions for desegregating public accommodations; initiating school-desegregation suits; establishing agencies to mediate racial conflicts; improving the economic status of blacks; and empowering the government to withhold funds from federally supported programs and facilities in which discrimination occurred.

Massive resisters in Congress reacted to the proposed legislation with alarm. Mississippi senator James Eastland called the bill a "complete blueprint for a totalitarian state" while Georgia senator Richard Russell prepared for a Congressional filibuster. As the leader of the southern delegation in successful campaigns to weaken federal civil rights legislation in the past, most notably the 1957 Civil Rights Act, Richard Russell was the natural choice to again lead the segregationist defense.[5]

Never a race-baiting or red-baiting firebrand, Russell was nonetheless a committed segregationist and anti-Communist. In arguing against Kennedy's proposed legislation, the ardent southern nationalist declared that federal enforcement of black civil rights in the South was worse than anything proposed by Thaddeus Stevens or Charles Sumner. Like carpetbaggers one hundred years before, Russell claimed, "outside agitators" backed by the "naked power" of the federal government were threatening "immediate and

---

4. Act No. 3, 1963, SG21074, Legislative Commission to Preserve the Peace Papers; House Bill No. 880, SG13842, Alabama State Sovereignty Commission Papers, Alabama Department of Archives and History; Wallace to Burleson, 25 September 1963, SG22381, F11, Wallace Papers; Howell to Wallace Memorandum, undated, SG22383, F18 and 19, Wallace Papers. Also see Carter, *Politics of Rage*, 232–33.

5. Quoted in Harvard Sitkoff, *The Struggle for Black Equality* (New York: Hill and Wang, 1981), 158.

revolutionary" changes in the region. If left unchecked, he asserted, the federal government would permit nonwhites to dilute the Anglo-Saxon character of the United States and allow Communists to slip in among them.[6]

The southern bloc tightened ranks around Russell to challenge the civil rights bill but, as the Georgia senator realized, they could no longer muster the influence they once had. Southerners had been increasingly isolated from the Democratic Party since the Roosevelt administration. The party had increasingly sought the votes of labor unionists and racial minorities over those of the traditionally solid southern bloc. By the 1960s, liberals controlled the party's platform. In response, southern legislators had increasingly allied themselves with conservative Republicans. This tactic helped the southern delegation prevent significant civil rights legislation in the 1950s, but by the early 1960s segregation had begun to fall out of popular favor nationally. While white southerners overwhelmingly continued to disapprove of federal civil rights legislation, public-opinion polls taken after Birmingham showed that most Americans were beginning to support King's crusade and, subsequently, Kennedy's initiative.[7]

Russell and the southern bloc's only hope in the face of these overwhelming odds rested on a two-pronged defense. The southerners could try to bottle up the legislation in a committee where a southerner was chairman, preferably Eastland's Judiciary Committee. If this tactic did not work, they could try to gain Republican help in supporting a filibuster and in preventing changes to the cloture rules. Successful only in temporarily blocking the cloture-rule changes, the southern bloc could not control the committee procedures or lead a coordinated filibuster.[8]

Hoping against hope, southerners turned to red and black accusations.

6. *Congressional Record*, 85th Cong., 1st sess., 1957, 103, pt. 8:10771–75; *Congressional Record*, 88th Cong., 2nd sess., 1964, 110, pt. 11:14299–302; *Congressional Record*, 87th Cong., 2nd sess., 1962, 108, pt. 4:4153; *Congressional Record*, 85th Cong., 1st sess., 1957, 103, pt. 12:16659–62; *Congressional Record*, 80th Cong., 2nd sess., 1948, 94, pt. 5:6459–60, 6864; "Declaration of Constitutional Principles," 17 March 1956, III A, Box 27, Russell Papers, Richard B. Russell Memorial Library, University of Georgia; "Russell to Mizell," 30 April 1962, X, Box 186, Russell Papers; "Ervin to Mizell," 13 April 1962, X, Box 186, Russell Papers; Gilbert Fite, *Richard B. Russell Jr., Senator from Georgia* (Chapel Hill: University of North Carolina Press), 220, 283–84, 308–309, 337–38, 414; Robert Mann, *The Walls of Jericho* (New York: Harcourt Brace, 1996), 191–99.

7. George Gallup, *The Gallup Poll: Public Opinion 1935–1971* (New York: Random House, 1972).

8. Fite, *Richard Russell*, 407, 412–13.

Perhaps, they reasoned, conservatives would be swayed by the argument that the civil rights movement was Communist-inspired and join the fight against the civil rights bill. Never in the past had Russell believed this tactic promised any success, but for the first time in the summer of 1963, he investigated reports that Communists had infiltrated the Southern Christian Leadership Conference. His inspiration came from the new leader of the southern red scare, Alabama governor George Wallace.[9]

Before the Senate Commerce Committee in July 1963, Wallace and two of his colleagues in southern state government directly tied the proposed civil rights bill to an alleged red and black conspiracy. The committee asked Mississippi governor Ross Barnett, Arkansas attorney general Bruce Bennett, and Wallace to address concerns that the civil rights bill would infringe on the property rights of business owners who wished to preserve segregation practices on their premises. All three charged that the bill's biggest flaw was its furtherance of the Communist cause.

Barnett's and Bennett's speeches were generally tired and unconvincing. Barnett repeated wild charges that the movement was a Communist conspiracy and that President Kennedy was assisting the red plot with his civil rights bill. Similarly, Bennett reviewed race relations in Arkansas, making the still unsubstantiated claim that racial unrest in the state "was deliberately planned by the Communist Party as a part of the directive handed down by Moscow in 1928." Governor Wallace, however, struck a chord with the committee and the press. He attacked the civil rights legislation along the same lines as the other two but based his accusations on congressional sources and avoided painting the entire movement red.

The president's bill, Wallace argued, was "part of the drift toward centralized socialist control and away from the free enterprise system." By catering to the forces of integration, the legislation constituted a "mad scramble for the minority bloc vote" and a violation of states' rights. Moreover, in acquiescing to the demands of the civil rights movement, the federal government was possibly aiding subversives. "Is the real purpose of this integration movement to disarm this country as the Communists have planned?" the governor asked. The demonstrators "break laws, destroy

9. Russell to HUAC Chairman, 29 July 1963, Civil Rights Special, UnAmerican Activities Committee, X, Box 3, Russell Papers; Willis to Russell, 13 August 1963, Civil Rights Special, UnAmerican Activities Committee, X, Box 3, Russell Papers; Kennedy to Russell, 1 November 1963, Civil Rights Special, UnAmerican Activities Committee, X, Box 3, Russell Papers.

property, injure innocent people, and create civil strife" but still enjoy the "sympathy and approval" of the federal government. "I resent," Wallace continued, "the fawning and pawing over such people as Martin Luther King and his pro-Communist friends and associates." King, Wallace reported, had attended the "Highlander Folk School for Communist Training." His "top lieutenant," Fred Shuttlesworth, was then president of the Southern Conference Educational Fund, described by "the Senate Internal Security Subcommittee and the House Un-American Activities Committee as an organization 'set up to promote Communism' throughout the South." King had also recently lied about firing Jack O'Dell, "a known Communist." Finally, King had been photographed with Aubrey Williams "identified by a witness," according to a "congressional committee" report, "as one who had been a member of the Communist Party." Wallace conceded that Williams had denied the charge but pointed out that he had admitted to connections with "a number of Communist-front organizations." On these grounds, Wallace concluded, the Congress of the United States should "defeat in its entirety the Civil Rights Act of 1963."[10]

Wallace's remarks made front-page news in the *Washington Post,* and the *New York Times* ran long excerpts from the governor's opening statement. Each of the major television networks also featured Wallace as the voice of southern opposition to the Kennedy bill. Senators like Democrat Clair Engle of California praised the governor for "the way he presents his case. He's smart." Indeed, only two senators took exception to Wallace's presentation, and their objections were mild. Neither contradicted the Alabama governor's description of Highlander as a Communist training school or defended Aubrey Williams. Wallace had successfully softened the virulent racism and the anti-Communist paranoia of the Bennetts and Barnetts. While avoiding blanket accusations and tailoring his message to a conservative national audience, he capitalized on widespread concerns over private-property rights, states' rights, anti-Communism, and social disorder. In short George Wallace did a great deal to bring the southern red scare closer to the conservative mainstream.[11]

With the national spotlight temporarily focused on Wallace, the Demo-

---

10. *Hearings before the Committee on Commerce, U.S. Senate, 88th Congress, First Session, July 15, 16, 1963.* Also see Carter, *Politics of Rage,* 157–60, and David Garrow, *Bearing the Cross* (New York: William Morrow, 1986), 278–79.

11. Carter, *Politics of Rage,* 160–61.

cratic senator from Oklahoma Mike Monroney asked the FBI and the Justice Department to respond to the Alabama governor's accusations. In a carefully worded statement, attorney general Robert Kennedy replied that the government had no evidence that "any of the top leaders of the major civil rights groups are Communists or Communist-controlled. This is true as to Dr. Martin Luther King, Jr., about whom particular accusations were made, as well as other leaders."[12]

Kennedy's statement may have comforted liberals, but it did little to stop southern nationalist calls to expand investigations into the civil rights movement. Representative Albert Watson of South Carolina reentered into the *Congressional Record* a report based on the findings of Arkansas representative E. C. Gathings outlining the "Subversive Character of the NAACP." And Senator Strom Thurmond of South Carolina (then a Democrat) declared that he was convinced that the civil rights demonstrations were part of a Communist conspiracy. Thurmond even suggested that the upcoming March on Washington for black civil rights was Communist-led.[13]

Thurmond's statement was the first of many he would make on the issue in the days leading up to the late-August march. Early in the month, the one-time Dixiecrat presidential candidate worked vigorously to keep concerns over a red and black conspiracy alive in Congress by repeating and expanding on the accusations of Wallace and company. On August 2 and again on August 7, Thurmond entered into the *Congressional Record* several newspaper articles alleging Communist influence in the sit-ins, freedom rides, protest marches, and civil rights rallies across the country. His most telling charges, however, came on August 13. The senator's accusations focused on longtime civil rights activist, close King associate, and principal organizer of the upcoming March on Washington, Bayard Rustin. Ostensibly correcting the "distorted and slanted reporting of the *Washington Post*," which praised the civil rights leader's record as a nonviolent protester and organizer, Thurmond painted a picture of Rustin that was less than heroic.[14]

12. "Government Has No Evidence Civil Rights Leaders Are Reds," *New York Times*, 26 July 1963, p. 1; "RFK Says Mixers Not Communists," *Mississippi Clarion-Ledger*, 26 July 1963.

13. "Leftist Sparks D.C. Marchers," *Jackson Daily News*, 27 July 1963; *Congressional Record*, 88th Cong., 1st sess., 1963, 109, pt. 11. See also "Thurmond Cites Red Bid to Form CORE Chapter," *The State*, 27 September 1961.

14. *Congressional Record*, 88th Cong., 1st sess., 1963, 109, pt. 10:13968–13975.

Thurmond delved deep into the activist's past. Rustin had been arrested for resisting the draft during World War II and had been convicted in California on "sexual perversion" charges. He had also been a member of the Com- munist Youth League and had been placed at Communist meetings as late as 1958. From 1955 to 1960, Rustin had acted as a secretary to Martin Luther King—the same King, Thurmond pointed out, who had lied about firing Hunter Pitts (Jack) O'Dell, "an admitted Communist." Finally Rustin was working closely with socialist A. Philip Randolph in organizing the upcoming March on Washington. Randolph and King, according to Thurmond, were sponsors of the Highlander Center in Tennessee (formerly the Highlander Folk School), which had been closed by the state "on the grounds of immorality." After entering several more articles into the record, the South Carolina senator concluded: "I am not satisfied and many people across this country are not satisfied with the Attorney General's efforts to whitewash the question of Communist influence or involvement in these Negro demonstrations which have been turning into race riots. . . . The evidence I have presented . . . and the evidence which has been presented in the Commerce Committee hearings . . . demonstrate the need for a searching and thorough investigation of this entire question by Congress, before any action is taken on the civil rights legislation which was sent to Capitol Hill as a direct result of these demonstrations."[15]

Thurmond's description of Rustin was accurate, if somewhat incomplete. Rustin had in fact been a committed civil rights activist with a controversial background. While living in Harlem as a young man, Rustin had run in Communist circles. He was drawn to Communism after the show trial of August Yokinen, a party member charged by the Communist International with acting discourteously toward three blacks at a Harlem nightclub. Rustin regularly attended the integrated social clubs run by Communists and did indeed eventually join the Communist Youth League. As a talented folk singer, Rustin was an effective recruiter for the group. He was also a capable organizer and rose quickly in the League's ranks.

When Adolf Hitler invaded the Soviet Union in June 1941, the Central Committee of the American Communist Party ordered Rustin to cease his efforts as an activist for black civil rights. Communists, by Central Committee dictate, could not be diverted from the all-out drive to defeat Hitler. The next morning, Rustin resigned from the party. He subsequently sought

15. Ibid, pt. 11:14836–44.

out A. Philip Randolph and offered his services. Randolph had recently become the most prominent black activist in the country when he publicly threatened to lead a massive march on Washington if President Roosevelt did not end racial discrimination in the defense industries. Rustin had worked on the march with Randolph for only a few days when Roosevelt signed an executive order mandating fair hiring practices on defense jobs. Randolph then referred Rustin to A. J. Muste at the Fellowship of Reconciliation (FOR).

FOR hired Rustin as its youth secretary. At the same time, he went to work for the FOR offshoot Congress of Racial Equality (CORE). Both organizations emphasized the anti-colonial aspects of Gandhian nonviolence, a philosophy Rustin took as his own. In 1943 he went to jail for refusing duty in a military hospital; he spent the rest of the war behind bars. Upon his release Rustin headed the Free India Committee and was arrested several times for picketing the British Embassy in Washington. In 1947 he joined a CORE-sponsored freedom ride through the South, the precursor to the 1961 rides. Again he went to jail, this time for violating North Carolina's segregation laws. After serving several months on a chain gang, Rustin journeyed to India and Africa to work with anti-colonialists such as Kwame Nkrumah of Ghana. Back home in the early 1950s, he led protests in New York against the Korean War.

Rustin liked to drink and party with the New York literati. He lived in Greenwich Village and fit well in its bohemian culture. Rustin was also homosexual, a fact accepted in the Village but frowned upon outside its confines. FOR leaders respected and liked him but understood that his homosexuality, if made public, would compromise the group's public standing. In January 1953, when California police arrested Rustin and two other men on morals charges (oral sodomy, according to Los Angeles police officials), he again went to jail and resigned from FOR. Adrift once more, Rustin moved to the South and joined Martin Luther King's Montgomery movement. From that vantage point, he helped form the Southern Christian Leadership Conference (SCLC) and organize many of that group's campaigns as well as other movement events, most significantly the 1963 March on Washington.[16]

16. Jervis Anderson, *Bayard Rustin: Troubles I've Seen* (New York: HarperCollins, 1997). Also see Taylor Branch, *Parting the Waters: America in the King Years, 1954–1963* (New York: Simon and Schuster, 1988), 168–73.

When confronted by Senator Thurmond, Rustin chose carefully which elements of his past he would share with the press. He responded to the South Carolinian's allegations by acknowledging his pacifism during the war and his association and subsequent split with the Communist Youth League. He denied having ever been to the Soviet Union as Thurmond alleged but said he "would have been proud" to have joined members of the Non-Violent Action Committee in Red Square. The protesters, Rustin explained, were condemning nuclear testing by the Soviet government and denouncing the absence of political democracy in the country. Thurmond's misleading statements on this issue, Rustin fired back, were a "disgrace to the United States Senate and a measure of the desperation of the segregationist cause." Rustin remained quiet about the morals charges in California. While he felt he might be forgiven for his political affiliations, he understood that his homosexuality could end his work on the march, as it had with FOR.[17]

To the leaders of the 1963 March on Washington, Rustin had acquitted himself well. There would be no purging this time. Martin Luther King publicly praised Rustin's abilities and achievements while A. Philip Randolph, for whom Rustin worked on the march, declared his "complete confidence in Bayard Rustin's character, integrity, and extraordinary ability." Any indiscretion he may have committed in California, Randolph declared, did not void or overwhelm his "ongoing contribution to the struggle for human rights." Finally in attacking Rustin, Randolph argued, Thurmond had overstepped the bounds of decency in his obsession "to discredit the movement."[18]

King's and Randolph's confidence in Rustin was well placed. The march itself was a tremendous success, much to the chagrin of southern segregationists. On August 28, more than two hundred thousand peaceful demonstrators gathered in Washington. From the Lincoln Memorial, the nation's top civil rights leaders voiced the grievances and frustrations of blacks in their quest for political and social equality. It was at this venue that Martin Luther King delivered the most stirring and historic speech of the long struggle:

17. "Thurmond Assails," *New York Herald Tribune*, 14 August 1963; Statement by Bayard Rustin, 14 August 1963, 8:0817, Rustin Papers, Library of Congress.

18. "Negro Rally Aide Rebuts Senator," *New York Times*, 16 August 1963, p. 10.

I have a dream that one day on the red hills of Georgia the sons of former slaves and the sons of former slaveowners will be able to sit down together at the table of brotherhood.

I have a dream that one day even the State of Mississippi, a state sweltering with the heat of injustice, sweltering with the heat of oppression, will be transformed into an oasis of freedom and justice. I have a dream that my four little children will one day live in a nation where they will not be judged by the color of their skin but by the content of their character. I have a dream today.

I have a dream that one day down in Alabama with its vicious racists, with its Governor having his lips dripping with the words of interposition and nullification—one day right there in Alabama, little black boys and black girls will be able to join hands with little white boys and white girls as sisters and brothers.

I have a dream today.

King's speech was transcendent. It restored the hope of nonviolent activists, regained the confidence of those sympathetic to the cause but wary of its confrontational stand in Birmingham, and rallied congressional support for the civil rights bill. The speech also reassured many that the movement for black civil rights was neither radical nor violent but in the best tradition of American democracy.[19]

Roy Wilkins had predicted before the march that when Rustin took over as its organizer, the SCLC worker's background would be used to discredit the movement in general. In reality, however, Thurmond's revelations about Rustin may have been a plus for the movement. Ultimately, according to march worker Tom Kahn, the arch-segregationist's attack on Rustin seemed to have done more good than harm in drawing participants to the event. The northern press had proven more sympathetic to Rustin than to the southerner. While Thurmond's attack may have bolstered already existing support in the South, it had won few new converts and alienated many in other parts of the country.[20]

In the longer run, however, Wilkins's fears also proved valid. Thurmond continued to hammer away with accusations against King, adding the civil rights leader's association with Anne and Carl Braden and the SCEF to the

19. Sitkoff, *Struggle for Black Equality,* 163–64.

20. Kahn to Stembridge, 19 August 1963, 7:0698, Rustin Papers; Garrow, *Bearing the Cross,* 276.

long list of charges of Communist cooperation. Always sensitive to the prevailing political winds, FBI director J. Edgar Hoover took the opportunity to pressure Attorney General Robert Kennedy into authorizing wiretaps of King's home and offices. Hoover, of course, had compiled his own files on Bayard Rustin as well as Jack O'Dell and Stanley Levinson. He believed as the southerners did that Communists had significantly influenced the movement. But Hoover's evidence was incomplete, and he did not want to make his files public for fear of compromising his agents before more incriminating evidence was forthcoming. Moreover, a public campaign by Hoover really was not necessary. Southerners such as Thurmond, Wallace, Bennett, Gathings, Eastland, and others, who often worked from FBI files leaked to them, served the director's purposes perfectly.[21]

Robert Kennedy and John Kennedy both recognized the significance of the public charges against King. The accusations, if widely believed, would affect the administration's reputation as anti-Communist as well as its chances of passing the civil rights bill. Thus did Robert Kennedy grant the FBI director's request for the King wiretap in early October 1963. The attorney general, at the same time, also signed off on an FBI request to wiretap Bayard Rustin.[22]

With Hoover, Thurmond, Wallace, and others pursuing King and the SCLC in Washington, James Eastland hoped to add the evidence that would once and for all end the move toward federally enforced civil rights legislation. The Mississippi senator had for years been searching for a smoking gun that would convince the nation of a red and black conspiracy. In the fall of 1963, he believed he had come closer than ever to finding it. On October 4 state and city police in New Orleans raided the offices of the Southern Conference Education Fund (SCEF). They also searched the homes and private offices of the organization's executive director James Dombrowski, its treasurer and attorney Benjamin Smith, and Smith's law partner Bruce Waltzer. The raids had come at the request of Louisiana's Joint Legislative Com-

---

21. *Congressional Record*, 88th Cong., 1st sess., 1963, 109, pt. 12:15797–808.

22. Michael Friendly and David Gallen, *Martin Luther King Jr: The FBI File* (New York: Carroll and Graf, 1993), 28–44; Garrow, *Bearing the Cross*, 287–307; Arthur M. Schlesinger Jr., *Robert Kennedy and His Times* (Boston: Houghton Mifflin, 1978), 352–67; Kenneth O'Reilly, *Hoover and the Un-Americans* (Philadelphia: Temple University Press, 1983), 94–97. See also Carl M. Brauer, *John F. Kennedy and the Second Reconstruction* (New York: Columbia University Press, 1977), 286–87; Victor Navasky, *Kennedy Justice* (New York: Atheneum, 1971), 136–47.

mittee on Un-American Activities (LUAC), formerly the Joint Legislative Committee on Segregation. While police ransacked their offices, Dombrowski, Smith, and Waltzer were arrested for violating Louisiana's Subversive Activities and Communist Control Law as well as the state's Communist Propaganda Control Act. They were charged with managing a subversive organization and distributing Communist propaganda.[23]

State officials had planned the raids months before the event. Like Eastland they hoped that the SCEF papers would provide clear evidence of a Communist conspiracy in the southern civil rights movement. Moreover, they trusted, the conviction of the three, especially Dombrowski, would shift the blame for racial conflict in the South and help undermine pending civil rights legislation. To accomplish these ends, officials believed, the raid would have to gain attention in Washington but at the same time be kept out of the hands of federal officials, including the FBI. As LUAC legal counsel Jack Rogers explained to the press, while he and the committee had complete confidence in J. Edgar Hoover, they did not trust Attorney General Bobby Kennedy and "his friend" Martin Luther King. For exposure in the nation's capital, LUAC looked instead to a person they deemed eminently trustworthy, Senator Eastland.

The personnel, financial, and membership records of SCEF were a coveted prize indeed for Eastland. In 1954 his Senate Internal Security Subcommittee (SISS) had attempted to secure lists of contributors and supporters of the organization and failed. Ten years later the subcommittee would finally have the opportunity to investigate the backgrounds of every person involved with the group. On the day following the Louisiana raid, the SISS subpoenaed the state police in Baton Rouge, demanding release of the Education Fund's records. The exchange had in all likelihood been prearranged. The subpoenas were dated October 4, the day of the raid.[24]

The letters and correspondence of James Dombrowski seemed the mother lode of the seized material. A founding member and administrator of the Highlander Folk School, an executive director of the Southern Conference for Human Welfare (SCHW), and a principal organizer of the offshoot Southern Conference Education Fund, he had been a target of red and

23. "Fact Sheet on the Raid and Arrests," 10 October 1963, Box 4, SCEF Raids Folder, Braden Papers, University of Tennessee.

24. Ibid.; Frank Adams, *James A. Dombrowski: An American Heretic, 1897–1983* (Knoxville: University of Tennessee Press, 1992), 270.

black investigations since the 1940s. In his various roles Dombrowski had provided a crucial connection between the civil rights movement and groups that southern segregationists most suspected of Communist subversion. Dombrowski himself was not a Communist but a Christian Socialist. Nonetheless he and the groups he led had embraced Communist friends, shared some of their radical ideas, and actively pursued leftist causes. His latitudinarian affiliations would plague him throughout his career.

Southerners had labeled Dombrowski a Communist even before the creation of Highlander School and the SCHW. In 1929, while attending graduate school at Union Theological Seminary, he had traveled to Elizabethton, Tennessee, to observe textile strikes there. At a Chamber of Commerce meeting, the young activist had challenged civic leaders who were calling for a forced end to the strike. He proclaimed a vision of the world where humans applied the ethics of Jesus to order society in a more equal fashion, particularly in industry. The following day, as Dombrowski was en route to the now famous strikes in Gastonia, North Carolina, he was arrested and charged as an accomplice in the murder of the Gastonia chief of police. Acting on the assumption that he was working with the National Textile Workers' Union—the heavily Communist organization leading the strike— southern newspapers reported that he was a Communist. Local authorities eventually released Dombrowski and dropped the charges, but the red label stuck.

In later years southerners would have more to be suspicious of than just the Gastonia incident. In addition to his positions with Highlander, the SCHW, and SCEF, Dombrowski had traveled to the Soviet Union and had been an active, sometimes radical, member of the Socialist Party. In 1934 he had joined the Revolutionary Policy Committee for Socialists, which called for adherents to abandon their gradualist approach and "act as a militant working-class party." He was also a committed and open popular fronter willing to "work with anyone who was going my way with a socialist philosophy." This stance brought Dombrowski trouble from both conservative critics and liberal anti-Communist allies. Indeed, several New Orleans members of the SCHW specifically named Dombrowski as the catalyst of their break from the group. The director, they claimed, had become an ineffective leader "because of his willingness to cooperate with persons whose motives are not above suspicion."[25]

25. Adams, *Dombrowski.*

But even more important to southerners, Dombrowski was a dedicated activist for black civil rights. The bus boycotts in Montgomery, Tallahassee, Birmingham, and other southern cities had inspired him to organize his own drive in New Orleans in the fall of 1956. When he delivered petitions to local officials asking the New Orleans transit authority to end segregation on trolleys and buses in early 1957, city newspapers immediately reported that many of the signers were members of SCEF, an organization that had been "investigated for Communistic activities." Local southern red scare leader Leander Perez added that the desegregation effort was in keeping with Communist designs to "foment violence and strife between two races . . . by forcing them into intimate contact." Undaunted by the charges, Dombrowski continued his crusade for black civil rights, pushing for school desegregation in Arkansas, voting rights in Mississippi, and civil rights legislation in Washington. Everywhere he appeared, though, the Communist label followed him. By the early 1960s, virtually every major civil rights venue in the South had been tainted by Dombrowski and his connections.[26]

Dombrowski's October 4 arrest in New Orleans was not his first, but it was in some ways his most harrowing. He was sixty-five years old and could only walk with the help of a cane. In addition, as he learned while making a phone call from his jail cell, police had held his wife at gunpoint and threatened to kill his dog when they raided the couple's home. Dombrowski's frayed nerves calmed a bit when a policeman escorted SCEF lawyer Ben Smith to his cell. But when Dombrowski asked his attorney, "When are you going to get me out of here?" Smith revealed that he was in the cell not as legal counsel but as a prisoner. Eventually the two gained their freedom and were met by a horde of news-people and cameras outside the courthouse.[27]

The arrests constituted a critical moment for SCEF. Movement activists had long criticized the group for not purging itself of Communist affiliations. But civil rights leaders across the South almost unanimously denounced the Louisiana police action. The Louisiana ACLU called it "a dangerous act of political repression." Student Nonviolent Coordinating Committee (SNCC) officials added that the action constituted "another demonstration of lawlessness and defiance of authority by segregationists." The state sedition laws in Louisiana, according to the group, were illegal,

26. Ibid., 241–42.
27. Ibid., 262–67.

being of the same type that the Supreme Court had outlawed in *Pennsylvania v. Nelson* and *NAACP v. Alabama*. Martin Luther King saw a dangerous trend in the arrests. The "smear tactics against efforts to bring about true brotherhood of man in the South" used by Wallace, LUAC, and others, King argued, "have shown signs of increasing intensity during recent months." Fred Shuttlesworth went a step further, adding that the raids were "part of a three-state conspiracy in Alabama, Mississippi, and Louisiana . . . to frustrate the drive for freedom by civil-rights organizations." He then called for SCEF contributors and friends to lobby the attorney general to return the organization's papers.[28]

Shuttlesworth's concern over the case was both personal and political. At the time of the raid, he was the president of SCEF. He had met Dombrowski in early 1957 when the SCEF director visited the Shuttlesworth family at its recently bombed-out home in Birmingham. Dombrowski had offered the organization's help in rebuilding and had asked Fred to become a member. Aware of Dombrowski's record as a civil rights advocate, Shuttlesworth had agreed to join the organization. A short time afterward, during Carl Braden's trial in 1958 and 1959, he had replaced Aubrey Williams as head of the group.

While he was head of SCEF, Shuttlesworth had become one of the most prominent civil rights leaders in the country. He had been an NAACP leader in Alabama until 1956, when the state's attorney general, John Patterson, had effectively banned the group. Shuttlesworth had then created his own Alabama Christian Movement for Human Rights in Birmingham. Through this organization, he had moved on to help found the SCLC. But he did not gain national prominence until the 1963 Birmingham protests. Eclipsed only by King, he was the principal organizer and catalyst for the city's desegregation drive.[29]

Shuttlesworth's leadership role in SCEF and his fame as a civil rights leader made him and the numerous groups he represented perfect targets for red and black investigators. Like Williams and Dombrowski, he was devoted to the idea that the fight for black civil rights and the defense of ac-

28. "Fact Sheet on the Raid and Arrests," 22 November 1963, Box 4, SCEF Raids Folder, Braden Papers; Shuttlesworth to Friends of SCEF, 8 October 1963, Box 4, SCEF Raids Folder, Braden Papers; "News from SCEF," 5 October 1963, Box 4, SCEF Raids Folder, Braden Papers.

29. See Andrew Manis, *A Fire You Can't Put Out: The Civil Rights Life of Birmingham's Reverend Fred Shuttlesworth* (Tuscaloosa: University of Alabama Press, 1999).

cused Communists went hand in hand. As president, he took up SCEF's sideline struggle against HUAC, calling it "an extra burden" but one that had to be borne. Actually, under Shuttlesworth's leadership, it became more than just "an extra burden" for SCEF. Instead of allocating financial support to campaigns directly challenging racial discrimination, SCEF devoted most of its funds in 1961 to defending Carl Braden's Supreme Court case.[30]

Movement conservatives would not overlook Shuttlesworth's support of alleged Communists. His contribution to the struggle in Birmingham had given SCEF new respectability among civil rights leaders, but some NAACP and SCLC officials were still concerned. Gloster Current, director of branches for the NAACP, for instance, cornered Shuttlesworth in an Atlanta airport waving a Jackson, Mississippi, newspaper column reading "Negro Pastor Heads Communist Front." At that point the Birmingham leader had just been elected president of SCEF. Current declared that the movement could not afford to be mixed up with reds. Shuttlesworth stood up to Current but was sensitive to the danger he posed to movement solidarity. He later told Roy Wilkins and Martin Luther King that he would give up his associations with the NAACP and SCLC if they thought it prudent. Neither King nor the usually cautious Wilkins believed any break was necessary. Shuttlesworth remained aware, however, that he was on thin ice.[31]

Because of his leadership role in SCEF, the October 4 raids in New Orleans alarmed Shuttlesworth in particular. That he would be a prime target became apparent when LUAC chairman James Pfister noted that he was an NAACP member, SCLC leader, and "close associate of Martin Luther King," and thus a principal liaison between groups and individuals recently scrutinized for their Communist ties. LUAC counsel Jack Rogers also emphasized Shuttlesworth's leadership role in SCEF, a group that he claimed acted as "the equivalent of a big holding company" through which "Communists infiltrated racial movements."[32]

In the weeks following the October raids, southern nationalists repeated Rogers's and Pfister's charges in every available forum. George Wallace appeared on NBC's "Today" show brandishing pictures of Carl and Anne Braden, Dombrowski, and Myles Horton, charging the four with responsibility for the Birmingham atrocities. The New Orleans Citizens' Council, at the

30. Adams, *Dombrowski*, 239–49.
31. Ibid., 260; Manis, *A Fire You Can't Put Out*, 397–98
32. Ibid., *Dombrowski*, 266–67.

same time, publicly praised the arrests of SCEF leaders and picketed the organization's offices with signs reading "Communist Headquarters of the South." Congressman Joe Waggonner Jr. of Louisiana also added his indictment of Fred Shuttlesworth as a "Communist-fronter" to the *Congressional Record*. Finally LUAC announced its intention to hold hearings to evaluate the material taken in the raids.[33]

Just days later, however, the segregationists' momentum stalled. Louisiana district court judge Bernard Cocke dismissed the charges against Dombrowski, Smith, and Waltzer, maintaining that LUAC had proceeded on opinion rather than evidence. The raids on SCEF as well as the offices and homes of the three defendants were, according to Cocke, illegal. Fearful that the judge would call for the state to return the SCEF documents, LUAC proceeded with plans to transfer the boxes containing seized material to Senator Eastland. SCEF attorneys were well aware of LUAC's intentions and immediately went to federal court in quest of an injunction enjoining the state from releasing the documents to the SISS. The request, however, came late on a Saturday afternoon. The court, following its normal procedure, had suspended action until the following Monday. LUAC sent the SCEF records to Mississippi that Sunday. Dombrowski and the SCEF attorneys, anticipating an Eastland smear campaign, vowed not "to let him get by with it."[34]

By the end of October 1963, Dombrowski and SCEF had filed additional suits in Louisiana and in U.S. District Court in Washington, D.C. They requested a further injunction restraining Eastland from using the SCEF documents and asked for half a million dollars in damages for false arrest and illegal seizure of property. Taking a cue from Shuttlesworth's claim that Mississippi, Louisiana, and Alabama representatives had plotted to undermine the civil rights movement, the injunction suit charged that Eastland and LUAC were part of a "conspiracy." The brief explained that the segregationists were hoping to "avoid the decisions of the United States Supreme Court prohibiting the enforced production of membership lists of organizations seeking enforcement of minority rights."[35]

33. "Urgent SNCC Memo," 5 October 1963, Box 4, SCEF Raids Folder, 3, Braden Papers; "News from SCEF," 16 October 196, Box 4, SCEF Raids Folder, 3, Braden Papers; *Congressional Record*, 88th Cong., 1st sess., 1963, 109, app. A6552–A6553.

34. "New Developments," undated, and "News from SCEF," 25 October 1963, Box 4, SCEF Raids Folder, Braden Papers.

35. "Eastland Is Sued," *New York Times*, 2 November 1963; "3 Ask $750,000," *New Orleans Times-Picayune*, 29 October 1963; "News from SCEF," 31 October 1963; and "Fact Sheet," 6 November 1963, Box 4, SCEF Raids Folder, Braden Papers.

The conspiracy theory had merit. SISS counsel J. G. Sourwine would later admit that Eastland had ordered SCEF records moved to Mississippi while court action to prevent their removal was pending. Eastland and LUAC then shared the SCEF documents with the Mississippi State Sovereignty Commission. Indeed, the SSC director spent a weekend in March with Jack Rogers for just that purpose. The commission in turn leaked several documents to *Jackson Advocate* editor Percy Greene. Greene, a black journalist who often cooperated with the SSC, ran articles and editorials stating that he had documented evidence of Martin Luther King's connections to SCEF. According to Greene this proved without a doubt that the civil rights movement was affiliated with Communists. The SSC arranged for the rest of the Jackson press to pick up the story from the *Advocate*. The news, the commission believed, would be more "effective" with a black author. That same month SSC officials passed the information on to Eli Howell, director of Alabama's Sovereignty Commission.[36]

That segregationists were hoping to "avoid" the decisions of the Supreme Court on the issue is without question. Eastland, of course, had been a longtime, vocal critic of the Court. As recently as May 2, 1962, the Mississippi senator had risen before his colleagues in the Senate to chart recent decisions of the high court involving subversive activities, including *Pennsylvania v. Nelson*. He had concluded that the results revealed a "grim picture" of the Court's overall decisions on "the Communist conspiracy." "The Court," he declared, "must be restricted."[37]

Duplicating Eastland's strategy, LUAC decided to take action before the Supreme Court had the opportunity to strike down Louisiana's Communist-control laws. LUAC chairman James Pfister, who was running for reelection to the state legislature at the time, pressed ahead with hearings on SCEF in early November. The proceedings would be closed to spectators but

36. "Leaders Protest SCEF Attack," *Southern Patriot*, January 1964; Memo: Johnston to File, 24 March 1964, ID# 9-1-2-69-1-1-1, Mississippi State Sovereignty Commission Files, Mississippi Department of Archives and History; Memo: Johnston to File, 2 April 1964, ID# 9-1-2-70-2-1-1, Mississippi State Sovereignty Commission Files; King Check, ID# 99-93-0-3-1-1-1, Mississippi State Sovereignty Commission Files. See also Memo: Johnston to File, 18 August 1964, Box 136, Mississippi State Sovereignty Commission Papers, McCain Library, University of Southern Mississippi; "Report of Principal Activities and Policies," 1 September 1964, Box 136, Mississippi State Sovereignty Commission Papers, McCain Library.

37. *Congressional Record*, 87th Cong., 2nd sess., 1962, 108, pt. 6:7599–7607.

open to the press, allowing a number of the documents seized in the October raids to become public. In its summary report, LUAC reproduced several letters, photographs, and check stubs taken from the SCEF files.

The report was in many ways typical of southern legislative committee offerings on SCEF. LUAC argued that, according to the standards set out by J. Edgar Hoover in his book *Masters of Deceit,* "the SCEF is in fact a Communist front!" The organization had connections to other fronts, had associates identified as Communist Party members, and had followed the Communist Party line, particularly on race issues. To reinforce these points, the committee drew on the testimony of two witnesses. The first was Major Homer Bryant of the Caddo Parish sheriff's office. Bryant recited the standard line on SCEF, describing once again the connection of the organization to the SCHW and these groups' citation record before the SISS. He identified the SCEF leadership as James Dombrowski, Carl and Anne Braden, Fred Shuttlesworth, Aubrey Williams, and Benjamin Smith. He then described the associations of each with civil rights groups and Communist fronts. The committee's other witness was Rev. C. H. Kilby, a Methodist preacher from Tracy City, Tennessee. Kilby, like Bryant, had nothing but old news to tell. He recounted the front record of the Highlander Folk School and James Dombrowski's connection to it.

But in addition to the reiteration of familiar charges against SCEF, the report brought to light the lengthy testimony of committee counsel Jack Rogers. Unlike the others, Rogers offered documents from the SCEF files to support LUAC's case. Included were a Communist Youth League card reported to belong to Myles Horton, a letter from Dombrowski to President Eisenhower asking amnesty for those convicted under the Smith Act, and a letter from Robert Williams, an African American Communist expatriate living in China, to Carl Braden. According to the latter document, the SCEF periodical the *Southern Patriot* had published an article by Williams. Rogers accurately noted that Williams had been a prominent radio propagandist for Communist Cuba. The committee counsel also reviewed documents linking SCEF lawyer Benjamin Smith to the National Lawyers Guild, a Communist front according to the Justice Department, and identifying Anne and Carl Braden—who were described by FBI, SISS, and HUAC witnesses as Communists—as strategists for SCEF's civil rights campaign. Finally, Rogers entered into the record papers linking SCEF to the SCLC, including a fund check made out to Martin Luther King, as well as documents connecting Dombrowski to Lee Lorch; the Bradens and Shuttlesworth to King; and

King to O'Dell. The paper trail suggested in the most tangible way to date that SCEF was at the center of a civil rights network in the South that had ties to Communists and fellow travelers.[38]

Three days after LUAC published its findings from the November hearings, Lee Harvey Oswald shot and killed President John F. Kennedy. Despite celebrations by the radical right, especially its segregationist components, the assassination undermined the effort to depict the civil rights movement as Communist inspired and led. Just as red and black investigators were beginning to gain the attention of the national media, Kennedy's death pushed them out of the headlines. Moreover Kennedy's successor Lyndon Johnson would prove to be as strong a supporter of black civil rights as the nation had ever seen. Johnson used the assassination to bolster the resolve of liberals and traditional conservatives in Congress to pass the Civil Rights Act as a tribute to the nation's fallen leader. So strong was the image of Camelot that criticism of Kennedy's administration, including its efforts in civil rights, was tantamount to slander against a martyred American hero.

The momentum southern nationalists had built in the summer and fall was never regained after the president's death. But a momentary hope existed that the assassination itself would help the segregationist and anti-Communist cause. Unanswered questions about the events in Dallas had created a new sense of paranoia. Many speculated that Communists had engineered the death of the president. In right-wing circles this theory was bolstered by the fact that a gunman, possibly the same one who had killed the president, shot General Edwin Walker on the same day as Kennedy, in the same city.

Edwin Walker was himself a well-known segregationist and anti-Communist. A West Point graduate, World War II and Korean War combat veteran, and career serviceman, he had resigned from the army in 1961 amid allegations that he was using John Birch Society pamphlets in his troop-in-doctrination program. Walker claimed to have left for other reasons, including the infiltration of the government by Communists and the use of American military forces for what he called "non-military ventures." Among these ventures was the use of troops in Little Rock, Arkansas, in

38. "Activities of the Southern Conference Educational Fund, Inc., in Louisiana," Report No. 4 of the Joint Legislative Committee on Un-American Activities, 19 November 1963, RG46, Subject File, SCEF 1956–1963 Folder, Senate Internal Security Subcommittee Papers, National Archives.

1957, a force Walker himself had reluctantly led. Out of the army, Walker had become a vocal advocate of far-right causes in Dallas. He accused the Kennedy administration of, among other things, helping the United Nations gain control of American troops and weapons. Through the UN, Walker charged, the international Communist conspiracy was attempting to gain control over the United States military. The NAACP and Martin Luther King, he said, were acting as agents of the UN.

In 1962 Walker called for volunteers to meet the federal threat in Oxford, Mississippi, just before the mayhem there erupted. During the ensuing clashes, local officials arrested him and charged him with inciting students to riot. Local prosecutors eventually dropped the charges because of a lack of evidence, but the incident made Walker something of a celebrity among southern reactionaries.

After the Ole Miss debacle, Walker would capitalize on his new popularity. In early 1963 he joined Rev. Billy James Hargis's nationwide tour, "Operation Midnight Ride," as a keynote speaker. Hargis was an ultraconservative Christian fundamentalist from Tulsa, Oklahoma, who made red and black accusations the core message of his sermons. In articles published by his own occasional paper the *Christian Crusader*, he had been a vocal critic of the Kennedy administration's civil rights initiatives, U.S. participation in the United Nations, and left-wing influences in the National Council of Churches. The tour, he declared, would resemble that of Paul Revere in 1775, but instead of warning of advancing redcoats, he and his speakers would warn of advancing reds.[39]

On the road Walker would declare to delighted segregationist audiences that the Ole Miss riots were more comic than tragic. "The students had a lot of fun on campus, plenty of laughs, a good time," he told an audience in Jacksonville, Florida. Ignoring the fact that two men had been killed and many others injured, he added, "I wouldn't call it a riot, just student high spirits." But while he downplayed student culpability in the riots, Walker blamed Communist leaders for stirring up the trouble.[40]

When forensics tests revealed that the bullet fired at Walker at his home in Dallas very probably came from the rifle used by Oswald to kill the presi-

39. James Gsell, "Gen. Walker and Rev. Hargis Will Make 'Conservative' Ride," *Daily Texan*, 20 February 1963; William K. Wyant Jr., "Walker to Join Him on Tour, Crusade Leader Hargis Says," *St. Louis Post-Dispatch*, 13 February 1963.

40. "Gen. Walker Finds Miss. Riot Just 'Lot of Fun,'" *Chicago Defender*, 9 March 1963.

dent, right-wingers and southern nationalists were both alarmed and excited. When Oswald's wife told FBI agents that her husband had tried to kill Walker because of the threat that the outspoken segregationist and anti-Communist posed to American Communist causes, they believed that they had their conspiracy. Oswald was indeed a devoted Communist who had lived in the Soviet Union and been a vocal advocate of Cuban Communism on his return to Louisiana. But many questions remained unanswered. Was there direct evidence that the assassin was an agent of the Soviet Union, Cuba, or some other nation, or was he a deluded maniac acting on his own? Oswald, of course, never had the chance to answer these questions. The Warren Commission concluded that he had been the lone gunman, but his motivation remained unclear. Filling the void of unanswered questions was an atmosphere of speculation and fear not unlike that which had fueled America's various red scares.[41]

The problem for southern nationalists, however, was that segregationists and the radical right were equally suspect in the assassination of the president. Walker himself had been a zealous Kennedy-basher. The effort to link Oswald to Walker was in part an attempt to deflect suspicions that Oswald was somehow the dupe of radical segregationists who hoped to end the president's civil rights initiatives. When it failed, red and black hunters remained vulnerable.

But even if the leaders of the southern right had been able to capitalize on the general paranoia in the aftermath of the Kennedy assassination, their own recklessness would have done them in. This soon became evident in the litigation over Senator Eastland's handling of the SCEF papers. At first the case proceeded smoothly for the Mississippi senator. Accepting the argument that Eastland was immune from prosecution because of a constitutional dictate forbidding the courts from considering speech or debate in Congress as evidence, the district court in Washington dismissed Dombrowski's case. But on appeal the Supreme Court agreed that while Eastland enjoyed the privilege of legislative immunity, SISS attorney J. G. Sourwine

---

41. "Gen. Walker Is Resigning," *Houston Post*, 13 April 1961; "Many Things Disturb Walker," *Dallas Texan*, 31 January 1962; "Walker Charges Conspiracy to Put US Forces under UN," *Dallas Morning News*, 21 March 1962; "Support Barnett, Gen. Walker Says," *Dallas Times Herald*, 27 September 1962; "U.S. Drops Its Charges on Walker," *Houston Post*, 22 January 1963; "Walker Rakes UN As Center for Spies," *Houston Chronicle*, 28 February 1963; "Same Gun Used, Experts Believe," *Dallas Times Herald*, 19 December 1963.

did not. This opened the subcommittee to more scrutiny than it had bargained for. Sourwine testified that he had obtained the SCEF records from the Louisiana committee by using blank subpoenas signed by Eastland. The SISS, he admitted, had never specifically authorized the subpoenas for the documents. The U.S. Court of Appeals in Washington subsequently ruled that the action was illegal.[42]

Despite the victories over Eastland and Louisiana's Communist-control laws, clearing Dombrowski and his colleagues proved no simple task. In January a three-judge federal court voted two to one to uphold the constitutionality of Louisiana's Subversive Activities Act. Immediately thereafter state prosecutors had the three SCEF leaders indicted for violating the law. By June, however, the legal winds began to shift. That month a Criminal District Court judge decided that the evidence taken in the October SCEF raid could not be used in court against Dombrowski, Smith, and Waltzer. The police, he ruled, had exceeded their authority in seizing more than the search warrants specified. Almost a year later, the Supreme Court provided the finishing touches. The Court concluded in a five-to-two decision that the registration sections of Louisiana's Communist-control laws were unconstitutional. The three SCEF workers were at long last out of the legal thicket.[43]

But in some ways the damage had already been done. As Martin Luther King testified before the federal court overseeing the SCEF case in January, "the fear of such possible accusations, regardless of their lack of basis in fact, effectively deters many who would otherwise be disposed to participate (in integration activities) . . . consequently, the work of such a civil rights organization as SCEF is as effectively hampered and stymied by charges and indictments as it would be by conviction of its officers and members." Nevertheless, Louisiana officials would have much preferred a conviction of a SCEF official. Only then would they have had the legal framework to prosecute others in the civil rights movement on similar charges.[44]

42. *Dombrowski v. Eastland*, 387 U.S. 82 (1967); "News from SCEF," 30 January 1964, Box 4, SCEF Raids Folder, Braden Papers.

43. "La. Red Control Law under Fire," *New Orleans Times-Picayune*, 16 June 1964; "Court Rejects SCEF Evidence," *New Orleans Times-Picayune*, 17 June 1964; "Louisiana's Anti-Red Law Voided," *Louisville Courier-Journal*, 27 April 1965; *Dombrowski v. Pfister*, 380 U.S. 479 (1965). See also Adam Fairclough, *Race and Democracy* (Athens: University of Georgia Press, 1995), 323–26.

44. "Leaders Protest SCEF Attack," *Southern Patriot*, January 1964.

194] It was a mark of the segregationists' determination that despite their inability to produce a smoking gun in the SCEF papers, successfully implicate
Martin Luther King in a Communist plot, or win a conviction against Dombrowski, they continued to lobby against the passage of the Civil Rights Act
using the same red and black accusations. Alabama's Commission to Preserve the Peace voiced its opinion of the 1964 civil rights bill in early
March, just after the House of Representatives approved it and sent it on to
the Senate. Southern nationalist to the core, the Peace Commission argued
that the civil rights bill of 1964 was not an "anti-South bill" but an "anti-
American bill." It would create a "federal dictatorship" controlling local institutions, eliminate "private property," destroy the "guaranteed right of
trial by jury," force the nation to bear the "impossible burden" of creating a
racial balance, and waste time and money through endless litigation. More
ominously the bill, according to the report, would make the "Communist
Party Platform seem most conservative." The civil rights measure would
ensure the Communist demands for "full racial, political, and social equality for the Negro Race" by abolishing any remnant of Jim Crow in the
South.[45]

As proof of the radical motives behind the bill, the report claimed that
its principal architects had "associations with groups and individuals identified with the communist apparatus or the communist 'solar system' of
fronts." Senator Paul Douglas of Illinois, according to the Peace Commission, had been a member of the Socialist Party in the 1930s and served on
the executive committee of the International Labor Defense, "officially
identified as a legal arm of the communist party." This had been true
enough, but the commission, in typical fashion, failed to account for the
senator's changing political identity and failed to separate his liberalism
from the overall Communist Party line. In fact, by the 1940s Douglas was
clearly an anti-Communist. He had even been a coauthor of the provision
of the McCarran Internal Security Act allowing the government to intern
those deemed likely to engage in sabotage or espionage in times of emergency. The Peace Commission made equally tenuous assertions about Congressman Emanuel Celler of New York who, according to the report, had
ties to such groups as the National Committee to Combat Anti-Semitism,
also labeled by HUAC as Communist-infiltrated. While the commission ar-

---

45. "The 1964 Civil Rights Bill . . . Its Pattern . . . Its Architects," CPP Resolution, 11
March 1964, SG 21073, Alabama Legislative Commission to Preserve the Peace Papers.

ticle claimed that it had not attempted "to place guilt or to impute Un-American motives" to these men, it suggested that they had been advocating the Communist Party line, a clearly false accusation even given the [195 rather limited parallels between Communist and liberal stances on racial equality. No knowledgeable person would accept the assertion that associations such as the ones held by Douglas and Celler were "sufficient cause to give pause in consideration of the bill now in the Senate."[46]

Douglas and Celler were, according to the Alabama Peace Commission document, perfect examples of those J. Edgar Hoover listed as "well meaning but thoroughly duped." Hoover would never have included these men in this group, at least publicly, but he did put Martin Luther King, a major force behind the civil rights bill, squarely in this category, minus the "well meaning" accolade. By the time Alabama legislators published the report, Hoover had committed the full force of his agency to exposing Communists in the civil rights movement. His suspicion of King and his cohorts grew into obsession as the FBI director refused to countenance any doubt about the guilt of the civil rights leadership. When assistant director William Sullivan reported to Hoover that there had been little to no Communist involvement in the March on Washington, the director was incredulous and indignant, stating, "This memo reminds me vividly of those I received when Castro took over Cuba. . . . I for one can't ignore the memos re King, O'Dell, Levinson, Rustin." Sullivan tried to backtrack, replying that "The Director is correct. . . . We were completely wrong." King should be marked "as the most dangerous Negro of the future in this nation from the standpoint of communism, the Negro and national security." Hoover continued to force Sullivan to grovel and put the agency on alert that the civil rights movement was to be targeted as a full-fledged threat to national security.[47]

Meanwhile the civil rights bill was forced to run a gauntlet of black and red investigators as it made its way through Congress. The Mississippi Sovereignty Commission, for example, underwrote the Coordinating Committee for Fundamental American Freedoms, the principal lobby against the civil rights legislation, and made sure that every congressman obtained a copy of LUAC's November report. But it was a column by widely read Wash-

---

46. Ibid.; "Anti-Red Amendment Proposed by Colmer," *Jackson Daily News*, 16 February 1964; Richard Fried, *Nightmare in Red* (New York: Oxford University Press, 1990), 196.

47. "The 1964 Civil Rights Bill . . . Its Pattern . . . Its Architects," SG 21073, CPP Papers; Fried, *Nightmare in Red*, 196; Branch, *Parting the Waters*, 903–904.

ington commentator Joseph Alsop that particularly disturbed movement leaders. The article in the April 15, 1964, editions of the *Washington Post* and the *New York Herald Tribune* said that an "unhappy secret" had been worrying Washington. The "charges of Communist influence, which have been hurled for so long by anti-civil rights racists," according to Alsop, had been "acquiring some color of truth." While older organizations such as the NAACP remained Communist-free, the SCLC, SNCC, and the Congress of Racial Equality (CORE) had all been implicated. Alsop argued that John Lewis of CORE, "though not a Communist, quite frankly believes in quasi-insurrectionary tactics." But it was King's relationships that were most disturbing. Not only had he employed the now notorious O'Dell, he had another relationship with a man "known to be a key figure in the covert apparatus of the Communist party."[48]

Alsop's remarks shocked King's closest advisers. A well-respected, moderate journalist had added new legitimacy to the southern segregationist charges against the civil rights movement's most conspicuous figure, a man whose authority depended in no small part on his reputation for moral and ideological rectitude. The day after the article came out, George Smathers, the politically moderate senator from Florida, entered it into the *Congressional Record* as part of his comments on the pending civil rights legislation. Smathers called on J. Edgar Hoover to clarify the matter for the Senate. A few days later, King grudgingly notified Burke Marshall and the Justice Department that his connections to Levinson had been eliminated.[49]

But the issue would not go away so easily. The morning after King's reassurance to Marshall, newspapers reported "secret" testimony that Hoover had given to a House subcommittee in January alleging Communist influence in the civil rights movement. The FBI director arranged for friends in the House to release the information after the Justice Department moved to block statements by Hoover on King. At the same time, Senator Thurmond made sure his colleagues were aware of Hoover's latest revelations during the Senate debates on the civil rights bill. Given Hoover's visibility and

48. "Report of Principal Activities and Policies," 1 September 1964, Box 136, Mississippi State Sovereignty Commission Papers, McCain Library. "An Unhappy Secret," *New York Herald Tribune* and *Washington Post*, 15 April 1964. See also Taylor Branch, *Pillar of Fire* (New York: Simon and Schuster, 1998), 241.

49. *Congressional Record*, 88th Cong., 2nd sess., 1964, 110, pt. 6:8223–24; "Smathers Asks Report on Reds," *Florida Times-Union*, 17 April 1964; Garrow, *Bearing the Cross*, 321–22.

credibility, Martin Luther King decided that he could no longer ignore the negative publicity. He had to face the accusations head on. Convening the press, King denied that he was under Communist influence, charged that [197 Hoover was aiding right-wing extremists with his allegations, and questioned the credibility of the FBI in its investigations of the civil rights movement. How could the public "accept the word of the FBI on communistic infiltration of the civil rights movement," King asked, "when it has been so ineffectual in protecting the Negro from brutality in the Deep South?" King then challenged the FBI director to produce real evidence if he had it and charged Hoover with plotting to sabotage the civil rights bill.[50]

Outside of the South, the associations of King, Shuttlesworth, Dombrowski, and others gave pause to many, but few were willing to accept the idea that their recently assassinated president's civil rights legislation was part of a red and black conspiracy. The House of Representatives passed the civil rights bill overwhelmingly, while the Senate voted in favor of the bill seventy-three to twenty-seven. Nays came almost exclusively from the South. Despite Alabama representative Albert Watson's last minute reiteration of the charges that the movement and the bill were Communist-inspired, President Lyndon Johnson signed the Civil Rights Act into law on July 2, 1964. It prohibited discrimination in most places of public accommodation, authorized the federal government to withhold federal funds to public programs practicing discrimination, banned discrimination by employers and unions, created an Equal Employment Opportunity Commission, established a Community Relations Service, and provided technical and financial aid to communities desegregating their schools.[51]

During the fight over the 1964 Civil Rights Act, segregationists had come closer than ever to creating a southern red scare that would capture the imagination of middle America. Ultimately, however, they failed to convince the nation, including a number of conservative Republicans who voted for the bill, that the act's originators and its provisions were Communist-inspired. Several factors were responsible. Despite the revelations concerning O'Dell, Levinson, Rustin, Dombrowski, and others, red and black investigators failed to show effectively how the Communist affiliations of

---

50. "Hoover Says Reds Exploit Negroes," *New York Times*, 22 April 1964, p. 30; "Report on Reds in Rights Movement Raises Eyebrows," *The State*, 5 May 1964; *Congressional Record*, 88th Cong., 2nd sess., 1964, 110, pt. 7:9183–85; Branch, *Pillar of Fire*, 293–95; Garrow, *Bearing the Cross*, 321–22.

51. *Congressional Record*, 88th Cong., 2nd sess., 1964, 110, pt. 11:14998–99.

these individuals directly and specifically affected the movement. Pointing out general similarities between the movement and the Communist Party line proved insufficient. In addition, the charges came from southern segregationist politicians rather than Hoover and the FBI. When Hoover eventually spoke up, it was too late. By late April the bill's success was already a foregone conclusion. The leaders of the southern red scare could not compete with the president's death. The assassination drew attention away from their accusations and ensured popular sympathy for the president's legacy, especially his civil rights legislation. Finally, the antics of Eastland and the SISS convinced many moderates that red and black investigators would use dubious, underhanded means to promote their cause. In trying to obtain the convictions of the SCEF leaders, they had put the American legal system to the test and lost. They would make the same mistake in challenging black voting rights, but they felt they had no choice. Once African Americans obtained and exercised the franchise, Jim Crow was doomed.

THE SOUTHERN RED SCARE AND
THE VOTING RIGHTS ACT OF 1965

7

BY THE TIME THE UNITED STATES SENATE BEGAN DEBAT-
ing the civil rights bill in the spring of 1964, a new generation of civil rights
activists had begun to assert themselves in the movement. They were
younger, more militant, and more politically radical. They viewed desegregation as a middle-class affair, remote from and unresponsive to the needs
of the black masses. Working primarily as field secretaries for the Congress
of Racial Equality (CORE) and the Student Nonviolent Coordinating Committee (SNCC) in Alabama and Mississippi, they believed the ballot box
held the key to empowering African Americans. Organizing on the local,
state, and national levels, they registered blacks to vote and ran black candidates for office. Eventually the Southern Christian Leadership Conference
(SCLC), the National Association for the Advancement of Colored People
(NAACP), and the Johnson administration joined the campaign and pushed
for federal legislation that was designed to eliminate discriminatory polling
practices.

With their political power base suddenly at risk, southern segregationists became increasingly reactionary. Racist arguments resurfaced that nonwhites were incapable of becoming responsible citizens of a democracy.
And as young activists poured into the South from the North, anxiety redoubled that a popular front of liberals, reds, and blacks was conspiring to
change the southern way of life. Southern red and black hunters insisted
that Communists and their fellow travelers directed the voting rights efforts. If they were not stopped, they desperately asserted, socialism would
surely reign in Dixie.

During the summer of 1964, the southern red scare reached its most
frantic and reckless point. Southern segregationists intensified their red and
black investigations and propaganda efforts in an attempt to undermine the
voting rights campaign, but they also, more than ever, used their findings to
have movement activists fired, jailed, and brutalized. Under the mounting
pressure, movement unity began to crack. The Voting Rights Act would sur-

vive, but the scare would leave a permanent fissure between liberal anti-Communists and radical activists leading the struggle for black equality.

In an address to a joint session of the legislature in early March 1964, Governor Paul Johnson proclaimed Mississippi's towns to be "the battleground chosen by the forces of rapid, revolutionary social change." To meet this challenge, Mississippi must not "fail to expand and equip [its] law enforcement organizations to maintain law and order." Johnson followed through on his pledge by becoming an active chairman of the State Sovereignty Commission (SSC). A policy statement proposed by the governor listed goals such as working with the FBI to pinpoint and publicly identify subversives in civil rights organizations and using the Sovereignty Commission as a "watchdog" over subversive individuals and groups in the state.[1]

Under director Erle Johnston, the Mississippi State Sovereignty Commission had been meeting these goals for years. With the help of James Eastland, J. B. Matthews, and others, the group had collected extensive files on suspected Communists and Communist fronts working in the state. Even before the addition of material from the Louisiana Un-American Activities Committee's October 1963 raid, the SSC's file on the Southern Conference Education Fund (SCEF) was among its largest. SCEF was at the forefront of subversive activity in the state, according to commission officials. SSC file reports indicated that fund field secretaries and "identified communists" Anne and Carl Braden had even proposed an "invasion" of Mississippi by civil rights workers, a plan that seemed to be bearing abundant fruit in the spring of 1964.[2]

That season marked the beginning of a full-scale project by the civil

1. "Address of Governor Paul B. Johnson," 3 March 1964, Box 94, Russell Davis Papers, Mitchell Memorial Library Special Collections, Mississippi State University; "Proposed Policy Statement," Box 143, Mississippi State Sovereignty Commission Papers, McCain Library and Archives, University of Southern Mississippi; "Proposed Statement to be Issued," Box 143, Mississippi State Sovereignty Commission Papers, McCain Library.

2. "At a hearing before . . . ," Box 136, Mississippi State Sovereignty Commission Papers, McCain Library; "Martin Luther King at Communist Training School," Segregation and Integration Collection, Mitchell Memorial Library Special Collections, Mississippi State University; "The Southern Conference Educational Fund," ID# 13-59-0-29-1-1-1 to 6-1-1, Mississippi State Sovereignty Commission Files, Mississippi Department of Archives and History; "Scrivner to Commission Members," 6 September 1962, Box 395, William M. Colmer Papers, McCain Library and Archives, University of Southern Mississippi; Erle Johnston, *Mississippi's Defiant Years* (Forest: Lake Harbor Publishing, 1990).

rights movement to register Mississippi blacks to vote. The brainchild of Student Nonviolent Coordinating Committee worker Robert Moses, the "freedom summer" project would bring in white and black students from across the country. The project was organized through the Council of Federated Organizations (COFO), a SNCC-dominated umbrella group that encompassed several of the civil rights bodies in the state. COFO had already launched a successful, student-aided "freedom vote" campaign under Moses's leadership in 1963. The campaign had tallied some eighty thousand votes from disfranchised blacks in a mock election featuring as candidates black activist Aaron Henry for governor and Tougaloo College chaplain Ed King for lieutenant governor. The exercise was designed to prove that Mississippi blacks wanted to vote but had been kept from registering. The summer project would duplicate the freedom-vote campaign on a larger scale, registering blacks to vote in the 1964 general elections.

By that time the connections between SCEF and the Mississippi movement under SNCC were extensive. In 1961 fund director James Dombrowski had supplied thirteen thousand dollars to bail out young civil rights protesters in McComb. Thereafter the group made annual donations of five thousand dollars to SNCC to support the work of white organizer Bob Zellner. At the request of Bob Moses, Carl Braden, while working for the fund, had also participated in civil-liberties and nonviolence workshops in the state. Anne Braden, moreover, had worked with James and Diane Nash Bevel to organize an educational center in the Delta. SNCC's work had been hampered after Mississippi newspapers ran stories that the group was associating with the Bradens. Liberals in the movement had also criticized SNCC for working too closely with the red-labeled SCEF. Nevertheless Moses and the group refused to break off the relationship.[3]

With the freedom-summer campaign looming, the SSC took advantage of the SCEF ties to the Mississippi movement. The commission focused specifically on the fund's association with Tougaloo College. Tougaloo had been a safe haven for Mississippi activists in the early 1960s. The school's president, Daniel Beittel, had welcomed SNCC and CORE workers on campus. Bob Moses had even worked with the school to set up literacy and work-study programs for Mississippi blacks who were also willing to partic-

3. John Dittmer, *Local People: The Struggle for Civil Rights in Mississippi* (Urbana: University of Illinois Press, 1995), 230–32.

ipate in the movement. As a result many of SNCC's field workers in the Jackson area were Tougaloo students and faculty members. Among them, the SSC learned, was John Salter.[4]

In late 1962 Salter, a young sociology professor at Tougaloo, had been the chief strategist for a boycott and direct-action campaign to end Jim Crow practices in Jackson. He had come to Mississippi from northern Arizona, where he had been a labor organizer. His father was a Micmac/Penobscot Indian, but Salter was considered white in Mississippi. After being arrested for picketing a Woolworth store in downtown Jackson as part of his campaign, Salter and his band of demonstrators received bail money from SCEF, the Gandhian Society, and New York attorney Victor Rabinowitz, all of whom were considered Communist sources by Mississippi segregationists. Because of these ties and his status as a white liberal intellectual at a school that openly supported civil rights, Salter gained an undeserved reputation as a Marxist.[5]

As Salter's campaign in Jackson wore on into late spring 1963, tensions in the city began to build. On May 28, a group of three black Tougaloo students sat down at a segregated lunch counter in the same downtown Woolworth where Salter had once been arrested. Soon a crowd gathered and began taunting, humiliating, and assaulting the students. When Salter joined the protesters, someone in the crowd yelled "I know you're a communist." Another shouted "Worse than that, he's a nigger lover." The crowd moved in and began beating Salter and the others, literally pouring salt in their wounds. The ugly event made national television news.[6]

Two weeks earlier, the SSC had taken inventory of its holdings on John Salter. The inventory revealed an extensive investigation. The SSC had sent letters to Mississippi senator James Eastland requesting FBI and Senate Internal Security Subcommittee (SISS) file information, to Tougaloo president Beittel demanding that he look into Salter's political associations, and to the professor's colleagues asking what they knew about Salter's Marxist affiliations. All that these inquiries revealed was that Salter might have been a Communist and may have once described himself as a "liberal Marxist." The SSC also discovered that Salter had once published an article in *Main-*

4. Ibid., 225–28.

5. John Salter, *Jackson, Mississippi: An American Chronicle of Struggle and Schism* (Hicksville: Exposition Press, 1979). Dittmer, *Local People*, 157–59.

6. Dittmer, *Local People*, 162–63.

stream magazine, a publication deemed subversive by HUAC. But the most promising material on Salter, according to the inventory, came from the Louisiana raids on SCEF. Documents from the raids had shown that Salter had worked closely with and even received money from Braden, Dombrowski, and others associated with the fund. The inventory's author commented that this material was "real good for action to withdraw accred[itation]" from Tougaloo.[7]

A year later John Salter was a field worker for SCEF, freedom summer was in the works, and the SSC was mounting a campaign against Tougaloo. In March 1964 the commission proposed to the Mississippi legislature that a bill be adopted to separate the Mississippi Accrediting Commission from the Southern Association in accrediting the state's schools. This would give the Mississippi Commission authority to deny sanction to Tougaloo regardless of what the Southern Association decided.[8]

Backing the request was a series of SSC reports on Tougaloo. Thanks largely to the LUAC raid material, the reports outlined in detail Salter's and Beittel's relationship with SCEF. They also noted the work done for SCEF by two female students at Tougaloo, Joan Trumpauer and Dorie Ladner. The commission then revealed the testimony of J. B. Matthews before the state's General Investigating Committee that SCEF was infiltrated with Communists. "This information which is documented," according to a concluding report, "proves that a member of the faculty at Tougaloo and at least two students have been directly or indirectly involved with activities of the Southern Conference Education Fund, Inc., a communist front organization." The report recommended that the legislature separate the authority of the Mississippi accrediting agency from the southern agency so that it might "deny accreditation to Tougaloo and prevent its graduates from teaching in Mississippi."[9]

The accreditation bill and the assumptions behind it were popular among Mississippi's segregationists. Most agreed with Erle Johnston, the SSC head and originator of the bill, that the state's blacks were not prone to

7. File Entitled John R. Salter, 12 May 1963, ID# 3-74A-0-3-1-1-1, Mississippi State Sovereignty Commission Files.

8. Report on Principal Activities and Policies from January 1, 1964, through August 31, 1964, 1 September 1964, Box 136, Mississippi State Sovereignty Commission Papers, McCain Library.

9. Tougaloo College Report (No. 1) and Tougaloo College Report (No. 2), Box 135, Mississippi State Sovereignty Commission Papers, McCain Library.

violence "unless stirred." In recent months Mississippi's "Negroes" had been provoked by SNCC, CORE, and COFO, groups Johnston was convinced had "Communist backing." Mississippians also agreed with the SSC director about the strategic importance of the bill. Johnston reasoned that denying Tougaloo accreditation was among the only remaining tools available to prevent civil rights reform in the state. Mississippi legislators readily enacted the bill into law.[10]

The accreditation measure gave the SSC the added negotiating tool it needed to shut down Tougaloo's civil rights activities. In April the SSC learned that the Tougaloo board of trustees would meet later that month. A few days before, SCC director Johnston flew to New York and met with three of the school's trustees. He presented them with documents that the SSC believed proved Tougaloo had become a "headquarters for operations by Carl and Anne Braden" and thus "an institution of agitation with known communists using college premises for workshops." Noting that the state and the college were on "a collision course," a not-so-veiled reference to the accreditation issue, Johnston suggested that a crisis might be avoided if Beittel were replaced as president and the civil-disobedience activities of college chaplain Ed King were curtailed. The day after the annual trustees' meeting, Beittel accepted a forced resignation. Tougaloo kept its charter and Ed King, but with Beittel gone the institution lost its position at the center of Mississippi civil rights activity.[11]

The State Sovereignty Commission's exploitation of the Tougaloo activists' ties to SCEF may not have been the only factor in Beittel's demise. Historian John Dittmer has noted that the Tougaloo president's fate may have been determined in part by Brown University president Barnaby Keeny. Keeny had recently become a major patron of Tougaloo. According to Dittmer he had used his influence to have Beittel removed. Still, the SSC's role in the board's decision cannot be discounted. The commission's efforts constituted a very real and successful use of the southern red scare on an insti-

10. Johnston to Buchanan, undated, ID# 9-33-0-4-1-1-1, Mississippi State Sovereignty Commission Files; Investigations and Research, Box 136, Mississippi State Sovereignty Commission Papers, McCain Library.

11. "Information about Dr. A. D. Beittel," ID# 1-84-0-20-1-1-1 to 2-1-1, Mississippi State Sovereignty Commission Files; Investigations and Research and Report on Principal Activities and Policies from January 1, 1964, through August 31, 1964, 1 September 1964, Box 136, Mississippi State Sovereignty Commission Papers, McCain Library.

tution supporting civil rights activism at a crucial time in the movement's history.[12]

A no less advantageous and timely coup for Mississippi segregationists [205 involved the National Lawyers Guild (NLG), but in this instance massive resisters had to do little more than sit back and watch. At the request of SNCC, the guild decided to send several students and lawyers to Mississippi in 1964 to represent civil rights workers arrested during the freedom-summer campaign. The State Sovereignty Commission got wind of the guild's plans and, well aware of the group's reputation as a Communist front, hoped to use the information to its advantage. But in the end, the commission hardly needed to lift a finger. The freedom-summer campaign staggered as liberal anti-Communist allies of the movement blasted SNCC for cooperating with the red-controlled Lawyers Guild.[13]

Unlike SCEF, the National Lawyers Guild had been listed with HUAC and the U.S. attorney general as a subversive organization. And in fact it had been dominated by Communists since the early 1950s and had used the bulk of its resources defending Communists in court. Founded in 1937 by a coalition of liberal and radical attorneys, the NLG had lost most of its liberal members in 1939 when the majority turned back a series of amendments renouncing Communism and reorganizing the organization's national board. Most of those who remained trickled out as the NLG became a target of anti-Communists. Following Khrushchev's secret speech and the Soviet invasion of Hungary in 1956, membership dwindled to about six hundred, but the organization rebounded a decade later as it focused on the civil rights movement and the war in Vietnam.[14]

Bob Moses's announcement that SNCC and COFO would begin accepting assistance from the Lawyers Guild in early 1964 made liberal anti-Communist supporters of black civil rights bristle. COFO's legal backers including the Legal Defense Fund and the Lawyers Constitutional Defense

12. Dittmer, *Local People*, 234–36.

13. See, for instance, "Carlisle to Johnson," 22 July 1964, "Johnston Memo on Benjamin Smith," 25 September 1964, Box 136, Mississippi State Sovereignty Commission Papers, McCain Library; "Investigations and Research," Box 136, Mississippi State Sovereignty Commission Papers, McCain Library.

14. Guenter Lewy, *The Cause That Failed: Communism in American Political Life* (New York: Oxford University Press, 1990), 283–87. And see Ann Fagen Ginger and Eugene M. Tobin, eds., *The National Lawyers Guild: From Roosevelt through Reagan* (Philadelphia: Temple University Press, 1988).

Committee immediately objected. The National Council of Churches, itself frequently red-baited by segregationists, also criticized Moses's acceptance of guild help. Finally Andrew Young, who was then representing Martin Luther King at COFO meetings, suggested that fighting the "red issue" and segregation at once in Mississippi was a losing proposition. SNCC and Moses, however, refused to be moved.[15]

When COFO announced its decision, freedom-summer leader Allard Lowenstein was busy organizing recruits for Mississippi's voter-registration drive. Lowenstein, a young white academic and activist who had committed himself to the fight for black equality after witnessing racist oppression in Southwest Africa, had first come to Mississippi after the assassination of Medgar Evers. Among his first contacts was Tougaloo's Ed King, who sent his visitor on to meet Bob Moses. The conversations between Moses and Lowenstein had produced the ideas for the freedom vote and, eventually, freedom summer. Both agreed that the summer project would need the help of white student recruits from the North, so Lowenstein used his connections at Stanford, Yale, Harvard, and other universities to muster volunteers.[16]

A disciple and former aide of Hubert Humphrey, Lowenstein was as committed to anti-Communism as he was to black civil rights. Indeed, he opposed Communist influences in the movement on both philosophical and practical grounds. Totalitarian Stalinists, he insisted, could not be legitimate defenders of civil rights; it was anathema to their ideology. At the same time, the identification of Communists with the movement caused huge public-relations problems. Charges that it was a tool of subversion hurt the movement's public image and its claim to the moral high ground. Lowenstein realized that for politicians sympathetic to the cause, this translated into a "go-slow" environment on civil rights issues. Thus from the outset he had criticized SNCC's involvement with the NLG, SCEF, and Highlander Folk School.[17]

15. Taylor Branch, *Pillar of Fire* (New York: Simon and Schuster, 1998), 273; Clayborne Carson, *In Struggle: SNCC and the Black Awakening of the 1960s* (Cambridge: Harvard University Press, 1981), 105–107; Dittmer, *Local People*, 229–31.

16. Branch, *Pillar of Fire*, 121–23.

17. William Chafe, *Never Stop Running* (New York: Basic Books, 1993), 189–210; James Findlay Jr., *Church People in the Struggle* (New York: Oxford University Press, 1993), 28; Gregory Stone and Douglas Lowenstein, *Lowenstein: Acts of Courage and Belief* (New York: Harcourt Brace Jovanovich, 1983), 23.

Lowenstein became so upset at Moses's announcement that SNCC would refuse to break ties with the Lawyers Guild that he ended his association with COFO and encouraged Stanford, Yale, Harvard, and University of Oregon students to withdraw as freedom-summer volunteers. In a rage he even went so far as to tell Stanford students that Moses and his organization were "being run by Peking." Lowenstein's defection meant the movement had lost a valuable recruiter and promoter with excellent connections in Washington. It had also lost more than a few freedom-summer volunteers.[18]

While the Mississippi Sovereignty Commission did not create the rift over the Communist issue within the movement, it was more than willing to help widen it. Indeed, the SSC's work on "freedom summer" had only just begun. In May 1964, the Mississippi state legislature passed a "criminal syndicalism" bill in anticipation of the student invasion. The bill outlawed subversive propaganda and political organization. The Sovereignty Commission only needed to dig up the necessary evidence. To this end the commission redoubled its investigative efforts. Director Johnston recommended that the "exposure of Communists among racial agitators be top priority for the Investigative Department." Governor Johnson agreed.[19]

The Sovereignty Commission sent several investigators into the field to gather information on COFO and the freedom-summer activities. One even posed as a summer voter-registration worker. Identified in reports only as Operator 79, the agent lived in the Morehouse Apartments in Jackson with student volunteers and kept tabs on everything from COFO's financial status and administration to individual workers' sexual habits. His priority, however, was to gain the confidence of movement radicals. He reported in mid-June that he had "convinced all of the staff that I am Anti-American and I am rapidly turning Communist." This, he went on, had won him much respect and a job as an instructor for "both new and old" staff members. It also gained him the friendship of movement workers, including a "confirmed socialist," a woman willing to commit acts of sabotage in the United States once the "right time" presented itself, and another whose husband was an organizer for the Communist Party.[20]

In later reports, Operator 79 stated that he had found "pro-Cuban and

18. Chafe, *Never Stop Running*, 193; Dittmer, *Local People*, 233–34.

19. Johnston to Johnson, undated, Box 136, Mississippi State Sovereignty Commission Papers, McCain Library; Dittmer, *Local People*, 307.

20. Report of Operator #79, 15 June 1964, ID# 9-32-0-14-1-1-1, Mississippi State Sovereignty Commission Files.

pro-Russian hardback novels," a "complete history of Russia," and a button with the logo of a "strongly Communist" group out of California called the SPU. He also revealed that he had met Emmy Shather and Casey Haden, two "great promoters of the 'revolution'" who were planning a school for women that would teach socialism and Marxism. "COFO," he finally reported in August, "has started lecturing Socialism to the Negro public."[21]

Besides Operator 79 the SSC employed other agents and informants who concentrated on linking Communists to the movement. Some, such as 79, infiltrated the movement to obtain information while others, such as Edgar Downing, an amateur anti-Communist researcher in California, provided the commission access to his files. The SSC also regularly subscribed to Communist and Communist-front publications using John Kochitzky, whose "Russianish" sounding name, the commission reasoned, would not look out of place on the mailing list. But the SSC's regular investigators, Andy Hopkins and Tom Scarborough, handled the bulk of the fieldwork. The two became the primary liaisons between local law enforcement agencies and the state commission.[22]

The SSC had always cooperated with local as well as federal bodies such as Eastland's SISS to expose Communists in the movement, but the degree to which they coordinated their efforts was never greater than in the summer of 1964. The commission and its allies orchestrated investigations, press releases, congressional speeches, and local prosecutions to provide the maximum public impact. The more success the alliance had in discrediting the summer project as Communist-dominated, SSC director Erle Johnston suggested to Governor Johnson, the fewer Mississippi blacks would join COFO and its registration drive. "Negroes as a race are very religious," Johnston reasoned, "and anything Communist sounds like Godless atheism." In late July SSC officials working with Eastland and local law enforcement acted on these assumptions. Concentrating on Holly Springs, Moss

21. Report of Operator #79, 19 June 1964, ID# 9-32-0-15-1-1-1 to 2-1-1, Mississippi State Sovereignty Commission Files; Report of Operator #79, 3 July 1964, Box 136, Mississippi State Sovereignty Commission Papers, McCain Library; Report of Operator #79, 10 August 1964, Box 136, Mississippi State Sovereignty Commission Papers, McCain Library.

22. Report on Activities, 21 July 1964, ID# 9-31-2-7-1-1-1, Mississippi State Sovereignty Commission Files; Johnston to File, 17 December 1964, ID# 3-30A-1-80-1-1-1, Mississippi State Sovereignty Commission Files; Investigations and Research and Report on Principal Activities and Policies from January 1, 1964 through August 31, 1964, 1 September 1964, Box 136, Mississippi State Sovereignty Commission Papers, McCain Library.

Point, and Drew, they put together a campaign designed to severely weaken COFO's registration efforts.[23]

The program hinged on a July 22 speech by Eastland in the Senate concerning "Communist infiltration into the so-called civil rights movement." According to the senator, "recent developments, including arrests of demonstrators at Moss Point, Holly Springs, and Drew, Mississippi," had provided "evidence of Communist participation and leadership" in the freedom-summer campaign. Eastland argued that new and more militant groups had come to power in the national movement while older organizations were "pushed toward the background." "Second generation agitators" led the new movement and maintained their power by proving their militancy in the nation's cities and the American South. Their efforts, the senator warned, were culminating in an "invasion" of Mississippi. Where Communists had been almost unheard of in the state previously, they were now cropping up in its smallest communities.[24]

In Holly Springs, Eastland reported, a professional agitator named Larry Rubin had been active. He was a member of the Communist-dominated Fair Play for Cuba Committee and the cousin of Danny Rubin, a youth organizer for the Communist Party of the United States. Eastland also presented as evidence of Rubin's Communist affiliations an address book containing the names of a number of persons with known Communist Party and front connections. The address book had been spirited away from Rubin when Marshall County sheriff's deputies and SSC investigator Tom Scarborough questioned him about a recent assault. Eastland also obtained background information on Rubin from the SSC. The commission had been investigating Rust College in Holly Springs since June and was well informed about freedom-summer participants in the area. Indeed, as it had with Tougaloo, the SSC had collected some "rather shocking" information regarding "Communistic activities" on campus, enough to take before the Rust board of trustees. Like Beittel at Tougaloo, Rust College's president was forced to resign.[25]

---

23. Johnston to Johnson, undated, Box 136, Mississippi State Sovereignty Commission Papers, McCain Library.

24. *Congressional Record*, 88th Cong., 2nd sess., 1964, 110, pt. 13:16593–97.

25. Scarbrough, Marshall County Investigation, 24 July 1964, Box 136, Mississippi State Sovereignty Commission Papers, McCain Library; Investigations and Research, undated, Box 136, Mississippi State Sovereignty Commission Papers, McCain Library; Report on Principal Activities and Policies from January 1, 1964, through August 31, 1964, 1 September 1964, Box 136, Mississippi State Sovereignty Commission Papers, McCain Library.

Local law enforcement and the SSC also furnished information to East-land concerning the arrest of Ronald Ridenour in Moss Point. Ridenour, Eastland revealed to his Senate colleagues, had been "kicked out of Costa Rica in 1964 for carrying Communist literature into that country." But the most significant contributions the SSC made to Eastland's red and black hunting campaign involved the lawyers representing demonstrators in Drew. Among them were George Crockett, a member of the National Law-yers Guild; Maynard Omerberg, a close associate of the Civil Rights Con-gress; Ben Smith, attorney for the Southern Conference Education Fund; and Frank Pestana who, according to the California Committee on Un-American Activities, was active in "virtually all of the major Communist-front organizations in southern California." These "legal carpetbaggers," according to Eastland, were at the forefront of the Communist conspiracy in Mississippi.[26]

Eastland's case against Communists working with the Mississippi movement, especially those in Drew, was the result of an elaborate network of local officials whose efforts were coordinated through the SSC. County sheriffs would report the names, addresses, and activities of local activists to the commission. The SSC would then research their backgrounds and pass the information on to Eastland, the press, or the state legislature's Gen-eral Investigating Committee to be distributed to the public. In the case of Drew, the SSC worked with the city's mayor, W. O. Williford, to set up a trial court to make its information about Communists in the local move-ment available to the press. The court's hearings were then coordinated to coincide with Senator Eastland's speech.[27]

The SSC predicted that the press coverage of the Drew hearings and Eas-tland's speech would deal "an effective blow against those racial agitators with communist backgrounds or associations." But the prediction grew out of a desperate need in Mississippi for some publicity that would draw the nation's attention away from the disappearance of three freedom-summer workers in Neshoba County. Michael ("Mickey") Schwerner, Andrew Goodman, and James Chaney had come up missing during a trip to investi-

26. Sourwine to Johnston, 1 April 1965, RG 46, Subject Files, MFDP 64–65, Senate Inter-nal Security Subcommittee Papers, National Archives; *Congressional Record*, 88th Cong., 2nd sess., 1964, 110, pt. 13:16593–97.

27. Johnston to Glazier, 23 July 1964, Investigations and Research, undated, and Report on Principal Activities and Policies from January 1, 1964, through August 31, 1964, 1 Sep-tember 1964, Box 136, Mississippi State Sovereignty Commission Papers, McCain Library.

gate a church burning near Philadelphia. They had been gone for a month when Eastland delivered his speech.[28]

The Mississippi senator carefully worked the three into his monologue. While Schwerner, Chaney, and Goodman may not have been conscious participants in the Communist cause, Eastland declared, the trio had subconsciously aided and abetted Communist Party activity in working for the movement. Eastland even conjured the possibility that the missing activists had concocted a hoax to be used as a publicity stunt, a theory that J. Edgar Hoover had himself recommended to Lyndon Johnson in the aftermath of the trio's disappearance. There was "just as much evidence," Eastland argued, that they were "voluntarily missing" as there was that they had been abducted.[29]

Mississippi red and black investigators leaped to support the notion that the "disappearance" of Schwerner, Chaney, and Goodman was the result of a Communist conspiracy. The two white activists in the group both had ties to left-wing groups and individuals. Goodman had grown up in a leftist New York household with connections to HUAC-prosecuted Communists. He had also attended the progressive and integrated Walden School from 1946 to 1961. Schwerner, like Goodman, was a New York native and Walden attendee; in addition, he was Jewish and looked to white Mississippians like a beatnik, which many Southern reactionaries associated with radicalism. The Mississippi Klan even identified Schwerner simply as "goatee," associating his facial hair with deviant political if not personal behavior. Schwerner was also a social worker and an experienced CORE volunteer who had the power to influence local blacks, a fact that automatically made him suspicious to many Mississippians. Finally, his family's use of Martin Popper, a "longtime Communist legal eagle" who had come to national attention defending members of the Hollywood Ten, only furthered speculation about the activist. Chaney, a black Mississippi native, had no such ties to the left, although he was clearly under the influence of the infamous Schwerner.[30]

But any chance Mississippi segregationists had of portraying the disappearance of Schwerner, Chaney, and Goodman as a Communist-planned publicity stunt, evaporated in early August when the FBI found the bodies of

28. Johnston to Glazier, 23 July 1964, Box 136, Mississippi State Sovereignty Commission Papers, McCain Library.

29. *Congressional Record*, 88th Cong., 2nd sess., 1964, 110, pt. 13:16593–97.

30. Ibid., 16596; Dittmer, *Local People*, 247. See also Seth Cagin and Philip Dray, *We Are Not Afraid* (New York: Macmillan, 1988).

the three buried in an earthen dam southwest of Philadelphia, Mississippi. Instead of pulling in its horns, the SSC leadership criticized the FBI for covering up the fact that Chaney had been found with a badge linking him to a black Communist arrested for inciting riots in New York. Publicly red-baiting the three martyred civil rights workers, the FBI realized, would not have played well outside of Mississippi.[31]

James Eastland had closed his July speech by praising white Mississippi's restraint in dealing with the summer invasion, but in the same breath he seemed to imply that there was a limit to that patience: "That the people of Mississippi are holding their tempers so well, that their natural human urge to defend themselves is being so tightly restrained, that they have been so little moved to counteraction in the face of such provocation, I say is to their everlasting credit." While Eastland and southern red and black hunting politicians did not openly advocate violence, they professed to understand the motivation behind it. At the least they condoned racial violence; at the most they helped create the paranoid delusions that drove it. Eastland and company provided a justification for beating and killing that did not carry the stigma of pure racism. Those who lashed out against civil rights workers were, in their estimation, acting on a human impulse to defend themselves against the greatest of modern evils, Communism. For Eastland and those who shared his extreme vision, the maiming of civil rights workers could be labeled a patriotic duty.[32]

Threats of violence against civil rights workers often accompanied anti-Communist rantings. In one instance Fred Shuttlesworth's family, then living in Cincinnati, received a series of phone calls threatening mayhem and highlighted by shouts of "Communist! Communist!" One caller put it simply: "Bombs fly in Hiroshima. Bombs fly in Alabama. Bombs fly in Ohio. Communist, Communist, Communist." More telling red and black rhetoric accompanied many of the most famous acts of violence against civil rights workers in the 1960s. The same night President Kennedy announced his support for pending civil rights legislation, Citizens' Council member Byron De La Beckwith shot and killed Mississippi NAACP leader Medgar Evers. Days before De La Beckwith had declared to locals in Greenwood, Mississippi, that the world was in the hands of Communists; he invited

31. "Jackson Mississippi," 5 August 1964, Box 136, Mississippi State Sovereignty Commission Papers, McCain Library.
32. *Congressional Record*, 88th Cong., 2nd sess., 1964, 110, pt. 13:16597.

them to let him know "if I can kill a nigger for you." In another example, white spectators attending a George Wallace speech on Communism and the Civil Rights Act of 1964 used folding chairs to beat bloody three black protesters who tried to interrupt. Finally, James Earl Ray, the man who would assassinate Martin Luther King, was an ardent anti-Communist and Joe McCarthy booster.[33]

But no better example exists of a civil rights worker being brutalized for his alleged Communist ties than that of Bob Zellner. A white Alabama native, Zellner had been SCEF's representative on SNCC's staff since 1961. As such he became a prime target of red and black haters. The Mississippi SSC, the Louisiana Un-American Activities Committee, and Alabama law-enforcement officials all kept close tabs on his activities. During an October 1961 march in support of a SNCC registration drive in McComb, Mississippi, Zellner had his eyes gouged and was kicked unconscious after local police refused to protect him from an angry white mob. Four months later he was jailed in Baton Rouge, Louisiana, and charged with criminal anarchy. Guards at the jail threw Zellner in with sixty-five inmates and told the prisoners that he was a "Communist who tried to smuggle obscene literature on race-mixing" into the state. He was subsequently threatened with sharpened spoons and razors and repeatedly beaten. Guards and inmates also doused him with water or slapped his feet every time he tried to fall asleep and paraded him before tours of high school students who had come to the jail to see "the nigger-loving Communist."[34]

That red-baiting provided a justification for violence in the South was not lost on SNCC or the Communist Party. Just after the FBI found the bodies of Schwerner, Chaney, and Goodman in Mississippi, *The Worker* re-

33. Smith to Robert Kennedy, 26 June 1963, Attorney General Files, Box 9, Civil Rights 6/16–6/30/63 Folder, Robert Kennedy Papers, John F. Kennedy Library; Andrew Manis, *A Fire You Can't Put Out: The Civil Rights Life of Birmingham's Reverend Fred Shuttlesworth* (Tuscaloosa: University of Alabama Press, 1999), 330; Dan Carter, *The Politics of Rage* (New York: Simon and Schuster, 1995), 216–17; Gerald Posner, *Killing the Dream: James Earl Ray and the Assassination of Martin Luther King, Jr.* (New York: Random House, 1998), 109.

34. Bob Zellner, telephone interview with author, 12 February 2002; "At a hearing . . . ," undated, Box 136, Mississippi State Sovereignty Commission Papers, McCain Library; Malone to Major, 12 May 1962, ID# 1-98-0-8-1-1-1, Mississippi State Sovereignty Commission Files. See also Carter, *Politics of Rage*, 227–28; Frank T. Adams, *James A. Dombrowski: An American Heretic, 1987–1983* (Knoxville: University of Tennessee Press, 1992), 255–57.

ported that anti-Communist and segregationist attacks in the state had risen to a level that "could well result in additional deaths of civil rights workers." The article quoted SNCC volunteer Jerry Tecklin as saying that "it wasn't enough that they killed Goodman, Schwerner, and Chaney, they're creating a red hysteria that may lead to a repeat performance." Tecklin was referring directly to the late-July campaign by Eastland, the SSC, and local newspapers to charge that the freedom-summer movement was Communist driven. The article may have exaggerated the possibility of a direct cause-and-effect relationship between the southern red scare and violence. It served the party's interest to publicly denounce anti-Communists as racists and fascists. But the article made a valid argument when it insisted that southerners determined to brutalize civil rights workers were attempting to legitimize their activities by posing as anti-Communists.[35]

Although violence was a concern for the movement, the political ramifications of the Communist label were even more daunting. The Mississippi registration campaign came to a climax in the late summer of 1964. Although the movement had successfully begun an effort that would eventually change the face of southern politics, COFO only managed to register some twelve hundred blacks to vote. Moreover, African Americans had been successfully barred from participating in precinct, county, and state conventions. But COFO would not give up. It enrolled some sixty thousand blacks in the Mississippi Freedom Democratic Party (MFDP) and laid plans to contest the seats of the lily-white, segregationist Mississippi Democratic Party at the national convention in Atlantic City. This effort, movement officials worried, would surely be compromised if the Communist charge gained any greater popularity.

The election of 1964 was as important to white southern segregationists as it was to southern blacks. Alabama's Commission to Preserve the Peace called the contest for the presidency "the last great battle of individual rights against the master state." The "Counterfeit Confederate" Lyndon Johnson and the forces of "big government" had captured the national Democratic Party. The new leadership was, according to the Peace Commission, catering to "radical groups and minority segments cynically directed by left-wing forces." Indeed, a victory by Johnson Democrats would be nothing less than a triumph for a "Communist Coalition" that included SNCC, CORE, the NAACP, the NCC, and the SCLC. By the end of the summer, the once

---

35. "Redbaiting Gives Death an Assist in Mississippi," *The Worker*, 4 August 1964, p. 3

solidly Democratic white South was sidling up to Republican Barry Gold-water, whose opposition to federal civil rights legislation, defense of states' rights, and extreme anti-Communism appealed to their most sacred values. [215] Mississippi Sovereignty Commission director Erle Johnston summed up his region's political center: "While I am a Democrat—I think Goldwater is the man for our times. We can't afford to turn our country over to the Reds and the red-inspired blacks."[36]

This did not mean, however, that Mississippi would completely aban-don the Democratic Party and give up its seats at the national convention. Not only would such abdication constitute giving in to "the red-inspired blacks," it would legitimize the MFDP charges that the regular Democratic Party delegates from Mississippi had been elected in an undemocratic man-ner. It would also jeopardize future elections in the state, including the in-cumbency bids of James Eastland and all of the Mississippi congressmen. The state thus kept close tabs on the MFDP and did its utmost to under-mine the organization's efforts to be seated at the national convention.

In mid-August, just days before the Atlantic City convention opened, the Mississippi attorney general's office requested that the State Sover-eignty Commission compile a brief opposing the seating of the MFDP dele-gates. The commission had maintained extensive records of MFDP activity and quickly put together a report. It focused on three main points: first that the party was organized chiefly by nonresidents of the state, second that the delegation selected by the party was chosen by representatives of only forty of the eighty-two Mississippi counties, and third that among the organizers of the MFDP were people with Communist-front associations. In support of the third point, the SSC provided brief sketches of the front-related activi-ties of a dozen persons, many of whom had been listed in Eastland's July Senate speech. Four of those named, Maynard Omerberg, George Crockett, Lawrence Warren, and Benjamin Smith, were members of the National Lawyers Guild working on the freedom-summer project.[37]

36. Staff Study, July 1964, SG13842, Alabama State Sovereignty Commission Papers, Al-abama Department of Archives and History; Johnston to Buchanan, undated, ID# 9-33-0-4-1-1-1, Mississippi State Sovereignty Commission Files. See also "Hargis Rips Reds, Lauds Goldwater," *Atlanta Constitution*, 30 July 1964.

37. Johnston to Griffin, 18 August 1964, Box 136, Mississippi State Sovereignty Com-mission Papers, McCain Library; Mississippi Freedom Democratic Party: An Analysis by the State Sovereignty Commission, undated, Box 136, Mississippi State Sovereignty Com-mission Papers, McCain Library.

The State Sovereignty Commission material became part of a package that accompanied the delegation of regular Mississippi Democrats to Atlantic City. This, they hoped, would drive a stake in the heart of MFDP attempts to unseat the Mississippi delegation. The material changed few minds, but it contributed to a rift at the convention between liberals and the more radical members of the movement. The conflict arose when the Freedom Democratic Party accepted a compromise offer from vice-presidential hopeful Hubert Humphrey to seat two at-large delegates rather than replace the entire regular Democratic Party delegation from Mississippi and other southern states. Movement liberals leading the national Freedom Democratic Party (FDP), including Martin Luther King, Bayard Rustin, members of the National Council of Churches, and FDP counsel Joseph Rauh, a founding member of the liberal, anti-Communist Americans for Democratic Action (ADA), supported the compromise. Mississippi blacks headed by Bob Moses and Fannie Lou Hamer felt betrayed. The liberals had sold them out, they believed. Not only had they acquiesced to the seating of Mississippi segregationists, they had denied SNCC members the ability to choose who would sit as the two at-large delegates.

Immediately the MFDP leaders distanced themselves from the party's liberals and fired Rauh as COFO's attorney. Rauh and the ADA subsequently lashed out publicly against SNCC and the Lawyers Guild claiming that it was "immoral to take help from Communists." Bob Moses tried to counter the criticism but confirmed its premise in many minds when he stated that the "liberals getting upset at us was inevitable. We are raising fundamental questions about how the poor sharecropper can achieve the Good Life, questions that liberalism is incapable of answering."[38]

Perhaps indicative of the growing rift in the movement, southern blacks failed to make any headway in the fall elections. The registration efforts had intensified, but the black vote actually declined from previous years. The conservative white South, meanwhile, was still very much committed to preserving its racial and political traditions. While Lyndon Johnson triumphed in one the greatest electoral landslides in American history, Barry Goldwater carried five Deep South states including Alabama, Georgia, Loui-

---

38. Investigations and Research, undated, and Report on Principal Activities and Policies from January 1, 1964, through 31 August, 1964, 1 September 1964, Box 136, Mississippi State Sovereignty Commission Papers, McCain Library; Rowland Evans and Robert Novak, "Inside Report: Freedom Party Postscript," *New York Herald Tribune*, 1 September 1964; Dittmer, *Local People*, 292–302, 315–18.

siana, South Carolina, and Mississippi with nearly 60 percent of the vote. Moreover, not one liberal challenger unseated a southern segregationist incumbent.[39]

Despite these setbacks the MFDP continued to challenge the domination of Mississippi politics by white segregationists. It filed a notice of contest with the U.S. House of Representatives asserting that, owing to the systematic exclusion of blacks from the registration process, the five congressmen from Mississippi had not been fairly elected. In preparing the challenge, the MFDP continued to employ the help of the Lawyers Guild. Indeed, the group recruited some one hundred fifty attorneys in the guild's network to take depositions from blacks who failed to register because of segregationist harassment. Not surprisingly, this initiative drew fire from those congressmen whose seats were challenged.

Representative Prentiss Walker, for one, charged that the MFDP's "deposition caravan . . . is staffed with either known communists or those affiliated with communist front organizations." But again it was Senator Eastland who took point. In three speeches delivered before the Senate in February and March 1965, he railed against the MFDP and its lawyers. He singled out for particular scorn Morton Stavis, an NLG attorney and head of the deposition collectors. Eastland revealed that Stavis was not only connected to several front organizations but had also been a member of the Communist Party in the mid-1940s. There was, in addition, the infamous Benjamin Margolis who was acting as a lawyer for the Freedom Party. Margolis, Eastland insisted, was "an old time Communist and one of the deadliest men in the Communist Party." And, most damning, Victor Rabinowitz was a major financial contributor to the movement.[40]

Rabinowitz, especially, would later seem to validate Eastland's calls for concern. A committed longtime Communist, Rabinowitz would take over as president of the National Lawyers Guild in 1967 . Although he did not always see eye to eye with the younger generation of radicals, he would embrace the New Left, hoping that "in their emphasis on the freedom of the individual, perhaps the young are looking to the ultimate goal of Communism rather than to the intermediate station of Socialism."[41]

39. See Bernard Cosman, *Five States for Goldwater* (Tuscaloosa: University of Alabama Press, 1966).

40. *Congressional Record*, 89th Cong., 1st sess., 1965, 111, pt. 2:1943–53, 2580 and pt. 4:5443–52; Dittmer, *Local People*, 341.

41. Lewy, *Cause That Failed*, 284.

But as costly as Eastland's rhetoric was, the continued criticism of the MFDP from within the movement made even greater waves. After a preliminary House vote on the MFDP challenge in January, NAACP head Roy Wilkins publicly charged that "Chinese communist elements" had infiltrated the Student Nonviolent Coordinating Committee. The NAACP leadership had long been at odds with the SNCC-led COFO, both in Mississippi and at the national level. Infighting over the Communist issue in the Mississippi movement would again develop late the following summer. After a young SNCC worker was killed while serving in Vietnam, the MFDP's official newsletter printed an article declaring that blacks should not serve in Southeast Asia. Mississippi journalist Hodding Carter III editorialized that the article was "close to treason," and MFDP heads Lawrence Guyot and Ed King were "deliberately collaborating in the communist line." Charles Evers of the Mississippi NAACP, meanwhile, followed in Roy Wilkins's footsteps and began denouncing members of the Mississippi Freedom Democratic Party as Communists. These statements came just weeks before the House again took up the MFDP challenge following seven months of procedural delays. The representatives, some swayed by the criticism of the Freedom Democrats and many convinced that enacting voting rights reform would make the challenge irrelevant, voted down the MFDP challenge 228 to 143.[42]

The criticism of the MFDP by more conservative members of the civil rights establishment came just as they were competing to regain leadership of the movement. Younger, more radical, and more militant groups such as SNCC and CORE had largely taken charge of the voting rights campaigns in Mississippi and Alabama. Traditionalists attempted to hold on to power by denouncing these organizations' ties to Communists. Their hope was to endear themselves to liberal, anti-Communist moderates who were leading the effort to have Congress enact national voting rights legislation.

With Martin Luther King under the red and black investigators' microscope, the SCLC was in no position to join in the criticism of the leftist up-and-comers. Nevertheless the organization hoped to maintain a leadership position in the voting rights campaign. By late 1964 it had devised a plan to force the federal government to adopt a strong voting rights law. Hoping to repeat the success of the campaigns in Birmingham and elsewhere, King looked again to provoke racist brutality against nonviolent protesters. The

42. Dittmer, *Local People*, 341, 351–59.

most likely place to stage the desired scenario, King decided, was Selma, Alabama. "Selma," he wrote in the *New York Times*, "has succeeded in limiting Negro registration to the snail's pace of about 145 persons a year. At this rate, it would take 103 years to register the 15,000 eligible Negro voters of Dallas County." Moreover Selma had already been the scene of violent beatings of civil rights workers at the hands of sheriff James G. Clark's deputies.[43]

The realization of King's plans in Selma was made possible to some degree by his ability to come to terms with J. Edgar Hoover. The war of words between the two had continued into November 1964 when Hoover publicly labeled King "the most notorious liar" in America. The FBI director was convinced that King aid Stanley Levinson had been intimately involved with the Communist Party's financial dealings. In addition he had learned from wiretaps that King and other SCLC leaders had been less than faithful husbands. The civil rights leadership's claim of moral superiority, in short, was a farce, Hoover declared. King shot back at Hoover, arguing that the FBI director had "apparently faltered under the awesome burden, complexities, and responsibilities of his office." Realizing the damage that their feud was doing to both of them, the two met in early December to hammer out some kind of accommodation. King told newsmen after the meeting that he and the director had reached "new levels of understanding." While they actually never came to any lasting rapprochement, King did assure the FBI head that he had a strong personal dislike of Communism; their feud—its public phase at least—momentarily subsided.[44]

No such understanding had been recorded with southern segregationists, however. Mississippi representative John Bell Williams, taking a cue from Hoover, confronted Attorney General Nicholas Katzenbach in the presence of President Johnson, demanding that the administration make public what was contained in the FBI file on Martin Luther King. Katzenbach reportedly lied, responding that there was no file on King. But Alabama's law-enforcement and investigative agencies had continued to keep tabs on King along with a number of civil rights leaders and groups suspected of Communist subversion. The state's Department of Public Safety

43. Harvard Sitkoff, *The Struggle for Black Equality* (New York: Hill and Wang, 1981), 187–88.

44. "King Rebuts Hoover Charges," *New York Times*, 20 November 1964; "Hoover, Dr. King Meet, See New Understanding," *Washington Post*, 2 December 1964; David Garrow, *Bearing the Cross* (New York: William Morrow, 1986), 261–62.

maintained rolls of "individuals active in civil disturbances." King's entry listed among his associates "Left Wing Pro-Communist Groups." A Peace Commission report estimated that the civil rights leader had "amassed the staggering total of more than 60 Communist front affiliations since 1955." Another commission profile warned state law-enforcement officials that King was "totally under the direction of the Communist Party." That Alabama segregationists would intensify their scrutiny of the civil rights leader during the voting rights campaign in Selma was a foregone conclusion, but it was troublesome to the movement nonetheless.[45]

King arrived in Selma in early January 1965, just weeks after accepting the Nobel Peace Prize. He announced that the movement would not be "asking" but "demanding the ballot." King led hundreds to register at the Dallas County Courthouse in daily marches over the next two months. Although Sheriff Clark controlled his temper, thousands of black demonstrators were arrested, drawing the attention of the national media. Finally in early March, the Selma movement's campaign to provoke an incident bore fruit. On the sixth of that month, King called on blacks to march from Selma to Montgomery to present a petition of grievances to the governor. Governor Wallace responded that such a demonstration would not be tolerated. A short time later, King told followers that he would not go ahead with the march, but his decision had little to do with Wallace's reaction. President Johnson had made it clear that he disapproved of the civil rights leader's move, while the Justice Department had warned him of Klan death threats.

But King was not the only leader in Selma. SCLC staff director Hosea Williams and SNCC's John Lewis would step in and carry out the demonstration. On March 7 black protesters gathered and began their journey out of town. After stopping the procession at the Pettus Bridge leading out of Selma, troopers and deputies savagely attacked a line of protesters. Watching on television the nation responded with a storm of indignation. Sympathy marches cropped up in several cities as thousands converged on

45. Memo: Sourwine to Eastland, 22 March 1965, RG46, Name File 3, MLK 1965, Senate Internal Security Subcommittee Papers; Individuals Active in Civil Disturbances, undated, SG22394, Wallace Papers, Alabama Department of Archives and History; Communists in Civil Rights, 20 October 1964, SG21073, Legislative Commission to Preserve the Peace Papers, Alabama Department of Archives and History; Carter, *Politics of Rage*, 233–34. See also Charles Eagles, *Outside Agitator* (Chapel Hill: University of North Carolina Press, 1993), 142–43.

Washington to push for federal intervention. Overwhelmed by the response, King called for a second march on the ninth.[46]

President Johnson, hoping to prevent a repeat performance, sent Com- munity Relations Service head Leroy Collins to meet with King and at the same time summoned Governor Wallace to the White House. Wallace walked into the Oval Office determined not to be intimidated by the famous "Johnson treatment." Taking a seat the governor seized the initiative, arguing straight away that law and order were dissolving in Alabama because of voting rights movement "malcontents," many of whom, he claimed, had been trained "in Moscow or New York." "You cannot deal with street revolutionaries," Wallace complained "First, it is a front seat on a bus; next, it's a takeover of parks; then it's public schools; then it's voting rights; then it's jobs; then it's distribution of wealth without work."

At this Johnson leaned forward, towering over the diminutive governor, his nose inches from Wallace's face, and launched into a monologue that did not let up for an hour. He explained the need to end racism, overhaul the welfare system, and break the cycle of poverty enveloping the South. At one point Wallace's right-hand man Seymore Trammell interrupted, declaring that the problem at hand was "the racial agitators and the growing menace of the Communist demonstrators in Alabama." The president pushed a pencil and tablet into Trammell's hands and said, "Here! Take notes." Johnson then lit into Wallace. "George," he asked, "why are you doing this? . . . Why don't you let the niggers vote?" When Wallace tried to explain that the county registrars would not allow it, the president angrily replied, "Don't you shit me, George Wallace."[47]

Wallace left the meeting subdued and silent, but a day later he was his old defiant self. He declared on CBS's *Face the Nation* that the national media had been ignoring the real issue in Alabama, "the infiltration of this so-called civil rights movement by members of the Communist conspiracy." Nevertheless the president had brokered a deal with Alabama authorities and King that the civil rights leader would lead his followers across the Pettus Bridge, stop when halted by troopers, pray briefly, and then order his marchers to turn around. The second Selma march went as scripted, leaving King the unenviable job of explaining to movement workers why they had not continued to Montgomery. But King did not come away from the inci-

46. Sitkoff, *Struggle for Black Equality*, 189–90.
47. Carter, *Politics of Rage*, 252–53.

dent empty-handed. On March 15 the president delivered a televised address to a joint session of Congress, eloquently urging passage of a voting rights bill. Johnson also prevailed on federal district judge Frank Johnson to give judicial sanction to a massive Selma-to-Montgomery march.[48]

On March 18 Wallace rose before a joint session of the Alabama legislature and denounced the demonstrators as nothing more than "mobs, employing the street warfare tactics of the Communists." He would not spend state money to protect the marchers. The president responded by federalizing the Alabama National Guard, thus ensuring the safety of the protesters along the fifty-mile route. The march was among the most triumphant of the civil rights movement. Some twenty-five thousand made the trip, singing, laughing, and clapping along the way. Civil rights activists would remember it as one of their greatest victories.[49]

Alabama segregationists would recall the event differently. State representative Bill Dickinson called the Selma campaign a celebration of lawlessness and debauchery. Among the Selma marchers with genuinely good intentions, he argued, were "adventurers, beatniks, prostitutes, and similar rabble." Only the Communist Party, he declared, could put such a "diverse group together into a formidable force." Citing the participation of Carl Braden, Abner Berry, James Peck, Bayard Rustin, and Martin Luther King, the congressman concluded that the "Communist Party and the Communist apparatus" had been the "undergirding structure for all of the racial troubles in Alabama for the past three months." Governor Wallace was so pleased with the speech that he had it reproduced and distributed throughout the state.[50]

Two days later, Alabama congressmen Jack Edwards and John Buchanan added that there existed "ample evidence that those affiliated with Communist-front organizations and identified with the Communist Party have in fact been active in Alabama in recent days." Buchanan's broadside drew particular attention in Washington. He was a member of the House Un-American Activities Committee (HUAC) and his comments came on the heels of committee chairman Edwin Willis's announcement that HUAC would begin investigations of the Ku Klux Klan in the South. Indeed, south-

---

48. Ibid., 254; Sitkoff, *Struggle for Black Equality*, 191–94.

49. Carter, *Politics of Rage*, 255–56.

50. *Congressional Record*, 89th Cong., 1st sess., 1965, 111, pt. 5:6113–14; Carter, *Politics of Rage*, 260.

erners on the committee were determined that the probe include extremism of all kinds. Willis went out of his way to make it clear that "elimination of the influence of the Klans alone will not bring the peace and order we all desire. There are other racial agitators at work in all parts of the country. The Committee is aware that Communist influence is at work in this field." Based on this and Buchanan's statements, critics of HUAC claimed the committee's Klan investigation was insincere, designed only to divert public criticism from a parallel investigation of Communists in the civil rights movement. The administration, caught between the two sides, sent Attorney General Nicholas Katzenbach to help quiet the debate by stating that while leftist groups had tried to inject their ideologies into the movement, they had been largely unsuccessful.[51]

Meanwhile the Alabama State Sovereignty Commission hoped to prove Katzenbach wrong. The SSC launched a project to develop a documentary film on the Selma-to-Montgomery march in early April. Employing a Dallas film company, the commission spent some thirty-five thousand dollars on production costs. The purpose had been to show that the march was a "world-wide attention-gaining device" that fulfilled "Communist objectives." The result was a poorly produced piece of propaganda that combined confusing narration with rather innocuous footage of civil rights leaders' speeches and Selma marchers milling about. Perhaps aware of the film's shortcomings, the SSC distributed it with a list of persons and organizations pictured and their affiliations with Communist causes. Included were the time-tested accusations against Martin Luther King, Fred Shuttlesworth, Bayard Rustin, Carl Braden, Hunter Pitts O'Dell, James Dombrowski, Benjamin Smith, and James Peck.[52]

While the film failed to draw the national attention Alabama red and black hunters had hoped for, a Peace Commission written report to the Alabama legislature did get noticed. But interest in the report came largely

51. *Congressional Record*, 89th Cong., 1st sess., 1965, 111, pt. 5:6767; Willis to Sikes, 19 August 1965, C46 B182 F7, Willis Papers, Southwest Louisiana State University; "Face the Nation," 4 April 1965, C46 B182 F2, Willis Papers; "Rights Groups Free of Red Rule—Katzenbach," *Washington Post*, 4 April 1965.

52. Final Billing, 29 July 1965, SG 13843, Alabama State Sovereignty Commission Papers; Synopsis of the Treatment, undated, SG13842, Alabama State Sovereignty Commission Papers; Script, "We Shall Overcome," undated, SG13843, Alabama State Sovereignty Commission Papers; Selma-Montgomery March Forward, undated, SG13842, Alabama State Sovereignty Commission Papers. See Carter, *Politics of Rage*, 260.

from the outlandish nature of its charges. The commission claimed that SNCC was "extensively Communist dominated," CORE was "an important arm of the pro-Communist conspiracy," and the SCLC was "substantially under control of Communists." These patently false characterizations drew an immediate response from the leaders of the groups mentioned. Martin Luther King blasted the report as "another attempt to evade the fact that democracy does not exist in Alabama." SNCC's public information director Julian Bond added that it was a "typical response from a typical Southern legislature." And CORE director James Forman stated that the accusations were "nothing but rubbish" but were to be expected from a committee made up of members "elected from counties with extremely low Negro registration."[53]

The United States Congress was equally unmoved by the southerners' insistence that the voting rights movement was a vehicle for the forces of international Communism. In August President Johnson signed the revolutionary Voting Rights Act into law. Under the measure federal examiners registered qualified voters and suspended devices such as literacy tests. "The lock on the ballot box for blacks had been broken," wrote civil rights historian Harvard Sitkoff.[54]

It was ironic that segregationist southerners labeled "Communist" the premier symbol of democracy, voting. But they never felt that theirs was a contradictory stance. They held a vision of democracy that had as its base the racist notion that blacks were unfit for citizenship. Indeed, they came to believe that the conservative South stood as the last barrier against a growing flood of social and political change that would ultimately lead to Communist control. They therefore spent a great deal of time, money, and effort in preventing a revolution at the ballot box. In doing so they also supported the notion that the violent defense of southern segregation was a patriotic duty. Ultimately the damage the southern red scare was able to inflict on the movement's legislative accomplishments was minimal. Few outside of right-wing circles were convinced that Communist influence in the movement was the driving force behind the voting rights bill. An already existing ideological rift within the civil rights establishment, how-

53. "Report in Alabama Rips Rights Groups As Red-Dominated," *Washington Post*, 30 June 1965; "Rights Groups Assail Alabama 'Witch-Hunt,'" *Washington Evening Star*, 30 June 1965.
54. Sitkoff, *Struggle for Black Equality*, 197.

ever, magnified what little southern segregationists were able to achieve. The split between liberal anti-Communists and younger radicals who were willing to accept Communist support allowed southern red and black hunters to drive a wedge into the movement. With rioting in urban black ghettos and the increasing alliance of the movement with the New Left over the next three years, they would continue to drive the wedge deeper.

8

ON AUGUST 11, 1965, JUST FIVE DAYS AFTER PRESI-
dent Johnson signed the Voting Rights Act, rioters took to the streets of
Watts, Los Angeles's largest black ghetto. The Watts uprising and subsequent outbreaks of violence in America's inner cities were the result of
many converging forces. The civil rights movement created the expectation
among African Americans that they would gain equal access to the American dream, but legislation did little to improve the conditions of blacks living in the urban North, Midwest, and West. In Philadelphia, Chicago, and
Detroit, African Americans lived in ghettos created by political and economic institutions controlled by racist whites. Ghetto dwellers received in-
adequate and unequal funding for sewers, streets, and schools while jobs
moved to the suburbs or to smaller towns. African Americans were left
stranded, excluded from white housing by unwritten covenants. In crum-
bling, rat-infested apartments, families disintegrated, young people dropped
out of school, drugs became commonplace and crime epidemic. One ghetto
after another exploded under the pressure in the summers of 1965 and 1966.

At the same time black-power advocates began winning the hearts and
minds of many African Americans. They turned from the teachings of Martin Luther King and the leadership of the Southern Christian Leadership
Conference (SCLC) and the National Association for the Advancement of
Colored People (NAACP) to embrace the teachings of Malcolm X and the
other ancestors of black-power ideology. They preached black pride and self-
reliance and argued that blacks could only liberate themselves spiritually,
politically, and economically through violent struggle. "If someone puts a
hand on you," Malcolm X told his followers, "send him to the cemetery."

The militancy embodied in the new philosophy began to spread through
the African American community in 1966. Members of the Student Nonviolent Coordinating Committee (SNCC) elected the radical Stokely Carmichael president over John Lewis, a pacifist. Similarly, the Congress of Racial
Equality (CORE) replaced James Farmer, an advocate of nonviolence, with

the militant, confrontational Floyd McKissick. They would change the movement from the inside out. They would reject mainstream American liberalism as the guiding force for racial reform. Real changes, they argued, would only result when blacks took pride in their own communities, created their own economic and political infrastructure, and committed themselves to permanent reform, even if it meant armed struggle. The time had come, Carmichael told a Greenwood, Mississippi, audience, for "Black Power! Black Power!"

With racial violence ravaging American cities and the black-power movement gaining momentum, southern segregationists instinctively looked for reds behind the unrest. This time their search proved easier. Evidence that Communist ideology had begun to permeate the struggle for black equality was abundant. The new leaders of the movement publicly embraced leftist radicalism. Carmichael and other black-power advocates brandished as a primary rhetorical device the prediction that black liberation would only be gained through the violent overthrow of American capitalism. Their speeches frequently alluded to the teachings of Communist icons Che Guevara, Ho Chi Minh, and Mao Tse-tung as guides to black equality. They also openly allied themselves with the New Left, a group of intellectuals and college students that embraced Marxist denunciations of liberalism, racism, and imperialism and opposed American involvement in the Vietnam War.

Given the overtly radical stance taken by black-power leaders, the contention that African Americans and Communists were together working for revolutionary change in the United States could no longer be dismissed as the reckless, politically motivated ravings of massive resisters. Indeed, segregationists would feel somewhat vindicated as the southern red scare gained a degree of national acceptance under the banner of law and order in the late 1960s.

Nothing pleased red and black hunters more than a November 19, 1965, Gallup poll declaring that an overwhelming majority of Americans believed that Communists had been involved in both anti–Vietnam War and civil rights demonstrations. While the segregationists could claim the results of the survey were partially due to their diligence in promoting the issue, the responses to the poll were also the result of recent events. That fall mainstream America, still reeling from the Watts riots, heard Martin Luther

King, the most recognizable leader of the civil rights movement, criticize American involvement in Vietnam.[1]

King first called for a negotiated settlement to the widening war in Vietnam in early March 1965. Bayard Rustin and Stanley Levinson had both told King that he had a responsibility to speak out on issues of war and peace, particularly on the growing conflict in Vietnam. The violent confrontation in Southeast Asia, King would tell Howard University students in Washington, D.C., was "accomplishing nothing." Indeed, he insisted, it was drawing resources away from the Johnson administration's War on Poverty, a crucial program needed to empower impoverished blacks.

Over the next few months, the civil rights leader would intensify his campaign to end the war. In July he publicly called for negotiations with the Vietcong and a quick settlement of the conflict so that the U.S. could concentrate on the pressing poverty issue. The following month he announced that he intended to send letters to the leaders of North Vietnam, South Vietnam, China, the Soviet Union, and the United States calling for peace talks. Finally, in September King met with United Nations ambassador Arthur Goldberg to present his case on Vietnam and request that the U.S. end its opposition to the admission of Communist China to the UN.[2]

King's criticism of the war in Vietnam and his support for China's admission to the UN was in no way motivated by an allegiance to Communism or even the more radical positions of the New Left. Rather, as a proponent of nonviolence and international peace, he felt a moral obligation to take the posture he did. But southern segregationists realized that King's stance on the issues fit nicely into their characterization of him as a Communist and the movement as a tool of Moscow. South Carolina senator Strom Thurmond called it a "disgrace" that Ambassador Goldberg would even meet with "troublemakers" like King and his aide Bayard Rustin, a "documented" Communist.

Southern nationalists understood that by blasting King's positions as un-American, they could bolster their own credentials as patriots. Not that they callously supported the war in Vietnam to justify their attacks on King. While many from the region objected strongly to American military adven-

1. Gallup Poll, 19 November 1965, Box 71, HU6 10/28/65–12/20/65, White House Central File, Johnson Presidential Papers, Lyndon Baines Johnson Library. See also Dan Carter, *The Politics of Rage* (New York: Simon and Schuster, 1995), 306.

2. David Garrow, *Bearing the Cross* (New York: William Morrow, 1986), 394, 425–45.

tures abroad, once the country had become involved in Vietnam they felt, as Georgia senator Richard Russell put it, that the U.S. could not afford to "tuck tail and run." Moreover, they understood that the consequences for [229 pulling out of Southeast Asia could very well include further Communist aggression around the world. But while they may have been genuine supporters of the war effort, white southerners were not averse to making political gain out of the conflict. That opportunity seemed particularly ripe in 1965 when some 80 percent of Americans felt it was "very important" to keep South Vietnam from going Communist.[3]

But the gains for southern segregationists at King's expense were only part of the problem for the civil rights leader. Even more serious were the frowns of his liberal allies such as the Democratic senator from Connecticut Thomas Dodd, who warned of the repercussions of King's anti-Vietnam stance: "The enemies of the civil rights movement have repeatedly made the charge that Dr. King is under Communist influence. I have myself defended Dr. King against this charge. But by the stand he has now taken on the whole series of vital foreign policy issues, I gravely fear that Dr. King has provided his own enemies and the enemies of the movements he heads with ammunition that they will know only too well how to use." Dodd's statement stunned King. The movement leader told friends that he would return to a focus on civil rights. "I have to find out how I can gracefully pull out so that I can get on with the civil rights issue because I have come to the conclusion that I can't battle these forces who are about to defeat my influence," he said. King anticipated that "they will take the Communist China thing and what Dodd said and use it to say that I am under the influence of Communists." The civil rights leader's decision turned out to be a sound one. A few months later, a *Washington Post* survey indicated that many Americans felt that movement groups criticizing American involvement in Vietnam were hurting the cause for black rights.[4]

While King's stance on Vietnam and China confirmed for some that the

---

3. Russell to Neff, 1 December 1965, Inter-Vietnam, Neff, SH, Russell Papers, Richard B. Russell Memorial Library; Russell to Wolfson, 4 January 1966, Inter-Vietnam, Wolfson, Louis E., Russell Papers; LBJ to Russell, 27 May 1964, Container 4, 3519a, 3520a, 3521a, LBJ Telephone Transcripts, Lyndon Baines Johnson Library; Terry Anderson, *The Sixties* (New York: Longman, 1999), 64.

4. *Congressional Record*, 89th Cong., 1st sess., 1965, 111, app. A5300; "Anti-Viet Stand Hurts Civil Rights Movement," *Washington Post*, 11 April 1966; Garrow, *Bearing the Cross*, 445.

movement sympathized with international Communist causes, the Watts riots had convinced others that Communism had taken root in America in the guise of black power. In the wake of the violence, black anti-Communist columnist George Schuyler blamed Martin Luther King and others for having created the atmosphere of civil disobedience that led to the reckless disregard for police authority in Los Angeles. Meanwhile Karl Prussian, a former Communist turned FBI informant, wrote pamphlets and articles on the riots that gained wide distribution in the South. The Watts "insurrection," he argued, came about at the hands of the "Communist civil rights movement" and its "revolutionary" ally President Johnson.[5]

Johnson and his Great Society welfare initiatives had been under attack from the right for encouraging laziness, criminality, and disrespect for the law since the 1964 election. Riots in the black neighborhoods of New York, New Jersey, Illinois, and Pennsylvania in the summer lead-up to the election seemingly confirmed their suspicions. Hoping to save votes he thought he had lost as a result of the urban unrest, Johnson turned to J. Edgar Hoover, who still garnered tremendous respect from the right, for help. He asked the FBI director, among other things, to "get in there and see about the communist groups." The president anticipated that the search for Communist influence in the riots would get Hoover on board with the administration and appease right-wing critics.

Johnson also expected that evidence of Communist infiltration among the more radical groups in the movement would prove useful. He could make public the information to discredit rioters and purge the movement of those who defected from his civil rights program. Johnson had already had Hoover investigate the Mississippi Freedom Democratic Party for just such a purpose.

Not surprisingly Hoover eagerly accepted the president's charge. He and a coauthor handpicked by Johnson, anti-Goldwater Republican Thomas E. Dewey, produced a 1964 report that furthered both the president's and the director's agendas. The report stated that poverty and discrimination were the principal causes of the current black unrest. Johnson's Great Society

---

5. "Negro Author Blames Riots on Civil-Rights Leaders," 26 August 1965, RG 46, Name File 3, Martin Luther King 1965, Senate Internal Security Subcommittee Papers, National Archives; "Watts Insurrection—Result of Communist Civil Rights Movement," August 1965, SG22401, Wallace Papers, Alabama Department of Archives and History; "Communist Influence in the Los Angeles Riots," undated, Box 2, Citizens' Council/ Civil Rights Collection, McCain Library and Archives, University of Southern Mississippi.

programs were designed to address such problems and, therefore, implicitly deserved the continued support of the American people. But the Dewey Report also stated that Communists had participated in the riots once the violence had gotten under way. While not evidence of a "Communist inspired" revolution, it was enough to justify continued diligence. Johnson would request information on Communist influence behind the riots the summer following Watts, and the FBI director would use this and future requests to continue to expand his surveillance apparatus.[6]

Ironically in lending support to Hoover's hunt for a red and black conspiracy, Johnson was supplying southern conservatives with a tool for criticizing his administration. In the summer of 1966, James Eastland specifically used Hoover's investigations of black subversives to bolster his and his fellow Mississippians' case against the civil rights movement and the Great Society. Eastland's Senate Internal Security Subcommittee (SISS) reproduced a special twelve-page statement quoting Hoover's testimony that American Communists "will step forward even more boldly hoping to infiltrate and influence civil rights organizations." The groups Hoover cited as most susceptible to Communist infiltration, Eastland and others would make clear, were the same ones spearheading the Great Society in the South.[7]

Southern conservatives were by then in full revolt against the president's reform agenda. Programs like Medicaid, Job Corps, and Head Start, they argued, infringed on states' rights by instituting a Communist-like central welfare state run by a huge federal bureaucracy. Moreover, as the Great Society targeted and employed blacks in the South, segregationists added that the programs were part of a conspiracy to aid minorities at the expense of the white majority. The issues easily fused together to revitalize the southern red scare. The Great Society, southern red and black investigators concluded, aided the Communist plot to redistribute the region's wealth and turn the racial hierarchy upside down.

By the summer of 1966, the southern crusade against the president's domestic programs was in full swing. In Mississippi the State Sovereignty

6. Katzenbach to Johnson, 17 August 1965, Box 13, FI President 1965, Katzenbach Papers, John F. Kennedy Library; Kenneth O'Reilly, *"Racial Matters"*: The FBI's Secret File on Black America (New York: Free Press, 1989), 229–38; Richard Gid Powers, *Secrecy and Power: The Life of J. Edgar Hoover* (New York: Free Press, 1987), 422–23.

7. "FBI Chief Tells Eastland Group of Red Strategy for Subversion," *Mississippi Clarion-Ledger,* 9 August 1966.

Commission (SSC), with the help of Senators John Stennis and James Eastland, targeted the Child Development Group of Mississippi (CDGM). One
of the nation's pioneer Head Start programs, the CDGM employed hundreds to provide poor children with preschool training, medical care, and
two hot meals a day. The Office of Economic Opportunity granted the group
$1.5 million to serve six thousand children through eighty-four centers in
the state. The CDGM immediately drew the attention of segregationist officials when it named Daniel Beittel its head. Beittel had remained in the
state even after he had been charged with harboring Communist agitators
at Tougaloo College and had been dismissed as the school's president. Adding to its vulnerability, the CDGM relied heavily on the cooperation of civil
rights activists working with local people in the state. Indeed, CDGM staff
members openly identified themselves with the Mississippi Freedom Democratic Party (MFDP).

Throughout 1965 the Sovereignty Commission had kept close tabs on
the MFDP and CDGM in their home bases in Mt. Beulah. It had in fact managed to place two informers in the CDGM home office. Through these spies
the SSC learned that Myles Horton, the infamous Highlander Communist,
was an instructor in the town. The commission duly arranged for press releases revealing as much. SSC friends in the state press, meanwhile, compared Head Start with programs in "Soviet Russia" and "Red China," and
its allies in Congress voted against funding the poverty program.[8]

In early 1966 when Southern Conference Education Fund leaders and alleged Communists Carl Braden and Benjamin Smith attended MFDP meetings in Jackson, the SSC sounded the alarm. The commission immediately
sent word to James Eastland in Washington about Braden and Smith; it also
sent him minutes from an MFDP meeting in which Freedom Democratic
Party leader Lawrence Guyot had approved sending an invitation to Herbert
Aptheker, "an identified California communist," to address the group. It
also sent reports to Senator John Stennis concerning CDGM personnel and
the mismanagement of group funds. Both Eastland and Stennis used the information in an effort to discredit the movement and its connections to the
Great Society programs in Mississippi. When the federal Office of Economic
Opportunity (OEO) granted the CDGM an additional $5.6 million over the
veto of Governor Paul Johnson, Eastland charged that the money was fund-

---

8. Dittmer, *Local People: The Struggle for Civil Rights in Mississippi* (Urbana: University of Illinois Press, 1995), 370–71.

ing "the extreme leftist civil rights and beatnik groups in our state, some of which have definite connections with Communist organizations."[9]

Mississippi segregationists were eventually able to stem the flow of fed- eral contributions to the CDGM through continued political pressure and by seizing control of the state's Community Action Programs. The SSC was also able to choke off private funding. It provided information about Communists in the CDGM to a liberal charitable organization called the Field Foundation which was considering a large contribution to the group. Swayed in part by Mississippi red hunters, the foundation's board decided against the contribution.[10]

Like the Mississippi SSC, the Alabama legislature's Commission to Preserve the Peace also scrutinized civil rights leaders of Great Society programs. In July 1966, the Peace Commission issued reports on the Black Panther Party in Lowndes County, Alabama. They claimed that SNCC, the Black Panther Party, the Lowndes County Freedom Organization (LCFO), and the Lowndes County Christian Movement for Human Rights, which had just been approved for a quarter-million-dollar grant from the OEO, were one and the same. Under the groups' leaders, who included Stokely Carmichael, James Forman, John Lewis, John Hulett, and Robert Strickland, the OEO funds had been used to support an apparatus "opposed to our Vietnam policy, and revolutionary in character."[11]

Because of his national reputation, his ambition, and his flair for demagoguery, George Wallace was in the best position to help create and take advantage of the white backlash forming in the wake of the urban rioting. Specifically, the governor understood that violence resulting from racial conflict and unrest over the Vietnam War provided a national law-and-order issue that was tailor-made for a seasoned red and black hunter. Speaking before the Fraternal Order of Police in August 1966, Wallace claimed that the riots in American cities had nothing to do with poverty or racism. They were instead a direct result of plans developed by a "conference of world guerilla warfare chieftains in Havana, Cuba," where Communists daily

9. Memo: Johnston to File, 14 January 1966, ID# 2-165-5-25-1-1-1, Mississippi State Sovereignty Commission Files, Mississippi Department of Archives and History; Dittmer, *Local People*, 375.

10. Investigations and Research, Box 136, Mississippi State Sovereignty Commission Papers, McCain Library and Archives, University of Southern Mississippi.

11. Strickland Conclusions, undated, and Report of the CPP, 14 July 1966, SG22401, Wallace Papers.

plotted an American revolution. The Peace Commission report was for Wallace another "alarming example of what is going on in this Nation today. . . . We have evidence hereof the federal government financing those who advocate actions which border on treason."[12]

The reports were thoroughly misleading, although not to the extent that OEO head Sargent Shriver suggested in a reply to Wallace's accusations. After the Selma-to-Montgomery march, SNCC workers including Stokely Carmichael had indeed taken it on themselves to organize a voter-registration campaign in predominantly black Lowndes County. They had also created the LCFO and taken on the Black Panther as its symbol. But the organization had been designed as a political party rather than a militant racial-separatist group. As Shriver indicated, the Lowndes County Christian Movement for Human Rights had been organized long before the LCFO arrived. Shriver did not acknowledge, however, that the groups shared a single chairman, John Hulett.[13]

In fact, the Alabama reports did not exaggerate the "revolutionary" backgrounds of some of the leaders in the Lowndes movement. Indeed, they rather underestimated its most important member, Stokely Carmichael. Carmichael had grown up in the Bronx, New York, where he established and maintained close associations with a number of young radicals as well as informal ties with several Marxist student organizations. Moreover, as a Howard University student he had become an admirer of the democratic-socialist ideas of Bayard Rustin and Tom Kahn of the League for Industrial Democracy and had participated in demonstrations against HUAC. Later, as a SNCC worker, Carmichael was among those who criticized the larger civil rights movement and especially Martin Luther King for capitulating to government pressure that forced the resignation of Jack O'Dell.[14]

The Alabama Peace Commission reports on Lowndes County also made only passing reference to Carmichael's use of revolutionary rhetoric, even though it had become increasingly prominent in his speeches. When a local deputy killed civil rights worker Jonathan Daniels, a friend of Carmichael,

12. Statement of Governor George C. Wallace, 19 July 1966, SG22401, Wallace Papers; Carter, *Politics of Rage,* 305.

13. Statement by Sargent Shriver, 20 July 1966, SG22401, Wallace Papers; Clayborne Carson, *In Struggle: SNCC and the Black Awakening of the 1960s* (Cambridge: Harvard University Press, 1981), 165–66. See also Emily Stoper, *The Student Nonviolent Coordinating Committee* (New York: Carlson, 1989), 15.

14. Carson, *In Struggle,* 105, 162–65.

he raged. "We're going to tear this county up," he told an audience in Lowndes County, "then we're going to build it back, brick by brick, until it's a fit place for human beings." Carmichael showed the same rhetorical [235 brashness in his criticism of black participation in the Vietnam War effort. The Vietcong, he claimed, were not the enemy of African Americans; southern racists were. If the military gives a black man a gun, he shouted at a Montgomery audience, "and tells him to shoot his enemy and if he don't shoot Lurleen and George and little junior, he's a fool."[15]

In a sense Carmichael and others in the Student Nonviolent Coordinating Committee, were doing the Alabama commission's work for it. Indeed, by 1966 SNCC's open alliance with the New Left and the anti-war movement had become popular knowledge as the press, including publications formerly friendly to the organization, criticized the leftist orientation of the group's rhetoric. Columnists Rowland Evans and Robert Novak blasted SNCC as "substantially infiltrated by beatnik left-wing revolutionaries, and—worst of all—by Communists." And *Newsweek* observed that while SNCC was too diverse to accept any organized ideology, it would, like other liberal movements, "have had to banish Communists from their midst or take the bitter consequences." While SNCC responded with a reiteration of the group's nonexclusion policy, some in the organization were nevertheless concerned that the red-baiting was finally taking its toll and that the group's fund-raising abilities were being hampered.[16]

Perhaps even more damaging to the movement in general, the red and black investigating campaigns of southerners in key domestic security positions in Congress, particularly James Eastland in the SISS and Edwin Willis in HUAC, gained a level of legitimacy they had not seen since the early Cold War. Their rehabilitation could be attributed in part to the white backlash sweeping the nation. In June 1966, when a white hardware contractor from Memphis shot James Meredith on his walk to "challenge the all pervasive and overriding fear" among Mississippi blacks who were still unsure it was safe to register to vote, the event became a rallying point for the civil rights movement. It also introduced the nation to black militancy. Along with the more conservative Martin Luther King of the SCLC and Roy Wilkins of the NAACP, SNCC's new chairman Stokely Carmichael and CORE's new director Floyd McKissick came to Meredith's aid. Carmichael and McKissick

15. Ibid., 165; Carter, *Politics of Rage*, 306.
16. Carson, *In Struggle*, 180–90.

had both come to power as symbols of a new regime committed to introducing the South to the black nationalism of Malcolm X. They took up the plea for black pride, identified the struggle with that of oppressed colonial peoples abroad, and rejected the movement's previous emphasis on integration, interracialism, and nonviolence. In the demonstrations that followed, Carmichael issued his mesmerizing call for "black power." "It's time we stand up and take over," he told followers. Then glaring at white onlookers, he warned "Move on over, or we'll move on over you."[17]

Although they awakened pride in the black community and even changed the way African Americans thought of themselves, the calls for revolution and rejection of nonviolence, which went hand in hand with the calls for black power, frightened whites and undermined movement support. As Carmichael observed, "to most whites, Black Power seems to mean that the Mau Mau are coming to the suburbs at night." Groping for explanations many whites turned with new interest to the charge that reds and blacks had mounted a conspiracy in the South. When Senator Eastland disclosed Sovereignty Commission investigations "revealing" Communist participation in the Meredith marches, his charges that black-power pleas in the South and urban race riots in the North were Communist attempts to "foment revolution in the United States" no longer seemed so far-fetched.[18]

Immediately following the Meredith shooting, John Ashbrook, the Republican congressman from Ohio and a HUAC member, declared his intention to push for hearings on "Negro hate groups." His call for action was symbolic of the growing alliance between northern conservatives and southern segregationists on law-and-order issues. Like the Ku Klux Klan, Ashbrook suggested, black hate groups were becoming equally capable of violent action and needed to be stopped. As evidence of the danger, he cited a June 1966 *Life* magazine story titled "Plotting a War on Whitey."

The article, which was reprinted in the *Congressional Record*, focused on black extremists who made up "a secret revolutionary elite" bent on bringing about "a summer of chaos—'Wattses, lots of them—only worse, much worse.'" These gun-carrying, Molotov cocktail–throwing militants,

17. Dittmer, *Local People*, 389; Harvard Sitkoff, *The Struggle for Black Equality* (New York: Hill and Wang, 1981), 212–17. See also Stokely Carmichael and Charles Hamilton, *Black Power: The Politics of Liberation in America* (New York: Vintage Books, 1992).

18. *Congressional Record*, 89th Cong., 2nd sess., 1966, 112, pt. 13:16563; Investigations and Research, Box 136, Mississippi State Sovereignty Commission Papers, McCain Library; Sitkoff, *Struggle for Black Equality*, 212–17.

the story argued, were "much closer to the mood of the 'brothers on the streets' than the establishment leadership is." Among them were Marxists and Maoists from the Progressive Labor Movement, Black Muslims, and other black-nationalist groups. But the most "influential and feared of the black revolutionary groups," the article went on, was the Revolutionary Action Movement (RAM). According to the story, RAM's leader was a former marine, NAACP leader, and North Carolina civil rights activist Robert F. Williams, who was then exiled in Cuba. Under Williams, the article suggested, RAM was organizing a revolutionary elite that would bring the guerilla warfare tactics of Lenin, Mao, and Che Guevara to the black masses, in turn setting off a new wave of rioting in American cities.[19]

Robert Williams, indeed, significantly influenced RAM and the black-nationalist movement nationwide. He had also long been a target of southern red and black investigators. Born in 1925 in Monroe, North Carolina, Williams had moved to Detroit at seventeen to work for the Ford Motor Company. There in 1943 he and his brother had battled white mobs in one of the worst race riots in U.S. history. A year later, Williams was drafted; he served in a segregated unit until 1946, when he returned home to again face rampaging whites. This time, however, the young army private would cradle a carbine. For the next seven years, Williams moved around, working again in auto plants in Detroit, studying psychology at three different black colleges, and writing articles for newspapers, including Detroit's edition of the *Daily Worker.* In 1953 he reenlisted in the armed forces, this time in the Marine Corps, where he served sixteen miserable months. Back home in Monroe in 1955, Williams joined the NAACP and quickly rose to become the head of the local chapter, just after the local Klan had intimidated the group so badly that it was reduced to only six members.[20]

Over the next four years, Williams rebuilt the NAACP branch back to some two hundred members. The core of the group consisted of black veterans and farmers, all well armed and not easily frightened. The group and Williams gained national and international prominence in 1958 when they used a local incident called the "kissing case" to highlight the American racial dilemma for a cold-war audience. The case centered on the conviction

19. *Congressional Record*, 89th Cong., 2nd sess., 1966, 112, pt. 10:12604–608.

20. Timothy Tyson, "Robert F. Williams, 'Black Power,' and the Roots of the African American Freedom Struggle," *Journal of American History* 85 (September 1998): 546–50. Also see Timothy Tyson, *Radio Free Dixie: Robert F. Williams and the Roots of Black Power* (Chapel Hill: University of North Carolina Press, 1999).

and imprisonment of two young black boys caught playing a kissing game with a young white girl. Williams and his followers fired off press releases and set in motion a huge publicity campaign that drew immediate support from a number of radical groups, including the Socialist Workers Party. Williams never joined this Trotskyite organization but accepted its logistical assistance in spreading the case across the country. He eventually drew the attention of the White House and the State Department, both of which expressed alarm at the damage that was being done to U.S. foreign relations by the incident. He also attracted the scrutiny of North Carolina governor Luther Hodges who, with the help of the FBI, initiated a smear campaign that asserted the whole affair was the handiwork of a "Communist-directed front."[21]

The "kissing case" put Williams on a collision course with the steadfastly anti-Communist NAACP hierarchy. The national and regional directors worried that if the group were "identified with communism, the Ku Klux Klan and the White Councils will pick up the charge that we are 'reds' and use it as a club to beat us to death." Equally disturbing to the national NAACP leaders was Williams's open repudiation of nonviolence. When a North Carolina jury acquitted two white men accused of beating and sexually assaulting a pregnant black woman, an angry Williams told reporters it was time to "meet violence with violence." Roy Wilkins immediately removed Williams as head of the Monroe NAACP. Defending himself at the association's national convention in 1959, Williams insisted that he had never meant to advocate acts of war but said he could no longer stand aside while the southern judicial system refused to protect black women and children. The audience, however, sided with Thurgood Marshall, who had approached the FBI about investigating Williams's Communist connections and with convention speaker Governor Nelson Rockefeller, who praised the NAACP for "rejecting retaliation against terror" and "repulsing the threat of communism to invade your ranks." The convention delegates upheld Williams's suspension.[22]

Williams returned to Monroe, where he continued to organize the community around the ideas of black economic advancement, black pride, inde-

---

21. Tyson, "Robert F. Williams," 550–56. See also Robert F. Williams, "Why I Propose to Return to Racist America," *Crusader*, December 1967, Box 6, Civil Rights Other Folder, North Carolina State Bureau of Investigation Papers, North Carolina State Archives.

22. Tyson, "Robert F. Williams," 556–58. See also "Why I Propose to Return to Racist America."

pendent black political action, black identification with anti-colonialism in the Third World, and "armed self-reliance." There the mainstream movement and southern segregationists continued to criticize him and label him an instigator of violence. Still holding Williams at arm's length, the SCLC and SNCC—then still nonviolent—launched a campaign for local desegregation in Monroe in 1961. When a white mob attacked and badly beat campaign picketers in front of the Union County Courthouse, angry blacks gathered near Williams's home. A white married couple, apparently lost at just the wrong moment, tried to drive through the mob but were stopped and threatened with their lives. Williams rescued the two whites and led them into his house, where he insisted they remain until the crowd cooled off. White authorities later used the incident to charge the activist with kidnapping.[23]

Williams and his family made their escape to New York City, then Canada, and eventually to Cuba, evading scores of FBI agents along the way. From 1961 to 1964, Williams lived in Cuba, working as a propagandist for Radio Havana. His program, called *Radio Free Dixie,* could be heard as far away as Harlem and Watts. Senator Eastland referred to Williams in a July 1964 Senate speech on Communist infiltration of the civil rights movement as the Cuban version of "Lord Haw Haw." His daily radio broadcasts, according to Eastland, flooded the South with propaganda, "specifically inciting to racial violence." Williams's shows, the senator proclaimed, had declared that nonviolence was dead and called for blacks to stockpile lye bombs.[24]

In fact Williams's programs had contained the rhetoric of armed self-defense, as had his publication *The Crusader,* which became a handbook for SNCC workers increasingly skeptical of nonviolence. His book *Negroes with Guns* subsequently became an important intellectual influence on Huey P. Newton and the Oakland, California, Black Panther Party. His calls for black liberation contained repeated references to Marxist leaders from Mao Tse-tung to V. I. Lenin. But for Williams Communism was secondary to black power. In *Negroes with Guns* he wrote, "The Marxists have participated in the human rights struggle of Negroes, but Negroes need not be told by any philosophy or by any political party that racial oppression is wrong.

23. Tyson, "Robert F. Williams," 558–64. See also "Why I Propose to Return to Racist America."
24. *Congressional Record*, 88th Cong., 2nd sess., 1964, 110, pt. 13:16596.

Racial oppression itself inspires the Negro to rebellion." He admitted that "Jim Crow discrimination and racial segregation may very well be based on economic exploitation," but he argued it was beside the point in organizing the black community.[25]

Indeed, after befriending Che Guevara and Fidel Castro during his three years in Cuba, Williams had begun to grow uneasy about Soviet control over the Communist regime there. Moreover his criticism of the American Communist Party had aroused the suspicion of his hosts. So in 1964 he traveled to Vietnam, where he swapped stories with Ho Chi Minh and wrote anti-war propaganda aimed at African American soldiers. A year later the Williams family relocated to Beijing, where they met with Mao and continued with the publication of *The Crusader*. There Williams sometimes indulged in a more revolutionary rhetoric, depicting black saboteurs and guerilla enclaves waging war against the United States government. It was these extremist statements that drew the attention of the Revolutionary Action Movement, which named Williams president-in-exile.[26]

The *Life* article on RAM and Williams was but one of many that fueled the white backlash and gave credence to southern segregationists' charges that black-nationalist elements in the civil rights movement had embraced Communists as revolutionary models and allies. But while the backlash against black power helped continue the southern red scare, southern segregationists also helped themselves by moderating their rhetoric and letting black militants such as Williams and Carmichael discredit the movement on their own. HUAC leader Edwin Willis, although a segregationist from the Deep South, had always been careful not to overstate Communist influence in the civil rights movement. When a group of John Birchers, Citizens' Council members, and representatives of the religious right presented a petition to his committee requesting an investigation of the SCLC, SNCC, CORE, and the Black Muslims in May 1966, Willis responded with typical restraint. He replied that HUAC's policy was only to investigate groups if there existed "reliable evidence that they are dominated, controlled or sub-

---

25. "The Deprived: Rebellion in the Streets," *Crusader*, Summer 1969, Box 6, Civil Rights Other Folder, North Carolina State Bureau of Investigation Papers, North Carolina State Archives; Floyd B. Barbour, *The Black Power Revolt* (Boston: Extending Horizons Books, 1968), 155–57; Robert Williams, *Negroes with Guns* (New York: Marzani and Munsell, 1962).

26. William Worthy, "The Red Chinese American Negro," *Esquire*, October 1964; Tyson, "Robert F. Williams," 567–68.

stantially infiltrated with Communists." According to the Louisiana representative, while Communists had tried to exploit the civil rights movement,
they had achieved "very little real success." The committee would consider
the petition following normal procedure, but Willis pledged not to let the
case be "used a forum for gossipers, name-callers, hate-mongers, race baiters, or character assassins from any quarter." Willis's caution gained red and
black investigators much-needed respect among those in the political mainstream. Consequently when more rioting occurred in the black sections of
Cleveland and other cities over the summer, his decision to lead HUAC in
an investigation of "planned and organized violence by subversive elements" in the riot areas drew little criticism.[27]

Even James Eastland tried to tone down his accusations. Rather than
painting the civil rights movement red with broad strokes, as he had done
routinely in the past, Eastland focused on individual Communists. He
hoped the more specific charges would broaden his appeal to a national audience then beginning to embrace law-and-order messages. In a May 1966
speech in the Senate, he predicted that states across the union would "feel
the effects of the poison spread by subversives." "Because of such activities," he anticipated, "riots and efforts to destroy all effective law enforcement may well visit the North, South, East, and West of this country." He
went on to claim, as he had many times before, that Mississippi had been
and was continuing to be attacked by Communists, most recently through
the administration's poverty program. But he was careful to add, "I am not
going to make a blanket charge that any organization or its members are
Communist." Moderation ill suited Eastland, however. Immediately thereafter he launched into a long speech criticizing the OEO's indirect support
of the Poor People's Corporation and the Mississippi Freedom Democratic
Party, which, he charged, included members tied to anti–Vietnam War protests, the Communist Party, and Communist fronts.[28]

The legitimacy of the civil rights struggle further eroded in the eyes of
most whites in 1967 as movement leaders continued to protest the war in
Vietnam; black rioters ravaged Detroit, Newark, and other cities; and black
nationalists expressed themselves in increasingly radical ways. Early that

27. *Congressional Record*, 89th Cong., 2nd sess., 1966, 112, pt. 9:11657; Memo from
Willis, 26 May 1966, C46, B181, F5, Willis Papers, University of Louisiana at Lafayette;
Virginia Representative William Tuck, C46, B181, F5, Willis Papers; HUAC Press Release,
3 October 1966, C46, B181, F7, Willis Papers.
28. *Congressional Record*, 89th Cong., 2nd sess., 1966, 112, pt. 8:9638-41.

year, Martin Luther King reiterated his opposition to the war, despite the continued support for the struggle to preserve a non-Communist South Vietnam among a majority of the populace. Beginning in February King gave a series of speeches denouncing the war. The most controversial of these came in early April in Atlanta. There King condemned America's conduct in harsh terms, openly denouncing U.S. policy for siding with "the wealthy and the secure while we create a hell for the poor" in Vietnam and for leading the country inevitably toward the occupation of Southeast Asia "as an American colony." Calling for an immediate end to all bombing and an agreement to withdraw all foreign troops from Vietnam, King declared that if the United States were "to get on the right side of the world revolution, we as a nation must undergo a radical revolution of values."[29]

Criticism of King's speech came from virtually every quarter. Friends such as A. Philip Randolph and Bayard Rustin would refuse to join the civil rights leader in criticizing the Johnson administration's policies in Southeast Asia, while Roy Wilkins quickly distanced his organization from King's. The *Washington Post* condemned the speech as "not a sober and responsible comment on the war," and concluded that King had "done a grave injury to those who are his natural allies." The *New York Times*, meanwhile, decried any combining of the civil rights and peace movements and rebuked King for his "reckless" comparison of American military methods with those of the Nazis. Finally *Life* magazine denounced the speech as "demagogic slander that sounded like a script for Radio Hanoi."[30]

At the same time, the Johnson administration and J. Edgar Hoover's FBI exchanged their own opinions of King's stance. Presidential adviser, former Americans for Democratic Action president, and committed liberal anti-Communist John Roche told Johnson that King "had thrown in with the commies" because he was "in desperate search for a constituency." The "Communist-oriented 'peace' types," he added, had "played him [King] like a trout." FBI director Hoover added more ominously that King's recent utterances had made it clear that "he is an instrument in the hands of subversive forces seeking to undermine our nation." Presidential press secretary George Christian, meanwhile, informed the president that he had contacted black columnist Carl Rowan who had long been suspicious of King's Com-

---

29. Garrow, *Bearing the Cross*, 545–53.
30. Ibid., 553–54.

munist ties and their possible effect on the movement. Several days later Rowan wrote that King had lost all tactical skill and, without naming Levinson, had been "listening most to one man who is clearly more interested in embarrassing the United States than in the plight of either the Negro or the war-weary people of Vietnam."[31]

Southern segregationists were delighted. Louisiana representative Joe T. Waggonner gloated to his colleagues in the House that King's "dedication to Communist goals" had finally been recognized. "Now that the civil rights movement has lost its glamor," Waggonner explained, King's "earlier training at such gatherings as the Communist Highlander Folk School has called him on to another field, to serve another Communist end, mobilizing support for Peking and Hanoi in their war against South Vietnam." Waggonner snarled at those who had not heeded the warnings of southern red and black investigators. Adding *Washington Post* stories on King's recent speeches to the *Congressional Record*, he declared that the civil rights leader's "pejorative behavior must be recorded, against the day when we are asked why we allowed this man to do what he has done."[32]

While they continued to lash King for his denunciation of American involvement in Vietnam, leaders of the southern red scare moved on to new targets. To a degree King's continued adherence to nonviolence insulated him. Segregationists sensed that public opinion might be more easily swayed against black, leftist, anti-war groups advocating armed self-defense. The change was most dramatically revealed in a January 1967 report of the Southern Association of Investigators (SAI), a group that included members of state sovereignty commissions and state bureaus of investigation across Dixie. The SAI warned that the "strongly pro-communist" SNCC and CORE had emphasized black power over King's nonviolence and noted the burgeoning alliance between the civil rights movement and the anti-war protesters, including the "militant pro-left" Students for a Democratic Society (SDS). The civil rights movement, the report concluded, was "at a point of drastic change." Due to "public revulsion" at its radicalization, the movement was losing "financial support" and could no longer support "protest marches and mass demonstrations." Vigilant Americans should "look instead for more hard core organizing of black power groups

31. Ibid., 554–55.
32. *Congressional Record*, 89th Cong., 2nd sess., 1966, 112, pt. 8:H5041.

and their satellite groups" who as "professional militants" posed an even
greater threat to local law enforcement than the "unprofessional zealots" of
244] the older movement.[33]

The agencies making up the SAI had their marching orders. While still
scrutinizing groups such as the SCEF and the SCLC, the Mississippi State
Sovereignty Commission, for one, moved many of its resources to investigating Communist ties to SNCC and the Black Panther Party. It even paid
Edgar Downing in Long Beach, California, to take pictures and make record-
ings of speeches by Stokely Carmichael, members of SNCC, and other
groups operating on the University of California at Berkeley campus. The
Alabama legislature's Commission to Preserve the Peace, meanwhile, con-
centrated on the SDS and Vietnam War protesters, as did Louisiana's Joint
Legislative Committee on Un-American Activities. The North Carolina
State Bureau of Investigation worked up an extensive report on "Subversive,
Extremist, and Black Nationalist Organizations." Included were the Black
Panther Party, CORE, RAM, SDS, and SNCC, all of which, according to the
report, professed Communist sympathies or adhered to revolutionary ideol-
ogies.[34]

At the same time, the FBI continued its investigations of Communists
in the civil rights and anti-war movements, paying particular attention to
groups comprised by the New Left. Although Hoover could never prove the
SDS was directly allied to international Communism, he had better luck
with the DuBois Clubs of America, a Communist-dominated campus front.

33. SAI Confidential Report, 15 January 1967, ID# 2-126-2-6-6-1-1, Mississippi State
Sovereignty Commission Files.

34. Jurors Order Sedition Trial, 12 September 1967, ID# 6-69-0-4-1-1-1, Mississippi
State Sovereignty Commission Files; Hopkins Investigation, 2 June 1967, ID# 13-0-5-63-1-
1-1, Mississippi State Sovereignty Commission Files; The pattern of the rioters, 31 July
1967, ID# 9-31-7-5-2-1-1, Mississippi State Sovereignty Commission Files; Downing to
Johnston, 30 October 1967, ID# 9-37-0-8-4-1-1, Mississippi State Sovereignty Commission
Files; SAI Newsletter, 12 October 1965, SG21074, Legislative Commission to Preserve the
Peace Papers, Alabama Department of Archives and History; Oppenheimer and Freeman
Files, undated, SG21074, Legislative Commission to Preserve the Peace Papers; Special Re-
port on Campus Unrest, November 1968, SG17137, Legislative Commission to Preserve
the Peace Papers; *Congressional Record*, 90th Cong., 1st sess., 1967, 113, pt. 15:19933–38;
Subversive, Extremist, and Black Nationalist Organizations, undated, Box 6, White Left
Groups Misc. File, North Carolina State Bureau of Investigation Papers, North Carolina
State Archives. See also SNCC, undated, Box 5, Civil Rights Other File, North Carolina
State Bureau of Investigation Papers, North Carolina State Archives.

The DuBois Clubs were, for J. Edgar Hoover, the "new blood for the vampire of international communism." The Justice Department agreed and attempted to have the group register with the Subversive Activities Control Board as a Communist-front organization. The Bureau also kept close tabs on black nationalists, especially those associated with SNCC, RAM, the Black Muslims, and the Black Panthers.[35]

The FBI's preoccupation as it investigated these groups was their members' participation in summer rioting. After the summer of 1966, Hoover began preparing semimonthly summaries of possible racial violence in major urban areas. He expected another long, hot summer in 1967. In a confidential report issued in the spring of that year, Hoover discussed potential unrest in more than fifty American cities. Of particular concern to the FBI director were the increasing links between the civil rights movement and war protesters in riot areas. While the riots over the past three years had been "spontaneous eruptions of mob violence," Hoover wrote, "incessant agitation and propaganda on the part of communists and other subversives and extremists have definitely contributed to Negro unrest and fomented violence." He added, "Demagogues like Martin Luther King, Stokely Carmichael, Floyd McKissick, Cassius Clay, and Dick Gregory have fanned the fires of racial discord and animosity." Their campaigns in coordination with the anti-war movement, he concluded, "helps to promote communist aims and programs in the United States and abroad."[36]

Republicans used Hoover's accusations to highlight the Great Society's permissiveness and attack the Johnson administration for failing to maintain law and order. They peppered the White House with questions about red and black collusion. Spiro Agnew, the Republican governor of Maryland, charged that subversive conspirators had planned and coordinated the riots while the administration sat idly by. Former president Dwight Eisenhower added that the FBI had been too constrained by the Justice Department to prevent the disorder.

Southerners joined in. Representative John Rarick of Louisiana worked to keep alive fears of RAM and Watts and argued to his colleagues that pov-

35. W. E. B. DuBois Clubs of America, February 1967, Confidential File, Box 57, HU6, White House Central File, Johnson Presidential Papers; Powers, *Secrecy and Power*, 428–29; O'Reilly, "*Racial Matters*," 274–94.

36. Racial Violence Potential in the United States This Summer, 23 May 1967, Confidential File, Box 56, HU2, White House Central File, Johnson Presidential Papers; O'Reilly, "*Racial Matters*," 238.

erty and ignorance were "far less the causation" of the riots than "education
and subsidization by anti-American forces." Alabama representative John
Buchanan, meanwhile, pushed for investigations into OEO involvement in
the "alarming epidemic of civil disorders which had swept across the cities
of America."

246]

The Johnson administration cringed at the growing agreement between
Republicans and southerners on the riots, the Great Society, black power,
and the alleged red and black conspiracy. Especially alarming to LBJ was the
thought that someone like SISS leader James Eastland would lead Republicans and southerners in public investigations that would make the most of
law-and-order criticisms of the administration. In early 1967 Eastland was
moving in that direction. He proclaimed that the anti-war movement had
come to be controlled by "Communists and extremists who favor the victory of the Vietcong and are openly hostile to the United States," and promised to "carry the ball" on the Senate's riot investigations. After HUAC head
Edwin Willis confirmed the president's fears in a letter warning that just as
the Republicans had been able to blast the Democrats for being "soft" on
Communism, so too would they portray his administration as being " 'soft'
on law enforcement and respect for law and order," Johnson moved to establish his own National Commission on Civil Disorders and put at its head
the moderate governor of Illinois, Otto Kerner.[37]

The Kerner Commission identified the social and economic difficulties
facing blacks in the inner cities as the essence of the problem there and suggested sweeping reforms in employment, education, welfare, and housing.
It paid only passing attention to J. Edgar Hoover's warnings about the "catalytic effect of extremists," including members of SNCC, the SCLC, SDS,
and a range of black-nationalist and Communist-front groups. Determined
not to let liberals move the law-and-order issue out of the national lime-
light, Hoover looked to a southern congressman to challenge the president's
commission. Both the SISS and HUAC were conducting their own investigations into the riots, but instead of James Eastland or Edwin Willis, Hoover
turned to Arkansas senator John L. McClellan, who chaired Joe McCarthy's
old Permanent Subcommittee on Investigations (PERM). An experienced
red and black investigator himself, McClellan shared his southern col-

37. *Congressional Record*, 90th Cong., 1st sess., 1967, 113, pt. 15:19934; *Congressional
Record*, 90th Cong., 1st sess., 1967, 113, pt. 17:22284–85; *Congressional Record*, 90th
Cong., 1st sess., 1967, 113, pt. 21:28846–50; Anderson, *The Sixties*, 80; O'Reilly, "*Racial
Matters*," 238–49.

leagues' concern for law and order but was less of a lightning rod for public controversy.[38]

Even before the Senate voted to fund his inquiry, McClellan announced
that he would focus on "law enforcement rather than the social causes underlying the disorders." As part of this strategy, the Arkansas senator brought Communist infiltration of the civil rights movement back to the forefront. Of particular use were the papers of Margaret and Alan McSurely, obtained from a Pike County, Kentucky, prosecutor after the state police raided their home. The two were poverty workers and organizers for the Southern Conference Education Fund (SCEF). While the state charged the McSurelys, like the Bradens fourteen years earlier, with violating a state sedition statute, McClellan's committee discovered a link between the couple and the Nashville riots. Stokely Carmichael, PERM revealed, had addressed a SCEF staff meeting and spoken at Vanderbilt University just days before the event. The SCEF link, McClellan contended, connected Carmichael and the Communists to the Nashville riots. Moreover, because the McSurelys were poverty workers, the thread could be tied further to the Great Society. PERM would summon the McSurelys and secure their indictment for contempt of Congress after the couple failed to answer questions regarding their political affiliations.[39]

McClellan's focus on Stokely Carmichael reflected a growing preoccupation in red and black hunting circles. Carmichael's call for "black power" coupled with his loose connection to the Lowndes County poverty program in Alabama, a charge that he had incited a riot in Atlanta, and his vow to go to jail rather than be drafted made him a symbol of all that southern conservatives abhorred. Eastland's SISS kept a close eye on his activities, as did local officials in the South. Like McClellan, Tennessee officials were particularly interested in Carmichael's involvement in the Nashville riots. Not only did they note his connections to SCEF, they linked him to the Highlander Folk School as well. Carmichael had visited the school close on the heels of the Nashville riot and had been quoted as saying that the idea for "black power" had come from Highlander founder Myles Horton. While Horton did not exactly teach Carmichael the concept, the school's staff agreed with the SNCC leader that whites could best help blacks by helping poor whites. Carmichael would later be charged with inciting the riot in Nashville, and the Tennessee house of representatives would even pass a

38. O'Reilly, *"Racial Matters,"* 249–52.
39. Ibid., 252–54.

resolution requesting that the attorney general revoke his citizenship and have him deported.[40]

At the same time J. Edgar Hoover began his own campaign against Carmichael. Before a House Appropriations subcommittee, the FBI director linked the black power leader to RAM, an organization "dedicated to the overthrow of the capitalist system in the United States, by violence if necessary." Hoover went on to charge that Carmichael had "been in frequent contact with Max Stanford, field chairman of the Revolutionary Action Movement, a highly secret all-Negro, Marxist-Leninist, Chinese Communist-oriented organization which advocates guerilla warfare to obtain its goals." In addition Carmichael also "afforded Stanford assistance and guidance in forming a Black Panther party in New York City," according to Hoover.[41]

Confronted with these charges, Carmichael challenged the FBI to prove them and then refused to discuss the matter further. He understood that an admission would only fuel speculation. Carmichael and Stanford had indeed known each other as teenagers in Harlem and as budding black activists had continued to stay in contact. But Stanford's and RAM's influence on Carmichael, particularly at the time of Hoover's testimony, was rather limited. SNCC separatists in Atlanta who had become RAM supporters were in fact involved in a bitter struggle with Carmichael when Hoover made his speech. At the same time that he was smearing Carmichael for his links with RAM and other radical elements, the FBI director may have actually been trying to exacerbate this internal turmoil. Later that summer Hoover would include members of SNCC, RAM, and other groups in a "Rabble Rouser Index." Those on the index would become primary targets of the FBI's Counterintelligence Program (COINTELPRO). As with the Communist Party, these groups were infiltrated by agents who would exploit existing conflicts with an eye to discrediting and destroying the organizations from within.[42]

40. Carmichael Jailed, Eastland Bids U.S. Act against Carmichael, and Report of CPP, 14 July 1966, RG46, Name File 2, Carmichael 1966, Senate Internal Security Subcommittee Papers; "Stokely Involved in Secret Talks," *Nashville Banner*, 7 April 1967; "Carmichael Highlander Visit Told," *Knoxville Journal*, 23 May 1967; "Deport Carmichael, Demands Tenn. Legislature," *Washington Post*, 11 April 1967; "Carmichael Charges Police Began Riot," *Washington Post*, 31 May 1967; John M. Glen, *Highlander: No Ordinary School* (Knoxville: University of Tennessee Press, 1996), 258.

41. "Carmichael Tied to Leftist Group," *New York Times*, 16 May 1967.

42. "FBI's Charges Brushed Aside by Carmichael," *New York Newsday*, 18 May 1967; Carson, *In Struggle*, 261-63; O'Reilly, *"Racial Matters,"* 277.

Representative Fletcher Thompson of Georgia used the occasion of Hoover's speech to call for a Justice Department investigation of Carmichael. What Thompson did not know was that the Johnson administration already had plans to commit the full range of the intelligence community to pursuing Carmichael. By the early summer of 1967, President Johnson was caught between a strange alliance of right and left. Critics from the right had questioned his ability to keep law and order amid the national turmoil, while radical black nationalists refocused their wrath on liberal reformers rather than southern racists. Liberals, they argued, posed the real threat to a successful black revolution by keeping the masses at bay with scraps of reform. Caught in this vise, Johnson had become increasingly frustrated. He told advisers that left-wing critics of the administration were all radicals, revolutionaries, or criminals and asked Hoover to step up his efforts to find a central theme in the civil disturbances. Johnson's national-security adviser Walt Rostow, meanwhile, mobilized the rest of the nation's intelligence community.[43]

Top-secret intelligence reports on the range of black-activist organizations reached the president's desk in the summer of 1967. National-security agents reported on Robert Williams's propaganda and his connections to RAM. Army intelligence, meanwhile, produced a lengthy document on SNCC claiming that the group had been influenced by "communist support and infiltration," and had become so extreme that it could "no longer be considered a civil rights group." And the Central Intelligence Agency followed with a paper on the "International Connections of US Peace Groups," which included SNCC and the SDS among groups with "Significant International Communist Contacts." Many of the reporting agents even adopted the rhetoric of southern red and black investigators. One intelligence official reported that "outside trained agitators" had incited the riots in Detroit and Newark; they in turn had been "exploited" by the Soviet Union. None of the reports, however, could give the president what he wanted—conclusive proof that the riots had been organized and carried out by a Communist-led united front.[44]

43. "Georgian Calls for Probe," 18 May 1967, RG 46, Name File 2, Carmichael Jan–Jun 1967, Senate Internal Security Subcommittee Papers; O'Reilly, *"Racial Matters,"* 239–45; Hugh Davis Graham, *The Civil Rights Era: Origins and Development of National Policy, 1960–1972* (New York: Oxford University Press, 1990).

44. CI Special Report on SNCC, 10 October 1967, Box 5, Civil Rights, Anti-War Folder, National Security File, Johnson Presidential Papers; Rostow to Johnson, 27 July 1967, Box 5, Civil Rights, Anti-War Folder, National Security File, Johnson Presidential Papers; Cur-

It was in its pursuit of Carmichael, however, that the intelligence community came closest to satisfying Johnson. Between July and December the young black-power advocate made a foreign tour that had many in the administration discussing the possibility of criminal prosecution. After speaking at a conference in London, Carmichael moved on to Cuba, where he attended the Organization of Latin-American Solidarity meeting. His statements crossed the president's desk at a steady clip, just as news of racial rebellion in Detroit hit the nation's newspapers. "Cuba had permitted us to observe many kinds of tactics employed in its struggles which we can adapt to ours," Carmichael told Havana audiences. The struggle of blacks in the U.S., the militant speaker said, was "the same struggle that is taking place in other parts of the world against oppression, racism, and imperialism." African American activists would use "any means necessary against the capitalist structure" as the movement progressed toward "an urban guerilla war." Indeed, he continued, the current riots were a "form of guerilla warfare inspired by the Guevara policy of creating other Vietnams to bring down capitalism and imperialism."[45]

Carmichael spent a weekend with Fidel Castro in Cuba after the conference adjourned then moved on to Moscow, then China—meeting briefly with Robert Williams—and then to North Vietnam, where he was a guest of Ho Chi Minh. Foreign-intelligence reports to the White House revealed that in Vietnam Carmichael had broadcast speeches to American servicemen via Radio Hanoi. "Colored GIs," he asked, "why then did you come to fight and die here halfway around the world from your homeland?" "To hell with the white man," he declared in another address; Vietnam was "his war: let him fight it." Indeed, it was "for the birds," he went on. "Lady Bird, Lyndon Bird, and all the other birds. . . . Our blood must be shed only for our people." From Vietnam Carmichael flew on to Africa, where he met prominent independence-movement leaders including Sekou Touré and Kwame Nkrumah. Nkrumah's socialist pan-Africanism appealed to Carmi-

---

rent Racial Disturbances and Possible Implications, 24 July 1967, Box 5, Civil Rights, Anti-War Folder, National Security File, Johnson Presidential Papers; CIA Report on International Connections of US Peace Groups, 15 November 1967, Box 2–3, US Peace Groups Folder, National Security File, Johnson Presidential Papers.

45. Special Memorandum on Stokely Carmichael's Activities and Statements Abroad, 9 August 1967, Box 5, Civil Rights, Anti-War Folder, National Security File, Johnson Presidential Papers.

chael as the ideal system for the liberation of all blacks, including African Americans. He returned to the United States in mid-December 1967.[46]

Carmichael's praise for Communist movements worldwide was not [251 without limits. He was particularly critical of bourgeois elements in the American Communist Party. But his purpose while on his trip had clearly been to identify the black revolutionary movement in the U.S. with Third World Communist attempts to end "white Western imperialism." Indeed, while in Africa he had clearly identified blacks as the leaders of proletarian revolution in the United States. When an African interviewer asked if black power would inevitably become part of the "class struggle irrespective of the question of racism," he replied with an emphatic "yes." The time would come, he argued, "when black and white workers will be involved in a common struggle against economic exploitation." "Black Power," he declared, "is the vanguard of the struggle against capitalism in the United States."[47]

With Carmichael's speeches abroad gaining daily coverage in the American press, the White House came under intense pressure to do something about him. As early as August, administration officials considered legal action. President Johnson hoped that a successful prosecution would put other black militants on notice that there was a limit to treasonous activity against the United States, but Attorney General Ramsey Clark worried that such action would only make Carmichael a martyr. Undersecretary Nicholas Katzenbach laid out the situation for the president in late December. Only one avenue of prosecution warranted serious consideration, he argued. Carmichael, while in Havana and Hanoi, had clearly violated a 1799 statute called the Logan Act. The act made it a crime to "communicate with an agent or official of a foreign government with the intent of 'defeating the measures of the United States.'" But given the "public relations and legal difficulties" of using the statute, which had never been the basis of criminal prosecution and was so broadly and loosely phrased as to be "unconstitutionally vague," Katzenbach "would not recommend prosecution." He

46. Carmichael Speech Airgram, 27 September 1967 and Carmichael Statement to Negro Servicemen, 5 November 1967, Box 5, Civil Rights, Anti-War Folder, National Security File, Johnson Presidential Papers; Carson, *In Struggle*, 275–77.

47. Special Memorandum on Stokely Carmichael's Activities and Statements Abroad, 9 August 1967, Box 5, Civil Rights, Anti-War Folder, National Security File, Johnson Presidential Papers; "Carmichael: Socialism the Basis for Unity," *Militant*, 11 December 1967; Carson, *In Struggle*, 274–76.

would, however, suggest later that Carmichael's speeches be used in prosecuting him for obstructing the draft.[48]

Ultimately the government was only able to seize Carmichael's passport after he returned to the United States. But the militant activist's statements abroad did affect the black-power leader's support at home. His identification of the black struggle with Communism abroad exacerbated rifts in the already bitterly fragmented SNCC staff. As in the Communist Party, the nuances of balancing race and class emphases within the ideological framework of the movement had created competing factions, jealous of their rivals' power. SNCC leaders eventually called their representative abroad and "ordered him to shut up." Carmichael would eventually be expelled from SNCC for not conforming to the group's constantly shifting ideological stance.[49]

The Johnson administration's pursuit of Carmichael and other members of the black-power movement revealed the president's desperate need for an explanation for the riots. Proof of some coordinated leftist effort behind the turmoil would not only help him politically but would help ease the personal angst he felt. Although he had originally signed off on investigations of Communists in the civil rights movement for political reasons, by 1968 Johnson had become more personally involved. He now hoped that evidence of Communists in the riot mobs would explain the increasing black militancy in the country. That the president was a southerner and an anti-Communist explains this to a degree but, perhaps more important, Johnson had sacrificed a great deal in pioneering civil rights reform. He felt betrayed when violence tainted the cause. According to Harry McPherson, the president believed that some conspiracy of the left had to have been at work for black Americans to disgrace the administration by rioting. Why would "good Negroes" go around shooting people unless they were inspired by " 'bad Negroes, bad white people, Communists,' or whatever."[50]

Ironically, Johnson's views were to a large degree those of a reviving con-

---

48. Bowdler to Rostow, 2 August 1967 and Memo on Possible Criminal Prosecution of Stokely Carmichael, 20 December 1967, Box 5, Civil Rights, Anti-War Folder, National Security File, Johnson Presidential Papers; "LBJ-Clark Differ on Handling Stokely," *Washington Post*, 5 December 1967.

49. "Carmichael Gives Up Passport," *Washington Post*, 12 December 1967; Carson, *In Struggle*, 276.

50. T. H. Baker, interviewer, Oral History of Harry McPherson, Tape 7, 9 April 1969, pp. 5–6, Lyndon Baines Johnson Library.

servative coalition, the voting alliance of southern Democrats and Republicans that LBJ had devoted his political life to breaking up. A September 1967 *Congressional Quarterly* poll revealed that southern Democrats were [253 still largely committed to the belief that reds and blacks had conspired to create racial turmoil in the country. When asked if "outside Negro agitators" were of "great importance," "some importance," or "insignificant" in creating the riots, 62 percent of them said "great importance." Asked the same question about "Communist agitation" behind the riots, almost 40 percent marked "great importance." Republicans generally agreed, tallying 59 percent and 20 percent respectively. Northern Democrats, meanwhile, only registered 17 percent on "outside Negro agitators" and less than 1 percent on "Communist agitation." The poll clearly marked an alliance of Republicans and southern Democrats on the red and black issue. Significantly, it was one of the many topics concerning law and order and other social-welfare platforms on which the groups could agree and which they could carry into the national elections in 1968.[51]

"If a single event can be picked to mark the dividing line" of the sixties, *Life* editorialized, "it was Watts." It had, according to *Life*, "ripped the fabric of lawful democratic society and set the tone of confrontation and open revolt." Southern red and black investigators needed little more than to ride the "white backlash" that emerged after the riots. After Watts, urban leaders such as Los Angeles mayor Sam Yorty began claiming that requests for War on Poverty funds coming from the riot-torn area were a result of "Communist agitation." Segregationists suddenly realized that they had allies outside of the South and that red and black issues played a significant role in the law-and-order politics of the late 1960s. Indeed, even the otherwise restrained and self-conscious Edwin Willis finally felt that he could legitimately claim that the nation's civil disorders had been planned and organized by a united alliance of Communists and Communist fronts. By 1968 southern segregationists no longer had to fight to have their claims taken seriously.[52]

51. "Congress, Governors, Mayors Polled on Riots," *Congressional Quarterly*, 6 September 1967. See William Billingsly, *Communists on Campus* (Athens: University of Georgia Press, 1999).

52. Reds Linked to Demonstrations, 21 March 1968, C46, B183, F4, Willis Papers; Willis to Gomillion, 13 February 1968, C46, B185, F6, Willis Papers; American Legion Address, 6 September 1968, C46, B183, F7, Willis Papers; Anderson, *The Sixties*, 74–75.

EPILOGUE

BY 1968 AMERICA'S "SILENT MAJORITY" NO LONGER needed southerners to tell it that blacks and reds were taking advantage of the civil unrest in the United States. With Tet proving to many the futility of continuing the war in Vietnam, young leftists mobilized once again to advocate an end to the conflict and replace it with a social and political "revolution" at home. Their rhetoric, coupled with mounting urban unrest, put conservatives on alert. Such was the mood in early April when James Earl Ray shot and killed Martin Luther King. "When white America killed Dr. King," Stokely Carmichael declared, "she declared war on us." Riots swept dozens of cities including Boston, Detroit, New York's Harlem, and, worst of all, Washington, D.C. Nationwide seventy-five thousand troops patrolled the streets, hoping to keep order. Thousands were injured and forty-six killed. Robert Kennedy's assassination in Los Angeles in June and rioting at the Democratic National Convention in Chicago in August moved the nation further toward chaos. Americans suddenly longed for calm and stability.[1]

To some degree, by the fall of 1968, a "Southernization" of American politics, as historian Dan Carter put it, had occurred. The country's conservative candidates were champions of God, country, law, order, and tradition—all longtime southern political mainstays. Indeed, many put their trust in that most prominent guarantor of southern nationalist values, George Wallace. The Alabama governor won 13 percent of the electorate in the general presidential election, an amazing showing for a third-party candidate. His opposition to black civil rights carried all of Dixie, but his hard-nosed commitment to order in the streets also played well nationwide. Indeed, racial fears across the country had become linked to general concerns over social unrest. Richard Nixon, the other conservative candidate in the presidential race, knew it and exploited it. He publicly distanced himself from the race issue during the campaign in order to distinguish himself from the extremist Wallace, but in private he anticipated that the election

---

1. Terry Anderson, *The Sixties* (New York: Longman, 1999), 108–109.

was "all about law and order and the damn Negro-Puerto Rican groups out there." His victory in part confirmed this political instinct.[2]

With the victory of law, order, and Nixon in the 1968 election, southern- ers found less and less use for red and black investigations. The win reassured some in the region that the federal government would no longer be used in support of liberal causes. But it was the changing nature of the civil rights movement that increasingly made the southern red scare unnecessary. With many of its legal and legislative objectives won in the South, the movement turned northward, toward the cities. By the summer of 1968, internal bickering and the death of Martin Luther King had left the movement rudderless. By the end of that year SNCC was dead, CORE was dying, and the SCLC was falling apart. Moreover, Highlander and the SCEF were both shells of their former selves and had moved away from civil rights to focus once again on the plight of the rural poor. Black nationalists with a propensity for violence were simply hard to find in the South. National and international critics changed focus. With the shift of focus to northern urban areas, southerners no longer felt under siege. Red and black hunting became obsolete.[3]

Southern states began phasing out their red and black investigating commissions in the early 1970s. The most notorious of these, the Mississippi State Sovereignty Commission, continued under Governor John Bell Williams from 1968 to 1972, but his successor William Waller found that the commission provided "no real indispensable services to the people of the state." Waller vetoed the agency's appropriation in 1973 and officially ended its business. The Louisiana legislature followed suit and ended its own investigations around the same time. By the end of the 1970s, virtually all remnants of the notorious southern committees had disappeared.[4]

The decline of the commissions coincided with the end of the Citizens' Councils and the death or retirement of the most prominent national red and black hunters. The Councils had lost most of their members and influ-

2. Dan Carter, *The Politics of Rage* (New York: Simon and Schuster, 1995), 348.

3. Anderson, *The Sixties*, 110; Earl Black and Merle Black, *Politics and Society in the South* (Cambridge: Harvard University Press, 1987); Ray Arsenault, "The Folklore of Southern Demagoguery," in Charles Eagles, ed., *Is There a Southern Political Tradition?* (Jackson: University Press of Mississippi, 1996).

4. *New York Times*, 22 April 1973. See also "Sovereignty Commission Agency History," State Sovereignty Commission Papers, Mississippi Department of Archives and History; Yasuhiro Katagiri, *The Mississippi State Sovereignty Commission: Civil Rights and States' Rights in a Deep South State, 1956–1977* (Ann Arbor, Mich.: UMI Dissertation Service,

256]

ence as early as 1964. Despite a brief resurgence in the late 1960s, the groups never regained the influence they had previously wielded. Council members once prominent in southern politics, meanwhile, passed on to their reward. Louisiana arch segregationist, red-baiter, and Council head Leander Perez died in March 1969, and Council ally Stanley Morse died along with his Grass Roots League in 1975. Even more important, HUAC head Edwin Willis left the House in 1968, J. Edgar Hoover died in 1972, and SISS leader James Eastland retired from the Senate in 1978.[5]

Those leaders of the southern red scare who were left eventually fell victim to changes in southern and national politics. Blacks increasingly voted, and growing numbers of women and non-native southerners joined the region's electorate. Social attitudes also changed with the industrialization and urbanization of the South. The conservative white ruling elite could no longer control the region's political agenda. PERM chairman John McClellan would lose his reelection bid in 1978; George Wallace, once the leading spokesman for southern segregation and anti-Communism, remained a force in Alabama politics only after he softened his extremist image to better suit the mood of the 1970s and 1980s.[6]

It was also no accident that the end of the southern scare coincided with a period of detente in the cold war. Under the Nixon administration, the United States normalized relations with the Soviet Union and China, signed the first Strategic Arms Limitation Treaty, and pulled out of Vietnam. The tense relationship with Communists abroad that undergirded the scare at home relaxed. With the international threat diminished, few continued to consider the Communist Party a fifth column and a real threat to domestic security.

The demise of the southern red scare's leaders and their committees, councils, commissions, and bureaus thus was not entirely voluntary and did

1997); Adam Fairclough, *Race and Democracy* (Athens: University of Georgia Press, 1995), 465.

5. Neil McMillen, *The Citizens' Council: Organized Resistance to the Second Reconstruction, 1954–64* (Urbana: University of Illinois Press, 1971), 360–63; Glen Jeansonne, *Leander Perez: Boss of the Delta* (Baton Rouge: Louisiana State University Press, 1977), 361; Chronology, Morse Papers, South Caroliniana Library, University of South Carolina; Richard Gid Powers, *Secrecy and Power: The Life of J. Edgar Hoover* (New York: Free Press, 1987), 486.

6. Numan Bartley, *The New South* (Baton Rouge: Louisiana State University Press, 1995), 407; Kenneth O'Reilly, *"Racial Matters": The FBI's Secret File on Black America, 1960–1972* (New York: Free Press, 1989), 276; see also Carter, *Politics of Rage.*

not ultimately mark a triumph for the cause. Indeed, southern nationalists had failed in their primary purpose, the preservation of segregation as a fundamental part of the "southern way of life." Despite the return of conservatism to national politics and the incorporation of red and black fear into the law-and-order issues of the late 1960s, liberal turns during the decade had re-centered American politics, particularly on the issues of race and national security. Although some de facto segregation continued to exist in the South, the region became increasingly rational and respectable. The federal commitment to black civil rights, meanwhile, continued to grow with the institution of affirmative-action and busing programs designed to integrate the nation's schools and federal offices. The demise of HUAC and the SISS also indicated a parallel turn in mood. Under the weight of increasing criticism for its extremism, its irrelevance, and its ineptitude, Congress abolished HUAC in 1975. Two years later, for similar reasons, the Senate ended the SISS. At the same time, hearings before the Pike Committee in the House and the Church Committee in the Senate discredited a range of federal intelligence agencies. Most significant for the southern red scare, the Senate Select Committee on Intelligence under Democrat Frank Church of Idaho cited specific instances of harassment of civil rights leaders in concluding that the FBI record on secret activities demonstrated a "pattern of reckless disregard of activities that threatened our constitutional system."[7]

With the downfall of its principle instigators and the end of the federal and state agencies devoted to its principles, the southern red scare had almost ceased to exist by the time of the Carter administration. This did not mean that southern-nationalist pleas or red- and black-baiting ceased completely among all southerners. South Carolina representative Albert Watson continued to hound Carl and Anne Braden for their participation in the civil rights movement. Senator John Tower of Texas and Representative John Rarick of Louisiana also carried on the charges through the Nixon administration, linking alleged Communists to Great Society programs. But the issues on which the scare had been built—segregation, states' rights, domestic security, and law and order—faded both in the South and nationally, leaving little with which red and black hunters could work.[8]

7. Bartley, *New South*, 406–16; Richard Fried, *Nightmare in Red* (New York: Oxford University Press, 1990),196; Powers, *Secrecy and Power*, 487.

8. "Red Influence Seen in People's March," *Greenville News*, 22 May 1968; *Congressional Record*, 90th Cong., 2nd sess., 1968, 114, pt. 10:13240–42; *Congressional Record*, 91st Cong., 1st sess., 1969, 115, pt. 9:12204; *Congressional Record*, 91st Cong., 1st sess., 1969, 115, pt. 10:13839.

SELECTED BIBLIOGRAPHY

MANUSCRIPT COLLECTIONS

Alabama Department of Archives and History, Montgomery
Commission to Preserve the Peace Papers
State Sovereignty Commission Papers
George Wallace Papers

Duke University, Special Collections, Durham
J. B. Matthews Papers

Eisenhower Presidential Library, Abilene
John Foster Dulles Papers
Dwight D. Eisenhower Papers

Emory University, Woodruff Library Special Collections, Atlanta
Ralph McGill Papers

Florida State Archives, Tallahassee
Florida Legislative Investigation Committee Papers

Johnson Presidential Library, Austin
John Connally Papers
Lyndon Baines Johnson Papers

Kennedy Presidential Library, Boston
Nicholas Katzenbach Papers
John F. Kennedy Papers
Robert Kennedy Papers
Adam Yarmolinsky Papers

Library of Congress, Washington, D.C.
NAACP Papers
Bayard Rustin Papers

Library of Virginia, Richmond
Albertis Harrison Papers

Mississippi Department of Archives and History, Jackson
State Sovereignty Commission Papers
John Bell Williams Papers

Mississippi State University, Mitchell Memorial Library, Starkville

Citizens' Council Collection

A. E. Cox Papers

William Davis Papers

Segregation and Integration Collection

National Archives, Washington, D.C.

Senate Internal Security Subcommittee Papers

North Carolina State Archives, Raleigh

State Bureau of Investigation Papers

Texas State Archives, Austin

Public Safety Department Papers

University of Alabama, Hoole Special Collections, Tuscaloosa

Lister Hill Papers

University of Arkansas, Special Collections, Fayetteville

Harold Hantz Papers

Gordon McNeil Papers

Philip Trapp Papers

University of Georgia, Russell Library, Athens

Roy Harris Collection

Richard Russell Papers

Ernest Vandiver Papers

University of South Carolina, South Caroliniana Library, Columbia

William Jennings Bryan Dorn Papers

Olin Johnston Papers

Stanley Morse Papers

South Carolina Council on Human Relations

University of Southern Mississippi, McCain Library and Archives, Hattiesburg

Citizens' Council/Civil Rights Collection

State Sovereignty Commission Papers

William C. Colmer Papers

University of Louisiana at Lafayette, Special Collections, Lafayette

Edwin Willis Papers

University of Tennessee, Special Collections, Knoxville

Carl and Anne Braden Papers

University of Texas, Center for American History, Austin
Texas v. NAACP Papers

University of Virginia, Special Collections, Charlottesville
Defenders of State Sovereignty Collection

MICROFILM AND ON-LINE COLLECTIONS

Facts on Film. Nashville: Southern Education Reporting Service.
Mississippi Oral History Program, University of Southern Mississippi. <http://www-dept.usm.edu/~ocach/msohp.html>

GOVERNMENT DOCUMENTS

Communism in the Mid-South, Hearings before the Subcommittee to Investigate the Administration of the Internal Security Act and Other Internal Security Laws of the Committee of the Judiciary, Senate, 85th Cong., 1st sess., October 28, 29, 1957. Washington, D.C.: Government Printing Office, 1957.

Communist Infiltration and Activities in the South: Hearings before the Committee on Un-American Activities, House of Representatives, 85th Cong., 2d sess., July 29, 30, 31, 1958. Washington, D.C.: Government Printing Office, 1958.

Congressional Record

Eastland, James O. "The Supreme Court's 'Modern Scientific Authorities' in the Segregation Cases." Washington, D.C.: Government Printing Office, 1955.

Hearings before the Committee on Commerce. Senate, 88th Cong., 1st sess., July 15, 16, 1963. Washington, D.C.: Government Printing Office, 1963.

Hearings Regarding Communist Infiltration of Minority Groups before the Committee on Un-American Activities. House of Representatives, 81st Cong., 1st sess., July 13, 14, 18, 1949. Washington, D.C.: Government Printing Office, 1949.

Report on Civil Rights Congress As a Communist Front Organization. House of Representatives, 80th Cong., 2d sess., House. Washington, D.C.: Government Printing Office, 1948.

Report on Southern Conference for Human Welfare. House of Representatives, 80th Cong., 1st sess. Washington, D.C.: Government Printing Office, 1947.

Southern Conference Education Fund Inc. Hearings before the Subcommittee to Investigate the Administration of the Internal Security Act and Other Internal Security Laws of the Committee of the Judiciary. Senate, 83rd Cong., 2d sess., March 18, 19, 20, 1954. Washington, D.C.: Government Printing Office, 1955.

Subversion in Racial Unrest, Public Hearings of the State of Louisiana Joint Legislative Committee, March 6–9, 1957. Baton Rouge: Louisiana Printing Office, 1957.

Williams, John Bell. "The President's Infamous Civil Rights Program." Washington, D.C.: Government Printing Office, 1948.

SUPREME COURT CASES

Barenblatt v. United States, 360 U.S. 109 (1959).

Bates v. Little Rock, 361 U.S. 516 (1960).

Beilan v. Board of Education, 357 U.S. 399 (1958).

Braden v. United States, 365 U.S. 431 (1961).

Brown v. Board of Education, 349 U.S. 294 (1955).

Dombrowski v. Eastland, 387 U.S. 82 (1967).

Dombrowski v. Pfister, 380 U.S. 479 (1965).

Gibson v. Florida Legislative Investigating Committee, 372 U.S. 539 (1963).

Jencks v. United States, 353 U.S. 657 (1957).

Konigsberg v. State Bar of California, 353 U.S. 252 (1957).

NAACP v. Alabama, 91 U.S. 78 (1958) and 360 U.S. 240 (1959).

Pennsylvania v. Nelson, 350 U.S. 497 (1956).

Schware v. Board of Bar Examiners, 353 U.S. 232 (1957).

Service v. Dulles, 354 U.S. 363 (1957).

Shelton v. Tucker, 364 U.S. 479 (1960).

Slochower v. Board of Education, 350 U.S. 551 (1956).

Sweezy v. New Hampshire, 354 U.S. 234 (1957).

Watkins v. United States, 354 U.S. 178 (1957).

Yates v. United States, 354 U.S. 298 (1957), 355 U.S. 66 (1957), and 356 U.S. 363 (1958).

NEWSPAPERS

Arkansas Democrat, 1958–1960

Arkansas Gazette, 1958–1960, 1964

Arkansas Traveler, 1958–1959

Atlanta Constitution, 1957–1964

Augusta Courier, 1955–1956

Birmingham Independent, 1965

Birmingham Post-Herald, 1961

Charleston News and Courier, 1955–1964

Dallas Morning News, 1957, 1962

Florida Times-Union, 1960–1961

Houston Chronicle, 1963

Houston Post, 1961–1963

Jackson Daily News, 1955–1964

Knoxville Journal, 1967

Louisville Courier-Journal, 1965

Memphis Commercial-Appeal, 1947, 1957–1961

Miami Herald, 1958

Miami News, 1958

Mississippi Clarion-Ledger, 1961–1966, 1990

Mobile Journal, 1961

Nashville Banner, 1967

Nashville Tennessean, 1958–1961

New Orleans Times-Picayune, 1957–1964

New York Times, 1919, 1946–1967, 1973

Plaquemines Gazette, 1956

Richmond Times Dispatch, 1958

Tampa Tribune, 1956

Washington Post, 1957–1967

PERIODICALS, 1948–1968

AAUP Bulletin, 1959

The Citizen, 1962

The Citizens' Council, 1960

The Crusader, 1967–1969

The Dan Smoot Report, 1962

The Firing Line, 1957

The Militant, 1967

Race Relations Law Reporter, 1956–1957

The Southern Patriot, 1964

Southern School News, 1954–1962

The Worker, 1964–1965

BOOKS

Adams, Frank T. *James Dombrowski: An American Heretic, 1897–1983.* Knoxville: University of Tennessee Press, 1992.

Adams, Frank T., and Myles Horton. *Unearthing Seeds of Fire: The Idea of Highlander.* Winston-Salem: John F. Blair, 1975.

Anderson, Jervis. *Bayard Rustin: Troubles I've Seen.* New York: Harper Collins, 1997.

Anderson, Terry. *The Sixties.* New York: Longman, 1999.

Aptheker, Herbert. *The Negro People in America.* New York: International Publishers, 1946.

Barbour, Floyd B. *The Black Power Revolt.* Boston: Extending Horizons Books, 1968.

Barnard, William. *Dixiecrats and Democrats.* Tuscaloosa: University of Alabama Press, 1974.

Bartley, Numan. *The New South.* Baton Rouge: Louisiana State University Press, 1995.

————. *The Rise of Massive Resistance.* Baton Rouge: Louisiana State University Press, 1969.

Bates, Daisy. *The Long Shadow of Little Rock.* Fayetteville: University of Arkansas Press, 1987.

Bell, Daniel, ed. *The New American Right.* New York: Criterion Books, 1955.

Bennett, David. *The Party of Fear: From Nativist Movements to the New Right in American History.* Chapel Hill: University of North Carolina Press, 1988.

Billingsly, William. *Communists on Campus: Race, Politics, and the Public University in Sixties North Carolina.* Athens: University of Georgia Press, 1999.

Billington, Monroe Lee. *The Political South in the Twentieth Century.* New York: Scribner, 1975.

Braden, Anne. *The Wall Between.* New York: Monthly Review Press, 1958.

Branch, Taylor. *Parting the Waters: America in the King Years, 1954–1963.* New York: Simon and Schuster, 1988.

————. *Pillar of Fire: America in the King Years, 1964–1965.* New York: Simon and Schuster, 1998.

Brauer, Carl M. *John F. Kennedy and the Second Reconstruction.* New York: Columbia University Press, 1977.

Broadwater, Jeff. *Eisenhower and the Anticommunist Crusade.* Chapel Hill: University of North Carolina Press, 1992.

Buckingham, Peter H. *America Sees Red.* Claremont, Calif.: Regina Books, 1988.

Cagin, Seth, and Philip Dray. *We Are Not Afraid.* New York: Macmillan, 1988.

Carleton, Don. *Red Scare: Right-wing Hysteria, Fifties Fanaticism, and Their Legacy in Texas.* Austin: Texas Monthly Press, 1985.

Carmichael, Stokely, and Charles Hamilton. *Black Power: The Politics of Liberation in America.* New York: Vintage Books, 1992.

Carson, Clayborne. *In Struggle: SNCC and the Black Awakening of the 1960s.* Cambridge: Harvard University Press, 1981.

Carter, Dan. *The Politics of Rage: George Wallace, the Origins of the New Conservatism, and the Transformation of American Politics.* New York: Simon and Schuster, 1995.

————. *Scottsboro: A Tragedy of the American South.* Baton Rouge: Louisiana State University Press, 1969.

Chafe, William. *Never Stop Running.* New York: Basic Books, 1993.

————. *Civil Liberties and Civil Rights.* New York: Oxford University Press, 1980.

Chappell, David. *Inside Agitators: White Southerners in the Civil Rights Movement.* Baltimore: Johns Hopkins University Press, 1994.

Clowse, Barbara Barksdale. *Ralph McGill: A Biography.* Macon: Mercer University Press, 1998.

Colburn, David. *Racial Change and Community Crisis.* New York: Columbia University Press, 1985.

Collins, Charles Wallace. *Whither Solid South? A Study in Politics and Race Relations.* New Orleans, 1947.

Cosman, Bernard. *Five States for Goldwater.* Tuscaloosa: University of Alabama Press, 1966. [265

Cruse, Harold. *The Crisis of the Negro Intellectual.* New York: William Morrow, 1967.

Degler, Carl. *Place Over Time.* Baton Rouge: Louisiana State University Press, 1977.

Dittmer, John. *Local People.* Chicago: University of Illinois Press, 1995.

Donovan, Timothy, and Willard Gatewood. *The Governors of Arkansas.* Fayetteville: University of Arkansas Press, 1981.

Dudziak, Mary. *Cold War Civil Rights: Race and the Image of American Democracy.* Princeton: Princeton University Press, 2000.

Eagles, Charles. *Outside Agitator.* Chapel Hill: University of North Carolina Press, 1993.

Egerton, John. *Speak Now against the Day.* New York: Alfred A. Knopf, 1994.

Fairclough, Adam. *Race and Democracy.* Athens: University of Georgia Press, 1995.

Fariello, Griffin. *Red Scare: Memories of the American Inquisition, An Oral History.* New York: W. W. Norton, 1995.

Faust, Drew Gilpin. *The Creation of Confederate Nationalism: Ideology and Identity in the Civil War South.* Baton Rouge: Louisiana State University Press, 1988.

Findlay, James, Jr. *Church People in the Struggle: The National Council of Churches and the Black Freedom Movement, 1950–1970.* New York: Oxford University Press, 1993.

Franklin, John Hope. *From Slavery to Freedom.* New York: Random House, 1969.

Fried, Richard. *Nightmare in Red.* New York: Oxford University Press, 1990.

Friendly, Michael, and David Gallen. *Martin Luther King Jr: The FBI File.* New York: Carroll and Graf, 1993.

Garrow, David. *Bearing the Cross.* New York: Vintage, 1986.

Gellhorn, Walter. *The States and Subversion.* Ithaca: Cornell University Press, 1952.

Genovese, Eugene. *From Rebellion to Revolution: Afro-American Slave Revolts in the Making of the Modern World.* Baton Rouge: Louisiana State University Press.

Ginger, Ann Fagen, and Eugene M. Tobin, eds. *The National Lawyers Guild: From Roosevelt through Reagan.* Philadelphia: Temple University Press, 1988.

Glen, John M. *Highlander: No Ordinary School.* Knoxville: University of Tennessee Press, 1996.

Goodman, James. *Stories of Scottsboro.* New York: Vintage, 1995.

Goodman, Walter. *The Committee.* New York: Farrar, Straus and Giroux, 1968.

Graham, Hugh Davis. *Crisis in Print: Desegregation and the Press in Tennessee.* Nashville: Vanderbilt University Press, 1967.

———. *The Civil Rights Era: Origins and Development of National Policy, 1960–1972* . New York: Oxford University Press, 1990.

Griffith, Barbara S. *The Crisis of American Labor: Operation Dixie and the Defeat of the CIO.* Philadelphia: Temple University Press, 1988.

Grubbs, Donald. *Cry from the Cotton: The Southern Tenant Farmers' Union and the New Deal.* Chapel Hill: University of North Carolina Press, 1971.

Havard, William C., ed. *The Changing Politics of the South.* Baton Rouge: Louisiana State University Press, 1972.

Haynes, John Earl. *Red Scare or Red Menace?* Chicago: Ivan R. Dee, 1996.

Heale, M. J. *McCarthy's Americans.* Athens: University of Georgia Press, 1998.

Hietala, Thomas. *Manifest Design.* Ithaca: Cornell University Press, 1985.

Higginson, Thomas Wentworth. *Black Rebellion.* New York: Arno Press, 1969.

Horne, Gerald. *Black Liberation/Red Scare: Ben Davis and the Communist Party.* Newark: University of Delaware Press, 1994.

———. *Communist Front?* Rutherford: Fairleigh Dickinson University Press, 1988.

Horsman, Reginald. *Race and Manifest Destiny.* Cambridge: Harvard University Press, 1981.

Horton, Myles. *The Long Haul: An Autobiography.* New York: Teachers College Press, 1998.

Hunt, Michael. *Ideology and U.S. Foreign Policy.* New Haven: Yale University Press, 1987.

Hutchinson, Earl Ofari. *Blacks and Reds: Race and Class in Conflict, 1919–1990.* East Lansing: Michigan State University Press, 1995.

Jeansonne, Glen. *Leander Perez: Boss of the Delta.* Lafayette: University of Southwestern Louisiana, 1995.

Johnston, Erle. *Mississippi's Defiant Years.* Forest: Lake Harbor, 1990.

Kelley, Robin. *Hammer and Hoe: Alabama Communists during the Great Depression.* Chapel Hill: University of North Carolina Press, 1990.

Kellogg, Charles Flint. *NAACP: A History of the National Association for the Advancement of Colored People.* Baltimore: Johns Hopkins University Press, 1967.

Key, V. O., Jr. *Southern Politics in State and Nation.* New York: Knopf, 1949.

Klehr, Harvey. *Communist Cadre.* Stanford: Hoover Institution Press, 1978.

Klehr, Harvey, et al., *The Soviet World of American Communism.* New Haven: Yale University Press, 1998.

Kornweibel, Theodore, Jr. *"Seeing Red": Federal Campaigns against Black Militancy, 1919–1925.* Bloomington: Indiana University Press, 1998.

Kruger, Richard. *Simple Justice.* New York: Knopf, 1975.

Levenstein, Harvey A. *Communism, Anticommunism, and the CIO.* Westport, Conn.: Greenwood Press, 1981.

Lewy, Guenter. *The Cause That Failed: Communism in American Political Life.* New York: Oxford University Press, 1990.

Manis, Andrew. *A Fire You Can't Put Out: The Civil Rights Life of Birmingham's Reverend Fred Shuttlesworth.* Tuscaloosa: University of Alabama Press, 1999.

Marable, Manning. *Race, Reform, and Rebellion.* Jackson: University Press of Mississippi, 1991. [267

McCardell, John. *The Idea of a Southern Nation: Southern Nationalists and Southern Nationalism, 1830–1860.* New York: W. W. Norton, 1979.

McMillen, Neil. *The Citizens' Council: Organized Resistance to the Second Reconstruction, 1954–64.* Urbana: University of Illinois Press, 1971.

Mitchell, H. L. *Mean Things Happening in This Land.* Montclair, N.J.: Allanheld, Osmun, 1979.

Morris, Aldon. *The Origins of the Civil Rights Movement.* New York: Free Press, 1984.

Murray, Robert K. *Red Scare.* Minneapolis: University of Minnesota Press, 1955.

Myrdal, Gunnar. *An American Dilemma: The Negro Problem and Modern Democracy.* New York: Harper and Row, 1944.

Nahaylo, Bohdan, and Victor Swoboda. *Soviet Disunion: A History of the Nationalities Problem in the USSR.* New York: Free Press, 1990.

Navasky, Victor. *Kennedy Justice.* New York: Atheneum, 1971.

Oppenheimer, Martin. *The Sit-in Movement of 1960.* New York, Carlson Publishing, 1989.

O'Reilly, Kenneth. *Black Americans: The FBI Files.* New York: Carroll and Graf, 1994.

———. *Hoover and the Un-Americans: The FBI, HUAC, and the Red Menace.* Philadelphia: Temple University Press, 1983.

———. *"Racial Matters": The FBI's Secret File on Black America, 1960–1972.* New York: Free Press, 1989.

Oshinsky, David. *A Conspiracy So Immense.* New York: Free Press, 1983.

Ovington, Mary White. *The Walls Came Tumbling Down.* New York: Harcourt, Brace, 1947.

Posner, Gerald. *Killing the Dream.* New York: Random House, 1998.

Powers, Richard Gid. *Not without Honor.* New York: Free Press, 1995.

———. *Secrecy and Power: The Life of J. Edgar Hoover.* New York: Free Press, 1986.

Record, Wilson. *Race and Radicalism: The NAACP and the Communist Party in Conflict.* Ithaca: Cornell University Press, 1964.

Reed, John Shelton. *The Enduring South: Subcultural Persistence in Mass Society.* Chapel Hill: University of North Carolina Press, 1972.

Reed, Linda. *Simple Decency and Common Sense.* Bloomington: Indiana University Press, 1991.

Reed, Roy. *Faubus: The Life and Times of an American Prodigal.* Fayetteville: University of Arkansas Press, 1997.

Robinson, Cedric. *Black Marxism: The Making of the Black Radical Tradition.* Chapel Hill: University of North Carolina Press, 1983.

Salmond, John. *A Southern Rebel: The Life and Times of Aubrey Willis Williams, 1890–1965.* Chapel Hill: University of North Carolina Press, 1983.

Salter, John. *Jackson Mississippi: An American Chronicle of Struggle and Schism.* Hicksville, N.Y.: Exposition Press, 1979.

Schlesinger, Arthur M., Jr. *Robert Kennedy and His Times.* Boston: Houghton Mifflin, 1978.

Schrecker, Ellen. *Many Are the Crimes.* Boston: Little, Brown, 1998.

———. *No Ivory Tower.* New York: Oxford University Press, 1986.

Schuyler, George. *Black and Conservative.* New Rochelle, N.Y.: Arlington House, 1966.

Shannon, David A. *The Decline of American Communism.* Chatham, N.J.: Chatham Bookseller, 1959.

Simmons, Jerold. *Operation Abolition: The Campaign to Abolish the House Un-American Activities Committee, 1938–1975.* New York: Garland, 1986.

Sitkoff, Harvard. *The Struggle for Black Equality.* New York: Hill and Wang, 1981.

Solomon, Mark. *The Cry Was Unity: Communists and African-Americans, 1917–36.* Jackson: University Press of Mississippi, 1998.

Sosna, Morton. *In Search of the Silent South.* New York: Columbia University Press, 1977.

Stone, Gregory, and Douglas Lowenstein. *Lowenstein: Acts of Courage and Belief.* New York: Harcourt Brace Jovanovich, 1983.

Stoper, Emily. *The Student Nonviolent Coordinating Committee.* New York: Carlson, 1989.

Sullivan, Patricia. *Days of Hope: Race and Democracy in the New Deal Era.* Chapel Hill: University of North Carolina Press, 1996.

Tindall, George. *The Emergence of the New South, 1913–1945.* Baton Rouge: Louisiana State University Press, 1967.

Tyson, Timothy. *Radio Free Dixie: Robert F. Williams and the Roots of Black Power.* Chapel Hill: University of North Carolina Press, 1999.

Williams, Juan. *Thurgood Marshall: American Revolutionary.* New York: Random House, 1998.

Williams, Robert. *Negroes with Guns.* New York: Marzani and Munsell, 1962.

Woods, Randall Bennett. *Fulbright: A Biography.* New York: Cambridge University Press, 1995.

Woodward, C. Vann. *The Burden of Southern History.* Baton Rouge: Louisiana State University Press, 1968.

———. *The Origins of the New South.* Baton Rouge: Louisiana State University Press, 1951.

———. *The Strange Career of Jim Crow.* New York: Oxford University Press, 1957.

ARTICLES

"The Ultras: Ultraconservative Anti-Communism," *Time*, 8 December 1961.

Arsenault, Ray. "The Folklore of Southern Demagoguery." In Charles Eagles, ed., *Is There a Southern Political Tradition*. Jackson: University of Mississippi Press, 1996.

Gatewood, Willard, Jr. "The American Experience: The Southern Variable." In *The American Experience: Public Lectures in Honor of the Nation's Bicentennial*. Fayetteville: University of Arkansas Press, 1977.

Gellhorn, Walter. "Report on a Report of the House Committee on Un-American Activities." *Harvard Law Review* 60 (1947).

Graham, Hugh Davis. "Southern Politics since World War II." In John Boles and Evelyn Nolen, eds., *Interpreting Southern History*. Baton Rouge: Louisiana State University Press, 1987.

Grantham, Dewey W. "An American Politics for the South." In Charles Grier Sellers, Jr., ed., *The Southerner As American*. Chapel Hill: University of North Carolina Press, 1960.

Horne, Gerald. "The Red and the Black: The Communist Party and African-Americans in Historical Perspective." In Michael E. Brown et al., eds. *New Studies in the Politics and Culture of U.S. Communism*. New York: Monthly Review Press, 1993.

Hackney, Sheldon. "Southern Violence." *American Historical Review* 74 (February 1969).

———. "The South As a Counterculture." *American Scholar* 42 (spring 1973).

Johnston, Joyce. "Communism vs. Segregation: Evolution of the Committee to Investigate Communist Activities in South Carolina." *Proceedings of the South Carolina Historical Association*. Columbia: University of South Carolina, 1993.

Mosely, Donald. "Holt Ross, The Second President of the Mississippi State Federation of Labor." *Journal of Mississippi History* 34 (August 1972).

Murphy, Walter F. "The South Counterattacks: The Anti-NAACP Laws." *Western Political Quarterly* 12 (June 1959).

Phillips, Ulrich B. "The Central Theme of Southern History." *American Historical Review* 34 (October 1928).

Potter, David M. "The Historian's Use of Nationalism and Vice Versa." In *The South and the Sectional Conflict*. Baton Rouge: Louisiana State University Press, 1968.

Salmond, John A. "The Great Southern Commie Hunt." *South Atlantic Quarterly* 77 (autumn 1978).

Schrecker, Ellen. "McCarthyism and the Decline of American Communism, 1945–1960." In Michael E. Brown et al., eds., *New Studies in the Politics and Culture of U.S. Communism*. New York: Monthly Review Press, 1993.

Tyson, Timothy. "Robert F. Williams, 'Black Power,' and the Roots of the African American Freedom Struggle." *Journal of American History* 85 (September 1998).

Woods, Jeff. " 'Designed to Harass': The Act 10 Controversy in Arkansas." *Arkansas Historical Quarterly* 56 (autumn 1997).

DISSERTATIONS

Clark, Wayne Addison. "An Analysis of the Relationship between Anti-communism and Segregationist Thought in the Deep South, 1948–1964." Ph.D. diss., University of North Carolina, 1976.

Katagiri, Yasuhiro. "The Mississippi State Sovereignty Commission: Civil Rights and States' Rights in a Deep South State, 1956–1977." Ph.D. diss., University of Michigan, 1997.

INDEX

ground of, 182–84; and Christian So-
cialism, 183; and civil rights
movement, 8, 170, 183, 184, 201, 203;
and Highlander, 104, 106, 182; and
Louisiana raids, 181–84, 186–87, 189,
192–93, 197–98; and SISS investiga-
tion, 44–45; and Shuttlesworth, 185
Dorn, William Jennings Bryan, 71
Douglas, Paul, 194–95
DuBois Clubs, 244–45
DuBois, W. E. B., 59
Dulles, John Foster, 69
Durr, Clifford, 45–47
Durr, Virginia, 45–47

Eastland, James: background of, 25,
42–43; and Civil Rights Act of 1964,
172; and CORE, 151–52; and Great Society, 231–33; on Judiciary Committee, 173; and politics, 8, 43–44, 246;
and McCarthy, 42–43, 46; racism of,
43; rehabilitation of, 235–36, 241; retirement of, 256; and riots, 246; and
Robert Williams, 239; and SCEF, 56,
102 181–82, 187–88, 192–93, 198; and
SISS, 5, 43–47; and southern red scare,
58, 64, 65, 88, 151–53, 161, 181, 200,
202, 208–12, 213, 231–33; and state sedition, 108, 137; and Supreme Court,
54–56; and violence, 212, 213; and voting rights, 215, 217–18
Edmiston, Martha, 101–2, 109
education, 72–84, 92, 96, 102, 114, 132–
36, 140, 146, 153–55, 201–4, 209. *See
also* individual schools
Edwards, Jack, 222
Eisenhower, Dwight D., 38, 68–70, 91,
117, 135, 245
Elaine riots (Arkansas), 17–18
Emergency Civil Liberties Committee,

124, 137. *See also* House Committee
on Un-American Activities
Etheridge, Tom, 147, 154
Evans, Medford, 144
Evers, Charles, 218
Evers, Medgar, 206, 212

Fair Employment Practices Commission, 25, 35, 37
Farmer, James, 226
Faubus, Orval, 7, 23, 68, 72–73, 84, 126,
150
Federal Bureau of Investigation: and
Brown, 87–88; and Carmichael, 248;
and Church Committee, 257; investigation of Communists in civil rights
movement, 86–91, 108, 133, 159–68,
238–39, 248; as model for states, 85,
91–92, 98, 111, 114; priorities of,
88–89; and riots, 245–46; and southern
red scare, 5, 88, 91, 94, 98, 108, 111,
132, 182, 189, 202, 212, 244; and wiretaps, 181
Fellowship of Reconciliation, 134, 140,
178
Fisk University, 101–2
Florida, 116, 120–23, 142
Foreman, Clark, 34
Forman, James, 224, 233
Foster, William Z., 133
Freedom Democratic Party, 216, 217,
218
Freedom rides, 140, 150–53
Freedom Summer (1964), 1, 200–1, 203,
205–14
Friend, Edwin, 105–6

Garrison, William Lloyd, 13–14
Gates, John, 133
Gathings, E. C., 63, 88, 176
Gellner, Ernest, 4

26, 166–68, 175; ideology of, 44; PERM investigations of, 247; and SCHW, 44–45; and SCLC, 189; SISS investigations of, 44–47, 175, 182, 187–88, 192–93, 198; and SNCC, 201–4, 213; state investigations of, 128, 130, 139–40, 181–82, 184–85, 186–90, 192–93, 200, 202–4, 244

Southern Conference on Human Welfare, 29–31, 33–34, 44–45, 99, 127, 149, 171, 183

Southern Inter-Agency Conference, 158

Southern Manifesto, 66–67

southern nationalism: and black revolution, 40, 85; and civic vs. ethnic nationalism, 4; definition of, 1–4; effect on civil rights movement, 10, 84; national appeal of, 12, 27, 167, 194, 228–29, 254–55; and patriotism, 2–4, 228–29; and radical right, 113; siege mentality behind, 2, 71, 124; and southern segregation, 4–5, 14–15, 68, 257; and southern red scare, 2–5

southern red scare: beginning of, 35–38, 48, 84; and black revolution, 5, 54; decline of, 11, 255–57; discredited, 47, 145–46, 192–93, 223–24; effect on civil rights movement, 10, 48, 103, 113, 119, 130, 135, 142, 156–68, 180–81, 193, 199–200, 204–5, 207, 224; effect on cold war, 68–69, 237–38; evidence in support of, 48, 57, 58–60, 68, 84, 95, 111, 134–35, 140–42, 161, 164, 166–68, 169, 170, 181, 194–95, 196–98, 209–10, 223–24, 240–41; growth of, 49, 113, 175, 199, 231, 236, 240, 243, 253; investigation network, 5, 48, 85–86, 92–93, 111, 113, 188, 196, 208–10, 243–44; limited power of, 113, 115–16, 130, 136, 141–42, 169, 180–81, 193, 224; motives behind, 60, 134–35, 136,

184, 229, 231; national appeal of, 169, 175, 182, 190, 195–98, 223–24, 227, 235–36, 240–41, 245, 253, 254–55; and politics, 7–8, 44, 214–18, 229, 236; and the press, 147–49, 154, 164, 188–89, 190, 195–96, 214, 221, 236, 240; and racism, 96, 134–35, 142, 224; and radical right, 113; as scapegoat for region's problems, 71; and southern nationalism, 2–5; and subversive racial change, 12, 136; and violence, 17–18, 38, 199, 202, 212–14, 224, 227; wastefulness of, 9

Southern Regional Council, 57, 99–100, 120, 127, 129, 148, 149

Southern Tenant Farmers' Union, 23–24

southern way of life: as American way of life, 70; and civilization, 37; and race, 13, 29, 40, 96, 171, 257; and southern siege mentality, 2, 14, 27, 71, 111, 153–54, 199, 209

Soviet Union, 16, 22, 27, 89, 133, 179, 240, 249, 256

Sputnik, 68–70, 107, 113

Stalin, Joseph, 22, 132

Stanford, Max, 248

State Sovereignty Commission: Alabama, 5, 171–72, 188, 223–24; Arkansas, 126; Mississippi, 5, 95–97, 115, 144, 188, 195, 200, 202–4, 207–10, 212, 213, 215–16, 231–33, 236, 244, 255

states' rights: and Americanism, 51–52; and Communism, 37, 69–70, 150–52, 153, 154–56, 172–73, 174–75, 231; and sedition, 107–11, 137, 141; and southern nationalism, 2, 124, 194, 215, 257

States' Rights Party, 36–38, 42–43

Stennis, John, 232

Strom, J. P., 115–16

Student Nonviolent Coordinating Committee: associations of, 184, 196,

Lightning Source UK Ltd.
Milton Keynes UK
UKHW010656190521
383980UK00001B/111

9 780807 129265